T0259393

Advances

in COMPUTERS
VOLUME 57

Advances in
COMPUTERS

Information Repositories

EDITED BY

MARVIN V. ZELKOWITZ

Department of Computer Science
and Institute for Advanced Computer Studies
University of Maryland
College Park, Maryland

VOLUME 57

ACADEMIC PRESS

An imprint of Elsevier Science

Amsterdam Boston Heidelberg London New York Oxford
Paris San Diego San Francisco Singapore Sydney Tokyo

Academic Press
An imprint of Elsevier Science
525 B Street, Suite 1900, San Diego, California 92101-4495, USA
http://www.academicpress.com

First edition 2003

Library of Congress Cataloging in Publication Data
A catalog record from the Library of Congress has been applied for.

British Library Cataloguing in Publication Data
A catalogue record from the British Library has been applied for.

ISBN: 0-12-012157-3
ISSN (Series): 0065-2458

⊗ The paper used in this publication meets the requirements of ANSI/NISO Z39.48-1992 (Permanence of Paper).

Transferred to Digital Printing, 2010

Printed and bound in Great Britain by

CPI Antony Rowe, Chippenham and Eastbourne

Contents

On the Nature and Importance of Archiving in the Digital Age

Helen R. Tibbo

Preserving Digital Records and the Life Cycle of Information

Su-Shing Chen

Managing Historical XML Data

Sudarshan S. Chawathe

Adding Compression to Next-Generation Text Retrieval Systems

Nivio Ziviani and Edleno Silva de Moura

Are Scripting Languages Any Good? A Validation of Perl, Python, Rexx, and Tcl against C, C++, and Java

Lutz Prechelt

Issues and Approaches for Developing Learner-Centered Technology

Chris Quintana, Joseph Krajcik and Elliot Soloway

Personalizing Interactions with Information Systems

Saverio Perugini and Naren Ramakrishnan

Contents

Contributors

Sudarshan S. Chawathe is an Assistant Professor of Computer Science at the University of Maryland at College Park. He received his M.S. and Ph.D. degrees in Computer Science from Stanford University in 1994 and 1999. The Indian Institute of Technology, Kanpur awarded him a B.Tech. Degree in Computer Science and Engineering and the President's Gold Medal, in 1999. He received the CAREER award from the National Science Foundation in 2000. His current research focuses on semistructured data, data mining, and stream processing.

Su-Shing Chen received his Ph.D. from the University of Maryland, College Park. He is the James C. Dowell Research Professor in the Department of Computer and Information Science and Engineering at the University of Florida in Gainsville, Florida.

Joseph Krajcik is a Professor of Science Education at the University of Michigan and a co-director of the Center for Highly Interactive Computing in Education. He works with science teachers to re-engineer classrooms so that students engage in solving authentic, meaningful problems through inquiry and the use of learning technologies. A major aspect of his work involves the design of curriculum materials and computing tools that support inquiry.

Saverio Perugini is a Ph.D. candidate in the Department of Computer Science at Virginia Tech. He has been a student there since the fall of 1998 and served the department as a graduate teaching assistant and instructor over the years. Currently Perugini is researching programmatic techniques to support personal interactions in information systems with his thesis advisor, Naren Ramakrishnan. He intends to pursue a faculty position in a computer science department after graduation. Perugini is a 1998 BSCS graduate of Villanova University and has a Masters degree in Computer Science from Virginia Tech. His research interests include personalization, recommender systems, and data mining.

Lutz Prechelt is head of Process Management and head of Training and Technical Documentation at abaXX Technology, Stuttgart, Germany. Until March 2000, he worked as senior researcher at the School of Informatics, University of Karlsruhe, where he also received his Ph.D. in Informatics in 1995. His research interests include software engineering (in particular using an empirical research approach), measurement and benchmarking issues, and research methodology. He has performed several controlled experiments about topics such as design patterns, inheritance hierarchies, and the Personal Software Process (PSP). Earlier research interests included neural network learning algorithms, compiler construction for parallel machines, knowledge based systems, and natural language parsing. He is the editor of the Forum for Negative Results (FNR), which is a part of the Journal of Universal Computer Science (J.UCS).

Chris Quintana is an Assistant Research Scientist in the School of Education at the University of Michigan, where he works with the Center of Highly Interactive Computing in Education and the College of Engineering. Dr. Quintana's background is in computer science and human–computer interaction, and his research interests include the application of principles from human-computer interaction, software engineering, and information visualization to the design of educational technology. His current work includes developing design methods and scaffolding guidelines for learner-centered software, and exploring the development of scaffolded work environments on both desktop and handheld computers for K-12 learners.

Naren Ramakrishnan is an Assistant Professor of Computer Science at Virginia Tech. His research interests include problem solving environments, mining scientific data, and personalization. He is the recipient of a 2000 National Science Foundation CAREER award and the 2001 New Century Technology Council Innovation award. Ramakrishnan received his Ph.D. in computer sciences from Purdue University in August 1997.

Edleno Silva de Moura is an Associate Professor of Computer Science at the Federal University of Amazonas (UFAM) in Brazil, where he heads the Information Technology Research Group (GTI). He received a Ph.D. in Computer Science from the Federal University of Minas Gerais (UFMG), Brazil, in 1999, where his research activities were focused on applications of data compression for information retrieval systems. After finishing his Ph.D., he worked as an associate researcher at UFMG and as Chief Technology Officer for Akwan Information Technologies, a company specialized in developing information retrieval systems for the Web. He is the author of several papers in journals and conference proceedings covering topics in the areas of information retrieval, text indexing, text searching, text compression, and related areas. He is currently a technology consultant for Akwan.

Elliot Soloway is a Professor in the College of Engineering, the School of Information and the School of Education and is co-founder of the Center for Highly Interactive Computing in Education, a multidisciplinary project aimed at developing standards-based, inquiry-driven, technology-pervasive curriculum for K-12.

Helen R. Tibbo is an Associate Professor in the School of Information and Library Science at the University of North Carolina at Chapel Hill. She teaches courses in archives, records management, user services, and digital preservation and access. Her research focuses on information seeking and digital access in cultural heritage repositories.

Nivio Ziviani is a Professor of Computer Science at the Federal University of Minas Gerais (UFMG) in Brazil, where he heads the Laboratory for Treating Information (LATIN). He received a Ph.D. in Computer Science from the University of Waterloo, Canada, in 1982. He currently coordinates a five years project on Web and wireless information systems (called SIAM) financed by the Brazilian Ministry of Science and Technology. He is co-founder of two companies specialized in developing information retrieval systems for the Web, the Miner Technology Group and the Akwan Information Technologies.He is the author of several papers in journals and conference proceedings covering topics in the areas of algorithms and data structures, information retrieval, text indexing, text searching, text compression, and related areas. He has been chair and member of the program committee and also general chair of several conferences and is a member of ACM, EATCS, and SBC.

Preface

Advances in Computers has been continually published since 1960 and is the oldest series to provide an annual update to the continuously changing information technology field. Each volume presents from six to eight chapters describing new developments in software, hardware, or uses of computers. In this volume, the 57th in the series, subtitled *Information Repositories*, the focus is on the growth of information repositories, databases, and digital records. The seven chapters describe how one stores, retrieves and learns from the information now being entered into such large databases.

In Chapter 1, "On the Nature and Importance of Archiving in the Digital Age," Professor Helen R. Tibbo discusses the problems of preserving information. Besides making new discoveries, civilization needs the ability to access previous discoveries, hence the need for libraries. With books, the major problem was decay – books would disintegrate in several hundred years. However, as we enter the digital age, the problems are now different. How does one preserve digital information, especially as digital formats and media change every few years? How does one address intellectual property and ownership of such information? How do you address authenticity of the information? These and other questions are the focus of this chapter.

Chapter 2, "Preserving Digital Records and the Life Cycle of Information" by Su-Shing Chen continues the discussion of preserving information in the digital age that was the focus of the previous chapter. This chapter, however, focuses on the OAIS (Open Archival Information System) model, which takes an archivist view of preserving and accessing digital information.

"Managing Historical XML Data" by Professor Sudarshan S. Chawathe is the topic of Chapter 3. Not only must repositories hold large amounts of data, one must be able to access the right information when needed. The Extensible Markup Language (XML) is a data format that uses tags within the data to specify the type of information contained within a file. The familiar Hypertext Markup Language (HTML) of Internet websites uses a similar notation. Use of XML provides a structure that allows data to be stored and retrieved when needed. XML is becoming ubiquitous and its structure is the focus of this chapter.

Even though disk storage is growing annually and becoming cheaper in the process, it is still finite. As this is being written, 80 billion bytes of storage for a small personal computer disk are quite common. When you read this, there is no telling what the size may be. But it is still finite. However, new information is growing at a rate that even surpasses the growth rate of these disks. To address these issues, compression algorithms have been used to compress more information into fewer storage locations. How one squeezes more bits of information into fewer bits is the topic of Chapter 4. Professor Nivio Ziviani and Professor Edleno Silva de Moura discuss such compression algorithms in "Adding Compression to Next-Generation Text Retrieval Systems."

One important characteristic of an information repository is being able to extract needed information rapidly from a file. For many such applications, a scripting language is used to define a program that can process a file searching for particular records that meet some condition. Languages like Perl, Python, and Tcl are examples of such languages used for that purpose. The alternative is to write a program using a more standard language such as C or Java. Which approach is more efficient in getting the job done? In Chapter 5, "Are Scripting Languages Any Good? A validation of Perl, Python, Rexx, and Tcl against C, C++, and Java," Dr. Lutz Prechelt compares the two approaches.

Chapters 6 and 7 present different aspects of information repositories. In "Issues and Approaches for Developing Learner-Centered Technology" by Dr. Chris Quintana, Dr. Joseph Krajcik, and Professor Elliott Soloway, the authors discuss the use of computers for learning. Software is often designed so that experts on a topic can use software for that topic effectively. But researchers have come to understand that a learner-centered approach is needed for tools to help novices learn. This chapter discusses techniques useful for building products that aid in novices learning new technologies.

In the final chapter, entitled "Personalizing Interactions with Information Systems" by Saverio Perugini and Professor Naren Ramakrishnan, the authors discuss some of the issues that were presented in the previous chapter. Personalization refers to automatic adjustment of information content, structure, and presentation tailored to the individual. This allows, for example, a user to tailor a web browser to operate as desired, rather than having all users use a standard way to access information. This would have an effect on all users, experts and novices alike, of being able to use information resources more effectively.

I hope that you find these articles of interest. If you have any suggestions of topics for future chapters, or if you wish to contribute such a chapter, I can be reached at mvz@cs.umd.edu.

Marvin Zelkowitz
College Park, Maryland, USA

On the Nature and Importance of Archiving in the Digital Age

HELEN R. TIBBO

School of Information and Library Science
University of North Carolina at Chapel Hill
Chapel Hill, NC
USA
tibbo@ils.unc.edu

Abstract

Digital preservation and archiving stand as grand challenges of the first decade of the 21st century. Our cultural heritage, modern scientific knowledge, and everyday commerce and government depend upon the preservation of reliable and authentic electronic records and digital objects. Issues such as software and hardware obsolescence, media fragility, expensive metadata creation, and intellectual property rights place all of these materials at risk. The archival and computer science professions must come together to solve the complex technical, conceptual, social, legal, and economic challenges that endanger the longevity of all digital objects. Basic archival principles must be built into information creation and management software and information creators must recognize the need to exert responsible custody over the digital information objects they manage. Archiving, and the preservation tools to facilitate it, must become ubiquitous if society is to preserve its memory in the digital age.

Digital archives combined with new technologies will liberalise scholarship ... This vision of a rich information record just waiting to be harvested and processed by the technology-enabled researcher of the future depends upon the survival of digital data. Sadly, based on current experience, it is evident that not much of this digital material will survive. It is already impossible to find old documentation for early computers ... [1, p. 12].

1. Introduction

1.1 The Information Age?

It is not an illusion; these are truly exciting times in which we live. Scientists are mapping the complete set of human genes with the goals of predicting, preventing, and curing disease and defects. Data mining is facilitating connections and discoveries impossible only a few years ago. We correspond with international colleagues and friends instantly through email, chat programs, teleconferencing, and collaborative research tools. Our financial records and personal identities are stored in electronic databases enabling us to access our bank accounts from around the world to manage our assets more effectively. Digital libraries are facilitating scholarship [2–5] in rare and ancient materials such as the Beowulf manuscript online [6]. The World Wide Web (WWW) provides a global, multimedia platform for presenting and retrieving all manner of information and commodities [7]. Many of us are never "out of contact," as we carry our mobile phones, personal digital assistants, and digital beepers wherever we go. Many observers have called the late 20th and early 21st centuries the "Information Age," but this will only become a reality when we have the ability to preserve authentic digital information reliably for the duration of its value. Only with the perfection of digital archiving, when we will have long-term as well as transitory control over all manner of digital assets—electronic records, digital objects, and e-content[1]—will we enter a true "Information Age." Until then, with all our wired and wireless connections, networks, and webs, we will remain in the "Day of Networked Digital Access" wherein our ability to move large quantities of digits with great rapidity often seems to hold more value and fascination than does the information itself or knowledge we might glean from it.

Ironically, we may today be further from an Information Age than we were when most information lived on print media. While we still do many of the same things we have long done—write letters to friends, send pictures of dogs and babies, look up answers to questions at the library—networked digital communication has fundamentally changed the format and stability of the information objects we create and access. Written letters, photographs, ledgers, and diaries have documented our lives and have found their way to our attics and some to manuscript repositories where

---

[1] According to the *SAA Glossary* [67], a "record" is "a document created or received and maintained by an agency, organization, or individual in pursuance of legal obligations or in the transaction of business." An electronic record is one created or stored in digital form. The National Archives of Australia provides more detail but does not consider media as it defines a record as "that which is created and kept as evidence of agency or individual functions, activities and transactions. To be considered evidence, a record must possess content, structure and context and be part of a recordkeeping system" (http://www.aa.gov.au/recordkeeping/er/manage_er/what_record.html). "E-content" is any material in any medium or combination of media—text, graphic, audio, video—created or stored in digital form. Electronic records are one type of e-content, defined by their capacity to provide evidence. Kenneth Thibodeau generically defines a "digital object" as "an information object, of any type of information or any format, that is expressed in digital form." The objects may be simple as in many word processing files or highly complex multimedia web pages. Thibodeau further explains that "Every digital object is a physical object, a logical object, and a conceptual object, and its properties at each of those levels can be significantly different" [123,235].

historians use them to reconstruct a picture of the past decades or centuries. Paper records, when signed and certified appropriately, have assumed evidential status in our courts and fill organizational and governmental archives. Receipts on little slips of paper have supported our claims for reimbursement and tax deductions.

Digitally created and stored information is posing significant preservation and legal challenges to these scenarios, of which most people are unaware. While documenting their weddings, children's births, and annual vacations with digital photographs and video few individuals ponder "How much of this information, history, and heritage will we be able to pass to our children and grandchildren?" Most of us blithefully do our daily business at ATMs without thinking about what would happen to our digital identities and our directly deposited "paychecks" if electronic files were corrupted and the digital records ceased to be authentic and reliable. Few people can tell when an electronic record will be admissible as evidence in court or what weight judge and jury will give it, nor what, in the sea of digital files and electronic records should be kept, what discarded, and when.

The format, extent, and rapid exchange of information that digital technologies facilitate, along with the extreme fragility of the information we create are of dire consequence to the "memory of the information society" [8]. While most previous media have physically persisted for enough years for an archivist to assess an item's value reflectively in the latter stages of its life cycle, the transitory nature of digital materials has led many people to consider these the "digital dark ages" [9]. Peter Lyman and Brewster Kahle note that "the pace of technical change makes digital information disappear before we realize the importance of preserving it" [10]. These are all issues fundamental to the emerging field of digital preservation.

This fragility and evanescence of digital files and records requires archival and preservation decisions and actions be made close to, or at, the point of creation. Archival qualities, that is, the enduring value of some information, must be recognized early, if not at the time the information is produced; the need for immediate and continual preservation demands that digital creators and users be frontline appraisers and build preservation potential into the materials they produce, receive, and for which they are responsible. Whereas archiving has long been considered a post hoc activity to house and preserve documents of enduring value after their primary role was completed, archival principles and practices must now pervade the work of all information managers, from digital librarians to individuals keeping their own files and records. This is not to say that the need for archival repositories will disappear. Indeed, the presence of trusted repositories is the cornerstone of much electronic record preservation research and theory, but the seeds of preservation must be sown at the time of record creation for the early years of a digital object's life may well determine its ultimate destiny. Nine years ago, Margaret Hedstrom called for archivists to develop strategies to change individuals' record-keeping practices, increase their awareness of the value of documentary evidence, and to produce tools to help in these processes [11]. Little progress has been made on many of these fronts. Awareness of the archiving impulse must become as ubiquitous as the computer if today's digital data and electronic records are to survive as have the analog cultural, scientific, and business records of the past [12,13].

1.2   Archiving Digital Assets: The Need for Collaboration

As digital libraries evolve into digital archives, archivists working with computer scientists must adapt archival principles, such as provenance and responsible custody, that have stood the test of time to the digital environment and insinuate them within other domains including information technology and collections management. William Arms points out, "the field of digital archiving is new. The needs are beginning to be understood, but the methods are still embryonic—particularly in the field of archiving" [14, p. 245]. Stephen Griffin, a member of the National Digital Information Infrastructure Preservation Program (NDIIPP) and the program manager for the federal interagency National Science Foundation Digital Libraries Initiative (NSF/DLI), echoes this point, noting that archiving is a topic that is "least worked on and most perplexing" [15]. The National Association of Government Archives and Records Administrators' (NAGARA) Advanced Institute for Government Archivists, held at the University of Pittsburgh School of Library and Information Science 1989–1992, concluded that "[t]he archival management of electronic records is probably the most important, and certainly the most complicated, issue currently before the archival profession" [16].

Expertise from a wide range of information professionals must be applied to the digital arena if digital materials are to be preserved for as long as they continue to have value. Forming such a "metacommunity" that will have "unparalleled opportunities to enhance the processes of knowledge creation and use" [17, p. v] is essential to digital preservation, but promises to be a challenging task and will require extensive and reinforcing communication. William Arms notes that many in the computer science field who are experts in networking, systems, and information retrieval know little about the information management accomplishments of librarians and archivists. At the same time, librarians and archivists are often generally uninformed as to the developments in the computing domain [14, p. ix]. This needs to change; and does appear to be doing so, if only to a very small degree, with the development of conferences such as the ACM/IEEE Joint Conference on Digital Libraries (JCDL). The digital "library," however, is not a digital "archive," and little attention has yet to be paid to the full range of activities associated with preservation and archiving in the DL environment. For example, in the highly cited *Practical Digital Libraries: Books, Bytes and Bucks*, Michael Lesk defines *digital libraries* as "organized collections of digital information" [18]. He talks about traditional library preservation problems, but does not address the issues of digital longevity. Conversely, Seamus Ross speaks to the parochial perspectives librarians and archivists frequently hold regarding electronic information [19,20] and notes that until these communities recognize the need to preserve a "cross-section of our digital heritage, media manufacturers, system developers, and software designers will not be encouraged to introduce preservation capabilities or functionalities into their products" [1, p. 10].

This chapter provides an overview of archival principles and practices applicable to digital preservation and reviews work that holds significant promise for enabling the longevity of digital content and thus the transmission of our cultural, economic, and scientific heritage into the future. The tasks are so large, complex, and require such diverse knowledge, skills, and perspectives that they cannot be accomplished by any one professional community. Collaborations between the archival, information science, and computing science communities will facilitate theoretical, methodological, and practical developments necessary to achieve long-term digital preservation and thus true digital archiving.

This is a discussion of challenge and promise. While there are texts that discuss the issues associated with digitization projects and that provide guidance as to current best practices and approaches [21–25], the questions concerning long-term preservation vastly outnumber the answers. Great minds and large agencies around the world are seeking the answers as to how best to create, organize, describe, store, preserve, and make digital information persistently and appropriately accessible. This is truly an international response to an international problem. While data format and exchange standards are emerging and research agendas and policies are being set, little implementation has gone forth and much testing of models and practicalities lies ahead. Governments, universities, and digital organizations are creating new policy directions and "best practices" in a race with time to preserve the late 20th century's digital content, but no one yet knows how this will all turn out.

So, if there are as of yet few answers, why write this chapter? In many respects, the questions that underlie the success of digital preservation, digital libraries, and digital archives are just as important as the answers. New "best practices" will continue to emerge with new technologies and further research, but we can expect many of the fundamental questions and principles associated with optimized creation, preservation, and provision of access to digital information to remain constant for some time. We cannot wait for all the answers before exploring the issues. As Mary Feeney writes, "electronic information is fragile and evanescent" [26, p. 8].

There will be no easy or fast answers to high quality digital preservation and optimized provision of access to electronic materials, be they digital images of rare texts or corporate records essential to organizational accountability. Each type of digital resource appears to have its own set of digitization and preservation best practices [23,27]; each type of organization its own needs for data retention, functional requirements, and archival policy development. The NHPRC-funded Recordkeeping Functional Requirements or "Pittsburgh Project" studied organizational culture with the premise that organizations would find differing tactics to satisfy each record-keeping requirement identified [28–30]. Indeed, what is so challenging in writing a chapter such as this one, and in implementing effective digital archiving programs, is that preservation in the digital world encompasses the totality of information management issues throughout the life cycle or continuum [31–35] of any document or artifact. These range from technical issues of storage media [36] and open computing standards, to social and economic issues of intellectual property rights [37,38] and the value of intellectual capital of digital objects [39], to social and educational issues of the provision of pedagogically optimized access to digital materials [40–42]. The stress on "risk management" in the digital preservation literature tells us what to expect [43,44].

This chapter will first explore definitions of archiving and digital preservation, followed by a discussion of the importance of digital archiving and the aspects of digital information that make preservation so challenging. The remainder of the chapter will review work informed by the archival perspective that is defining the digital landscape and working to ensure the preservation of our cultural, economic, and scientific heritage, ending with a call for collaboration between archivists and computer scientists to solve the conundrum that is long-term preservation. It concludes by outlining the steps that will be necessary for ubiquitous digital archiving and long-term preservation to become realities.

2.   What Is Archiving?

Until recently, only archivists and scholars used and understood the terms "archiving" and "archives." In trying to book hotel reservations for the annual meeting of the Society of American Archivists (SAA), many members have had to explain what an archivist does and have been confused with everything from an anarchist to an anchovy! In general, the stereotype of the archivist was an old dusty person tending to old dusty papers that few people ever used—the "dead file" clerk. The times, however, are changing. With the Web, the boom in digital content, and searchability of large databases, the word, "archives" is everywhere. Suddenly, a term until quite recently seen as arcane is now firmly situated within the popular parlance and used by many professions [45]. The popular definitions of this term, however, are at variance with those the professional archival community have established based upon principles essential to the management and preservation of electronic as well as paper records. In 1991 Margaret Hedstrom noted that archivists had "literally lost control over the definition of archive" [46, p. 336]. Today, when the future of cultural heritage, scientific knowledge, and business and industry are clearly tied to the development and widespread adoption of digital archiving principles and practices, we must remove "literal" from her sentence.

The computer community, both professional and amateur, uses "archiving" to mean the act of storing copies of digital (usually non-current) data in an offline (but still electronic) environment [47, p. 26]. For example, many newspaper websites provide users the ability to search today's paper or their "archives," texts of papers published before the most recent one, broken into manageable clumps of material, covering a month or a year. A listserv's archive is composed of all the old (before the present day) messages. Database vendors such as Dialog [48] or Lexis-Nexis [49] may present large databases such as MEDLINE [50] in smaller, more searcher-friendly, chronological increments, with the older records being called back files or archival files. For much of the world, "electronic archiving" means storing digital data in segments (frequently chronologically) for future use apart from the most current data, or making back-up copies of files, frequently storing them on portable media such as tapes or disks.

For archivists, archiving is a complex process that can range across the lifecycle of information and that involves an array of different functions including, selecting, acquiring, arranging and describing, preserving (physical preservation), and providing access. Archiving always has the goals of *preserving* and *making accessible* documents, records, and other data of *enduring value*. Enduring value stems from a document or record's intrinsic attributes, the contextual documentation that surrounds it, its relationship to other records and entities, and assurance of its authenticity and reliability. David Bearman operationalizes the need for authentic records arguing that "archives and records management share a simple goal: providing for organizational accountability." He goes on to explain that "Accountability depends on being able to demonstrate managed access to information which is important for reasons of ongoing need or future evidence, from the time of creation" [51, p. 13]. Bearman links evidence to accountability through "managed access" that preserves reliable and authentic records. The motto of the United States National Archives and Records Administration (NARA) encapsulates the above discussion: "ready access to essential evidence" [52].

Most popular and computer-oriented usage of the term "archiving" oversimplifies an involved process and omits any notion of responsibility for the physical and intellectual longevity, authenticity and reliability, and future usefulness of the materials being stored. Hodge and Carroll in a report for the International Council for Scientific and Technical Information, note "The simple use of the noun "archive" does not result in an "organization being attentive to the archiving of the collection, or taking an archivist role" [53, p. 17]. In the Open Archives Information System (OAIS)

Reference Model the Consultative Committee for Space Data Systems defines an archive is "an organization that intends to preserve information for access and use by a Designated Community" [54, p. 1–8]. Here we see the concepts of preservation, access, and custody for use linked. In a discussion of the archival discipline, Luciana Duranti breaks out several aspects of the field that taken together comprise "archival science."

> Archival science comprises the ideas about the nature of archival material (i.e., archival theory) and the principles and methods for the control and preservation of such material (i.e., archival methodology). The analysis of archival ideas, principles and methods, the history of the way they have been applied over time (i.e., of archival practice), and the literary criticism of both archival analysis and history (i.e., archival scholarship) are also integral part of archival science. Thus, archival science can be defined as a system inclusive of theory, methodology, practice, and scholarship, which owes its integrity to its logical cohesion and to the existence of a clear purpose that rules it from the outside, determining the boundaries in which the system is designed to operate. [55, p. 39]

2.1   Digital Objects and Electronic Records

Until quite recently, American archives, especially those in large government and corporate organizations, processed collections differently from manuscript repositories that contained primarily personal papers [56–58]. The printing of the *SAA Basic Manual Series* in the late 1970s,[2] [59] the rise of the MARC/AMC (Machine Readable Cataloging/Archives and Manuscript Control) cataloging format in the 1980s [60–64], and the development of Encoded Archival Description (EAD) for presentation of electronic finding aids in the 1990s [65,66] have all contributed to a merging of archival, and especially, descriptive, practice between institutional archives and manuscript repositories. In the last two decades, the word, "archivist" has been widely applied to manuscript positions and "archiving" has been accepted as the blanket term regardless of the types of materials that are being kept. The 1993 *SAA Glossary* defines "archives" in this manner [67, p. 3].

Conversely, the rise of electronic records in the government and corporate sectors and the search for effective means of controlling and preserving them, especially preserving evidentiary value, may be once again separating archivists and curators. Kenneth Thibodeau observes, "One of the key elements that distinguishes archives from other institutions which preserve information is that archives' essential responsibility is to preserve and deliver authentic records to subsequent generations of users" [68].

---

[2]This series, published by SAA from 1977 through 1985 included 15 titles, some of which are still available at the SAA website: www.archivists.org. Most important in the early stages of "standardizing" descriptive practice, was David Gracy's guide to arrangement and description.

Margaret Hedstrom notes a "tension between those who assume that archives exist primarily to preserve authentic and reliable evidence for the practical benefits of society, and others who would encourage archivists to expand their definition of evidence and think imaginatively about its possible uses" [11, p. 90]. The Australian archival literature reflects this recognition [69].

Much of the schism between organizational archivists and manuscript curators centers on the definition of the term, "record" and its essential place in archiving. For the archivist, a record is "a document created or received and maintained by an agency, organization, or individual in pursuance of legal obligations or in the transaction of business" [67, p. 28]. The term describes any piece of "recorded information, regardless of medium or characteristics." An "authentic record" is "a record that is what it purports to be and is free from tampering or corruption" [70, p. 2]. An "electronic record," is "a record that is created (made or received and set aside) in electronic form" [70, p. 5]. Much discussion and research throughout the 1990s and into the 21st century has focused on establishing "recordness" and functional requirements that define information as being a record, as well as ensuring reliable and authentic records that can serve as evidence of organizational and personal behavior [51,71–73]. Kenneth Thibodeau explains how "records" differs from other "documents."

> Records are documents accumulated in the course of practical activities. As instruments and byproducts of those activities, records constitute a primary and privileged source of evidence about the activities and the actors involved in them. While records are often conceived in terms of textual documents, such as letters and reports, they can take any form. What differentiates records from documentary materials in general is not their form, but their connection to the activities in which they are made and received. If this link is broken, corrupted, or even obscured, the information in the record may be preserved, but the record itself is lost. [68]

The broader perspective articulated in the SAA's position statement, "Archival Roles for the New Millennium" [74], which envisions the term "archiving" and archival principles, including authenticity and reliability, being applied to the retention and disposition of the full range of digital files and objects, not merely clearly defined "records" from institutional entities, underlies this chapter. As David Bearman has observed, archiving should attempt to identify human actions that are worth remembering, not just those documents with legal standing [75]. Thus archival principles and practices have value for the individual dealing with a flood of electronic mail and the digital library endeavoring to maintain its collections over time as well as for those at national and corporate archives.

2.2   Preservation, Access, and Archiving

Traditionally, *preservation* and *archiving* have had two distinct definitions with preservation being a necessary component of, but not equivalent to, the totality of archiving. Ritzenthaler notes that for many archivists, "preservation is the very cornerstone upon which archival institutions are founded" [76, p. 1]. The *SAA Glossary* defines preservation as "The totality of processes and operations involved in the stabilization and protection of documents against damage or deterioration and in the treatment of damaged or deteriorated documents" [67, p. 27]. Recent use of these terms in the electronic world seems to be converging to "refer to the long-term storage, preservation, and access to digital information" [53, p. 17]. According to Paul Conway, "in the digital world preservation is the creation of digital products worth maintaining over time" [77, p. 4 of online version]. This is because preservation, and thus any hope of future archiving, must begin at the time of creation of digital objects or at least at the point of acquisition. The InterPARES Preservation Task Force's Final Report goes a step further in revealing how the concept of preservation has evolved from the print to the digital arena, how it must be pushed to the beginning of the digital object's life cycle, and how it must involve access. In a significant departure from traditional archival practice, the Task Force explains, "it is not possible to preserve an electronic record: it is only possible to preserve the ability to reproduce the record" [78, p. 9]. Because electronic preservation demands migration or some other form of reproduction, "the process of preserving an electronic record goes well beyond keeping it safely in storage. The process of preservation begins with the initial act of storage and extends through reproduction of the record" [78, p. 9].

Ritzenthaler, working from the print paradigm, observes a "classic conflict" between preservation and access that "must be arbitrated by the custodians and caretakers of archival records" [76, p. 1]. Conway, focusing on the digital environment, argues that preservation *is* access and that the end goal is to preserve not merely the digital object, but access to the digital object [77, p. 26 of online version]. As broad terms, both *archiving* and *preservation*, encompass the management of many subcomponents necessary to keep materials alive for future use. Both archiving and preservation involve more than simply keeping the bit-stream intact and decipherable; these terms imply responsible custody of both the physical and intellectual aspects of digital objects of enduring value. For digital materials this means preserving content, context, and access through the life cycle of the record and centers on the notion of permanence [79].

Archiving, irrespective of the media on which information is recorded, involves a substantial commitment from the archives (or other body serving the archival function). This commitment comes at a high cost because of the labor-intensive nature of such archival functions as maintaining the authenticity of the materials, describing them in metadata so as to preserve their context and usefulness and to make them retrievable and accessible, and preserving them physically. These tasks are no less expensive for electronic materials than they are for their print counterparts. Indeed, the massive quantities of digital materials, the need to capture their digital qualities for future replication and access, and the process of describing their content and context may require more effort than traditional description of print resources has entailed. Several large-scale digitization projects begun in libraries and archives in the mid-1990s have estimated the cost of long-term preservation of the digital assets they have created, but actual costs are unclear at this time [80–84]. RLG does provide an extensive costing worksheet [85] and Kenney and Rieger present a detailed costing formula in *Moving Theory into Practice* [23, p. 137–139; 169–175]. Price and Smith have called for the use of business models that involves risk assessment and management for digitization project [86]. Most of these estimates and projections cite production of metadata as the most costly element in digitization projects and in preserving digital assets. Automated methods of producing technical, administrative, and preservation metadata will go far in reducing these costs and are an essential element in the deep infrastructure necessary for ubiquitous digital preservation. In summary, archiving is a process of stewardship over materials of enduring value that ensures longevity of use and utility; not just preservation of the physical object.

On its website, the Society of American Archivists lists seven enduring roles and responsibilities for archivists:

1. Manage cost-effective archival programs for the selection, retention, and use of both electronic and paper documentary materials.
2. Ensure that an authentic and reliable record is created and available for use.
3. Evaluate the universe of available documents and record-keeping systems to select those to preserve for future use.
4. Preserve and document the context and arrangement of the materials retained for long-term use.
5. Provide descriptive tools, such as registers, indices, and databases, to allow records-keepers, researchers, archivists, and others to locate and identify the information and evidence in archival holdings.
6. Preserve information and evidence in a protective environment and in a format or media that will remain usable over time.
7. Promote and help people use archives to explain the past, support accountability for the present, and provide guidance for the future [74].

Elements essential to digital preservation can be extracted from each of these points. This chapter highlights only those areas in which archivists provide the most unique and salient perspectives and where the most work toward ensuring digital longevity has gone forth: appraisal of digital materials; establishing and ensuring authenticity and reliability; descriptive tools, standards, and metadata; physical and technical preservation; and provision of access. In many cases, individuals who contribute extensively toward our understanding of what digital archiving means are not archivists, but they work from within the archival paradigm and apply its principles, practices, and perspectives.

3. Why Digital Archiving Is Important: Society, Memory, and Cultural Heritage

Although it sounds melodramatic, the future course of modern society rests upon our ability to perfect the archiving of digital data. We will need to develop viable and cost effective technical procedures; create local, national, and international policies and strategic plans to govern these procedures, develop open standards to facilitate data exchange; figure out how to best manage the entire process; and find the collective will to pay for all this. The search for technical answers is well underway; standards and policies are being developed, as are management models. Given the magnitude of the problem and the dire consequences of our failure, however, a very modest number of people worldwide are engaged in this quest. Most institutions working on electronic data archiving research and development projects are underfunded; competition for resources is keen. The political will and financial support does not yet appear evident on a large scale, but when more corporate and government data fall to the ravages of time and e-commerce does not function well, support will come, albeit in a reactive rather than proactive fashion. Corporate risk and loss of longitudinal data will be key. The challenge, if today's cultural and scientific heritage is to be preserved, is to build the technologies and infrastructure to preserve digital assets, not simply try to rescue them after near disaster.

Digital data is everywhere; electronic records lie at the core of operations for business, financial, governmental, scientific, academic, and cultural enterprises today. Digital technology is truly amazing, but as with most other complex entities, carries the seeds of its own destruction. Mary Feeney notes that, "The short term benefits of digital objects—manipulation, distribution, duplication, linking—are immense, but the long-term viability of such objects is fraught with difficulty because of the ever-changing technology needed for their storage and use." These conditions lead to the "increasing concern about the potential loss of our 'collective memory' in the Digital Age" [26, p. 8–9]. Peter Lyman and Brewster Kahle observe, "Like oral culture, digital information has been allowed to become a medium for the present, neither a record of the past nor a message to the future" [10]. Jeff Rothenberg observes that "digital information lasts forever—or five years, whichever comes first" [87, p. 2].

In 1998 at the Time & Bits Conference that focused on digital preservation, Peter Lyman and Howard Besser asked "What kind of picture of life in the late twentieth century could the historians of the future uncover, if the only lasting record of our time were printed on paper?" and provided numerous examples of significant loss of digital cultural heritage that had already occurred [88]. It seems clear that in answer to their question, digital data in all formats and media, is forming "an increasingly large part of our cultural and intellectual heritage" [26, p. 8] and will be essential to the historical and intellectual record of our time as well as to the present day functioning of society.

Seamus Ross notes that where once most digital information was generated within government and private organizations, implying that such environments provide at least the potential for control and preservation, the general public is now creating an enormous body of information on the Internet and Web [1, p. 22]. This documentation will be extremely important for future historians trying to understand late 20th century and early 21st century life and culture, but little is being done to preserve it or develop personalized preservation systems. With the exception of Brewster Khale's pioneering web archiving project, the Internet Archives with his "Wayback Machine" and the Long Now Foundation, very few organizations are effectively archiving their own websites [89–91]. There also appears to be little or no effort being made to capture the nature of virtual communities as they spring up and subside on the Web [1, p. 22]. McClure and Sprehe also found that US government agencies were not identifying materials they published on the web of enduring value and were not planning for their preservation [92]. Since McClure and Sprehe's report, the Smithsonian Institution did commission a study of the best approaches to preserving its web resources [93].

Ross and Gow (1999) in *Digital Archaeology: The Recovery of Digital Materials at Risk*, part of the JISC/NPO Studies on the Preservation of Electronic Materials series, provide numerous examples of digital data loss and recreation through extreme and expensive measures, collectively termed, "digital archaeology" [94]. Examples include recovery of the Challenger space shuttle data tapes and recovery of politically sensitive electronic records after German re-unification. While several of these stories have "happy" endings, in that at least some data was rescued and significant technical and managerial lessons were learned for the future preservation of digital data, although all at substantial financial cost, they all point to the incredible fragility of digital data. Other, not so happy stories tell of the loss of the first electronic mail message and Landsat photographs of the Amazon basin in the 1970s, now essential to understanding changes in the rainforest [95–97]. Perhaps most unsettling is that these case studies document data loss at major institutions that should logically be expected to have better resources, knowledge, and motivation to preserve digital information than many smaller organizations. Undoubtedly the day-to-day preservation situation in smaller, less well-heeled institutions is far worse.

Our collective memory; our cultural heritage now captured in digital artifacts; and the very functioning of society in respect to commerce, health care, and government all hinge on our ability to develop digital strategies and policies, perfect preservation techniques, and educate corporations and citizens with regards to their role and stake in electronic data archiving. David Levy has cited the "current inability to preserve digital information" as "a major impediment to the adoption of digital forms on a grand scale" and has called for heroic measures to improve digital preservation [98]. In essence, digital society cannot go forward without the assurance of digital preservation.

4.   The Challenges of Digital Data Archiving

4.1   Abundance and Proliferation of Digital Information and Formats

The problem exists at every level, from small business to great archival institutes to the ordinary household. You can't simply cram all this information in a box and stick it in the attic, because the attic is already jammed, as are the basement and all the closets. [99]

Each year new statistics appear estimating the size of the Web; each year the number skyrockets, and although the growth curve may not be as steep now as it was just a few years ago, the overall size of the Web is stunning and there is no sign that growth will stop. As of January 2000, Inktomi Corporation and NEC Research Institute announced the result of a study that verified the "surface" Web, the static, publicly available part visible to search engines, had grown to more than one billion unique, indexable pages, with close to 6.5 million servers worldwide. Close to 55% of the top-level domains for web addresses were .com with 87% of all documents in English [100]. As of January 2001, the "How Much Information?" Project webpage at the School of Information Management and Systems (SIMS), University of California at Berkeley, stated that the surface web consisted "of approximately 2.5 billion documents," with a growth rate of "7.3 million pages per day. They further estimated the total amount of information in the surface Web to be between 25 and 50 terabytes of information" [101]. SIMS based these estimates on Cyveillance studies and projections in mid-2000. Cyveillance calculated the size of an average web page at 10,060 bytes [102]. OCLC's Web Characterization Project estimated 8,745,000 websites[3] existed in 2001, an 18% increase over their 2000 figure [103]. The Pew Internet and American Life Project provides extensive links to Internet statistics [104] as does the Congressional Internet Caucus [105].

While constantly growing, the Web changes in other ways that makes it an evolving rather than archival environment. Pages change and other pages and entire sites disappear. This fluid and mutable state of the Web is problematic for researchers, especially historians. For example, much of the documentation concerning and "presence" of many of the failed dotcoms of the 1990s only existed in web pages. Brewster Kahle, through Internet Alexia and the Internet Archive, is working to preserve snapshots of the World Wide Web. The Internet Archive presently contains over 10 billion web pages from 1996 through mid-2002 or more than 100 terabytes of information [89–91]. Snapshots capture some of the information available on the Web, and Kahle's unique project is valuable to anyone trying to find a page that no longer exists on the current Web, but this approach does not preserve the dynamic nature of the Web.

The Web while enormous, ever spreading, and firmly in the public's consciousness, is but one part of all the digital data existing today. Not only is the "hidden" or "deep" web, that part which search engines do not index due to matters such as password protection and dynamic database generation, many times larger than the visible web, non-web files and databases from desktops to vast corporate, financial, and government data warehouses, present staggering accumulations of digital records. As of September 2001, BrightPlanet, a provider of Internet content infrastructure and search data to web-enabled businesses, estimated the size of the hidden or "deep" web at 400 to 550 times larger than the publicly available web that search engine robots can probe. They note that the deep Web "contains 7,500 terabytes of information, compared to 19 terabytes of information in the surface Web" and that "sixty of the largest deep websites collectively contain about 750 terabytes of information— sufficient by themselves to exceed the size of the surface Web by 40 times" [106– 108]. Lyman and Varian state that there are 550 billion web-connected documents in the deep web [109]. Moreover, they state that as of 1999, "The world produced between 1 and 2 exabytes[4] of unique information per year," [101] and estimate that 93% of all information produced in 1999 was in digital format [110]. These statistics reveal the immensity of the Web, the extent of all "born digital" [10] information, and hold several implications. Finding relevant material on the Web is already difficult, frequently discouraging, and often a process of diminishing returns. If this vast

---

[3] A distinct location on the Internet, identified by an IP address, that returns a response code of 200 and a Webpage in reply to an HTTP request for the home page. The Website consists of all interlinked Webpages residing at the site's IP address.

[4] An exabyte is a billion gigabytes or 10^{18} bytes.

and burgeoning accumulation of data is not organized and preserved in a meaningful way, soon locating useful information may be pure luck.

While such born digital files may be well organized (although this is doubtful), typically little has been done to preserve them. Huge stores of governmental, financial, business, scientific, and cultural data hang in the balance, awaiting reliable preservation and the benefit of archival disposition based on the principles of the sanctity of evidence, provenance, the life cycle of records, the organic nature of records, and the hierarchy of records and their description [17]. Indeed, these documents await electronic records management and active archival treatment that involves appraisal, physical and intellectual preservation, and description that provides context for use and an effective means of accessibility. Kenneth Thibodeau of the National Archives and Records Administration sums up the stakes for NARA and the United States in unequivocal terms:

> Information in digital form poses critical challenges for the National Archives and Records Administration (NARA). While many other institutions are facing such challenges, NARA's situation is different because of the special requirements that apply to archival institutions, NARA's unique role in the Federal Government, and the scale and diversity of the Government's programs. NARA views success in facing these challenges as entailing nothing less than building the archives of the future. In sober terms, unless we succeed in surmounting these challenges there will not be a National Archives of the United States for the digital era. [68]

Along with the scale of the problem, the proliferation of increasingly complex digital objects needing archiving serves continuously to complicate the situation. Thibodeau summarizes the situation at the National Archives:

> The challenges NARA faces are further compounded by the scope and scale of its responsibilities. The Federal Government is a large, complex entity engaged in a bewildering variety of activities. The records NARA is responsible for preserving range from those produced in enacting laws to the personnel files of veterans, from the conduct of foreign affairs to the investigations of independent counsels; from the interdiction of narcotics to the topography of the United States. The president, the congress, the courts, and federal agencies employ a practically unlimited and continually changing variety of computer systems, digital media, and applications in conducting their business. The only reasonable assumption NARA can make is that preserving the electronic records of the Federal Government requires the ability to preserve virtually every class of digital object that has been, or may be created. Beyond that, NARA needs to contend with explosive growth in the quantities of electronic records it needs to preserve. The first accession of electronic records into the National Archives was in 1970. Since then, holdings of electronic records have grown exponentially, and the available data indicates that exponential growth will continue in the future. [68]

At the same time, a vast body of print and other analog works awaits digitization for use by broader audiences, both scholarly and popular. Seamus Ross notes that creating digital versions of print resources is expensive but "there are substantial gaps between the demand for resources and those which already exist in digital form, as well as the available expertise and skills for their creation" [111]. Funding and planning for digitization efforts from organizations such as the Library of Congress, the NHPRC, and the Institute for Museum and Library Services (IMLS) in the United States, as well as Joint Information Systems Committee (JISC) in the United Kingdom and the National Library of Australia, along with other national libraries indicates recognition of the need to digitize significant cultural materials for access to worldwide audiences. In April 2001, the Cultural Heritage Applications Unit of the Information Society Directorate General of the European Commission brought together an expert panel from member states and drafted the Lund Principles and Lund Action Plan [112]. The Lund Principles aim to ensure that the cultural heritage of Europe is made available in digital form through a cooperative infrastructure for digitization among member nations. Here are more materials that await preservation in addition to, and at times, in place of, their originals.

Yet few preservationists see digital copies of print works as preservation copies. Indeed, as Yakel points out, many individuals view the term "digital preservation" as an oxymoron [113]. The issues discussed in the remainder of this section illustrate why most archivists consider microfilming and printing on acid free, buffered paper to be the only generally acceptable preservation methods for endangered print materials at the opening of the 21st century [114,115]. In contrast, Clifford Lynch notes that "the digital collection ... is the locus of stewardship for digital preservation" [116].

4.2   Media & File Fragility & Decay

All information storage media has a lifespan, although this varies greatly from one technology to another. Conway discusses the irony and dilemma posed by the capacity and inherent instability of modern media:

> The earliest known evidence of writing—pictorial signs on sun-dried clay tablets—originated roughly 6,000 years ago. Tens of thousands of examples of Sumerian and Babylonian writing exist today in the world's major research centers. Archaeologists unearth hundreds more every year. From ancient times to the present, the entire technology of writing has undergone steady evolution. Today, we have the capacity to store detailed bit-mapped images of hundreds of books on an optical disk the size of a coaster. This capacity to record and store gives rise to one of the central dilemmas of recorded history: Our capacity to record information has increased exponentially over time while the longevity of the media used to store the information has decreased equivalently. [117]

Throughout his writings on preservation, Paul Conway describes preservation as a combination of prevention of loss (deterioration), renewal of usability (treatment), and extension of the usefulness of information content (reformatting). He argues that these goals of preservation remain constant whether the medium is paper or electronic, but in the digital world the timeframe shifts dramatically. Results of tests conducted by the National Media Laboratory for the U.S. Department of Defense eloquently support Conway's observation. Van Bogart [118] reports media life expectancy, under various preservation conditions (temperature and humidity) for various types of magnetic tape, optical disks, paper, and microfilm. At 86 °F and 60% humidity no magnetic tape reliably holds data for more than 6 months; optical disks survive reliably for a year; acid-free, buffered paper survives 10 years; and archival quality silver microfilm lasts 30 years. At ideal conditions of 50 °F and 25% humidity the best magnetic tape and optical disks may reliably retain data for 20 years; microfilm for 200 years; and buffered paper for 500 years. Porck and Teygeler observe that life expectancy (LE) testing of audio- and videotape is "an important and difficult challenge" with "standardization of LE testing advancing slowly, and no serious insight or understanding, based on research by independent laboratories, is available to the public" [119]. Ross and Gow in their study of the potential for recovery of lost digital data or "digital archaeology," provide a caveat to all considering media longevity:

> Our initial understanding of the stability and life expectancy of particular types of media often depends upon the claims made by the media manufacturers themselves. These claims tend to reflect the exuberance of scientists compounded by the hype of their marketing teams. As a result it often proves difficult to make well-informed and secure decisions about technological trends and the life expectancy of new media. [94, p. iii]

In this study they found the stability of CD-R technologies highly overrated. Media fragility means that preservation in the form of copying to new media (refreshing) must take place early in a digital object's lifespan and be repeated frequently throughout its existence.

Beyond the vulnerabilities of the media itself such as signal dropout that occurs gradually over time with magnetic tape, digitally stored information is also inherently fragile and mutable. Given a hostile environment such as a fire, flood, or lightening all data can be destroyed in an instant. Manufacture defects often render entire disks unreadable without resort to some sort of rescue program. Short of total destruction, digital files are very easy to alter with the precise changes being hard to detect. This lack of "fixity" is a primary challenge to the authenticity of electronic records. Someone may intentionally inflict such data loss or accidentally cause it by erasing or writing one version of a file over another. Data loss may be detected at the time of the event, remain undetected until the file is accessed for use in the future, or go undetected at point of use.

4.3 Hardware, Software, and Media Obsolescence

As short as it may be, digital media life expectancy is not the primary impediment to long-term preservation of digital information. Thus far, most electronic media have outlived our ability to find machines on which to use them and the software with which to access file content. Jeffrey Rothenberg notes that for optical disk (CD), digital tape, and magnetic tape, the average time to obsolescence is a mere five years [87]. One need only think of 8-track tapes, 5-inch floppy disks, and mainframe computer tape formats to understand the situation. The 1990s saw the heyday of 3.5-inch floppy disks and two types of zip disks, all of which are rapidly being replaced by inexpensive read-write CD-ROMs for day-to-day data storage.

For many people and many organizations, the primary approach to preserving digital information is to fundamentally alter its format by printing everything of value to paper. This is clearly not a solution to the "digital" preservation conundrum, although most states have public records laws telling state employees to do just that with all significant documents and email messages. As simplistic as this seems, print versions of born digital objects are inherently different from their digital relatives. Print copies are not necessarily authentic copies nor do they always contain all the information found in the original, such as email headers, to preserve their evidential value. The "PROFS" and "GRS20" lawsuits in the 1990s brought by a group of private citizens and public interest groups against the Executive Office of the President, the US National Security Council and the Archivist of the United States largely turned on the definition of "record" and whether or not electronic mail messages constituted records, and more specifically, if they were records lacking header information [120–122]. Moreover, few people actually print out all important documents and especially email messages. Additionally, the contents and relationships found within dynamic databases and complex systems cannot be captured fully in paper snapshots.

Kenneth Thibodeau presents a lucid overview of the digital preservation methods used and under development in the last decade [123, p. 18]. He sorts these approaches on a continuum from attempts to preserve specific technology, as with emulation and computer museums, through data migration to new formats, to the preservation of digital objects as seen in the persistent archives approach. A wide variety of work is going forward along the spectrum Thibodeau draws.

At the "preserve technology" end of Thibodeau's scale lies the computer museum, wherein a repository (or individual) warehouses the hardware and software necessary to read any media they wish to store. This involves not only the space in which to keep these items, but also documentation for older systems so one knows how to run and fix them and the parts needed to keep them running. Over time, the museum needs to keep a good deal of hardware and software applications and versions thereof and refresh data, including the software programs, on new media (of the old type) on a scheduled basis. It must also keep a supply of the old media for this purpose but it is unclear how long its shelf life will be even if it has not been used to store data. Computer museums are probably best kept for historical, not functional purposes, although most offices keep some older computer equipment for access purposes once it is no longer in daily use. Along the same line, computer simulators that recreate the entire hardware and software environment of an earlier machine such as Edsac, 1949–50 built at the University of Cambridge [124] or the Ferranti Pegasus, 1956–1962 [125] provide more historical understanding of earlier computing capabilities than practicalities for digital preservation. The Science Museum in London has also successfully built the Difference Engine and printer from Charles Babbage's original 19th century plans [126].

Another proposed solution to technological obsolescence, emulation, also falls at the "preserve technology" end of Thibodeau's digital preservation methods scheme. Rothenberg was an early primary proponent of this approach [127]. He explains that hardware is not stored in this approach, but rather, the "specification of the hardware environment" required to run the software is also stored along with the data. More generically, hardware, software, processors, and operating systems may all be "emulated" and embedded with digital files that will use them for presentation and manipulation in the future. Bearman argues that this approach "preserves" the wrong things—hardware and software—rather than the authentic records themselves [128].

The Digital Rosetta Stone approach maintains documents in their original file formats along with a "metaknowledge archive" that would have information needed to recover digital data from superseded media [129]. The CAMiLEON project, a collaboration between the University of Michigan and University of Leeds, takes the opposing view, arguing that emulation is a valid and affordable method of digital preservation [130]. Ross and Gow provide evidence from a case study that emulation is challenging [94,29,30], but note that much of the work in emulation has been in the area of recreating arcade games and that this technique warrants further investigation. While game enthusiasts may desire an authentic arcade experience on their computers and hand-held devices, the issues and stakes are hardly the same as with the preservation of authentic electronic records, thus the work from the game domain may not translate directly to an evidential records/information environment.

Reformatting or refreshing data, a preservation solution mid-range between saving technology and saving objects, involves moving digital data from one storage medium to another, usually without having to open the software application that created the information [47, p. 27].[5] Starting with the premise that refreshing "cannot serve as a general solution for preserving digital information" the Commission on Preservation and Access (CPA) explained in a landmark report that

> copying depends either on the compatibility of present and past versions of software and generations of hardware or the ability of competing hardware and software product lines to interoperate. In respect of these factors—backward compatibility and interoperability—the rate of technological change exacts a serious toll on efforts to ensure the longevity of digital information. [97, p. 5]

More involved than simple reformatting, migration is the process of moving data from one computer platform or software program to another. Charles Dollar defines migration with an archival perspective, noting that it involves two primary activities: "(1) maintaining processable authentic electronic records and (2) migrating authentic electronic records from legacy information systems." Dollar explains that migration involves readable media, operational devices to read the media, target media and devices, and significantly, "proprietary legacy systems that lack export software functionality" [47, p. 31].

Migration, one of the most discussed strategies for preservation, necessarily involves changing the digital object over time. Researchers are working on several different approaches to migration, but they all share the common element of accepting that original digital objects cannot be preserved, only copies of the objects. Migration from older proprietary systems to newer versions or to open systems can be a very complicated, expensive, labor-intensive process that involves a good deal of programming, possible reduction of files to a lowest common data denominator such as ASCII (file standardization), and often data loss [127, p. 13]. Significantly for archivists, migration entails moving and altering the data targeted for preservation, thus raising serious questions as to maintenance of reliability and authenticity. Even very small changes, such as formatting that may be lost with a conversion from a proprietary application format to ASCII text, can change the meaning of a document (e.g., loss of bold and italic demarcation) and thus result in a copy that is not an authentic and reliable rendering of the original. The CPA notes that "the purpose of migration is to preserve the integrity of digital objects and to retain the ability for clients to retrieve, display, and otherwise use them in the face of constantly changing technology" [97, p. 6]. With all but the simplest of files, migration has not yet proven to be an archival preservation solution [97, p. 6]. Bearman, however, advocates more research into migration and its appropriateness and robustness given "unambiguous specifications of the source and target environments" [128].

---

[5] Charles Dollar notes that it may also involve transforming the character code from Binary Coded Decimal (BCD), Extended Binary Code for Data Interchange (EBCDIC) or Unicode to American Standard Code for Information Interchange (ASCII).

Some of the most promising and generalizable work in the technical aspects of digital preservation are in an advanced and comprehensive evolution of the migration approach, persistent archives, with work ongoing at the San Diego Super Computer Center in a NARA-funded project, "Collection-Based Persistent Digital Archives" [131,132]. These efforts, discussed below, seek to preserve complex objects without altering their authentic attributes.

In summary, we have yet to develop a reliable technique to preserve the bit streams of large volumes of electronic records and other digital data in ways that ensure they remain accessible, processable, and do not lose their authenticity and integrity with time. This is a key area in which archivists and computer scientists must collaborate. Ongoing research is discussed below.

4.4   Intellectual Property Rights

Many commentators on the progress of digital preservation predict that the technical challenges will be solved long before the legal and social ones. Chief among the legal issues involving digital preservation and access are intellectual property rights, privacy, and data security. The National Research Council in *The Digital Dilemma* concluded that "three technological trends—the ubiquity of information in digital form, the widespread use of computer networks, and the rapid proliferation of the World Wide Web—have profound implications for the way intellectual property (IP) is created, distributed, and accessed by virtually every sector of society" [133, Chap. 6]. The dilemma comes from the "promise and peril" of networked information that is natively easy to access; the peril from the ease of inappropriate use and reproduction and conversely from overly restrictive access controls. The problem appears so intractable because so many stakeholders are involved.

Libraries and archives have long preserved the analog cultural record by purchasing books and manuscripts and providing access to them under the doctrine of first sale, that is, a person or institution who purchases a work can make it available to others. This has worked well with tangible print items because only one person can read a book at a time, thus lots of libraries have had to buy lots of books and magazines and publishers have prospered. The fact that most published items are dispersed in many libraries has also served as a preservation safety net, with at least some institutions conserving most items of value. The national deposit system with the Copyright Office at the Library of Congress has gone far toward collecting the published cultural and scientific record in the United States. Materials in- and out-of-print have been made available to the public. Once copyright has expired, important works have been republished in the public domain and less valuable works have "naturally" expired. Archives have preserved unpublished original works by restricting access and thus wear, and in some cases publishing collections such as the *Thomas*

Jefferson Papers when they have either passed into the public domain or when the repository has held the copyright to the material.

Given current technologies, policies, and economics, the brevity of digital life and its ability to generate exact replicas of materials has made the system of copyright, originally devised "To promote the progress of science and useful arts, by securing for limited times to authors and inventors the exclusive right to their respective writings and discoveries" (Article 1, Section 8, *US Constitution*) a significant obstacle in the path of widespread digital archiving. First, publishers and content producers have successfully lobbied for longer copyright periods [134]—periods far longer than average digital lifespans, but for the most part, they have not taken on the role of archival repositories. Second, national [135] and international [136] copyright legislation prohibits the copying of a range of digital resources including computer programs. Unless trusted repositories, charged with preserving the published record, such as the Library of Congress and other research institutions, have the legal right to make copies of digital materials so that works can be migrated to new media and new versions of software, much will be lost. There is little hope of most commercial publishers preserving any but the more profitable materials in their catalogs for decades or more.

Although digital materials enjoy protection under lengthy copyright terms, there is no national system of copyright deposit of digital materials at the Library of Congress as there has been with printed works although there are plans for and examples of national depository systems for digital materials in other countries [137–141]. The depository system for printed materials facilitated the building of the Library of Congress collection and provided for open public access to these materials, without significantly diminishing the financial return for most publishers and authors. Open access to deposited digital materials that can be copied in a few keys strokes, however, is perceived as an economic threat to content producers. Until there is national deposit for electronic materials in the US it is unlikely that most digital publications will be systematically preserved even though they resided under copyright protection. The NRC report observes that "if archives cannot obtain the digital materials that need to be archived and if they cannot obtain clear legal authorization to manage them across time, then no amount of progress on the technical problems will make any difference" [133, Chap. 3].

Emulation presents even more elaborate intellectual property law problems than copying data files. The premise behind emulation is that the programs that produce the digital object must be preserved, copied, and interfaced with newer hardware and operating systems. Even if emulation proves to be an effective preservation strategy, copyright restrictions may make it useless if software producers do not allow repositories to copy and work with their applications. Yet copyright is not the only problem. Increasingly, companies are using licensing mechanisms, dependent on contract law and redressed through civil proceedings, to protect their software. Infringement of contractual arrangements generally result in financial penalties. Information technology companies are also protecting algorithms underlying their software using patent laws. Data security measures such as encryption and watermarking also present challenges at time of preservation but clearly unprotected networked data is at risk.

Protection of intellectual property rights, and ensuring privacy and security of digital assets from easy theft are all social and legal issues that have their resolution in technological as well as policy solutions. The NRC report notes that

> There are also a variety of important forces at work—regulations, markets, social norms, and technology—all of which must be considered and all of which may also be used in dealing with the issues. Knowing about the full range of forces may open up additional routes for dealing with issues; not every problem need be legislated (or priced) into submission. Individuals exploring these issues are well advised to be cognizant of all the forces at work ... [133, Chap. 6]

The NRC report reaches several conclusions and recommendations that involve the work of the all stakeholders in the digital dilemma, including cultural heritage institutions and the information technology community. These recommendations seek solutions workable and equitable for all while providing the framework within which digital preservation can occur.

5.   Early Agenda Setting

Concern for digital preservation and electronic data archiving emerged in the 1970s, with work to migrate the 1960 decennial census data to new, readable media and exploration of electronic records issues at the National Archives [142–144]. Concerns, uncoordinated efforts, a few state electronic records programs, and a small literature grew in the 1980s and early 1990s [145–155]. Even though there was not widespread activity in the electronic records nor digital preservation arenas, the realization by key individuals and organizations that the preservation of the cultural record was at stake, led to agenda setting that has greatly influenced most research and development in digital archiving and preservation to this day.

In the United States, the 1991 Research Issues in Electronic Records Working Group, sponsored by the Minnesota Historical Society and funded by a grant from the National Historical Publications and Records Commission (NHPRC), was the first and continues to be the most significant influence on digital archiving and electronic records management to date. This group examined issues related to the identification, preservation, and long-term use of electronic records and produced a national agenda for research in the archival management of such records [156]. The working group developed ten questions that constituted the basis of a research agenda that NHPRC has adopted as part of its strategic plan and electronic records funding priorities:

1. What functions and data are required to manage electronic records in accord with archival requirements? Do data requirements and functions vary for different types of automated applications?
2. What are the technological, conceptual, and economic implications of capturing and retaining data, descriptive information, and contextual information in electronic form from a variety of applications?
3. How can software-dependent data objects be retained for future use?
4. How can data dictionaries, information resource directory systems, and other metadata systems be used to support electronic records management and archival requirements?
5. What archival requirements have been addressed in major systems development projects and why?
6. What policies best address archival concerns for the identification, retention, preservation, and research use of electronic records?
7. What functions and activities should be present in electronic records programs and how should they be evaluated?
8. What incentives can contribute to creator and user support for electronic records management concerns?
9. What barriers have prevented archivists from developing and implementing archival electronic records programs?
10. What do archivists need to know about electronic records [156]?

NHPRC has and continues to support several projects, including the Pittsburgh Project [157], a test of the Pittsburgh Functional Requirements at Indiana University [158,159], the U.S. involvement in the InterPARES I and II work [160], the research at the San Diego Super Computer Center regarding the technical aspects of record migration through persistence strategies [161] and the Managing the Digital University Desktop Project at the University of North Carolina at Chapel Hill and Duke University [162] with funds earmarked for electronic records research. NHPRC's influence on electronic records management, started in 1991, continues today and in large part is just now returning results as these projects direct the next generation of research.

While the NHPRC funded some of the first work in the U.S. on electronic records research, it was not until the 1996 report of the Task Force on Archiving of Digital Information entitled, *Preserving Digital Information*, published by the Commission on Preservation and Access (CPA) and the Research Libraries Group (RLG), that much attention coalesced around the broader digital preservation crisis. This was the first widely read statement, and arguably the most influential to date, on this topic. Seven years later, authors and speakers at meetings around the globe are measuring accomplishments in digital preservation against this early agenda-setting document.

Significantly, the CPA report defines digital archives as a different type of organization from digital libraries:

> Digital archives are distinct from digital libraries in the sense that digital libraries are repositories that collect and provide access to digital information, but may or may not provide for the long-term storage and access of that information. [97, p. iii]

Today, libraries with digital assets are facing the need to preserve them, but little serious work has gone forth on preservation issues and techniques in individual repositories. The Task Force produced five major conclusions that remain relevant today:

- The first line of defense against loss of valuable digital information rests with the creators, providers and owners of digital information.

- Long-term preservation of digital information on a scale adequate for the demands of future research and scholarship will require a deep infrastructure capable of supporting a distributed system of digital archives.

- A critical component of the digital archiving infrastructure is the existence of a sufficient number of trusted organizations capable of storing, migrating and providing access to digital collections.

- A process of certification for digital archives is needed to create an overall climate of trust about the prospects of preserving digital information.

- Certified digital archives must have the right and duty to exercise an aggressive rescue function as a fail-safe mechanism for preserving valuable digital information that is in jeopardy of destruction, neglect or abandonment by its current custodian [97, p. 40].

A network of trusted digital repositories are essential to this vision of digital preservation in that it would be "collectively responsible for the long-term accessibility of the nation's social, economic, cultural and intellectual heritage instantiated in digital form ..." [97, p. iii]. Neither a certification system nor a network of trusted digital repositories exists today, seven years after the CPA report, but significant work has gone forward in establishing the characteristics and responsibilities of such repositories for large-scale, heterogeneous collections held by cultural organizations [163]. While relatively few creators, providers, and owners of digital information are seriously concerned with long-term preservation or at least few are taking significant steps to implement preservation programs, other groups worldwide are setting agendas and providing recommendations including the European Commission, the JISC in the United Kingdom, and the National Library of Australia. These are discussed in Section 7 below.

6. Archival Approaches to Ensuring Digital Longevity

Individuals and societies have successfully, if not always optimally, dealt with recorded information for a very long time. Organized archives have existed for more than 5,000 years, with recognizable libraries appearing at least 4,000 years ago [164–167]. Clearly, techniques and methods changed over time, especially with the introduction of printing 500 years ago, but reassuringly, those charged with keeping the tablets, papyri, manuscripts, and books have all performed the same functions of acquiring, appraising, arranging, describing, storing, preserving, and making accessible the information in their care. We stand faced with the same functional tasks in the digital world that librarians and archivists have long known. While the playing field has changed and the methods by which we will reach the "well-ordered digital age" will necessarily be different from how we have run print libraries and archives, many of the underlying questions, principles, and functions applicable in the past may well be relevant and inform the management of digital resources. In our rush to find new answers for the digital environment we must not dispense with established models and information management functions simply because they have applied to print culture.

Preservation of information that possesses enduring value is central to all that archivists do. Theirs is, by definition, a long-term perspective regarding information and records of human activity that no other professional group exhibits. This perspective, manifest in the traditional activities and functions of archival science, is indispensable in the quest to develop reliable and affordable means to ensure the longevity and authenticity of digital data.

6.1   Appraisal

"Appraisal," according to Bellardo and Bellardo, "is the process of determining the value and thus the disposition of records" [67, p. 2]. The InterPARES Project (International Research on Permanent Authentic Records in Electronic Systems) Appraisal Task Force, researching the preservation of authentic electronic records, defines it similarly: "Appraisal involves making a judgment or estimation of the worthiness of continued preservation of records." The Task Force notes that it also considered appraisal in a broader sense because it "is often, though not always, part of the act of acquisition of records by the entity responsible for their long-term preservation, the preserver." The "preserver" is "the juridical person whose primary responsibility is the long-term preservation of authentic records" [168, p. 8].

While somewhat different for personal papers collected in manuscript repositories and organizational records assessed for inclusion in archives, all appraisal involves establishing value. It is based upon many factors including documents' and objects' current administrative, legal, and fiscal use; their evidential and informational value, their arrangement and condition, their intrinsic value, and their relationship to other records. Appraisal has been called the archivist's "most intellectually demanding task" [169] and SAA has deemed it to be the archivist's "first responsibility" to select "records of enduring value" [170,171]. Ham notes that "what makes archival selection so critical is its finality. Because archival materials are usually unique, the archivist's decision about what to save and what to destroy, or to ignore and thereby assign to eventual loss, is irrevocable" [169, p. 1]. A complicating factor is that the secondary values that often imbue documents and records with "enduring value" are generally different from the primary values they exhibited in the active phase of their lifecycles. For example, land ownership records once proved who owned which parcels and thus who could profit from them; for the historians they can reveal a wide range of social and familial relations.

Conversely, appraisal is important in that it is only with the elimination of dross that relevant information and evidence can be located when needed. Contrary to popular perception, archives retain only five to ten percent of the total documentation that most organizations create. Given the enormity of digital materials that might be considered for long-term preservation, both sides of the appraisal coin—retention and elimination—are critical to the future of our cultural, corporate, and scientific record.

Archivists appraise materials based on a number of criteria or values. *Archival value* is defined in very specific terms that justify retaining and preserving selected materials over time. Archival value is manifested in several narrower values— administrative, fiscal, legal, intrinsic, evidential, and informational. *Administrative* or *operational value* is the "usefulness of records/archives for the conduct of current and/or future business" [67, p. 2]. *Fiscal value*, more specifically, is the "worth of records/archives for the conduct of current or future financial or fiscal business and/or evidence thereof" [67, p. 14]. Similarly, *legal value* is the "worth of records/archives for the conduct of current or future legal business and/or evidence thereof" [67, p. 20]. *Intrinsic value* relates to the inherent nature of the materials—age, content, signatures, seals, and other distinguishing elements that make them historically and commercially valuable. *Evidential value* is the "worth of documents/archives for illuminating the nature and work of their creator by providing evidence of the creator's origins, functions, and activities" [67, p. 19]. Finally, *informational value* "is the worth of materials "for reference and research deriving from the information they contain on persons, places, [and] subjects" [67, p. 18].

Some document and artifacts may exhibit several archival values and thus be in a strong position for retention; others are clearly of a transitory nature that should be disposed of when their immediate, active life is complete. While some materials, particularly those created in corporate or governmental settings, may possess very clear legal and evidential values and are often marked for retention based on regulatory statutes (warrant), selection of other items for retention is often highly subjective. This is particularly true in the case of determining informational value and especially in attempting to predict historical value. The archival community has been exploring how media, and especially the fact of being digital, influences or changes archival values and the appraisal process. The InterPARES project has done the most extensive exploration into the challenges of appraising, determining authenticity of, and preserving electronic records.

In the InterPARES I Project (1999–2001), a major international research initiative, archival scholars, computer engineering scholars, national archival institutions and private industry representatives collaborated to develop the theoretical and methodological knowledge required for the permanent preservation of authentic records created in electronic systems. The InterPARES I Project was based in the School of Library, Archival and Information Studies at the University of British Columbia. It continued the "UBC Project," "The Preservation of the Integrity of Electronic Records," that was conducted between 1994 and 1997 by archival researchers at UBC in collaboration with the US Department of Defense (DoD) [172]. The goal of this project was "to identify and define conceptually the nature and components of an electronic record and the conditions necessary to ensure its integrity, that is, its reliability and authenticity" [55, p. 43]. InterPARES I continues in the InterPARES II project (2002–2006) that will explore experimental, interactive, and dynamic records. Major funding sources include Canada's Social Science and Humanities Research Council, the American National Historical Publications and Records Commission, the National Archives and Records Administration of the United States, and the Italian National Research Council. The InterPARES I researchers worked in three teams that focused on core archival functions: Appraisal, Authenticity, and Preservation. The work of each will be presented below.

The InterPARES Appraisal Task Force set out "to determine whether the theory and methodology of appraisal for electronic records differs from that for traditional records, and what role the activities of appraisal play in the long-term preservation of electronic records" [168, p. 6]. After reviewing the existing literature on the appraisal of electronic records [173], the Task Force surveyed organizations regarding their appraisal of electronic records, and from these data developed a functional model for the selection of electronic records [168, p. 61].

The Task Force concluded that selection, involves four main activities: "(1) managing the selection function, (2) appraising electronic records, (3) monitoring electronic records selected for preservation, and (4) carrying out the disposition of electronic records." The appraisal activity contains the sub-functions of compiling information about the records, assessing the value of the records, determining the feasibility of preserving the records in an authentic state, and making the appraisal decision. Central to the technical aspects of appraisal, determining the feasibility of maintaining authentic records involves (1) determining the record elements to be preserved; (2) identifying the digital components to be preserved; and (3) reconciling preservation requirements with preservation capabilities. This step gathers information about the form, content, and context of the record, that may be observable in the record or its metadata, or implied organizational, legal, and technical environments that are necessary to determine that the record is accurate and reliable over time and that it can be accessed at some undetermined point in the future. The report concludes with discussion of the original research questions:

1. What is the influence of digital technology on appraisal?
2. What is the influence of the retrievability, intelligibility, functionality, and research needs on appraisal?
3. What are the influences of the medium and the physical form of the record on appraisal?
4. When in the course of their existence should electronic records be appraised? Should electronic records be appraised more than once in the course of their existence, and, if so, when?
5. Who should be responsible for appraising electronic records?
6. What are the appraisal criteria and methods for authentic electronic records [168, p. 6]?

A key recommendation acknowledges that "appraisal is a knowledge-intensive and research-intensive activity" and that appraisers must be provided with the proper training, tools, information, support, and resources to conduct the necessary research" [168, p. 36].

6.2 Authenticity and Evidence

Determining and ensuring the reliability and authenticity of archival materials, especially records with evidentiary value for organizations, is a primary responsibility of archivists. Heather McNeil provides an insightful discussion of the relationship between authenticity and evidence in *Trusting Records* [174]. Peter Hirtle notes that "Pure archival interest in records depends not on their informational content, but on the *evidence* they provide of government or business activity" [175, p. 11]. Glenda

Acland represents a similar perspective in Australian archival thought, noting the "pivot of archival science is evidence, not information" [176]. We need only to think of the controversy and legal debate over the White House electronic mail records from the Reagan administration to realize how important ensuring that archived electronic files are authentic to fulfill their evidentiary role in business, scholarship, and society [120–122]. The InterPARES Authenticity Task Force defines an authentic record as one "that is what it purports to be and is free from tampering or corruption" [177, p. 2]. Authenticity, and thus evidentiary value, resides in much of what encircles and enfolds records—their format, their provenance, and the change of custody that follows them.

Traditionally, archivists have sought to ensure authenticity of paper records at both the collection and item levels. At the collection level archivists have used the principles of provenance and original order and a documented chain of custody to preserve the context in which records were created. This has worked very well with large collections such as those at the National Archives. At the item level, archivists and scholars have used a variety of methods from the disciplines of diplomatics and paleography to determine the authenticity of paper records.

Provenance is a term with several levels of meaning. According to the *SAA Glossary*, "provenance" is: (1) The organization or individual that created, accumulated, and/or maintained and used records in the conduct of business prior to their transfer to a records center, archives, or manuscript repository" or "(2) Information regarding the origin and custodial history of documents" [67, p. 27]. Stemming from these notions of creator, ownership, and custody, the "principle of provenance" states "records/archives of the same provenance must not be intermingled with those of any other provenance" [67, p. 27]. It is based on the principle of *le Respect des fonds*, established in France in the 1840s [178]. In Germany in the 1880s the principle of provenance was established as a means of archival management to ensure the evidentiary value of records for the new school of critical historians [179]. The principle of original order also has a French derivation, *le Respect de l'ordre intérieure*. This principle states that records should be left in the order in which creators filed them, again with the goal of providing insight about the creator and context for the records. Additionally, maintaining provenance and original order make it easier to see gaps or odd inclusions in a series of records and thus provide some measure of authenticity at the collection or series levels.

Diplomatics, a form of literary criticism, and more specifically an "analytical technique for determining the authenticity of records issued by sovereign authorities in previous centuries," began to be formalized the 17th century in Europe [180]. Its purpose was to determine "the reality of the rights or truthfulness of the facts" and was used widely by the law profession, then by historians and archivists starting at the end of the 19th century with the rise of evidence-based history. Herein archivists and scholars would evaluate the authenticity of documents based on indicators such as paper and ink type, seals, signatures, and general form, e.g., a charter should look like typical charters and contain specific types of information.

The digital environment wherein copies are made with a click and changes are often hard to detect, poses many questions regarding authenticity of electronic records. Wendy Duff has noted that "as records migrate from a stable paper reality to an intangible electronic existence, their physical attributes, vital for establishing the authenticity and reliability of the evidence they contain, are threatened" [181]. Peter Hirtle asserts that the most important question facing archivists today is "how to ensure the authenticity of records in digital form" [175, p. 16]. It is unclear at this point whether the principle of provenance or the methods of diplomatics will be relevant to the preservation of electronic records, but ongoing research appears to afford these tools significant roles in determining authenticity among a range of necessary processes and methodologies.

A large part of determining a digital object's authenticity rests in defining the inherent and necessary characteristics that accomplish this task. For archivists this search started with efforts to determine the functional requirements of electronic records. The Recordkeeping Functional Requirements Project at the University of Pittsburgh (1993 to 1996) used case studies, professional standards, expert advice, and precedents to derive a set of functional requirements for records and recordkeeping that are necessary for the preservation of evidence in electronic format. The Pittsburgh project derived these elements in a context of literary warrant taken "from the law, customs, standards and professional best practices accepted by society and codified in the literature of different professions concerned with records and recordkeeping" [157]. From the functional requirements, the Pittsburgh researchers derived a set of production rules that "decompose each functional requirement into a form that is specific and observable" and metadata specifications that "describe how documentation of the content and structure of a record can link up and be retained with metadata that describes the context of its business transaction" [157].

The Pittsburgh project rested on the assumption that "recordness" and "evidentiality" must be built into the record system from the start if they are to be maintained throughout the life cycle of the record. Here the system and metadata substitute in large part for the archival repository. While this may represent the ideal situation, few documents are created within electronic records management systems that generate preservation metadata at the point of creation and it is unclear in the days of the Enron and Worldcom scandals how agencies and organizations preserve the authenticity of their own records. With significant simplification and a good deal of effort, Philip Bantin at Indiana University tested the Pittsburgh functional requirements [182,183]. Although a pioneering project that led to other research, the Pittsburgh study presented more complexity and demanded an unrealistic records creation environment for it to have extensive practical influence thus far.

The University of British Columbia (UBC) Project (1994–1997), "Preservation of the Integrity of Electronic Records" [172], used archival theory and diplomatics to assess how best to ensure record authenticity. Although the methods were quite different from those used in Pittsburgh, some of the findings were similar, namely, that the authenticity of records could best, or perhaps only, be preserved if they were produced in a system that facilitated the generation of specific preservation metadata at the point of creation. Conversely the UBC project is founded in the necessity of a trusted archival repository as the centerpiece of electronic record preservation.

The InterPares I Project, also sought to apply diplomatics to assessing and ensuring the authenticity of digital records along with case studies of existing electronic records systems. The primary outcomes from this research were a set of requirements "that support the presumption of the authenticity of electronic records before they are transferred to the preserver's custody" and a second set that "support the production of authentic copies of electronic records after they have been transferred to the preserver's custody" [177, p. iv]. Some of the most significant analysis within the Authenticity Task Force's Final Report is the comparison of the conceptual requirements for authenticity and existing national and international standards, placing the InterPARES findings in context and placing the usefulness of such standards for the preservation of authentic electronic records in question.

The International Standards Organization's "Draft International Standard on Records Management" (ISO/DIS 15489) exhibits some overlap with the InterPARES requirements for authenticity, but many points to ensure long-term preservation are missing. The "Design Criteria Standard for Electronic Records Management Software Applications" (DoD 5015.2-STD) from the US Department of Defense entirely focuses on active records and system functionalities, and does not address either authenticity nor long-term preservation of the records accommodated by the system in their active life [184]. The "Model Requirements for the Management of Electronic Records" or MoReq (Interchange of Data between Administrations (IDA program) from the European Commission is a model specification of requirements for ERMS (Electronic Records Management Systems) designed to be applicable throughout Europe [185]. There is greater mapping of requirements between the InterPARES requirements and MoReq, but the latter, as with the DOD ERMS criteria, stresses functionality over procedures and policies and speaks mainly to active records. This analysis illustrates that while these electronic records management standards may ultimately facilitate the preservation of electronic records prior to their deposit in a trusted repository, there is of yet no international standard for systems or software to support the long-term preservation of authentic electronic records. Much work for both the archival and computer science communities lies ahead.

6.3   Description, Metadata, and Standards

The term "metadata," meaning "data about data," is in wide use today, especially to denote information that describes web pages. Although the term became popular among information specialists only in the late 1980s, information managers, including librarians and archivists have been creating and using metadata for centuries. The tags that hung from scrolls in the Alexandrian Library contained metadata; library card catalogs are metadata databases; and archival finding aids are extensive sources of very rich metadata relating to archival collections.

The archival profession has created very distinctive forms of metadata to accommodate description, retrieval, and preservation of document collections. Of most note is the "finding aid" that can be anything from a brief summary of a collection to an extended description of the content and arrangement of a collection that facilitates researchers finding relevant documents in what could be hundreds of boxes (or disks) of material.

The hallmark of finding aids is collective and hierarchical description. Finding aids generally start with an overall description of the collection; a biographic sketch if the collection is composed of personal papers, or an institutional history if they are organizational files; series descriptions; folder lists; and occasionally, item level lists or descriptions, with each element inheriting the characteristics of the one of which it is a part. This hierarchical approach makes possible description of very large collections by eliminating the need to catalog each and every item—a prohibitive expense that can be justified only for the most important items.

Effective and efficient hierarchical arrangement and description are predicated on the principles of provenance and original order. Keeping files together from the same office of origin or creator and in the file order in which they come to the archives, not only reflects a good deal about the institution or person that created them, it generally provides a logical arrangement for all but the most disorganized files. Typically, there will be large files including correspondence, financial records, and writings in personal papers and equally distinct sets of records in institutional files. Archivists term these distinct units "series." Folders and items (analog or digital) fit into series while a number of series make up a collection, the contents and arrangement of which are described in the overall collection description and relevant history.

Daniel Pitti began work in 1993 at the University of California, Berkeley Library, that has resulted in the Encoded Archival Description Document Type Definition (EAD DTD) [186,187]. The goal of the initial project was to "investigate the desirability and feasibility of developing a nonproprietary encoding standard for machine-readable finding aids such as inventories, registers, indexes, and other documents created by archives, libraries, museums, and manuscript repositories to support the use of their holdings" [188]. Many archives were already contributing electronic "catalog" records to national online bibliographic utilities such as OCLC [189] or

RLIN (Research Libraries Information Network) [190] but archivists found these to be generally unsatisfactory because they failed to capture and represent the richness of archival description as finding aids had done. The creation of the EAD DTD and its subsequent adoption as a standard has allowed archives to place their finding aids on-line, providing rich collection description and hierarchical access to materials. Originally created for the Standard Generalized Mark-up Language (SGML), EAD is now XML (Extended Mark-up Language) compliant, facilitating easier access through most web browsers [191–193]. The Society of American Archivists and the Library of Congress maintain the EAD standard and provide a *Tag Library* [194] and *Application Guidelines* [195] on the LC website. Many organizations beyond archives are finding the hierarchical capabilities of EAD to be useful in describing their materials and are thus adopting an archival perspective in their information management practice. Presently, work is going forward on an "Encoded Archival Context" standard "for encoding and exchanging contextual information about the creators, subjects, and circumstances that contributed to the creation and use of archival materials" [196].

Beyond the efforts to provide users with direct networked access to finding aids, work is going forth in many projects to develop content and preservation metadata standards for digital materials. The Dublin Core (DC) is now a recognized international standard for descriptive or discovery metadata for digital materials [197,198]. Designed initially to provide access to web pages, DC is enjoying wider application and work is going forth on defining frameworks for the interoperability of metadata sets. A key feature of the DC is its extensibility and the management of this process. While discovery metadata assists in locating materials through search engines, "preservation" or "administrative" metadata stores information deemed necessary to the long-term preservation of digital objects. Categories of information include the software used to create the object, the number of pixels per inch for images, and a given image's relationship to others in a multi-image object. The METS (Metadata Encoding Transmission Standard) overview at the Library of Congress explains the importance of structural and technical metadata:

> Without structural metadata, the page image or text files comprising the digital work are of little use, and without technical metadata regarding the digitization process, scholars may be unsure of how accurate a reflection of the original the digital version provides. For internal management purposes, a library must have access to appropriate technical metadata in order to periodically refresh and migrate the data, ensuring the durability of valuable resources. [199]

Much of the work in preservation metadata is being conducted within the structure of the Open Archival Information System (OAIS) initiative [200]. The OAIS Reference Model, chartered by the Consultative Committee on Space Data Systems and led by

NASA [54], "is articulating the functionality and components of any system responsible for preserving any type of information over any length of time" [68]. The model is a draft ISO standard that "provides a high level framework for entities, functions, data flows and administrative activities" [68]. The OAIS Model contains an information model that broadly describes metadata necessary for long-term preservation and that works within the functional model of the archives. Data within the OAIS can either be the resource to be preserved or metadata associated with it. Within this generalized metadata model, information concerning the preservation of the data object is termed "Preservation Description Information" and consists of four types of information familiar within the archival community:

- *Reference Information*: enumerates and describes identifiers assigned to the Content Information such that it can be referred to unambiguously, both internally and externally to the archive (e.g., ISBN, URN).

- *Provenance Information*: documents the history of the Content Information (e.g., its origins, chain of custody, preservation actions and effects).

- *Context Information*: documents the relationships of the Content Information to its environment (e.g., why it was created, relationships to other Content Information).

- *Fixity Information*: documents authentication the mechanisms used to ensure that the Content Information has not been altered in an undocumented manner (e.g., checksum, digital signature) [54].

It should be noted that OAIS is a very high level model and that its translation into a working system take a great deal of effort and time. The digital archiving community must produce modularized, interchangeable, and portable tools that function within an OAIS environment before fully operable implementations will be possible.

In June 2002, The OCLC/RLG Working Group on Preservation Metadata published its report, "Preservation Metadata and the OAIS Information Model: A Metadata Framework to Support the Preservation of Digital Objects" [201]. This work represents a refinement, extension, and elaboration of a synthesis of four existing preservation metadata schemes developed by the CURL Exemplars in Digital Archives project (Cedars), the National Library of Australia (NLA), the Networked European Deposit Library (NEDLIB), and the Online Computer Library Center, Inc. (OCLC).

Cedars, a U.K. collaborative project that involved librarians, archivists, publishers, and repositories, was funded under phase three of the JISC Electronic Libraries Program (eLib). From April 1998 through March 2001, Cedars investigated the issues surrounding digital preservation and the responsibilities that research libraries and archives would have to assume to ensure continued accessibility to both digitized and born-digital materials [202]. Practical work focused on the creation of a

Distributed Archive Prototype, based on the OAIS system and the development of a metadata framework to enable long-term preservation of digital assets [203].

With funding from the European Commission's Telematics Application Programme, the NEDLIB (Networked European Deposit Library) project ran from 1998 through 2000 [204]. The Koninklijke Bibliotheek (National Library of the Netherlands) led eight national libraries in Europe, one national archive, and IT organizations and publishers in this project. NEDLIB developed a common architecture and basic tools for building deposit systems for electronic publications (DSEP). The project, built on the OAIS model, addressed "major technical issues confronting national deposit libraries that are in the process of extending their deposit, whether by legal or voluntary means, to digital works" [205]. NEDLIB extends the OAIS model by adding a dedicated preservation module that accommodates migration and emulation strategies and "preservation description information," including authenticity information and the preservation measures undertaken for a deposit copy.

Much of the work from the National Library of Australia has been conducted within the context of the PANDORA (Preserving and Accessing Networked Documentary Resources of Australia) Project [206]. PANDORA has established an archive of selected Australian online publications, including web pages, developed several model policies and procedures, and has created a logical data model for preservation metadata.

Also extending from the OAIS model, is the Digital Library Federation [207] Metadata Encoding Transmission Standard (METS) initiative, hosted at the Library of Congress. METS provides "an XML document format for encoding metadata necessary for both management of digital library objects within a repository and exchange of such objects between repositories" [199]. METS builds on the work of the Making of America II project (MOA2) that devised an encoding format for descriptive, administrative, and structural metadata for textual and image-based works [208]. A METS document consists of: descriptive metadata, administrative metadata, file groups, a structure map, and behaviors. METS includes coverage of administrative/preservation metadata designed for specific types of digital objects such as images and audio files through extension schemas [209].

Much of the work from the major archival projects studying long-term preservation of digital objects and records, including the Pittsburgh and InterPARES projects, focuses on the production and maintenance of metadata to establish the identity of electronic records and demonstrate their integrity and authenticity. The Pittsburgh Project sought appropriate metadata through an analysis of literary warrant. The InterPARES Authenticity Task Force's report includes both benchmark and baseline requirements to support the presumption of authenticity, many of which involve metadata that establishes a record's identity and its documentary, procedural, technological, provenancial, and juridical-administrative contexts.

6.4   Technical Preservation

While few archivists possess extensive technical backgrounds and knowledge, archivists are becoming involved in projects with computer scientists seeking solutions to the technical aspects of long-term preservation. As discussed above, two approaches to the problems posed by software and hardware obsolescence have received the most attention. Migration is the process of taking digital files and moving them to new hardware or software, thus potentially changing the presentation of the data, the ways it may be manipulated, and the data itself. Given a small store of files this may not be a difficult process, although individual treatment will not ensure uncorrupted transfer. Given the billions of files institutions such as the National Archives or a large digital library may hold, present day migration strategies are neither efficient nor do they ensure the preservation of authentic electronic records. Emulation is the process by which the data files remain constant and software is used to replicate or "emulate" the software applications or hardware that originally supported display and manipulation of the files.

At this time there is no clear solution to the challenges of technological obsolescence. Both of these approaches and those that fall between them in Thibodeau's classification discussed above require and deserve extensive research and development. It is essential that the archival perspective that stresses preservation of authenticity and reliability of records and information be present in all such research if long-term digital archiving is to become a reality.

The CAMiLEON (Creative Archiving at Michigan and Leeds: Emulating the Old on the New) project, a collaborative effort the School of Information, University of Michigan and the University of Leeds (UK), funded by JISC and the NSF, builds from the earlier JISC-funded Cedars project, and explores the potential of emulation as a means of reliably preserving authentic electronic records [210]. Herein, the approach is to preserve the "look and feel" of software-dependent digital objects.

In 1997, as part of its strategic plan, the US National Archives launched a collaborative approach to building its Electronic Records Archive (ERA) Program. Key partnership include the OAIS Initiative; the InterPARES Project; the Distributed Object Computation Testbed (DOCT), an interagency collaboration between the Department of Defense's Advanced Research Projects Agency and the U.S. Patent and Trademark Office; and the San Diego Supercomputer Center (SDSC). SDSC is working to invent "not only a preservation method, but an information management architecture built around the objective of preservation of arbitrarily structured sets of virtually any type of electronic record" [68]. In its "Collection-Based Persistent Object Preservation" and "Archivists' Workbench" projects, SDSC articulates a persistent object approach using XML information models. This approach is based on the OAIS model and tested on a one million message software-dependent e-mail collection. The major components of the SDSC persistent archive system are support for ingestion, archival storage, information discovery, and presentation of the collection. Contextual and hierarchical information about records is preserved in this system.

The Preservation Task Force of the InterPARES Project has produced the "Preserve Electronic Records" Model. Rather than prescribing a technical "solution," this model "provides an extensive, detailed and highly coherent framework for identifying and analyzing the specific challenges faced in implementing appraisal decisions that select specific bodies of electronic records to be preserved" [78, p. 18]. The *Preservation Task Force Final Report* goes on to note that "this framework guides the evaluation of technological options and the articulation of specific preservation strategies addressing both the archival and technological characteristics of the records to ensure the continuing availability of authentic copies of the records across time and generations of technology" [78, p. 18]. This framework is built on a premise that articulates the necessity of ongoing collaboration between the archival and computer science communities:

> This formulation of the problem of preserving electronic records clearly situates it not in technology, but in the interface between the goal of preserving electronic records and the technology on which they depend. Technology itself is not a problem. If we did not need to preserve records beyond the life expectancies of hardware, software and digital media, we would not have any preservation problem. Similarly, technology cannot determine the solution. It is archival and records management requirements, which define the problem. It must be archival and records management criteria which determine the appropriateness and adequacy of any technical "solution". [78, p. 18–19]

6.5   Information Needs and Behaviors

Most of the work to date in digital preservation has sought solutions based around the requirements of authentic records and electronic systems. These are important aspects in the success of any digital archiving effort, but are not sufficient by themselves to ensure preservation. Although the Commission on Preservation and Access (CPA) and Research Libraries Group (RLG) Task Force on the Archiving of Digital Information found in 1996 that "The first line of defense against loss of valuable digital information rests with the creators, providers and owners of digital information" [97, p. 40], very few studies have examined how individuals create, use, and manage digital documents. Tora Bikson has studied email usage [211] and an NHPRC-funded project that the University of North Carolina at Chapel Hill is currently exploring how university faculty, staff, and administrators are managing and preserving the digital documents they create and receive [162].

Understanding human information-creation, information-management, and information-seeking behaviors is essential to building optimized preservation systems that will facilitate long-term use as well as long-term storage of materials. Regardless how well electronic records management systems are designed around the needs of authentic records, if they are not built to accommodate human information management behaviors it is unlikely they will be used or used effectively. Much like former Speaker of the House Thomas "Tip" O'Neill's dictum, "All politics is local," the success of desktop records management and subsequent archiving of material presently depends on the individual and his or her specific information management behaviors. At this point very little is known about these behaviors and even less about how to optimize them to serve the historical, legal, financial, instructional and scholarly requirements of institutions. David Wallace's strongest conclusion from his study of e-mail policies is that there is a "glaring absence of electronic recordkeeping systems." But deployment is only part of the battle. Success of such systems depends on customizations to meet the needs of the specific user population. Wallace goes on to argue in the tradition of Rogers, that

> When electronic recordkeeping systems are developed and deployed, they will have to do so in specific reference to the recordkeeping context in which they reside. It is quite unlikely that such systems will be easily integrated into organizations in absence of customizations accounting for the various functions, terminologies, and series evident in organizations across society. There are no magic bullets, only context-sensitive desktop and system level implementations.[6] [212]

We must build systems, be they for electronic records management or management of image collections in digital libraries around the notion that digital preservation must be proactive, it must start at the time of object creation, and it must be compatible with human information behaviors. Herein is an area in which archivists, experts in user studies and user behavior, and computer scientists must pool their collective knowledge and approaches to the digital preservation problem. We must develop appropriate software that will facilitate digital preservation from the point of creation; extensive user education programs must be directed toward making society information management literate, starting in primary school.

We also need to know much more about how individuals from all walks of life will use the digital objects we are preserving. To date, archivists have conducted few user studies although there have been calls for them for almost two decades [213–217]. Archivists, librarians, and other information specialists must conduct numerous studies to determine how users and potential users are locating, assessing, and using the labors of digital preservation efforts. Some archivists are exploring how researchers

---

[6] At the April 6, 2001 Triangle ARMA meeting, John Hackett and Sherrill Gibson who are involved in deploying the CIA's "PERM" ERMS, stressed the need for understanding users' needs, system customization, and user education throughout the process if such systems had a chance of being successful. ("Getting Ready for Electronic Implementation." Powerpoint slides).

access the usefulness of electronic finding aids and digitized documents [218,219]. Others are studying how users find their repository online [220–222]. A collaborative project between the University of North Carolina at Chapel Hill and the University of Glasgow is studying how historians locate primary resources in the digital age [223].

7. The Future: Digital Dark Ages or a New Enlightenment

Every age has its grand challenges. Developing means for effective, efficient, and affordable archiving of digital assets stands as one of the most significant, thorny, complex and pressing problems we face at the beginning of the 21st century. We no longer have the luxury of saying that one day soon society will need to learn how to preserve digital information. Society as we know it is dependent upon digital data. The vast majority of information that the scientific, social, governmental, educational, and financial sectors create is now born digital. Patient records in hospitals are entirely electronic; paychecks and social security payments are electronic transfers that only appear in print on monthly banking statements; data from research projects seeking solutions to cancer, AIDS, and global warming are all in digital form; the Web is the only documented existence for entire communities of interest and the official publication vehicle for many corporate and educational organizations. Additionally, cultural institutions are preserving some of the most significant aspects of our cultural heritage heretofore embodied in analog media, such as print or works of art, through digitization programs. How many of these digital assets will exist in accessible form 100 years from now, or fifty years, or even ten years hence is unknown, but we can easily envision the difficulties that will arise and the cultural loss that will ensue if particular pieces of information are lost.

The solutions to the digital preservation conundrum, because of its multifaceted nature wherein technical, social, legal, and educational problems must be solved and infrastructures built, will require extensive and intensive communication between, and collaborative efforts from, a number of stakeholders and communities. The roles for archivists, computer scientists, and the information technology industry loom large in the work that lies ahead, but the most important outcomes will be syntheses and synergies from these groups. We already see some of this collaboration in the NHPRC-funded project at the San Diego Supercomputer Center that is seeking automatic means to classify and retrieve over a million e-mail messages from the first Bush presidential administration and in Department of Defense certified electronic records management systems and in the European Commission's MoReq specification. These efforts, however, are just the beginning of what must be accomplished.

In order for effective digital archiving to become a reality, and for today's digital objects to be accessible tomorrow, several steps must be taken, answers found, policies established, and information disseminated. Archivists and computer scientists will be integral players in the work that lies ahead, projects large and small.

7.1   Society Must Recognize, Understand, and Actively Support the Efforts to Solve the Challenges of Digital Archiving

While some archivists, computer scientists, and government and industry leaders have a growing awareness of the need to address the digital archiving dilemma and build national and international infrastructures to support its development, most individuals, including many archivists and computer scientists, are only vaguely aware of the situation. Those laboring to ensure the longevity of digital information must make the case for the importance of their work. This means not only conducting research, attending meetings, and writing papers but also widely publicizing the digital dilemma and the loss of cultural heritage, corporate assets, and scientific data that society faces. Some of this work is already occurring. The film, *Into the Future* [224], produced by the Council on Library and Information Resources and the American Council of Learned Societies in 1998, does an excellent job of capturing the essence of the grand challenge of digital preservation and its ramifications for society at large as have some newspaper and magazine articles [225–228]. Significantly, a search of the *New York Times* database for 1999–present on June 27, 2002, yielded only one article with the key words, "digital preservation" [229].

National and international infrastructures necessary to sustain digital preservation and long-term access to digital assets will not come without a hefty price tag. The research required to determine means and best practices for digital archiving along with education programs for information creators and keepers will be expensive and require large-scale funding, primarily from governmental organizations such as the National Science Foundation[7] in the United States and the European Commission.[8] In order for there to be extensive and adequate financial support from government funders for research in digital archiving and the management of electronic records, public awareness and the will to solve these problems must be greater than they are now.

In October 2001, UNESCO produced a draft resolution on digital preservation that augmented its 2002–2007 strategy to include launching "an international cam-

---

[7]NSF funds digital library and information science research through its Directorate for Computer and Information Science, and Engineering (CISE) (http://www.nsf.gov/home/cise/).

[8]The European Commission funds Information Technology research through its Information Society Directorate (http://europa.eu.int/comm/dgs/information_society/index_en.htm). It has "specific responsibility for increasing the understanding, development and uptake of information and communication technologies and their applications within the European Union."

paign to safeguard endangered digital memory and the drafting of guidelines for the preservation of digital heritage and for preserving materials in digital form" [230]. This resolution builds from UNESCO's 2002–2003 cross-cutting project, *Preserving Our Digital Heritage*, which called for a framework "for the identification, protection, conservation and transmission to future generations of the digital heritage, especially through the adoption of an international charter for the preservation of digital heritage." The 2001 resolution urges the UNESCO Director-General "to raise awareness among governments and other information producers and holders of the need to safeguard the digital memory of the world as much as possible in its authentic form" and "to encourage the Member States of UNESCO, governmental and non-governmental organizations and international, national and private institutions to ensure that preservation of their digital heritage be given high priority at the national policy level." The Society of American Archivists endorsed this statement, with SAA president Steven Hensen noting "The recommendations in the resolution should lay the foundation for positive moves towards the necessary policy and law to ensure the long-term preservation of this information. This, in turn, should give archivists, records managers, librarians, and other information professionals the sort of support they will require "to find ways to preserve these fragile, transient, and technology-dependent digital records . . . " [231].

Agencies and organizations concerned with information management, archiving of electronic records, and digital preservation in general, must redouble their efforts to publicize the situation and the need for increased funding. In the United States such organizations include, but are not limited to, the Library of Congress (LC), the National Archives (NARA), the Council on Library and Information Resources (CLIR), the National Historical Publications and Records Commission (NHPRC), the Institute for Museum and Library Services (IMLS), the Research Libraries Group (RLG), OCLC, the Society of American Archivists (SAA), the American Society for Information Science and Technology (ASIST), ARMA (Records Management), and the American Library Association (ALA). Such efforts must be collaborative on a worldwide basis with agencies such as Joint Information Systems Committee in the United Kingdom (JISC).

Significantly, the European Commission has recently funded ERPANET (Electronic Resource Preservation and Access NETwork), a project that is establishing a growing European consortium to make visible a wide range of high quality information concerning digital preservation as well as conducting training programs regarding best practices in digitization and digital archiving. ERPANET:

> is concerned with addressing the lack of awareness, fragmentation of knowledge and skills amongst the stakeholder communities about how to handle existing digital preservation problems, and how to plan effectively for the future. It aims

to address the lack of identification and focus on core research/problem areas
and bring coherence and consistency to activities in this area. [232]

The European Commission's *DigiCULT Report* recommended in point 62 that "the
European Commission should support actions to raise awareness for long-term
preservation of born digital resources outside the cultural heritage community." The
report goes on to explain that "such actions should address industry as well as all
other areas where born-digital material is created, to facilitate awareness at the beginning of the resource life-cycle, at the creation stage" [233]. The National Library
of Australia has also taken on the dissemination of information concerning digital preservation as one of its missions. The PADI (Preserving Digital Information)
website [234] is one of the most extensive subject gateways to digital preservation
resources worldwide while its PANDORA project discussed above is an extensive
testbed for archiving digital and web publications.

7.2   The Challenges That Electronic Records, and More Broadly, Digital Objects, Pose in Respect to Their Long-Term Preservation and Access Must Be Fully Explored as a Priority Research and Development Area That Receives Both Strategic Planning and Extensive Funding

Following from making digital preservation more visible to stakeholders and society at large, funders, especially government agencies, must recognize the urgent
nature of the digital archiving dilemma. Solutions to handling and preserving millions and millions of digital objects that governments, corporations, and educational
institutions alone produce each day is a staggering challenge that will require extensive, large-scale research and development projects. Governments must back these
efforts with large sums and must also labor on the public's behalf on issues such as
intellectual property rights. Monies must also be used to create educational programs
and train everyone who creates digital information how to preserve and archive it as
appropriate.

Because technologies will continue to evolve and media will become more complex and thus more fragile; because electronic information will continue to become
more dynamic, often created from multimedia databases at the point of use, research
and development will be ongoing tasks. The *DigiCULT Report: Technical Landscapes for Tomorrow's Cultural Economy Unlocking the Value of Cultural Heritage*
(2002) from the European Commission's Information Society Directorate-General is
an impressive example of government-sponsored research and analysis of the cultural heritage landscape and the effect emerging digital communication technologies
are and will have upon it. It concludes that "one of the issues that will not be solved

within the next five years is long-term preservation of complex digital objects." It goes on to observe that while "cultural heritage institutions will have a better understanding on how to actively manage the life-cycle of different media types, the available technological solutions and strategies will remain short-term answers for a long-term adventure" [233]. This echoes the finding from the InterPARES Preservation Task Force that technology was neither the problem nor the solution, but rather archival and records management requirements.

Despite the need for extensive research into all facets of practical digital archiving, a good deal of work has gone forth in the past decade since Margaret Hedstrom presented a research agenda for digital preservation in 1991 at the meeting that established the NHPRC electronic records agenda [46]. Much of this effort, however, has been in the form of uncoordinated, isolated, relatively small-scale projects and studies conducted in the United States, Europe, and Australia. These have produced valuable insights and generated numerous conferences, workshops, and working groups, that in turn, have produced a body of conference proceedings and journal articles. Because there is such a need to educate a critical mass of individuals and organizations concerning the present and desired state of digital archiving there has been much overlap of themes, presentations, and speakers found at these meetings and conferences around the world.

It appears that we have entered a period of affirmation. Digital archiving experts agree on many of the key issues and challenges and digitization best practices are fairly well established for digitizing images and text as witnessed at meetings such as the CLIR/DAI sponsored, "The State of Digital Preservation: An International Perspective" [235] and the DLM Forum's 2002 meeting in Barcelona, Spain, "Access and Preservation of Electronic Information: Best Practices and Solutions" [236]. Additionally, national and international standards bodies are establishing a number of technical and metadata standards to support archiving digital information.[9] It is now time to leverage the findings from small projects into large, coordinate, strategically planned and funded national and international efforts. Echoing the 1996 CPA/RLG report, The DigiCULT report recommends in point 58:

> National governments and regional authorities need to take immediate action on long-term preservation and formulate a strategy for digital preservation as part of a national information policy. The strategy should involve setting up a network of certified organisations to archive and preserve digital cultural resources. [233, p. 49]

The report goes on to add:

---

[9]For example, the OAIS initiative discussed above is a draft ISO standard; METS is an emerging standard; and EAD is also a standard.

A national preservation policy should include a clear idea of who should be responsible for the preservation of digital cultural heritage in the future. As digital preservation is a costly undertaking that requires great expertise, we recommend the establishment of a network of certified organisations that take care of different types of material. These organizations should closely cooperate at the national and international level and actively seek to participate in Research & Development trials to foster documentation and information exchange for guidelines. These organisations should also monitor all relevant developments, in the digital preservation area. Features of such certified trustworthiness could include: experience in digital archiving, participation in R&D activities, organisational stability and longevity. [233, p. 49–50]

National and international agendas continue to be set and a variety of national strategies formed concerning digital preservation [237]. Much of this agenda setting has taken place in the United Kingdom. In late 1995, The Joint Information Systems Committee and the British Library held a conference at Warwick where strategic action points were derived [238]. Subsequently, the National Preservation Office of the British Library established a Digital Archive Working Group which resulted in several studies and a strategic policy framework for creating and preserving digital collections that examined how different organizations were approaching stages in the life-cycle of digital resources [239]. This early planning resulted in one of the most visible digital preservation projects, Cedars. JISC funded Cedars through its eLib and Digital Preservation Focus programs [240]. In 1997, the Humanities Advanced Technology and Information Institute (HATII) at the University of Glasgow carried out a study of the opportunities and obstacles posed by the use of Information and Communications Technology (ICT) in the heritage sector in order to establish a funding policy [241]. One of the primary findings of this study was the need for national strategies in the heritage sector to direct resources for digitization and digital preservation projects. In 2001, another UK preservation-minded organization, the Digital Preservation Coalition (DPC), was established "to foster joint action to address the urgent challenges of securing the preservation of digital resources in the UK and to work with others internationally to secure our global digital memory and knowledge base" [242].

In December 2000, the US Congress passed legislation to establish the National Digital Information Infrastructure and Preservation Program (NDIIPP) in the Library of Congress [243]. Congress charged the LC to lead a national planning effort for the long-term preservation of digital materials and to work collaboratively with representatives of other federal, research, library, and business organizations. NDIIPP's work has involved four stages: stakeholder meetings to gather data, collaborative research agenda building, development of a conceptual framework, and scenario planning. The NDIIPP conceptual framework for a digital preservation infrastructure involves economic, political, social/cultural, legal, and technical factors. Friedlander provides a summary and analysis of achievements to date in the April 2002 *D-Lib Magazine* [15].

Also in April of 2002, the NSF/Library of Congress-sponsored workshop on "Research Challenges in Digital Archiving" met to work toward establishing a national infrastructure for long-term preservation of digital information. Topics of this meeting included the bit stream interpretation problem, architecture for repositories, and policy and economic models. Its goal, according to Hedstrom, was "to have a combination of academic researchers and people from industry who are actually building things like storage management systems to develop a set of research challenges that will excite the community of people who actually do research in this area" [244].

This meeting was a significant move forward as is the NSF/European Union (Delos) international task force to coordinate digital preservation research and development efforts on both sides of the Atlantic [245]. NSF has also partnered with JISC in a digital library funding initiative and the Deutsche Forschungsgemeinschaft (DFG) [246].

Because all technologies will change and digital objects will become increasingly complex, reassessment and agenda setting must continue for the foreseeable future, but this must not impede action at this time. With agendas emerging and evolving, it is now time for concerted, coordinated, collaborative research and development from the range of stakeholders in digital preservation from around the globe.

7.3 Preservation and Access Must Be Viewed as Having an Inseparable Relationship

Digital repositories must be designed around the principles of both immediate and long-term use. To date, much of the technical discussion associated with digital archiving has revolved around physical preservation and preserving the intellectual integrity of documents and digital objects. There also needs to be integration of use technologies, techniques, and policies into digital archiving design. Presumably, the digital library community will be helpful with insights from digital reference services [247,248]. It is important to remember that while archives are preserving materials for use in the future, the actual point of use is always in the present. Archiving solutions, including the design of metadata schemes for information retrieval, must be built at the nexus of authenticity requirements and existing and projected user needs and behaviors. In order to ascertain user needs the digital archivist must design and conduct extensive user studies.

Because digital archives will provide the possibility of instantaneous, worldwide interconnected access to materials from users' desktops, retrieval and presentation software must be constructed to optimize remote use of digital resources. Digital archives must also supply an array of educational and facilitative tools on their web-sites to support use of digitized materials and offer instructional guides and tutori-als [249]. Context must be preserved along with content so as to support both re-trieval and use of digital objects.

7.4   Archivists, Information Scientists, Librarians, Policy Makers, and Computer Scientists Must Address the Full Range of Issues Integral to Digital Preservation in a Coordinated and Collaborative Fashion

Throughout the digital preservation literature we see the litany of challenges asso-ciated with long-term preservation discussed earlier in this chapter. These, however, are not isolated problems that neatly fall into distinct categories such as technical, legal, and social. For example, technical developments such as new ERMS or emu-lation software must be placed within the larger social context of who will use them, how they will be financed, and what outcomes are desirable. Electronic record and data management systems are prime examples of technical solutions that theoreti-cally provide excellent mechanisms for document and information management, but which often fail in actual implementations because users perceive that they require too much time to use properly.

Other examples of necessary software development that should also involve an archival perspective are mentioned in the DigiCULT report, including means to cap-ture metadata at the point of digitization and integrate it with a collection manage-ment system; means to generate access and preservation metadata at the time of creation of born digital objects; and long-term preservation strategies for complex digital objects [233, p. 49].

Margaret Hedstrom, who is guiding the formulation of the research program asso-ciated with NDIIPP, argues that the first step to providing solutions is "to disaggre-gate the problem of digital archiving and to recognize that digital preservation spans issues in computer and information science research, development of technology and tools, evolving standards and practices, policy and economic models, and organiza-tional change." She continues, "At the same time, we have to be cognizant of how the various approaches or solutions will work together" [15].

Already organizations such as NSF, the Library of Congress, and the European Commission and projects such as ERPANET and InterPARES are bringing a range of stakeholders together who have vested interests in the success of digital archiving to set agendas and seek solutions. This is a good beginning but challenges the way we have traditionally worked and calls for extensive collaboration that is often difficult and time consuming. Peter Lyman and Brewster Kahle in calling for an action agenda note:

Our purpose is not so much to answer these questions in a definitive manner, but to organize a discussion between communities which must learn to work together if the problem of digital preservation and archiving is to be solved— computer scientists, librarians and scholars, and policy makers. This paper, then, is the product of a dialogue between a computer scientist/entrepreneur and a political theorist/librarian, and represents an attempt to create a common agenda for action. [10]

7.5   The Information Technology Industry Must Produce Tools to Support Digital Preservation and Access

Archivists and other heritage curators cannot preserve digital information themselves. Electronic records and digital objects are born of technology and their preservation must lie, in part, in technology. Archivists, librarians, policy makers, and educators cannot produce viable digital archiving solutions without software designed to support preservation. Lawrence Brandt, program director of the collaboration between the Library of Congress and the National Science Foundation's program in digital government, cautions that "systems that can result from research are not likely to be the robust systems an agency may eventually require. Thus, there will be a need beyond the research phase for work that converts a promising experiment into a reliable, operating system" [15].

"Forging strategic alliances with relevant agencies nationally and internationally, and working collaboratively together and with industry and research organisations, to address shared challenges in digital preservation" are primary goals of the Digital Preservation Coalition (DPC) in the U.K. At the DPC Forum with Industry on Future R&D for Digital Asset Preservation, June 5, 2002, [243] Neil Beagrie, JISC Program Director, noted that there are "major gaps in current products and services" and that there is a major "future role potentially for industry" [250].

7.6   The Notion of Responsible Custody of Digital Assets Must Pervade Society; Digital Archiving Must Become Ubiquitous

Due to the challenges of the vast production of information, media fragility and technological obsolescence, preservation and archival interventions in the digital environment requires earlier intervention than has been the case with print documents. As Seamus Ross argues, digital preservation needs to be proactive. If digital materials are to be preserved over the long-term, "preservation features need to be incorporated into them" and made an "integral element of the initial design of systems and projects" [1, p. 13]. We have seen this in the print world in the publication of books on acid-free paper, but for the most part, preservation has been a collection of activities, many environmental, and including conservation to restore deteriorating items, applied well after the fact of creation. Preservation, and sadly, most archiving, have been reactive, rather than proactive.

To be effective in the digital environment, archiving must be pushed back into the active lifespan of information objects. We see this approach already in use in the Australian theory of post-custodial archiving and the records continuum. This does not simply mean, however, that archivists must work with other information professionals, be they records managers or librarians, when documents and other digital objects have yet to come to archival custody. The implications are indeed a more radical departure from traditional archival thought and practice. First, the influence of the archivist and the archival role are greatly enhanced and extended because the archivist becomes a more visible presence in information management during the active phase of a digital object's life than was previously the case with paper documents as seen in the U.K.'s Public Record Office (PRO) EROS (Electronic Records in Office Systems) guidance materials [251]. Archival perspectives and planning need to be built into the creation and early management of all information that will enjoy long-term preservation. Ironically, in this process of extending the archivist's influence and control, there is a concomitant loss of control. Simply put, if creators of digital information do not take steps to preserve it early in its life, it will never reach any long-term preservation facility. This recognition leads to the need for concepts of responsible custody and archiving to pervade society. Basic archival principles must be built into information creation and management software and information creators must recognize the need to exert responsible custody over the digital information objects they manage. Fundamental archival concepts and activities, such as the creation of identifying and authenticating metadata as well as some form of data migration, must become commonplace and ubiquitous.

7.7   Archivists Must Take a Leading Role in Educating Society Regarding Digital Preservation

The need for ubiquitous digital archiving if significant cultural, scientific, and economic information is to be preserve, be it in digital libraries, international corporations, or in people's homes, creates a new and very challenging role for archivists. Along with working with computer scientists and the information technology industry to design systems that will reliably preserve authentic digital objects, archivists must become teachers. Information management literacy must be added to the profession's agenda.

ACKNOWLEDGEMENT

The author wishes to thank several colleagues and students for reviewing a draft of this text and providing very insightful comments.

REFERENCES

[1] Ross S., "Changing trains at wigan: digital preservation and the future of scholarship", in: *NPO Preservation Guidance Occasional Papers*, National Preservation Office, London, 2000. Available at http://www.bl.uk/services/preservation/occpaper.pdf.[10]

[2] Ellis M., "Constructing a glossary for *The Electronic Beowulf*", *Revue: Informatique et Statistique dans les Sciences Humaines* **33** (1997) 113–123. Available at http://www.uky.edu/~kiernan/eBeowulf/rissh-me.htm.

[3] Kiernan K.S., "The Conybeare-Madden collation of Thorkelin's *Beowulf*", in: Pulsiano P., Treharne E. (Eds.), *Anglo-Saxon Manuscripts and Their Heritage*, Ashgate, Aldershot, Hants, England and Brookfield, Vermont, 1997, pp. 117–136. Available at http://www.uky.edu/~kiernan/eBeowulf/con-mad/cony-mad.htm.

[4] Kiernan K.S., "Digital image processing and the *Beowulf* manuscript", *Literary and Linguistic Computing* **6** (1991) 20–27. Available at http://www.uky.edu/~kiernan/eBeowulf/ksk-llc.htm.

[5] Solopova E., "Encoding a transcript of the *Beowulf* manuscript in SGML", in: *Association for Computers and the Humanities/Association for Literary and Linguistic Computing Conference, University of Virginia*, 1999. Available at http://www.uky.edu/~kiernan/eBeowulf/allc-es.htm.

[6] *Electronic Beowulf*. Available at http://www.uky.edu/~kiernan/eBeowulf/guide.htm.

[7] Berghel H., Bank D., "The World Wide Web", in: Zelkowitz M. (Ed.), *Advances in Computers*, Vol. 4, Academic Press, San Diego, 1999, pp. 180–219.

[8] DLM-Forum, *Proceedings of the DLM-Forum on Electronic Records: European Citizens and Electronic Information: The Memory of the Information Society, Brussels, October 18–19, 1999*, European Communities, Luxembourg, 2000. Available at http://europa.eu.int/ISPO/dlm.

[9] Bergerson B., *Dark Ages II: When the Digital Data Die*, Prentice Hall PTR, Upper Saddle River, NJ, 2002.

[10] Lyman P., Kahle B., "Archiving digital cultural artifacts", *D-Lib Magazine* (1998). Available at http://www.dlib.org/dlib/july98/07lyman.html.

[11] Hedstrom M., "Electronic archives: Integrity and access in the network environment", in: Kenna S., Ross S. (Eds.), *Networking in the Humanities: Proceedings of the Second Conference on Scholarship and Technology in the Humanities, Elvetham Hall, Hampshire, UK, 13–16 April, 1994*, Bowker-Saur, London, 1994.

[12] McKemmish S., "Evidence of me ...", *Archives and Manuscripts* **24** (1) (1996) 28–45.

[10] All URLs accessible as of September 10, 2002.

[13] Upward F., McKemmish S., "Somewhere beyond custody", *Archives and Manuscripts* **22** (1) (1994) 136–149.

[14] Arms W.Y., *Digital Libraries*, MIT Press, Cambridge, MA, 2000.

[15] Friedlander A., "The national digital information infrastructure preservation program: Expectations, realities, choices and progress to date", *D-Lib Magazine* **8** (4) (2002). Available at http://www.dlib.org/dlib/april02/friedlander/04friedlander.html.

[16] National Association of Government Archives and Records Administrators, *Archival Administration in the Electronic Age: An Advanced Institute for Government Archivists*, NAGARA, Pittsburgh, PA, 1989. Co-sponsored by the School of Library and Information Science University of Pittsburgh and funded by the Council on Library Resources.

[17] Gilliland-Swetland A.J., *Enduring Paradigm, New Opportunities: The Value of the Archival Perspective in the Digital Environment*, Council on Library and Information Resources, Washington, D.C., 2000. Available at http://www.clir.org/pubs/abstract/pub89abst.html.

[18] Lesk M., *Practical Digital Libraries: Books, Bytes and Bucks*, Morgan Kaufman, San Francisco, 1997, ixx.

[19] Ross S., "Historians, machine-readable information, and the past's future", in: Ross S., Higgs E. (Eds.), *Electronic Information Resources and Historians: European Perspectives. The British Academy, London, 25 June 1926*, Max-Planck-Institut für Geschichte in Kommission bei Scripta Mercaturae Verlag, St. Katharinen, 1993, pp. 1–20.

[20] Ross S., "Consensus, communication, and collaboration: Fostering multidisciplinary cooperation in electronic records", in: *INSAR (Supplement II), Proceedings of the DLM-Forum on Electronic Records*, 1997, pp. 330–336. Available at http://europa.eu.int/ISPO/dlm/dlm96/proceed-en4.pdf.

[21] Besser H., Trant J., *Introduction to Imaging: Issues in Constructing an Image Database*, Getty Information Institute, Santa Monica, CA, 1995. Available at http://www.getty.edu/research/institute/standards/introimages/.

[22] Jones M., Beagrie N., *Preservation Management of Digital Materials: A Handbook*, The British Library, London, 2001. Available at http://www.dpconline.org/graphics/handbook/index.html.

[23] Kenney A.R., Rieger O.Y. (Eds.), *Moving Theory into Practice: Digital Imaging for Libraries and Archives*, Research Libraries Group, Mountain View, CA, 2000.

[24] Lee S.D., *Digital Imaging: A Practical Handbook*, Neal-Schuman, New York, 2000.

[25] Northeast Document Conservation Center, *Handbook for Digital Projects: A Management Tool for Preservation and Access*, Northeast Document Conservation Center, Andover, MA, 2000. Available at http://www.nedcc.org/digital/.

[26] Feeney M. (Ed.), *Digital Culture: Maximising the Nation's Investment: A Synthesis of JISC/NPO Studies on the Preservation of Electronic Material*, British Library Board, London, 1999. Available at http://www.ukoln.ac.uk/services/elib/papers/other/jisc-npo-dig/intro.html.

[27] Bennett J.C., "A framework of data types and formats, and issues affecting the long term preservation of digital material", in: *JISC/NPO Studies on the Preservation of Electronic Materials*, British Library Research and Innovation Centre, London, 1997. Available at http://www.ukoln.ac.uk/services/elib/papers/supporting/pdf/rept011.pdf.

[28] Bearman D., "Diplomatics, weberian bureaucracy, and the management of electronic records in Europe and America", *American Archivist* **55** (1992) 168–181.

[29] Cox R.J., "Re-discovering the archival mission: The recordkeeping functional requirements project at the University of Pittsburgh: A progress report", *Archives and Museum Informatics* **8** (1992) 279–300.

[30] Duff W., "Harnessing the power of warrant", *American Archivist* **61** (1998) 88–105.

[31] Upward F., "In search of the continuum: Ian Maclean's 'Australian experience' essays on recordkeeping", in: *The Records Continuum: Ian Maclean and Australian Archives First Fifty Years*, Ancora Press in association with Australian Archives, Clayton, Australia, 1994. Available at http://rcrg.dstc.edu.au/publications/fuptrc.html.

[32] Upward F., "Structuring the records continuum—Part one: Postcustodial principles and properties", *Archives and Manuscripts* **24** (2) (1996) 268–285. Available at http://rcrg. dstc.edu.au/publications/recordscontinuum/fupp1.html.

[33] Upward F., "Structuring the records continuum—Part two: Structuration theory and recordkeeping", *Archives and Manuscripts* **25** (1) (1997) 35. Available at http://rcrg. dstc.edu.au/publications/recordscontinuum/fupp2.html.

[34] McKemmish S., "Yesterday, today and tomorrow: A continuum of responsibility", in: *Proceedings of the Records Management Association of Australia 14th National Convention, 15–17 Sept 1997*, RMAA, Perth, 1997. Available at http://rcrg.dstc.edu.au/publications/recordscontinuum/smckp2.html.

[35] McKemmish S., Acland G., Ward N., Reed B., "Describing records in context in the continuum: The Australian recordkeeping metadata schema", *Archivaria* **48** (1999) 3–43.

[36] Council on Library and Information Resources and Library of Congress, *Building a National Strategy for Preservation: Issues in Digital Media Archiving. Commissioned for and sponsored by the National Digital Information Infrastructure and Preservation Program*, Council on Library and Information Resources & Library of Congress, Washington, DC, 2002. Available at http://www.clir.org/pubs/abstract/pub106abst.html.

[37] National Research Council, *The Digital Dilemma: Intellectual Property in the Information Age*, National Academy Press, Washington, D.C., 2000. Available at http://books. nap.edu/html/digital_dilemma/.

[38] NINCH (National Initiative for a Networked Cultural Heritage) Copyright Town Meetings webpage: http://www.ninch.org/copyright/.

[39] Ross S., "Report on 'Creation, preservation and access to electronic information: Economical and functional aspects'—Maintaining the value of intellectual capital", in: *INSAR (Supplement IV), Proceedings of the DLM-Forum on Electronic Records: European Citizens and Electronic Information: The Memory of the Information Society, Brussels, 18–19 October 1999*, European Community, Brussels, Belgium, 1999, pp. 318–321. Available at http://europa.eu.int/ISPO/dlm.

[40] Roes H., "Digital libraries and education: Trends and opportunities", *D-Lib Magazine* **7** (8) (2001).

[41] Zia L.L., "The NSF national science, mathematics, engineering, and technology education digital library (NSDL) program: A progress report", *D-Lib Magazine* **6** (10) (2000).

[42] Zia L.L., "Growing a national learning environments and resources network for science, mathematics, engineering, and technology education: Current issues and opportunities for the NSDL Program", *D-Lib Magazine* **7** (3) (2001).

[43] Lawrence G.W., Kehoe W.R., Rieger O.Y., Walters W.H., Kenney A.R., *Risk Management of Digital Information: A File Format Investigation*, Council on Library and Information Resources, Washington, D.C., 2000. Available at http://www.clir.org/pubs/abstract/pub93abst.html.

[44] Kenney A.R., McGovern N.Y., Botticelli P., Entlich R., Lagoze C., Payette S., "Preservation risk management for web resources: Virtual remote control in Cornell's Project Prism", *D-Lib Magazine* **8** (1) (2002).

[45] Cox R.J., "What's in a name? Archives as a multi-faceted term in the information professions", *Records & Retrieval Report* **11** (1995).

[46] Hedstrom M., "Understanding electronic incunabula: A framework for research on electronic records", *American Archivist* **54** (1991).

[47] Dollar C.M., *Authentic Electronic Records: Strategies for Long-Term Access*, Cohasset Associates, Chicago, 2000.

[48] Dialog website: www.dialog.com.

[49] LexisNexis website: http://www.lexisnexis.com.

[50] United States National Library of Medicine. Available at. http://www.nlm.nih.gov/hinfo.html.

[51] Bearman D., "Archival data management to achieve organizational accountability for electronic records", in: Bearman D. (Ed.), *Electronic Evidence: Strategies for Managing Records in Contemporary Organizations*, Archives & Museum Informatics, Pittsburgh, PA, 1994. Originally published in *Archives and Manuscripts* **21** (1) (1993) 14–28.

[52] National Archives and Records Administration. NARA's Vision, Mission, and Values. Available at http://www.archives.gov/about_us/vision_mission_values.html.

[53] Hodge G.M., Carroll B.C., "Digital electronic archiving: The state of the art and the state of the practice", Report sponsored by the International Council for Scientific and Technical Information, Information Policy Committee and CENDI, April 26, 1999. Available at http://www.icsti.org/99ga/digarch99_TOCP.pdf.

[54] Consultative Committee for Space Science Data Systems, *Reference Model for an Open Archives System (OAIS). Draft Recommendations for Space Data System Standards, CCSDS 650.0-R-2*, 2001. Available at http://www.ccsds.org/documents/pdf/CCSDS-650.0-R-2.pdf.

[55] Duranti L., "The impact of digital technology on archival science", *Archival Science* **1** (1) (2001). Available at http://www.kluweronline.com/issn/1389-0166/current.

[56] Berner R.C., *Archival Theory and Practice in the United States: A Historical Analysis*, University of Seattle Press, Seattle, 1983.

[57] O'Toole J.M., *Understanding Archives and Manuscripts*, Society of American Archivists, Chicago, IL, 1990, pp. 27–47.

[58] Posner E., *American State Archives*, University of Chicago Press, Chicago, 1964.

[59] Gracy D.B., *Archives and Manuscripts: Arrangement and Description*, Society of American Archivists, Chicago, IL, 1980.

[60] Bearman D., "Archives and manuscript control with bibliographic utilities: Challenges and opportunities", *American Archivist* **52** (1) (1989) 26–39.

[61] Bearman D., *Towards National Information Systems for Archives and Manuscript Repositories: The National Information Systems Task Force (NISTF) Papers, 1981–1984*, Society of American Archivists, Chicago, IL, 1987.

[62] Hensen S.L., "The use of standards in the application of the AMC Format", *American Archivist* **49** (1) (1986) 32.

[63] Lytle R.H., "An analysis of the work of the National Information Systems Task Force", *American Archivist* **47** (1984) 357–365.

[64] Martell S.H., Use of the MARC AMC Format by archivists for integration of special collections' holdings into bibliographic databases and networks, M.S.L.S. thesis, University of North Carolina at Chapel Hill, 1991.

[65] Pitti D.V., "Encoded archival description. An introduction and overview", *D-Lib Magazine* **5** (11) (1999). Available at http://www.dlib.org/dlib/november99/11pitti.html.

[66] Hensen S.L., "Archival cataloging and the Internet: The implications and impact of EAD", *Journal of Internet Cataloging* **4** (3/4) (2001) 75–95.

[67] Bellardo L.J., Bellardo L.L. (Eds.), *A Glossary for Archivists, Manuscript Curators, and Records Managers*, Society of American Archivists, Chicago, 1992.

[68] Thibodeau K., "Building the archives of the future: Advances in preserving electronic records at the National Archives and Records Administration", *D-Lib Magazine* **7** (2) (2001). Available at http://www.dlib.org/dlib/february01/thibodeau/02thibodeau.html.

[69] Cunningham A., "Beyond the pale? The 'flinty' relationship between archivists who collect the private records of individuals and the rest of the archival profession", *Archives and Manuscripts* **24** (1) (1996) 20–26.

[70] InterPARES Project, *The InterPARES Glossary. A Controlled Vocabulary of Terms Used in the InterPARES Project, No.2002.1*, University of British Columbia, Vancouver, Canada, 2002. Available at http://www.interpares.org/documents/InterPARES.

[71] Bearman D., *Electronic Evidence: Strategies for Managing Records in Contemporary Organizations*, Archives & Museum Informatics, Pittsburgh, PA, 1994.

[72] Cox R.J., "The record: Is it evolving?", *The Records and Retrieval Report* **10** (3) (1994) 1–16.

[73] Morelli J.D., "Defining electronic records: A terminology problem... or something more", in: Ross S., Higgs E. (Eds.), *Electronic Information Resources and Historians: European Perspectives. The British Academy, London, 25 June 1926*, Max-Planck-Institut für Geschichte in Kommission bei Scripta Mercaturae Verlag, St. Katharinen, 1993, pp. 83–91.

[74] Society of American Archivists, Archival Roles for the New Millennium, 1997. Available at http://www.archivists.org/governance/handbook/app_j3.asp.

[75] Bearman D., *Archival Methods*, Archives and Museum Informatics, Pittsburgh, PA, 1989, 59–67. Technical Report No. 9.

[76] Ritzenthaler M.L., *Preserving Archives and Manuscripts*, Society of American Archivists, Chicago, 1993.

[77] Conway P., "Overview: Rational for digitization and preservation", in: *Handbook for Digital Projects: A Management Tool for Preservation and Access*, Northeast Document Conservation Center, Andover, MA, 2000. Available at http://www.nedcc.org/digital/II.htm.

[78] InterPARES Preservation Task Force, Preservation Taskforce Final Report. October 31, 2001. Available at http://www.interpares.org/documents/ptf_draft_final_report.pdf.

[79] O'Toole J.M., "On the idea of permanence", *American Archivist* **52** (1) (1989) 10–25.

[80] Puglia S., "The costs of digital imaging projects", *RLG DigiNews* **3** (5) (1999). Available at http://www.rlg.org/preserv/diginews/diginews3-5.html#feature.

[81] Hendley T., "Comparison of methods & costs of digital preservation", British Library Research and Innovation Report 106. BLRIC, British Library, London, 1998. Available at http://www.ukoln.ac.uk/services/elib/papers/supporting/pdf/hendley-report.pdf.

[82] Tanner S., Joanne J.L., "Digitisation: How much does it really cost?", in: *Digital Resources for the Humanities 1999 Conference*, 1999. Available at http://heds.herts.ac.uk/resources/papers/drh99.pdf.

[83] Kingma B., "The costs of print, fiche, and digital access: The Early Canadiana Online Project", *D-Lib Magazine* **6** (2) (2000). Available at http://www.dlib.org/dlib/february00/kingma/02kingma.html.

[84] Ashley K., "Digital archive costs: Facts and fallacies", in: *DLM Forum '99*, 1999. Available at http://europa.eu.int/ISPO/dlm/fulltext/full_ashl_en.htm.

[85] RLG worksheet for estimating digital reformatting costs, 1998. Available at http://www.rlg.org/preserv/RLGWorksheet.pdf.

[86] Price L., Smith A., *Managing Cultural Assets from a Business Perspective*, Council on Library and Information Resources, Washington, D.C., 2000. Available at http://www.clir.org/pubs/abstract/pub90abst.html.

[87] Rothenberg J., Ensuring the longevity of digital information. Rand Corporation. February 22, 1999, 2. Available at http://www.clir.org/pubs/archives/ensuring.pdf. This paper is an expanded version of the article "Ensuring the longevity of digital documents" that appeared in the January 1995 edition of *Scientific American* **272** (1) (1999) 42–47.

[88] Lyman P., Besser H., "Defining the problem of our vanishing memory: Background, current status, models for resolution", in: MacLean M., Davis B.H. (Eds.), *Time & Bits: Managing Digital Continuity*, Getty Conservation Institute & The Long Now Foundation, Los Angeles, CA, 1998, p. 11. Available at http://www.longnow.org/10klibrary/TimeBitsDisc/tbpaper.htm.

[89] Waybackmachine, http://www.waybackmachine.org/.

[90] Longnow Foundation, http://www.longnow.org/.

[91] Kahle B., "Preserving the Internet: An archive of the Internet may prove to be a vital record for historians, businesses and governments", *Scientific American* **276** (3) (1997) 82–83.

[92] McClure C.R., Sprehe T.J. Guidelines for electronic records management on state and federal agency websites, 1998. Available at http://istweb.syr.edu/~mcclure/guidelines.html.

[93] Dollar C., Archival Preservation of Smithsonian Web Resources: Strategies, Princi-
      ples, and Best Practices, 2001. Available at http://www.si.edu/archives/archives/dollar
      %20report.html.

[94] Ross S., Gow A., "Digital Archaeology: Rescuing Neglected and Damaged Data Re-
      sources", in: *JISC/NPO Studies on the Preservation of Electronic Materials*, British
      Library Board, London, 1999. Available at http://www.hatii.arts.gla.ac.uk/Projects/
      BrLibrary/rosgowrt.pdf.

[95] Eisenbeis K.M., *Privatizing Government Information: The Effects of Policy on Access
      to Landsat Satellite Data*, Scarecrow Press, Metuchen, NJ, 1995.

[96] National Research Council, *Preserving Scientific Data on Our Physical Universe:
      A New Strategy for Archiving the Nation's Scientific Information Resources*, National
      Academy Press, Washington, D.C., 1995.

[97] Waters D., Garrett J., Preserving Digital Information, Report of the Task Force on
      Archiving of Digital Information Commissioned by the Commission on Preserva-
      tion and Access and the Research Libraries Group, May 1, 1996. Available at http://
      www.rlg.org/ArchTF/.

[98] Levy D.M., "Heroic measures: Reflections on the possibility and purpose of digital
      preservation", in: *Digital Libraries 98*, ACM, Pittsburgh, PA, 1998, p. 152.

[99] Achenbach J., The too-much-information age. Washington Post, March 12, 1999, A1.

[100] Inktomi and NEC Research Institute. Web surpasses one billion documents, 2000.
      Available at http://www.inktomi.com/new/press/2000/billion.html.

[101] Lyman P., Varian H.R., How much information? Internet—summary, 2001. Available
      at http://www.sims.berkeley.edu/how-much-info/internet.html.

[102] Cyveillance. Internet exceeds 2 billion pages, July 10, 2000. Available at http://www.
      cyveillance.com/web/newsroom/releases/2000/2000-07-10.htm.

[103] OCLC. Web Characterization Project. Available at http://wcp.oclc.org.

[104] Pew Internet and American Life Project, Net resources—Internet statistics, 2002. Avail-
      able at http://www.pewinternet.org/netresources/index.asp.

[105] Net Caucus. Internet Statistics, 2002. Available at http://www.netcaucus.org/statistics/.
      Founded in the spring of 1996, the Congressional Internet Caucus is a bi-partisan group
      of members of the House and Senate working to educate their colleagues about the
      promise and potential of the Internet.

[106] Complete Planet. "Deep Web" website: http://www.completeplanet.com/help/help_
      deepwebFAQs.asp.

[107] "Invisible Web Gateways" web search at http://websearch.about.com/internet/websearch/
      cs/invisibleweb1/.

[108] SearchEngineWatch, Invisible web, 1999. Available at http://www.searchenginewatch.
      com/sereport/99/07-invisible.html.

[109] Lyman P., Varian H.R., How much information? Executive summary, 2001. Available
      at http://www.sims.berkeley.edu/how-much-info/summary.html.

[110] Lyman P., Varian H.R., How much information? Charts, 2001. Available at http://www.
      sims.berkeley.edu/how-much-info/charts/charts.html.

[111] Seamus R., "Preservation and networking in the aid of research", in: Coppock T. (Ed.), *Information Technology and Scholarship: Applications in the Humanities and Social Sciences*, British Academy, Oxford University Press, 1999, p. 318.

[112] IST Web. "eEurope: creating cooperation for digitisation. LUND PRINCIPLES." Available at http://www.cordis.lu/ist/ka3/digicult/lund_principles.htm.

[113] Yakel E., "Digital preservation", in: *Annual Review of Information Science and Technology (ARIST)*, Vol. 35, ARIST, Medford, NJ, 2001, p. 337.

[114] Weber H., Dörr M., *Digitization as a Method of Preservation? Final Report of a Working Group of the Deutsche Forschungsgemeinschaft*, Commission on Preservation and Access and the European Commission on Preservation and Access, Amsterdam, Washington, D.C., 1997, p. 3. Available at http://www.clir.org/pubs/abstract/pub69.html.

[115] Smith A., *Why Digitize?*, Council on Library and Information Resources, Washington, D.C., 1999. Available at http://www.clir.org/pubs/abstract/pub80.html.

[116] Lynch C., "Digital collections, digital libraries and the digitization of cultural heritage information", *First Monday* **7** (5) (2002). Available at http://www.firstmonday.dk/issues/issue7_5/lynch/index.html.

[117] Conway P., *Preservation in the Digital World*, Commission on Preservation and Access, Washington, D.C., 1996, p. 3. Available at http://www.clir.org/pubs/reports/conway2/index.html.

[118] Van Bogart J.W.C., *Magnetic Tape Storage and Handling: A Guide for Libraries and Archives*, Commission on Preservation and Access and National Media Laboratory, St. Paul, MN, 1995.

[119] Porck H.J., Teygeler R., *Preservation Science Survey: An Overview of Recent Developments in Research on the Conservation of Selected Analog Library and Archival Materials*, Council on Library and Information Resources, Washington, D.C., 2000, p. 34.

[120] Armstrong v. Executive Office of the President et al. Brief for appellant. May 17, 1996. Available at http://www.citizen.org/litigation/briefs/FOIAGovtSec/articles.cfm?ID=873.

[121] Bearman D., "The implications of *Armstrong v. Executive Office of the President* for the archival management of electronic records", *American Archivist* **56** (1993) 674–689.

[122] Pasterczyk C.E., "Federal e-mail management: A records manager's view of Armstrong v. Executive Office of the President and it's aftermath", *Records Management Quarterly* **32** (2) (1998) 10–22.

[123] Thibodeau K., "Overview of technological approaches to digital preservation and challenges in coming years", in: *The State of Digital Preservation: An International Perspective. Conference Proceedings. Documentation Abstracts, Inc. Institutes for Information Science, April 24–25, 2002, Washington, D.C.*, Council on Library and Information Resources, Washington, D.C., 2002. Available at http://www.clir.org/pubs/abstract/pub107abst.html.

[124] The Edsac Simulator. Available at http://www.dcs.warwick.ac.uk/~edsac/. Cited in [94, p. 28].

[125] Ferranti Pegasus Working Parties. Available at http://www.cs.man.ac.uk/CCS/pegasus/peghome.htm.

[126] BBC News, Babbage Printer Finally Runs, April 13, 2000. Available at http://news.bbc. co.uk/1/hi/sci/tech/710950.stm.

[127] Rothenberg R., *Avoiding Technological Quicksand: Finding a Viable Technical Foundation for Digital Preservation*, Council on Library and Information Resources, Washington, D.C., 1999. Available at http://www.clir.org/pubs/abstract/pub77.html.

[128] Bearman D., "Reality and chimera in the preservation of electronic records", *D-Lib Magazine* **5** (4) (1999). Available at http://www.dlib.org/dlib/april99/bearman/04bearman.html.

[129] Heminger A.R., Robertson S.B., "Digital Rosetta Stone: a conceptual model for maintaining long-term access to digital documents", in: *Sixth DELOS Workshop: Preservation of Digital Information. ERCIM-98-W003*, European Research Consortium for Informatics and Mathematics, Le Chesnay, 1998, pp. 35–43. Available at http://www.ercim.org/publication/ws-proceedings/DELOS6/.

[130] Holdsworth D., Wheatley P., "Emulation, preservation, and abstraction", in: *CAMiLEON Project*, 2001. Available at http://129.11.152.25/CAMiLEON//dh/ep5.html. See *RLG DigiNews* (2001) 5/4 for a shorter version. Available at http://www.rlg.org/preserv/diginews/diginews5-4.html#feature2.

[131] Moore R., et al., "Collection-based persistent digital archives—Part 1", *D-Lib Magazine* **6** (3) (2000). Available at http://www.dlib.org/dlib/march00/moore/03moore-pt1.html.

[132] Moore R., et al., "Collection-based persistent digital archives—Part 2", *D-Lib Magazine* **6** (4) (2000). Available at http://www.dlib.org/dlib/april00/moore/04moore-pt2.html.

[133] National Research Council, *The Digital Dilemma: Intellectual Property in the Information Age*, National Academy Press, Washington, D.C., 2000. Available at http://www.nap.edu/html/digital_dilemma/.

[134] Sonny Bono Copyright Term Extension Act. S 505, P.L. 105-298, 11 Stat. 2827. Available at http://www.loc.gov/copyright/legislation/s505.pdf.

[135] U.S. Copyright Office. The Digital Millennium Copyright Act of 1998. Summary, December 1998. Available at http://www.loc.gov/copyright/legislation/dmca.pdf.

[136] The WIPO Copyright Treaty. Available at http://www.wipo.int/treaties/ip/wct/index.html.

[137] Henriksen B., "Legal deposit from the Internet in Denmark: Experiences with the law from 1997 and the need for adjustments", in: *Preserving the Present for the Future: Strategies for the Internet Conference*, 2001. Available at http://www.deflink.dk/upload/doc_filer/doc_alle/1023_BNH.doc.

[138] Hakala J., "Electronic publications as legal deposit copies", *Tietolinja News* (1999). Available at http://www.lib.helsinki.fi/tietolinja/0199/legaldep.html.

[139] Lariviere J., Guidelines for legal deposit legislation, 2000. Available at http://www.ifla.org/VII/s1/gnl/legaldep1.htm.

[140] The Royal Library. National Library of Sweden. Kulturawr3: About the Project, 2002. Available at http://www.kb.se/ENG/kbstart.htm.

[141] Nieuwenburg B., Project deposit of Dutch electronic publications (DNEP). Available at http://www.kb.nl/kb/ict/dea/index-en.html.

[142] Dollar C.M., "Computers, the National Archives, and researchers", *Prologue* **8** (1) (1976) 29–34.

[143] Fishbein M.H., "Report on the Committee on Data Archives and Machine Readable Records—Fiscal year 1973", *APDA* **1** (2) (1973) 5–10.

[144] Fishbein M.H., "ADP and archives: Selected publications on automatic data processing", *American Archivist* **38** (1975) 31–42.

[145] Hedstrom M., Kowlowitz A., "Meeting the challenge of machine readable records: A state archives perspective", *Reference Studies Review* **16** (1–2) (1988) 31–40.

[146] Bearman D., Hedstrom M., "Reinventing archives for electronic records: Alternative service delivery options", *Electronic Records Management Program Strategies, Archives and Museum Informatics Technical Report*, No. 18, 1993, pp. 82–98.

[147] Committee on the Records of Government, Report sponsored by the American Council of Learned Societies, Social Science Research Council, and the Council on Library Resources, Council on Library Resources, Washington, D.C., 1985.

[148] Dollar C.M., *Archival Theory and Information Technologies: The Impact of Information Technologies on Archival Principles and Methods*, University of Macerata Press, Macerata, 1992.

[149] Lesk M., *Image Formats for Preservation and Access: A Report of the Technology Assessment Advisory Committee to the Commission on Preservation and Access*, Commission on Preservation and Access, Washington, D.C., 1990.

[150] Lesk M., *Preservation of New Technology: A Report of the Technology Assessment Advisory Committee to the Commission on Preservation and Access*, Commission on Preservation and Access, Washington, D.C., 1992.

[151] Lynch L., *Accessibility and Integrity of Networked Information Collections*, Office of Technology Assessment, Congress of the United States, Washington, D.C., 1993.

[152] Mallinson J.C., "Preserving machine-readable archival records for the millennia", *Archivaria* **22** (1986) 147–152.

[153] Mohlhenrich J. (Ed.), *Preservation of Electronic Formats: Electronic Formats for Preservation*, Highsmith, Fort Atkinson, WS, 1993.

[154] National Academy of Public Administration, The Effects of Electronic Recordkeeping on the Historical Record of the U.S. Government: A Report for the National Archives and Records Administration, National Academy of Public Administration, Washington, D.C., 1989.

[155] Neavill G.B., "Electronic publishing, libraries, and the survival of information", *Library Resources & Technical Services* **28** (1984) 76–89.

[156] http://www.archives.gov/nhprc_and_other_grants/electronic_records/research_issues_contents.html.

[157] Pittsburgh Project website. Formerly at http://www.lis.pitt.edu/~nhprc/. Due to a site crash, available only through Brewster Kahle's Waybackmachine: www.waybackmachine.org ([89] above).

[158] Bantin P., "Strategies for managing electronic records: Lessons learned from the Indiana University electronic records project", in: *ECURE 2000 Conference: Preservation and Access for Electronic College and University Records, Ari-*

zona State University, Phoenix, AZ, 2000. Available at http://www.asu.edu/it/events/ ecure/bak/ecure2000/bantin-presentation/index.htm.

[159] University Archives. Electronic Recordkeeping at Indiana University. NHPRC Funded Electronic Records Project, Phase II, 2000–2002. Available at http://www. indiana.edu/~libarch/ER/.

[160] U.S. InterPARES Project website: http://is.gseis.ucla.edu/us-interpares/index.html.

[161] San Diego Supercomputer Center. Methodologies for Preservation and Access of Software-dependent Electronic Records website: http://www.sdsc.edu/NHPRC/.

[162] University of North Carolina at Chapel Hill. School of Information and Library Science. "Managing the Digital University Desktop" website: http://ils.unc.edu/ digitaldesktop/index.html.

[163] RLG, "Trusted digital repositories: Attributes and responsibilities", Research Libraries Group, Mountain View, CA, 2002. Available at http://www.rlg.org/longterm/ repositories.pdf.

[164] Casson L., *Libraries of the Ancient World*, Yale University Press, New Haven, CT, 2001.

[165] Harris M.H., *History of Libraries in the Western World*, Scarecrow Press, Metuchen, N.J., 1984, 12–13.

[166] Posner E., *Archives in the Ancient World*, Harvard University Press, Cambridge, MA, 1972.

[167] Reichmann F., *The Sources of Western Literacy: The Middle Eastern Civilizations*, Greenwood, Westport, CT, 1980.

[168] InterPARES Appraisal Taskforce, Appraisal Taskforce Final Report, October 31, 2001. Available at http://www.interpares.org/documents/aptf_draft_final_report.pdf.

[169] Ham F.G., *Selecting and Appraising Archives and Manuscripts*, Society of American Archivists, Chicago, IL, 1993, p. 1.

[170] Society of American Archivists. Committee on Goals and Priorities, *Planning for the Archival Profession*, Society of American Archivists, Chicago, IL, 1986.

[171] Cox R.J., Samuels H.W., "The archivist's first responsibility: A research agenda to improve the identification and retention of records of enduring value", *The American Archivist* **51** (1988) 28–51.

[172] Duranti L., MacNeil H., "The protection of the integrity of electronic records: An overview of the UBC-MAS research project", *Archivaria* **42** (1996) 46–67. The UBC Project website is at http://www.interpares.org/UBCProject/index.htm.

[173] Eastwood T., Appraisal of Electronic Records: A Review of the Literature in English, May 30, 2000. Available at http://www.interpares.org/documents/interpares_ ERAppraisalLiteratureReview.pdf.

[174] MacNeil H., *Trusting Records: Legal, Historical and Diplomatic Perspectives*, Kluwer Academic, Dordrecht, The Netherlands, 2000.

[175] Hirtle P.B., "Archival authenticity in a digital age", in: *Authenticity in a Digital Environment*, Council on Library and Information Resources, Washington, D.C., 2000. Available at http://www.clir.org/pubs/reports/pub92/pub92.pdf.

[176] Acland G., "Managing the record rather than the relic", *Archives and Manuscripts* **20** (1) (1992) 57–63.

[177] InterPARES Authenticity Task Force, Authenticity Task Force Final Report, October 28, 2001. Available at http://www.interpares.org/documents/atf_draft_final_report.pdf.

[178] Gränström C., "The Janus Syndrome", in: *The Principle of Provenance: Report from the First Stockholm Conference on Archival theory and the Principle of Provenance, 2–3 September 1993*, Swedish National Archives, Stockholm, Sweden, 1994, p. 13.

[179] Erlandsson A., "The principle of provenance and the concept of records creator and record", in: *The Principle of Provenance: Report from the First Stockholm Conference on Archival theory and the Principle of Provenance, 2–3 September 1993*, Swedish National Archives, Stockholm, Sweden, 1994, p. 33.

[180] Duranti L., *Diplomatics: New Uses for an Old Science*, Scarecrow Press, Lanham, Md, 1998.

[181] Wendy D., "Ensuring the preservation of reliable evidence: A research project funded by the NHPRC", *Archivaria* **42** (1996) 28–45.

[182] Bantin P., "Developing a strategy for managing electronic records: The findings of the Indiana University electronic records project", *American Archivist* **61** (2) (1998) 328–364.

[183] Bantin P., "Strategies for managing electronic records: A new archival paradigm? An affirmation of our archival traditions?", *Archival Issues* **23** (1) (1998) 17–34.

[184] Department of Defense (DOD) Standard 5015.2 for records management systems. Available at http://www.archives.gov/records_management/initiatives/dod_standard_5015_2.html.

[185] Model Requirements for the Management of Electronic Records. MoReq Specification, March 2001. Prepared for he IDA Programme of the European Commission by Cornwell Affiliates. Available at http://www.cornwell.co.uk/moreq.pdf.

[186] Pitti D.V., "Encoded archival description: The development of an encoding standard for archival finding aids", *American Archivist* **60** (3) (1997) 268–283.

[187] Ruth J.E., "The development and structure of the encoded archival description (EAD) document type definition", *Journal of Internet Cataloging* **4** (3/4) (2001) 27–59.

[188] Network Development and MARC Standards Office. Library of Congress. Encoded Archival Description Official Website. Available at http://lcweb.loc.gov/ead/eadback.html.

[189] OCLC is a nonprofit membership organization serving 41,000 libraries in 82 countries and territories around the world. It is headquartered in Dublin, Ohio. Available at www.oclc.org.

[190] Research Libraries Information Network website: www.rlin.org.

[191] Hensen S.L., "NISTF 2 and EAD: The evolution of archival description", *American Archivist* **60** (3) (1997) 284–296.

[192] Kiesling K., "EAD as an archival descriptive standard", *American Archivist* **60** (3) (1997) 344–354.

[193] Fox M.J., "Stargazing: Locating EAD in the descriptive firmament", *Journal of Internet Cataloging* **4** (3/4) (2001) 61–74.

[194] Society of American Archivists and the Library of Congress, EAD Tag Library for Version 1.0, 1998. Available at http://lcweb.loc.gov/ead/tglib/tlhome.html.

[195] Society of American Archivists and the Library of Congress, EAD Guidelines for Version 1.0, 1999. Available at http://lcweb.loc.gov/ead/ag/aghome.html.

[196] Encoded Archival Context (EAC) website. Available at http://www.library.yale.edu/eac/goalsandworkplandraft.htm.

[197] Dublin Core Metadata Initiative Website. Available at http://dublincore.org/index.shtml.

[198] Dekkers M., Weibel S.L., "Dublin Core Metadata Initiative progress report and workplan for 2002", *D-Lib Magazine* **8** (2) (2002). Available at http://www.dlib.org/dlib/february02/weibel/02weibel.html.

[199] Library of Congress. Metadata Encoding and Transmission Standard (METS) Official Website, METS: An Overview and Tutorial, 2001. Available at http://www.loc.gov/standards/mets/METSOverview.html.

[200] Chen S.-S., "Preserving digital records and the life cycle of information", in: Zelkowitz M. (Ed.), in: *Advances in Computers*, Vol. 57, Elsevier, San Diego, 2003, pp. 69–107.

[201] The OCLC/RLG Working Group on Preservation Metadata, Preservation Metadata and the OAIS Information Model: A Metadata Framework to Support the Preservation of Digital Objects, 2002. Available at http://www.oclc.org/research/pmwg/pm_framework.pdf.

[202] Cedars Project. The Cedars Project Report. Executive Summary, 2001. Available at http://www.leeds.ac.uk/cedars/pubconf/papers/projectReports/cedarsrepmar01exec.html.

[203] Cedars Project. Metadata for Digital Preservation: The Cedars Project Outline Specification Draft for Public Consultation, 2002. Available at http://www.leeds.ac.uk/cedars/documents/Metadata/cedars.html.

[204] Networked European Deposit Library (NEDLIB). Available at www.konbib.nl/nedlib.

[205] Van der Werf-Davelaar T., "Long-term preservation of electronic publications: The NEDLIB project", *D-Lib Magazine* **5** (9) (1999). Available at http://www.dlib.org/dlib.

[206] National Library of Australia and Partners. PANDORA Archive. Available at http://pandora.nla.gov.au/index.html.

[207] Digital Library Federation website: www.diglib.org.

[208] Making of America 2 website: http://sunsite.berkeley.edu/MOA2/.

[209] Library of Congress. AV Prototype Project Working Documents, 2002. Extension Schemas for the Metadata Encoding and Transmission Standard web page. Available at http://lcweb.loc.gov/rr/mopic/avprot/metsmenu2.html.

[210] CAMILEON website: http://www.si.umich.edu/CAMILEON/.

[211] Bikson T.K., Law S.A., "Electronic mail use at the World Bank: Messages from users", *The Information Society* **9** (2) (1993) 89–124.

[212] Wallace D.A., "Recordkeeping and electronic mail policy: The state of thought and the state of the practice", in: *SAA 1998 Annual Meeting*, 1998, 31 p. mss. Paper draft: http://www.mybestdocs.com/, found under "guest authors".

[213] Conway P., "Facts and frameworks: An approach to studying the users of archives", *American Archivist* **49** (1986) 393–407.

[214] Conway P., *Partners in Research: Improving Access to the Nation's Archive: User Studies at the National Archives and Records Administration*, Archives and Museum Informatics, Pittsburgh, PA, 1994.

[215] Dearstyne B.W., "What is the use of archives: A challenge for the profession", *American Archivist* **50** (1987) 76–87.

[216] Maher W.J., "The use of user studies", *The Midwestern Archivist* **11** (1986) 15–25.

[217] Turnbaugh R.C., "Archival mission and user studies", *The Midwestern Archivist* **11** (1986) 27–33.

[218] Yakel E., "Listening to users", *Archival Issues*, forthcoming.

[219] Tibbo H., "Learning to love our users: A challenge to the profession and a model for practice", *Archival Issues*, forthcoming.

[220] Duff W.M., Johnson C.A., "Accidentally found on purpose: Information seeking behavior of historians in archives", *Library Quarterly*, forthcoming.

[221] Tibbo H.R., Meho L.I., "Finding finding aids on the World Wide Web", *American Archivist* **64** (1) (2001) 61–77.

[222] Southwell C., "How researchers learn of manuscript resources at the Western History Collections", *Archival Issues*, forthcoming.

[223] Tibbo H.R., "Primarily history: Historians and the search for primary source materials", in: *JCDL'02, July 13–17, 2002, Portland, OR*, ACM, New York, 2002, pp. 1–10.

[224] Sanders T., *Into the Future: On the Preservation of Knowledge in the Digital Age*, Commission on Preservation & Access and the Council of Learned Societies, Washington, D.C., 1998. Available at http://www.clir.org/pubs/film/film.html#future.

[225] O'Brien D., "The digital black hole?", *Sunday Times (London)* **17** (March 17, 2002).

[226] McKie R., Thorpe V., "Digital Domesday Book lasts 15 years, not 1,000", *The Observer* (March 3, 2002), Observer News Pages, p. 7.

[227] Millar S., "Urgent need to save digital heritage, say campaigners", *New Media Age* (April 11, 2002) 26.

[228] "Keeping hold of the intangible", *The Guardian (London)* (February 28, 2002) 11, Guardian Home Pages.

[229] Hafner K., "Saving the nation's digital legacy", *New York Times* (July 27, 2000) G.1, Late Edition (East Coast).

[230] UNESCO, Resolution on Digital Preservation. Available at http://unesdoc.unesco.org/images/0012/001239/123975e.pdf.

[231] Hensen S., Endorsement of the UNESCO Resolution on Digital Preservation. Available at http://www.archivists.org/statements/UNESCO-resolution.asp.

[232] Erpanet (Electronic Resource Preservation and Access Network) website: http://www.erpanet.org/about/main.htm.

[233] European Commission, Directorate-General for the Information Society, 2002. The DigiCULT Report: Technological Landscapes for Tomorrow's Cultural Economy: Unlocking the Value of Cultural Heritage, European Commission, Luxembourg, 51. Available at http://www.salzburgresearch.at/fbi/digicult/.

[234] National Library of Australia, PADI: Preserving Access to Digital Information. Available at http://www.nla.gov.au/padi/.

[235] Council on Library and Information Resources, *The State of Digital Preservation: An International Perspective. Conference Proceedings. Documentation Abstracts, Inc. Institutes for Information Science, April 24–25, 2002, Washington, D.C.*, Council on Library and Information Resources, Washington, D.C., 2002. Available at http://www.clir.org/pubs/abstract/pub107abst.html.

[236] DLM-Forum, "DLM-Forum 2002. @ccess and Preservation of Electronic Information: Best Practices and Solutions", May 7–8, 2002. Available at http://europa.eu.int/historical_archives/dlm_forum/index_en.htm.

[237] Hedstrom M., "The role of national initiatives in digital preservation", *RLG DigiNews* **2/5** (1998). Available at http://www.rlg.org/preserv/diginews/diginews2-5.html #feature2.

[238] JISC/British Library. "Long term preservation of electronic materials." A report of a workshop organised by JISC/British Library, held at the University of Warwick on 27/28 November 1995. British Library R&D Report 6238. The British Library, London. Available at http://www.ukoln.ac.uk/services/papers/bl/rdr6238/paper.html.

[239] Beagrie N., Greenstein D., "A strategic policy framework for creating and preserving digital collections", *British Library Research and Innovation Report 107*, The British Library, London. Available at http://www.ukoln.ac.uk/services/elib/papers/supporting/pdf/framework.pdf.

[240] Joint Information Systems Committee homepage: http://www.jisc.ac.uk/JISC eLib. The Electronic Libraries Programme homepage: http://www.ukoln.ac.uk/services/elib/.

[241] Ross S., Economou M., "Information and communications technology in the cultural sector: The need for national strategies", *D-Lib Magazine* (1998). Available at http://www.dlib.org/dlib/june98/06ross.html.

[242] Digital Preservation Coalition website: http://www.dpconline.org/graphics/index.html.

[243] Library of Congress. Digital Preservation. NDIIPP website: http://www.digitalpreservation.gov/ndiipp/.

[244] Hedstrom M., National Science Foundation "Workshop on Research Challenges in Digital Archiving: Toward a National Infrastructure for Long-Term Preservation of Digital Information", Warrenton, VA, April 12–13, 2002. Available at http://www.digitalpreservation.gov/ndiipp/repor/repor_pres.html.

[245] Hedstrom M., Ross S., "EU(DELOS)-NSF Working Group on Digital Archiving and Preservation", *D-Lib Magazine* **8** (9) (2002), See also NSF project site: http://www.dli2.nsf.gov/internationalprojects/eu_future.html. See also for more information: http://www.si.umich.edu/digarch.

[246] NSF Digital Library Initiative Phase 2. Available at http://www.dli2.nsf.gov/intl.html. NSF-JISC: International Digital Libraries Collaborative Research and Applications Testbeds. Available at http://www.nsf.gov/pubs/2002/nsf02085/nsf02085.pdf. NSF-DFG: International Digital Libraries Research—a Joint Funding Program from the Deutsche Forschungsgemeinschaft (DFG) and the National Science Foundation (NSF). Available at http://www.dfg.de/foerder/biblio/neues/dfg_nsf.pdf.

[247] Tibbo H.R., "Interviewing techniques for remote reference: Electronic versus traditional environments", *American Archivist* **58** (1995) 294–310.

[248] LeFurgy W.G., "Levels of service for digital repositories", *D-Lib Magazine* **8/5** (2002). Available at http://www.dlib.org/dlib/may02/lefurgy/05lefurgy.html.

[249] Katte J., "Reaching out to researchers: A model for web-based user education for archives and manuscript collections", Master's thesis, 2002, University of North Carolina at Chapel Hill.

[250] DPC website: Future R&D for Digital Asset Preservation. DPC Forum with Industry, June 5, 2002. Beagrie N., Trends and future opportunities, 2002. Available at http://www.dpconline.org/graphics/events/presentations/pdf/industryforum02_NB.pdf.

[251] The National Archives. Public Records Office, EROS Programmme. Guidelines on the Management and Appraisal of Electronic Records, 1998. Available at http://www.pro.gov.uk/recordsmanagement/eros/guidelinesfinal.pdf.

Preserving Digital Records and the Life Cycle of Information

SU-SHING CHEN

Department of Computer Information Science and Engineering
University of Florida
Gainesville, FL 32611-6120
USA

Abstract

In the Information Age, digital records are prevalent in every day life, from government, business, and education to banking, healthcare, and entertainment. While we have invested significant time and effort to create and capture information in the digital form, and are making great strides towards making digital information available in every community across the world, we do not have the ability to make this information available across generations of information technology, making it accessible with future technology and enabling people to determine whether it is authentic and reliable. This paper reports on the current status of digital preservation, an emerging field involving computer science, information technology, library science, and archival science. Digital preservation must be considered in a broader context, namely the life cycle of information. In the life cycle of information, we describe all essential factors for preserving digital records, including not only formats, structures, and types of digital records but also access software services, computing environments, even security keys and authenticity signatures and certificates of the records. Our finding is that preservation of digital records will be a major undertaking, but feasible solutions do exist.

1. Introduction

"The Tao that can be told is not the eternal Tao. The name that can be named is not the eternal name."
—Lao Tsu in Tao Te Ching, 1500 BC

This paper will discuss the preservation of digital records or the longevity of digital records as described eloquently in [12]. We are facing a fundamental paradox in digital preservation for the records that can be preserved may not be the eternal records. On the one hand, we want to maintain digital information intact as it was created, but on the other we want it to be accessible in a dynamic context of use [2]. Why the rapid progress being made in information technology today to create, capture, process and communicate information in the digital form threatens the accessibility in the near future? This is because hardware and software products are being upgraded and replaced roughly every eighteen months, and companies in the information technology sector report that the majority of products and services they offer did not exist five years ago. For cost-effectiveness and media decay, we have to change hardware and software products from generation to generation, and records have to migrate from original forms. The digital environment has fundamentally changed the concept of preservation. Traditionally preservation in physical objects (e.g., paper) means keeping things unchanged. For instance, we can still read the Rosetta Stone of Ptolemy V in hieroglyphic, demotic, and Greek today. However if we could succeed in holding on to digital information without any change, the information would become increasingly harder, if not impossible, to access. Even if a physical medium could hold digital information intact, the formats in which information is recorded digitally do change and the hardware and software to retrieve the information from the medium often become obsolete. Since this rapid change will continue for the foreseeable future, what are the requirements and strategies of preserving digital records? Namely, if not the "eternal" records, what are we preserving then?

The reality seems that we will not preserve all digital records, but only the essential information for our society's memory. It is an extremely tough situation for the society to judge what to preserve and what not to preserve, because we are not able to know what will the future Information Age be. Since we do not know what kinds of information, applications, software and hardware will be in the future, how can we predict what to preserve and what not to preserve at the present? But there are two kinds of digital preservation! A distinction could be made between individual preservation and organizational preservation of digital records, for individual preservation is a great success of information technology. Not only we are able to create our own archives and collections up to terabytes, but also there are many downloadable materials for fair use from the Internet. We are living in an information-rich society. During one's lifetime, individual preservation of one's personal records is readily feasible by simply preserving all records that one encounters. But organizational preservation is a totally different story. It is like the Tower of Babel, a Babylonian City in the Bible. The information explosion creates unprecedented amount of digital records that organizations are ill equipped to manage and preserve. As the workflow processes grow exponentially complex and rely more heavily or solely on digital records, not knowing how to preserve them is a real threat to the very foundation of organizations. Therefore the organizational preservation of digital records is an important issue for the Information Society. The responsibility of preserving digital records lies on all organizations: government offices, companies, hospitals, and institutions. This paper is concerned with organizational preservation of digital records.

For this purpose, we must address preservation within the life cycle of information. The life cycle of information spans acquisition, indexing, collection, preservation, access, and utilization in a cyclic and dynamic manner [3]. If preservation is missed, then the life cycle will be jeopardized and organizations will fall to disarray in the long-term. Few recognize that the complexity of preservation lies at access and utilization of the life cycle, because users will have constant demands to implement more access services and applications (APIs), which complicate further the preservation. Each access or API utilized will need software preservation (see Section 5.3). Thus organizations must design and implement their preservation of digital records effectively and seamlessly in the life cycle of information so that their daily activities will remain functional in terms of the APIs. In the life cycle of information, organizations may decide what to preserve and what not to preserve based on the organizational missions. Organizations must be also responsible to maintain their software services and computing environments. In the Information Age, most organizations are strongly interconnected: business-to-business, business-to-government, and government-to-government. Certain regulations on preservation are necessary and should be established soon among organizations. Only in this context, the legal accountability of digital records will be maintained in terms of admissible evidence and due weight in a court of law.

The paper consists of several parts, each of which contains some sections. In the first part, we describe a brief history of archival science and records management in the 20th century. Next we discuss the role of organizations and its social impacts in preservation. In an organizational infrastructure, the second part presents an object-oriented framework of the life cycle of information for digital libraries or other information services as in [3]. It includes a basic account of information preservation, introducing the concepts of metadata, container, packaging, and other operations (e.g., indexing and access) of digital objects. In the third part, we describe preservation functions of a major ISO reference model of preservation: OAIS (Open Archival Information System) [1]. The OAIS Model takes an archivist perspective. Its life cycle of information is somewhat different from the digital libraries and information services perspective. Next we synthesize them into our object-oriented framework. In the last part, we discuss some important research issues of preservation: media migration, software preservation, and security and fixity measures in digital preservation. In the archivist community, few recognize the importance of digital security and fixity measures in preservation. Since digital records can be easily altered unlike paper records, their security and fixity attributes for proving user and record authenticity would require digital encryption, signature and related security keys. Easily we can see future scenarios that the public or private key to a preserved record is not preserved or lost after a considerable length of time, regardless of permanent preservation of the record or not. So preserving digital security and fixity measures for digital preservation is a new critical issue for archivists.

Due to the wide circulation of OAIS as an ISO reference model, this paper will present a significant portion of the OAIS model. We appreciate the approval by the CCSDS Secretariat, Program Integration Division, National Aeronautics and Space Administration, Washington, DC 20546 USA for the inclusion. If any of our interpretations and presentations is erroneous, CCSDS should not be responsible and we will assume full responsibility for the potential error. From the archivist and digital librarian perspectives [1,3], we will compare the differences in the life cycle of information. In this paper, the OAIS Model has a strong influence on the life cycle. We will not use exactly the OAIS terminology, rather in a more computer science fashion to maintain our neutrality of presentation at some places. Readers will easily find corresponding terms in [1].

2.   Archival Science and Records Management

We first describe some history notes of archival science and records management in the 20th century. Next we discuss the current status, the role of organizations and its social impacts on preservation.

2.1   Some Historical Notes

Before the digital revolution, archival science and records management had a stable life cycle of the so-called "paper trail". In earlier human history, archives and libraries were relatively identical, reserved for the learned scholars. The industrial revolution caused a demand for public libraries for the mass of citizens. Today's concept of digital libraries is that of public libraries, thus departing from archives and records management systems.

In the wake of digital revolution, two prominent archivists spoke about preservation of digital records. First, L. Duranti exposed to us the theory of Diplomatics practiced during the middle ages, particularly in the Roman Epistola [7]. The form of a record was analyzed as a methodology of administrative actions and functions that generated it. Diplomatics defined the record form as the complex of the rules of representation used to convey an official message. The theory turns out to be relevant to modern day practice: extrinsic and intrinsic elements of the record form are relevant to the metadata and structure of digital records, while administrative actions and functions are descriptions of workflow processes. Thus history seems to repeat again and again.

In Diplomatics, the extrinsic elements constitute the material make-up of the record and its external appearance: the medium, script, language, special signs, seals, and annotations. These elements carry significant amount of social, cultural, intellectual, economic, and technical information about the record. Among them, annotations are most relevant to modern day records. They include authentication, registration, notes and types of actions, and even registry number, classification number, and cross-references. The intrinsic elements are integral parts of the record including content and its presentation. In a formal structure, intrinsic elements have three classes: protocol, text, and eschatocol. An example of eschatocol in private records is a sequence of appreciation sentence, salutation, complimentary clause (e.g., "sincerely yours"), signature, qualification of signature, and secretarial notes. Official records have more unique eschatocols (e.g., those of European Monarchs).

Next, C. Dollar initiated a comparative study about what archivists and records managers should do in the Information Age in [5,6]. As a visionary, he argued that the two groups must understand how their disciplines engage in a joint enterprise.

He reviewed the common roots of archives and records management with the re-emergence of archives in North America in the 1940s and their subsequent divergence over the decades. He identified the common ground including records integrity, disposition, and accessibility over time, which is linked in a single unifying theme by the importance of contextual relations of digital records. Finally he called for the agenda of designing metadata systems as a means to ensure the contextual information is preserved. The Dollar vision is beginning to take shape today after almost a decade. Let us examine the current status in the next subsection.

2.2   Current Status

Digital preservation is definitely for all digital libraries, archives and records management systems. The report, "Preserving Digital Information", by J. Garrett and D. Waters from the library community is an important document on digital preservation [8]. It has influenced our current thinking significantly. Although there have been several other efforts (e.g., M. Hedstrom [9], J. Rothenberg [12], and many others), the most concrete follow-up action is taken by the Consultative Committee for Space Data Systems (CCSDS), which is an organization officially established by ten international space agencies (e.g., NASA) and twenty three observer agencies (e.g., USGS). The committee has produced two documents CCSDS 650.0-R-1 and CCSDS 650.0-R-2, entitled "Reference Model for an Open Archival Information System (OAIS)", issued on May 1999 and July 2001 respectively [1]. Open Archival Information System (OAIS) is an International Organization for Standardization (ISO) reference model. OAIS addresses a full range of archival information preservation functions including ingest, archival storage, data management, access, and dissemination. It addresses the migration of digital information to new media and forms, the data models used to represent the information, the role of software in information preservation, and the exchange of digital information among archives. It identifies both internal and external interfaces to the archive functions, and it identifies a number of high-level services at these interfaces. It provides various illustrative examples and some "best practice" recommendations. It defines a minimal set of responsibilities for an archive to be called an OAIS, and it also defines a maximal archive to provide a broad set of useful terms and concepts. Finally it provides some perspectives on preservation of not only digital information but also access services using software porting, wrapping, and emulation of hardware. Readers could download the document from the website [1].

The InterPARES Project is an international research initiative led by L. Duranti to develop the theoretical and methodological knowledge required for the permanent preservation of authentic records created in electronic systems [10]. The methodologies include diplomatic analysis, structured interviews, and systems analysis and design. A common object-oriented and relational modeling method (i.e., IDEF, originated from a DoD project at the University of British Columbia) guides the research activities. The project has investigated authenticity requirements, appraisal criteria and methodology, and preservation methodologies. For Phase 1, a preservation model and glossaries for authenticity, appraisal, and preservation have been developed. The project is currently in Phase 2 [10].

The Public Record Office of Victoria, Australia, has developed an excellent framework, called the Victorian Electronic Records Strategy (VERS) in March 1999 [15]. VERS is to assist public offices in managing their digital records. The strategy focuses on the information contained in digital records rather than the systems that are used to produce them. Under various provisions of the Public Records Act 1973, the Public Record Office Victoria and other public offices share the responsibility for the management of records in all formats and their long-term preservation. VERS defines a format to support: long life (i.e., preservation, accessibility, readability, and comprehensibility), evidence, disposal (i.e., appraisal, authorized, transfer, or destroy), and augmentation (i.e., "onion records"). Moreover VERS provides an extensive metadata scheme in XML format, which can be downloaded [15].

2.3   The Role of Organizations and Social Impacts

Throughout human history, organizations (e.g., governments, institutions, and companies) have established archives to preserve records for future use by themselves or public citizens. Each established nation has maintained its national archive. In the USA, NARA (National Archives and Records Administration) is a large enterprise with many distinguished experts (e.g., C. Dollar worked at NARA) (http://www.nara.gov). NARA serves as the archives for the US federal records by taking ownership of the records and preserving the information content and authenticity. Recently it has established the Electronic and Special Media Records Services Division, which appraises, accessions, preserves, and provides access to federal records in digital formats. In [1], several major archives have been described including NARA.

In general, organizations have very different requirements and implementations of their archives, which depend on the nature of organizations. For example, hospitals will maintain their patient records, school systems their student records, and companies their financial records. It seems that government regulations should determine whether organizations should preserve, how they preserve and what they preserve? In the social context, organizations are the functional entities of a society. Their accountability is manifested by the preservation of digital records. The auditing of preserved records is becoming a critical process to ensure social justice (e.g., few scandalous cases involving major US corporations in 2001 and 2002). The legal accountability of digital records may be maintained in terms of admissible evidence and due weight in a court of law.

Traditional archives, digital libraries, and records management systems should assume a variety of storage and preservation functions. Traditionally, preserved records have been in the forms of books, reports, maps, microfilms, photographs, analog sound tracks and films, which are readable, listenable and viewable directly by humans with the aid of various playing and projection devices. The preservation of physical and analog media has been to ensure long-term stability and accessibility (see media life expectancy in Table IV). The preservation of digital records takes on a different direction, because the technology advances so rapidly that hardware devices and software products are being upgraded and replaced constantly. Companies in the information technology sector report that the majority of their products and services they offer did not exist five years ago. Simultaneously, the explosive growth of information in digital forms has posed a severe challenge not only for traditional archives and their information providers, but also for many other organizations in the government, commercial and non-profit sectors.

Small to medium sized organizations are finding that they need to worry about information preservation functions typically of traditional archives associated with large organizations, because digital information can be easily lost or corrupted. The pace of technology evolution is further causing severe pressure on the ability of existing data structures or formats to represent information for the organizations in the future. The supporting information necessary to preserve the information is available or only available at the time when the original information is produced, but we are preserving for the future use. Organizations must start to preserve in long-term, otherwise their information will be lost forever. This paper describes the full life cycle of information so that a cost-effective long-term preservation strategy of information may be achieved.

Is the preservation of digital records really critical to organizations? The answer is definitely yes, but we must adjust our thinking creatively and innovatively. Otherwise, we might be falling into the Tower of Babel situation. It seems that information technology allows us to innovate in such a way that the preservation of digital records might be distributed instead of being centralized. That computing is highly distributed today (e.g., cluster and grid computing) is perhaps the best argument for distributing preservation also. In the introduction of this paper, we have discussed the distinction between individual preservation and organizational preservation of digital records. The phenomenon of enabling individuals to maintain their information resources may reduce the dependency on traditional archives and libraries as the sole sources of information. We should formulate the question of how much information should organizations preserve vs. how much information should individuals preserve?

Facing the ever-increasing cost of preservation, organizations need sound policies and strategies to preserve the essential information in the long-term. The life cycle of information is not only preservation and access functions, but rather covers the full workflow process in organizations. As a workflow process relies more heavily on digital records, not knowing how to preserve them will be a real threat to the very foundation of organizations. The constant changing of hardware and software products requires media migration of digital records and system upgrade of hardware and software. There are several critical issues facing organizations:

(1) Why organizations must preserve every digital record in very frequent technology changes?
(2) Could they ask third party archives to preserve for them?
(3) Could they develop a distributed strategy of preservation?
(4) Could they allow some digital records to be preserved by individual workers within an organization?
(5) Could preservation be not the full "look and feel" (word processing and access software) view of the record, but simply a sequence of text paragraphs that can be adequately represented by ASCII characters, or an XML document that can be displayed by some standard access software, such as PDF (see Section 3.1 and [15])?

The last issue is perhaps very unpopular to archivists (they demand the exactly same "look and feel"), but will be cost effective to organizations. The content will be defined, anyway, as the bit stream made up of these characters. The representation scheme associated with the content is only a description of how to interpret this bit stream as characters, together with any access software needed to adequately display and understand the meaning of the textual content (see Section 3.1). The complexity of representation scheme and access software will be discussed later in Section 5.3.

All these questions have social impacts and are organization-oriented, and thus difficult to address by the research community. The CCSDS reference model and VERS framework are reasonable approaches to digital preservation for large-scale organizations (e.g., government offices and space agencies). Although these are thoughtful approaches, the actual implementations will depend on government regulations and organizational commitments. It is not clear to us how small to medium sized organizations will conduct digital preservation? Their preservation strategies must rely on large-scale organizations with which they do business.

In spite of its complexity, digital preservation is being practiced today. The rapid advance in digital government and electronic commerce around the world will definitely push digital preservation into the forefront of Information Technology. We have seen electronic tax submissions, business transactions, government proposal handling, and many others already. We expect that the preservation operation will be an essential element in future computer architectures. A natural step in information processing operations, just as the "SAVE" operation, may be the ultimate goal of digital preservation, which is embedded in every hardware and software system. In the court of law, we have seen the legal accountability of electronic mails. In the future, we should see more digital records to be maintained in terms of admissible evidence and due weight. The social impacts of digital preservation will evolve and unfold for many years to come.

3.   Life Cycle of Information

Object-oriented methodology has emerged to be a standard representation scheme of information technology [13]. The information encapsulation principle provides a representation of digital records as objects [3]. It wraps the information content by its accompanying procedures, which are applied whenever necessary. Operations in the life cycle of information will be expressed as complex objects of "record" objects (generally speaking, workflow processes may be represented as complex objects). In an organizational infrastructure, we present the object-oriented framework of the life cycle of information. The life cycle consists of acquisition, indexing, collection, preservation, access, and utilization (see [3] for further discussions) in Fig. 1.

Due to the diversion of archives and libraries, the life cycle of information varies in emphasis and scope. Projects on preservation tend to present the life cycle from the archivist perspective. In the OAIS project [1], acquisition (i.e., ingest), preservation,

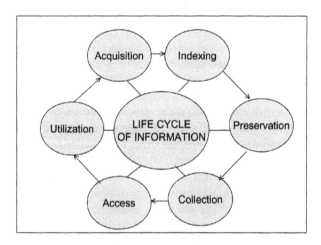

FIG. 1. Life cycle of information.

and access have been developed in details. In the InterPARES project [10], appraisal, authenticity, and preservation have been investigated. In [3], the life cycle of information has addressed the digital library and information service perspective. In a general framework of digital libraries, we have focused on the information encapsulation principle as a generalization of object-oriented programming for multimedia objects including: video, audio, image, text, virtual reality, and many other data types. We have emphasized the extensibility of objects as networked objects, whose sources may be distributed and networked. We have described the applicability of objects, for records are not static but dynamic in workflow processes. We have defined several important general operations (e.g., access and indexing) and supporting infrastructures (e.g., communications, preservation, semantics, and users) in the life cycle of digital libraries. In [3], preservation is considered as an infrastructure, which depends on specific implementations (e.g., the OAIS Model). What is needed is to develop a general life cycle of information model for all archivists, digital librarians, and computer scientists. This paper makes such an attempt on a component-based architecture of the life cycle of information (see Section 4.2). What we propose here is that the order of component operations in a life cycle of information may vary in Fig. 1 with rearrangements of components. Readers will see that the OAIS Model has the indexing operation only as a component of the acquisition (ingest) operation, while in a digital library, indexing is an important operation which covers various traditional library indexing (e.g., metadata, full-text, and catalog), content-based indexing, and indexing based on data mining and conceptual graphs.

3.1   Digital Records as Objects

In the object-oriented programming paradigm, an object has state, behavior and identity. The structure and behavior of similar objects are defined in their common class. An object is an instantiation of the class it belongs to and it inherits the variables of specific data types and associated software procedures. This includes procedures that support object definitions, structures, formats and the basic access and presentation operations. Each archive, digital library, or records management system contains a large number of classes of objects or records that form a class hierarchy. All such classes enjoy the inheritance property: A derived class inherits variables and associated procedures from its base class. The inheritance principle of object-oriented programming paradigm is an important concept as it provides programming by inheritance, polymorphism, and encapsulation. The information encapsulation principle provides a general representation scheme of various multimedia genres as content information of the life cycle. The multimedia data content is wrapped by its representation scheme and accompanying software procedures, which are applied

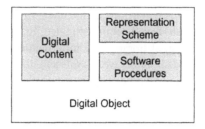

FIG. 2. The digital object concept.

whenever necessary. The representation scheme maps the bit streams of content information into understandable information of certain format, structure, and type. The accompanying software procedures execute specific functions on the content. Thus content information, representation scheme, and software procedures become modular and reusable. Digital objects are convertible and transformable, and operable under operations of the life cycle of information (Fig. 2).

A more detailed example of digital objects is depicted in Fig. 3, in which some common software procedures are described.

The surrounding procedures are essentially basic operations of the life cycle of information. Applications that operate on the digital objects do not need to know

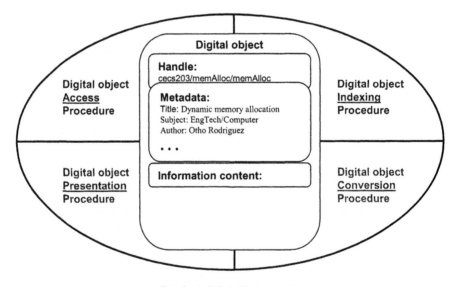

FIG. 3. A digital object example.

the specific variables and/or components of the digital objects. The object variables and components are accessed through the object's surrounding procedures. With the digital objects specified independently of its implementations, the information encapsulation principle is independent from various representation issues of the object definition. The variables and components of the digital objects may be changed without affecting the external applications. Therefore, in the information encapsulation principle, digital objects can be transformed into other objects of different definitions, structures and formats for reusability [3].

Since digital objects are encapsulated, they are active, dynamic, and extensible. They are active, because software agents may be embedded in objects so that objects may initiate activities. They are dynamic under a workflow process that is associated with accompanying software procedures of objects. For example, a workflow process in an organization will bring objects into the dynamics (or state transitions) of various transactional applications. They are extensible in the sense of multimedia content and networked sources. Any object can be augmented by other objects of multimedia content, which are coming from networked sources. It is common that a digital record pulls several networked records into itself, particularly in collaborative environments. The external applications and procedures operating on the digital objects can be used for various kinds of other relevant digital objects. This is the polymorphism principle, central to object-oriented programming paradigm. The procedures surrounding the digital objects also adhere to the polymorphism concept as it act as an "interchangeable black box" operating on different digital objects illustrated in Fig. 4.

This figure shows an example of the polymorphism concept for the information presentation operation. The digital object has a unique object handle, image content and the metadata file (XML encoded), which will be described in Section 3.3. The digital objects may be different, but the same procedure applying to them acts as a black box. The presentations (outputs) from the procedure will be different for the different digital objects.

In [1], the OAIS Model builds also upon this basic concept of digital objects. Its content is either physical or digital, and the representation scheme (i.e., representation information) allows the interpretation of the data into meaningful information. The multimedia digital content is composed of one or more bit sequences. The purpose of the representation scheme is to convert the bit sequences into more meaningful information. It does this by describing the format, structure, and type, which are to be applied to the bit sequences and that in turn result in more meaningful values such as characters, numbers, pixels, arrays, tables, etc.

These data, their aggregations, and mapping rules, which map from the underlying digital content to high-level structures, are referred to as the structure information of the representation scheme. The structure information is commonly identified by

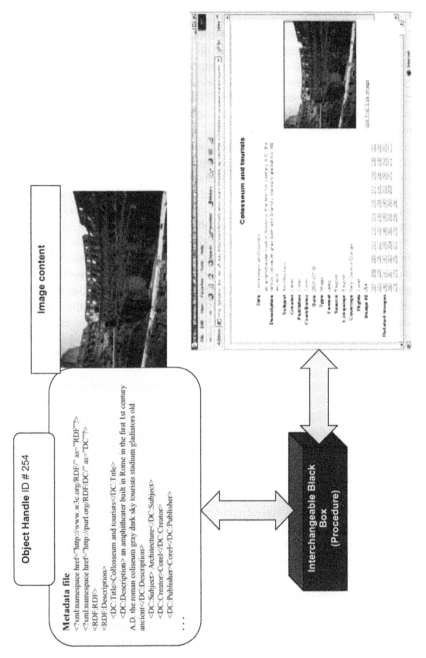

FIG. 4. An interchangeable black box.

name or by relative position within the associated bit sequences. The representation scheme provided by the structure information is usually insufficient to understand the digital content. The additional required information is referred to as the semantic information. Semantic information may be quite complex. It may include special meanings associated with all the elements of the structural information, operations that may be performed on each data type, and their interrelationships. Moreover the representation scheme may contain further associative references to other representation schemes.

In order to preserve a digital object, its representation scheme—both structural and semantic—must also be preserved. This is commonly accomplished when the representation scheme is expressed in text descriptions that use widely supported standards such as ASCII characters. If text descriptions are ambiguous, we should use standardized, formal description languages (e.g., XML markup languages in Fig. 4) containing well-defined constructs with which to describe the data structures. These markup languages will augment text descriptions to fully convey the semantics of the representation scheme.

Software procedures associated with digital objects commonly are access software and presentation (display or rendering) software. Access software presents some or all of the content information of a digital object in forms understandable to humans or computer systems. It may also provide some types of access service, such as transforming, manipulating, and processing, to another object and system (e.g., scientific visualization systems of time series or multidimensional arrays). The future existence and conversion of access software depend highly on the commercial viability, which is a very difficult prediction to make. Presentation software is able to display the content information in human-readable forms, such as the PDF display software to render the record human-readable. The PDF display software is wide available and used. Although it is not clear whether PDF will exist forever, its future commercial conversion is highly viable. Otherwise a PDF software emulator may be implemented. Since access software and presentation software are provided at the current desktop, their preservation is not carried out at each object level, but only at the environmental level. This difficult problem of long-term software preservation will be addressed later in Section 5.3.

It is tempting to use Internet-based access software to incorporate some of the representation scheme as a cost-effective means. Some web-based digital libraries or information services (of mostly HTML records) actually do use web access software even as the full representation scheme. Access software source code becomes at least the partial representation scheme of those digital objects. However one is concerned that such information may be mixed with various other processing and display algorithms, and may be incomplete since the code assumes an underlying operating environment. If executables of access software are used, without the source code,

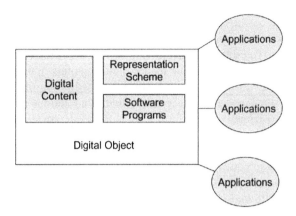

FIG. 5. Applications associated with a digital object.

such archives run the risks of losing the complete representation scheme. It is essentially more difficult to maintain an operating environment of software than to preserve records over time. Thus the operating environment must continuously support the software, in order to access the preserved records. The operating environment consists of the underlying hardware and operating system, various utilities, and storage and display devices and their drivers. A change to any of these will cause the software to cease function properly. Therefore preserving digital records is associated with preserving or at least maintaining their access and presentation software. Figure 5 depicts various applications associated with a digital object that require also preservation consideration.

This complicated situation can be significantly simplified if digital objects have a standard form so that access software and further applications can be easily executed. Currently the W3C (World Wide Web Consortium) is carrying out various XML activities supported by all computer companies [16]. If these activities can extend to include preservation operations of the life cycle of information described in this paper, a good deal of the software preservation issues will be much simplified. Other advantages of the XML standard include the object-oriented representation of digital objects, and various multimedia representation and interchangeable rendering schemes.

3.2   Bundling of Preservation Package

An important characteristic of preservation is the bundling of necessary preservation information to a digital object so that we can still access and retrieve the content

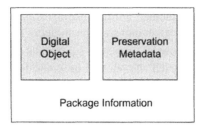

FIG. 6. Preservation package.

whatever the hardware, software, and media migration have changed the environment. The meta-information (information about information) of preservation information is essential to the concept of preservation package, which is a container of two types of information, content information and preservation metadata [1,14] (see references in [14]). The content information and preservation metadata are encapsulated and identifiable by the package information. The resulting package is made accessible by the indexing and collection operations of the life cycle. The conceptual preservation package is shown in Fig. 6.

The content information is the original target information of preservation. It consists of the digital content, its associated representation scheme, and software procedures. The preservation metadata applies to the specific content information. They are needed to preserve the content information, to ensure it is clearly identified, and to understand the context in which it was created. The OAIS preservation metadata is divided into four types: provenance, context, reference, and fixity. Briefly, they are described in the following:

- Provenance describes the history and source of the content information: who is the author, who has had custody of it since its origination, and its history (including processing history). This gives future users some assurance as to the reliability of the content. Provenance can be viewed as a special type of context information.

- Context presents how the content information relates to other information outside the information package. For example, it would describe why the content information was produced, what is the workflow process, and it may include a description of how it relates to another content information object that is available.

- Reference provides one or more identifiers, or systems of identifiers, by which the content information may be uniquely identified. Examples include an ISBN number for a book, or a set of attributes that distinguish one instance of content information from another. Further examples include taxonomic systems, reference systems and registration systems in digital libraries.

- Fixity provides a wrapper, or protective shield, that protects the content information from undocumented alteration. It provides the data integrity checks or validation/verification keys used to ensure that the particular content has not been altered in an undocumented manner. There are many fixity measures, such as CRC, checksum, Reed–Solomon encoding, digital signature, encryption, certificate, and watermarks.

The package information is the information, which binds, identifies, and relates the content information and preservation metadata either actually or logically. It is similar to the binding and cover of a book. These individual packages have to be indexed and collected into collection information of the archive. The collection information describes which collection does a package belong to and where to find the collection? Usually it is called meta-metadata in digital libraries. Within a collection, packages must be indexed so that they can be searched and retrieved. The indexing information may be a larger set of attributes or metadata, in addition to the preservation metadata, that are searchable in a catalog service [3] (see references in [3]). In OAIS, the preservation metadata or the total archival information over an indefinite period of time is called preservation description information (PDI) [1]. The PDI must include information that is necessary to adequately preserve the particular content information with which it is associated. It is specifically focused on describing the past and present states of the content information, ensuring it is uniquely identifiable, and ensuring it has not been unknowingly altered. In digital libraries where access is more frequent than archives, indexing and collection operations are very important. We will address them in Section 3.3. The larger set of attributes or metadata for search and retrieval in a catalog service may not be permanently preserved in full for they are not preservation metadata (PDI) of objects and search algorithms may evolve.

Some examples of preservation metadata (PDI) of OAIS are given in Table I [1].

The package information does not need to be preserved since it does not contribute to the content information or the preservation metadata (PDI). The preservation should avoid holding content information or PDI only in the naming conventions of directory or file name structures. These structures are likely to be used as package information. The package information is not preserved by migration. Any information saved in file names or directory structures may be lost when the package information is altered.

3.3   The Object-Oriented Framework

The life cycle of information is represented in an object-oriented framework in [3]. The life cycle consists of at least the following operations on information: acqui-

TABLE I
EXAMPLES OF OAIS PDI TYPES

Content Information Type	Reference	Provenance	Context	Fixity
Space Science Data	Object identifier	Instrument description	Calibration history	CRC
	Journal reference	Processing history	Related data sets	Checksum
	Mission	Sensor description	Mission	Reed–Solomon coding
	Instrument	Instrument	Funding history	
	Title	Instrument mode		
	Attribute set	Decommutation map		
		Software interface specification		
Digital Library Collections	Bibliographic description	Metadata of digitization	Pointers to related original documents	Digital signature
	Persistent identifier	Pointer to master version		Checksum
		Pointer to digital original		Authenticity indicator
		Metadata of preservation		
		Pointers to earlier versions		
		Change history		
Software Package	Name	Revision history	Help file	Certificate
	Author/Originator	License holder	User guide	Checksum
	Version number	Registration	Related software	Encryption
	Serial number	Copyright	Language	CRC

sition, indexing, collection, preservation, access, and utilization. In any organization, information is received from external transactional sources, generated by its own workflow processes, or accessed from information resources (e.g., libraries and archives). The life cycle starts, only after a record is acquired (ingested or initiated) by an organization. An acquired record will be preserved for long-term use. All preserved records are stored into appropriate collections, each of which is properly indexed for future access and utilization. The life cycle captures a spiral (rather than a linear) process, because acquisition follows utilization again in a repetitive pattern in Fig. 1. It is a common practice that a record used in the workflow with additional information will be acquired by the organization. In this case, the record may be either permanently archived or continuously processed in the workflow process.

The life cycle may be divided into three stages: (1) acquisition and indexing, (2) collection and preservation, and (3) access and utilization, although the division is not clearly drawn. In the life cycle of information, we need the integrated knowledge and training as archivists, librarians, and system managers. Traditionally, there are tensions between archivists and librarians, but they will diminish as the two converge. In Section 4.2, we propose a component-based architecture for the life cycle of information. Different organizations would have to build up their own deployments under this architecture. The life cycle is a continuous process of all three stages. As we examine closer into more detailed secondary and tertiary operations of the life cycle, we will see strong interdependencies among the three stages.

There are secondary operations of the life cycle, such as:

- conversion,
- transformation,
- communication,
- transmission,
- information mining,
- information integration,
- information presentation,
- storage,
- update,
- transfer.

These secondary operations may be embedded in various stages of the life cycle. Conversion and transformation of formats and structures of digital objects permit the interchange among them. They are used for instances in primary operations (e.g., preservation, access, utilization) and secondary operations (e.g., information presentation, information mining and integration). Communication and transmission send digital objects from computer hardware and storage systems through communications networks. They are needed perhaps in every operation of the life cycle. Information mining and integration extract concepts and mediate query results from networked sources into unified objects for users. They are essential to indexing and access operations. Information presentation brings information in useful manners to users in access and utilization operations. Storage, update, and transfer take place in almost every operation of the life cycle. Furthermore preservation permeates through all these secondary operations for we may need to preserve some or all software components associated with these secondary operations.

3.3.1 Information Indexing

In the next section, we will describe in more details some of these operations in the OAIS Model. Now we discuss operations that will not be described much there. First we discuss the indexing operation, which defines the structure of the life cycle of information. An organization decides how to index its records and allocate them into collections, usually depending on the hierarchical structure within the organization. There are two main indexing approaches: Information Retrieval (IR) and Database Management System (DBMS), which have recently merged much closer to a web-based DBMS system with both full-text and database query capabilities. The full-text indexing is based on the inverted file approach, namely keywords are indexed with links to records. The database indexing is based on attributes associated with records. Using DBMS and Library of Congress attributes, Dublin Metadata Core has become a popular indexing scheme of digital libraries and information services today [3] (Table II).

Dublin Metadata Core does not support preservation, package, and bundling. However it can be extended to a new metadata scheme for the life cycle of infor-

TABLE II
DUBLIN CORE METADATA

Element	Element Refinement(s)	Element Encoding Scheme(s)
Title	Alternative	–
Creator	–	–
Subject	–	LCSH, MeSH, DDC, LCC, UDC
Description	Table Of Contents, Abstract	–
Publisher	–	–
Contributor	–	–
Date	Created, Valid, Available, Issued, Modified	DCMI Period, W3C-DTF
Type	–	DCMI Type, Vocabulary
Format	Extent	–
	Medium	IMT
Identifier	–	URI
Source	–	URI
Language	–	ISO 639-2, RFC 1766
Relation	Is Version Of, Has Version, Is Replaced By, Replaces, Is Required By, Requires, Is Part Of, Has Part, Is Referenced By, References, Is Format Of, Has Format	URI
Coverage	Spatial	DCMI Point, ISO 3166, DCMI Box, TGN
	Temporal	DCMI Period, W3C-DTF
Rights	–	–

TABLE III
AN EXAMPLE METADATA SCHEME

General	Title, catalog/entry, language, description, keyword, coverage, aggregation
Provenance	Version, status, contributor, owner
MetaMetaData	Identifier, catalog/entry, contributor, owner, metadata scheme, language
Technical	Format, size (bytes), location, fixity, requirements (installation, platforms, software), duration
Pedagogical	Interactivity type, interactivity level, semantic density, intended end user role, age range, and description on how to be used
Rights	Cost, copyright, description of condition of use
Relation	Program, resource, reference, and context
Annotation	Person, date, description, comment
Classification	Taxon, taxon-path

mation. In [4], we have developed a metadata model for our digital libraries, which includes several essential elements about preservation as well as other elements not about preservation, derived from the IMS/IEEE Learning Object Metadata Standard [4]. The current version includes nine metadata elements, some of which can occur multiple recursive times (Table III).

In this scheme, we have created a specific provenance element to stress its importance. Fixity, such as check sum, becomes a technical sub-element nevertheless. The pedagogical element describes interactivity with users (e.g., education and entertainment), user age range, and other user-centered sub-elements, which are collection-oriented. The relation and classification elements and sub-elements are useful to supporting preservation. The relation element provides a place for preservation information: reference and context. Their use for archival bounds between objects, in a traditional archival process, is important. The classification element provides a principal mechanism for extending the object model by allowing it to reference taxonomies and describe associated taxon-path sub-elements corresponding to the object. Thus, classification provides multiple alternative descriptions of the object within the context and meaning of several taxonomies. Annotation allows further preservation comments on the record. This example has shown that a reasonable implementation for preservation metadata is feasible.

Multimedia objects add a new dimension to preservation. Diverse multimedia types have different file sizes and formats. Although the object-oriented approach allows multimedia objects to be manipulated equally as objects, they are technically

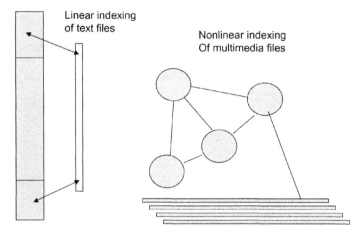

FIG. 7. Nonlinear indexing of multimedia data streams.

very different to be processed. For examples, a minute MPEG-2 video file has size 30 MB, a minute compressed audio file 10 MB, and a text file only 3 KB. When they are preserved as video/audio/subtitle of a movie, they need proper synchronization. In preservation metadata, various content and context elements are interdependent. The relationships are nonlinear in nature, thus are not searchable as the linear indexing of textual files or preserved packages (Fig. 7) [3].

For effective query, search, and retrieval, multimedia content-based indexing adds a great deal of complexity to the preservation metadata scheme. But special browsing products may be also used for discovery and search (e.g., thumbnails and images). The preservation of video content has to deal with the intensity $I(x, y, t)$ of pixel (x, y) at time t. Various MPEG compression formats have extra structures, such as (I, P, B) frames and subband coding (the decomposition of input signal into several narrow bands by band splitting with low-pass and high-pass filters). A Geographical Information System (GIS) has different features in its collections in terms of positions, and latitude and longitude variables. The USMARC (MAchine-Readable Catalog) of the US Library of Congress has a geographic subject subdivision catalog, but they do not encode complex geographic footprints (e.g., river basins and congressional districts) (see references in [3]). Archivists have not studied these issues.

3.3.2   Information Access and Utilization

Information access and utilization are the final stage of the life cycle serving users and organizations. Information access searches a catalog service of the indexed collections to retrieve queried objects from potentially networked storage resources. In-

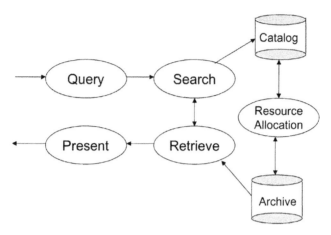

FIG. 8. Information access.

formation access has been extensively investigated and developed (see [3] and many references in current information retrieval, digital libraries, and web services literature). Figure 8 describes information access to catalog and archive services. Due to potentially large volumes in networked environments, a resource allocation service is needed to find the appropriate resources. Archivists tend to consider a central archival storage (e.g., the OAIS Model). We have relaxed somewhat the assumptions to networked access.

Information utilization is a part of workflow processes of an organization involving many application software procedures. This topic has not been fully studied from the preservation perspective. What we have discovered is that these utilization software procedures are directly related the preservation of digital records. Thus, the preservation of digital records becomes a more serious issue of preservation of associated application software. This issue should not be avoided, because the end results of utilization are newly created objects, some of which will be further acquired by organizational collections in the life cycle. Their associated software is an essential part of the life cycle.

4.   The OAIS Functional Model of Preservation

The OAIS functional model of preservation explains several important preservation functions within the life cycle. The model defines essential functional entities and the information flow of them. Note that the ingest node and the access node of the OAIS Model are exactly the acquisition and access operations of the life cycle. Some functions have counterparts in digital libraries and other information services. Administration, data management and preservation planning functions may be enlarged to similar functions of the entire life cycle of information. Here they are considered as functions within the preservation operation. Archival Storage will be handled by the secondary storage operation of Section 3.3.

The OAIS Model has explicitly described various functions and their subfunctions. In Section 4.2, we extract some important ones into components for a component-based architecture. It seems highly plausible that different organizations will deploy their archives, digital libraries, or records management systems in different infrastructures. The OAIS Model only presents a class of scientific archives. The proposed component architecture provides the flexibility and reusability for the deployments.

4.1   The OAIS Model

The OAIS model has six functional entities (in shaded blocks) and related interfaces (in arrows). Major information flows are shown in Fig. 9. The Preservation Planning and Administration functions receive inputs from and give outputs to the Management (not indicated in the figure) of the archive or the life cycle. Data Management is another function responsible to the Management.

The roles of the six entities in the OAIS Model are described as follows [1].

Acquisition (i.e., ingest) provides the services and functions to accept raw records from producers or from internal organizational units under Administration control and prepare the contents for Archival Storage and Data Management within the archive. Acquisition functions include receiving and performing quality assurance

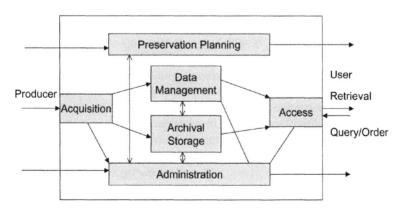

FIG. 9. The OAIS functional model.

(QA), generating a preservation package, which complies with the archive's data formatting and documentation standards, extracting indexing information (called package descriptive information) for inclusion in the archive database, and coordinating updates to the Archival Storage and Data Management. The extracted indexing information generally speaking may be different from the preservation metadata (PDI) and other indexing information of the record, which are extracted from collection and indexing operations of the life cycle. We find this piece of information unclearly defined by the OAIS Model. For first time readers, it may confuse with the PDI and packaging information within each package of Section 3.2. Since its objective is for aiding Access to a specific archive, it is essentially indexing information from the archivist perspective. So in the OAIS Model, the collection and indexing operations of digital libraries are essentially included in the Acquisition operation. In the InterPARES Model [10], appraisal is an important function, which is not covered in the OAIS Model. Appraisal is an important selecting process in archival science and records management, which disposes unwanted materials. In our more general life cycle model, appraisal should be included (e.g., VERS has a disposal function [15]).

Archival Storage provides the services and functions for the storage, maintenance and retrieval of packages. Archival Storage functions include receiving packages from Acquisition and adding them to permanent storage, managing the storage hierarchy, refreshing the media on which archive holdings are stored, performing routine and special error checking, providing disaster recovery capabilities, and providing Access to packages for users. Archival Storage is represented by the secondary storage operation of Section 3.3.

The following three functions serve the Management of the archive or the life cycle. We do not have counterparts defined yet in the primary and secondary operations of the life cycle in Section 3.3, thus they should be included in the preservation operation as functions or components in Section 4.2. In fact, we would prefer a single management system with these functions so that they can be coordinated more efficiently.

Data Management provides the services and functions for populating, maintaining, and accessing indexing information, which identifies and documents archive holdings and administrative data used to manage the archive. Data Management functions include administering the archive database functions (maintaining schema and view definitions, and referential integrity), performing database updates (loading new package information or archive administrative data), performing queries on Data Management to generate result sets, and producing reports from these result sets.

Administration provides the services and functions for the overall operation of the archive system. Administration functions include soliciting and negotiating submission agreements with producers, auditing submissions to ensure that they meet archive standards, and maintaining configuration management of system hardware and software. It also provides system engineering functions to monitor and improve archive operations, and to inventory, report on, and migrate/update the contents of the archive. It is also responsible for establishing and maintaining archive standards and policies, providing customer support, and activating stored requests.

Preservation Planning provides the services and functions for monitoring the environment and providing recommendations to ensure that the information stored remains accessible to the user community over the long term, even if the original computing environment becomes obsolete. Preservation Planning functions include evaluating the contents of the archive and periodically recommending archival information updates to migrate current archive holdings, developing recommendations for archive standards and policies, and monitoring changes in the technology environment and in the community's service requirements and knowledge base. The Preservation Planning also designs IP (Intellectual Property) templates and provides design assistance and review to specialize these templates into packages. Preservation Planning also develops detailed migration plans, software prototypes and test plans to enable implementation of Administration migration goals.

Access provides the services and functions that support users in determining the existence, description, location and availability of information stored, and allowing users to request and receive information products. Access functions include communicating with users to receive requests, applying controls to limit access to specially protected information, coordinating the execution of requests to successful completion, generating responses and delivering the responses to consumers. Since Access has been addressed in Section 3.3.2, we will not repeat any result in this section. The access control function will be separately addressed in Section 6.1 in conjunction with other security issues of preserved records in Section 6.2. This nascent topic has not been addressed in previous research on archives and digital libraries.

Acquisition is a process highly dependent on organizations. The OAIS Acquisition distinguishes an information package into three kinds: SIP (Submission Information Package), AIP (Archival Information Package), and DIP (Dissemination Information Package). The AIP is further broken into information components, called AIU (Archival Information Unit). In this paper, we do not make such a distinction.

4.2   A Component-Based Architecture

The OAIS Model has provided a maximal preservation model that consists of many useful functions, some of which are automated in the computer system, while others are conducted in human activities of the life cycle. When organizations finally realize their preservation policies and strategies, perhaps only partial models of

OAIS may be deployed for their life cycles of information. We propose a component-based architecture that can compose any partial list of functions as components of a deployment. We start with the primary operations of the life cycle: acquisition, indexing, collection, preservation, access, and utilization (not necessarily in the same order) of the object-oriented framework as in Section 3.3. The components of secondary operations, some of them are defined in the OAIS Model, are reconstructed here. Such architecture will be flexible enough to satisfy the varying requirements of diverse organizations and reusable by sharing component-based software. Earlier, we have discussed the complexity of preserving access and API software of digital records. Any preservation system that preserves access and API software must apparently be itself preserved in the advancement of technology and media migration. Consequently this component-based architecture seems to be the only way to go. We do not elaborate on the component-based software aspects here, but the importance is quite evident.

4.2.1   Acquisition

The acquisition operation will assume only the packaging function, not the indexing operation, of digital objects as in the OAIS Model. Acquisition has the receive submission function, which provides the appropriate capability of storage devices to receive submitted objects from the producer or from administration. The function may represent a legal transfer of custody for the content information to the archive, and may require that special access controls be placed on the contents (see Section 6.1). The quality assurance function validates (QA results) the successful transfer of the submitted objects to the staging area, which might include cyclic redundancy checks (CRC) or checksums associated with each data file, or the use of system log files to record and identify any file transfer or media read/write errors.

Acquisition has the generate package function. The generate package function transforms one or more submitted objects into packages that conform to the archive's data formatting and documentation standards. This may involve file format conversions, data representation conversions or reorganization of the content information in the submitted objects.

Our collection and indexing operations take over some acquisition functions of the OAIS Model. The generate indexing function extracts indexing information from the packages and from external sources to provide the full metadata set is now part of indexing operation of Section 3.3.1.

4.2.2   Collection

The collection operation is not explicitly but implicitly covered in the OAIS Model. It is highly relevant to Archival Storage of the OAIS Model. After information is acquired, indexed and preserved, each preservation package must be stored in permanent collections. Building physical file systems and maintaining permanent storages of a collection are major undertakings with technical load-balancing and other optimizations. The collection functions include the generate collection, resource allocation, update and transfer, and storage functions.

The generate collection function positions preservation packages into logical collections, based on their indexing information. Furthermore, when collections populate more and more physical storages, the resource allocation function will become necessary for finding and indexing the collections. We call such indexing information of collections meta-metadata (Table III).

The secondary update operation has shown up several times in the OAIS Model. It appears usually together with the transfer operation. For examples, the update function is responsible for transferring the preservation packages to the secondary storage operation for Archival Storage. Transfer of the preservation packages includes a storage request and may represent an electronic, physical, or a virtual transfer. After the transfer is completed and verified, the storage operation returns a storage confirmation indicating the storage identification information for the preserved package. The update function incorporates also the storage identification information into the transfer of indexing information for the preserved package and transfers it with a database update request to the catalog service (a database management system itself) and the database management system of the life cycle. In return, the data management systems provide a database update response indicating the status of the update. Database updates may take place without a corresponding storage transfer when the submitted package contains indexing information for a preserved package already in the Archival Storage. Similar update functions may take place in other components, however it may be reused with certain modifications.

The secondary storage operation has several functions taken from those of Archival Storage. Storage functions include communication, transfer, storage management, media replacement, error checking, and disaster recovery. Communication issues/receives requests and confirms transfers. Transfer performs the physical transfer from one storage or device to another. Storage management decides the anticipated frequency of utilization of data objects, assigns appropriate storage devices, and selects media types. There are many parameters and constraints: storage management policies, operational statistics, protection policies, required throughput rate, maximum allowed bit error rate, or special handling or backup procedures. It monitors error logs to ensure that preserved packages are not corrupted during transfers, provides operational statistics summarizing the inventory of media on-hand, available storage capacity in the various tiers of the storage hierarchy, and usage statistics.

The media replacement function provides the capability to reproduce the preservation packages over time. Within it, the content information, preservation metadata

(PDI), and other indexing information for search/retrieval should not be altered. The data constituting the packaging information may be changed. The migration strategy (i.e., refreshment, replication, repackaging, or transformation) selects the media type, storage, and architecture.

The error checking function provides statistically acceptable assurance that no components of the preservation package are corrupted during any internal storage data transfer. This function requires that all hardware and software provide notification of potential errors and that these errors are routed to standard error logs that are checked by the staff. The fixity information provides some assurance that the content information has not been altered as the package is moved and accessed. The storage facility procedures should provide for random verification of the integrity of preserved packages using various error checking mechanisms.

The disaster recovery function provides a mechanism for duplicating the digital contents of the collection and storing the duplicate in a physically separate facility. This function is normally accomplished by copying the archive contents to some form of removable storage media (e.g., digital linear tape and compact disc), but may also be performed via hardware transport or network data transfers.

4.2.3   Preservation

The preservation operation has three components: database management, administration, and preservation planning. The database management system should be closely integrated with the database management system of the life cycle of information. It carries indexing information and system information. Indexing information identifies and describes the holdings, and system information is used to support the life cycle operations. Many functions defined in the OAIS Model are traditional database capabilities, such as the capabilities to update various preservation information, to create, maintain and access customized user views, and to provide internal validation (e.g., referential integrity) of the contents. The database management functions are in accordance with the administration policies.

The OAIS administration functions are quite extensive as archives are concerned. Our view is that the administration variables should be decided by an individual organization for the lack of established general regulations. The current wisdom of administration, at least of the OAIS Model, seems to negotiate between producers and archives, and to mediate among user communities for establishing policies, standards, and strategies. Preservation planning is another function of the OAIS Model, which depends on an individual organization. Preservation planning designs package templates and migration plans, monitors technology and communities for change. We feel that administration and preservation planning might be merged in some way. Several administration variables are unique to preservation representing the entire range of information of the life cycle of the OAIS Model:

- Policy information that provides pricing information and availability constraints for ordering archived information.

- Request tracking information that records the progress of each user transaction with an archive.

- Security information that includes user names and any passwords or other mechanisms needed to authenticate the identity and privileges of archive users.

- Event based order information that provides the information needed to support repeating or future requests.

- Statistical information needed by archive Administration to determine future policies and performance tuning for more effective archive operation.

- Preservation process history information that tracks the migrations of packages, including media replacements and transformations.

- User profile information that enables the archive to maintain facts such as user name and address to avoid the user having to reenter these facts each time he enters a request.

- Accounting information that includes the data necessary for the operation of the archive as a business.

5.   Media Migration Issues

A key issue of preservation is media migration, which causes mainly the complexity of preserving digital records. Media migration issues are multi-layered. The first is when digital information is migrated across physical media and across formats. The second is when access services to digital information must be modified as technology changes. The third is when access services are ported to new systems and environments, and are wrapped to maintain consistent interfaces. The fourth is when access services are emulated to support legacy applications. At each layer, associated API software to these affected access services must also be modified accordingly. In Section 5.1, we will examine the necessity of media migration in the Information Age. In Section 5.2, we define, for the first layer, four types of media migration. Finally in Section 5.3, we discuss the preservation of access services software due to media migration and related environmental changes, for the three higher layers.

5.1   The Necessity of Media Migration

The paradox of digital preservation is mainly due to the necessity of media migration. The fast changing computer and digital storage media industries cause the

TABLE IV
MEDIA LIFE EXPECTANCY

Data Storage Type	Format/Technology	Common Life Expectancy (Years)	High Quality Life Expectancy (Years)
Magnetic Tape	Cartridge, Digital Linear Tape	5	20
CD-ROM	CD-ROM, WORM, CD-R	5	50
Paper	High quality	20	100
Microfilm	Archival	100	200

necessity of media migration: Any archive must eventually migrate much of its holdings to different media and/or to a different hardware or software environment to keep them accessible. Computer hardware and software must change, because media technology evolves. Conversely, media technology changes, because computer hardware and software evolve. This seems like a chicken-and-egg problem. Digital storage media can be kept at most a few decades before the probability of irreversible loss of data becomes too high to ignore. Under appropriate temperature and humidity parameters, Table IV estimates the life expectancy of data storage types.

Furthermore, the rapid pace of technology evolution makes many existing systems much less cost-effective after only a few years. Media migration is to transfer digital information from old media to new media and from old storage to new storage in order to preserve digital information based on several reasons:

(1) Cost-Effectiveness: The rapid pace of hardware (e.g., disk and tape drives) and software evolution provides greatly increasing storage capacities and transfer bandwidths at reducing costs. It also drives the obsolescence of some media types well before they have time to decay.

(2) User Requirements: The users will demand the benefits of new technologies and consequently raise their expectations of the types and levels of services they expect. The increased services may have new requirements. The user community may be continuously broadened, resulting in the need to revise the requirements.

(3) Media Decay: Digital media, over time, become increasingly unreliable as secure preservation of bits. Even those that are used with some level of error correction eventually need to be replaced. The result of media decay is that preserved records must be moved to newer media from time to time.

The paradox of digital preservation has become our way of life [2]. Although we have survived well in the Y2K problem, the social impacts of digital preservation will be costly and significant. In Section 2.3, we have mentioned the uncertainty of this evolution. But we must act now.

5.2   Media Migration Types

Administration and preservation planning must decide media migration. There are four well-known digital media migration types. The types, ordered by increasing risk of information loss, are [1]:

- Refreshment: A media replaces a media of the same type by copying the bits. The existing mapping infrastructure of archival storage is reused without alteration.

- Replication: With no change to the packaging information, content information and preservation metadata, the bits are preserved in the transfer to the same or new media type. Replication may require changes to the mapping infrastructure of archival storage.

- Repackaging: There is some change in the bits of the packaging information.

- Transformation: There is some change in the bits of the content information while attempting to preserve the full information content.

The smallest risk of information loss is under refreshment because none of the bits holding all the information are altered. There is also little risk of information loss under replication because none of the bits representing content information are changed. However if a new media type is involved there will be some changes needed in the mapping infrastructure of archival storage. The risk is that something may go wrong in the process and some unintended changes to bits may take place. Repackaging recognizes that some bit changes will take place, but these are mostly confined to information used to delimit the content information and preservation metadata, and so generally do not alter the information carried by them. Transformation changes some of the bits in the content information with corresponding changes in the associated representation scheme and software programs. The new information object is a new version of the previous object. The original version may be retained for verification of information preservation. The representation scheme defines the rules of the transformation from a base set of entities to a set of resulting entities. If the transformation is one to one, it is called reversible transformation. A simple example of reversible transformation maps the ASCII codes "A through Z" to the UNICODE UTF-16 codes for "A through Z". A non-reversible transformation is not one to one, such as a lossy image compression function. A new version is produced only after the transformation is done. Refreshment, replication, or repackaging does not produce any new version. However in the provenance metadata element of preservation metadata, such migration records of preserved records must be kept.

5.3   Access Software Preservation: From Despair to Hope

First we describe some depressing issues. Since preserved records are accessed through certain access services, and the user community may have developed further applications on top of the access services (see Section 3.1). Such APIs must be preserved in conjunction with access services software. As technology evolves, new hardware, media, and operating systems will make such APIs unusable. In order to maintain the same kind of APIs for its users, we will need to provide a wrapper interface around part of the new environment to match its services to the established API. The API will need to be adequately documented and tested to ensure that it delivers correctly the information content using the new access services software.

The user community wants usually to maintain the original "look and feel" of the preserved records as presented by a specified application or set of applications during utilization. This is also the archivist's perspective of digital preservation. We have made a great deal of costly efforts to maintain the "look and feel" (see our discussion in Section 2.3). As the computing environments evolve, the API or APIs will cease to function or will function incorrectly at some point. The preservation of the access services and API software would depend on whether or not the source code for the access services software is available. If the source code and adequate documentation on the API are available, the approach is to port the API to the new environment and attempt to ensure the correct functionality of it. However this approach has a high cost and benefit ratio. If the access services software is a proprietary package, which was widely used and available commercially, it is likely that there will be commercially provided conversion software which transforms the preserved records to other forms used by the new access services software having a similar "look and feel".

First, we may use the software emulation approach. If an API provides a well-known set of operations and a well-defined API for access services, the API could be adequately documented and emulated. If the user interface is primarily one of display or other devices, which affect human senses (e.g., image and sound), this reverse engineering will become difficult to quantify. It is possible that the API runs, but it functions incorrectly or unsatisfactorily. To guarantee the discovery of all such situations, it would be necessary to record the access services software's correctly functioning outputs as data sets, along with adequate representation scheme and preservation metadata so that the records could be correctly accessed. This would need to be checked with the results obtained after moving to a new environment. This will be very difficult if the API has many different modes of operation. Further, if the API's output is primarily sent to a display device, recording this data stream does not guarantee that the display looks the same in the new environment and therefore the combination of API and environment may no longer be giving fully correct information to the user. Maintaining a consistent "look and feel" may capture that "look and feel" with a separate recording to use as validation information.

Next, another approach is hardware emulation. One advantage of hardware emulation is that once a hardware platform is emulated successfully all operating systems and APIs that ran on the original platform can be run without modification on the new platform. However, this does not take into account dependencies on input and output and other (communication) devices. Hardware emulation has been used successfully when a very popular operating system is to be run on a hardware system for which it was not designed, such as running a version of Windows™ on an Apple™ machine. In this case, even when strong market forces encourage the approach, not all applications will necessarily run correctly or perform adequately under the emulated environment. For example, it may not be possible to fully simulate all of the old hardware dependencies and timings, because of the constraints of the new hardware environment. Further, when the API presents information to a human interface, determining that some new device is still presenting the information correctly is problematic. Once hardware emulation has been adopted, the resulting system is particularly vulnerable to previously unknown software errors that may seriously jeopardize continued information access services. Given these constraints, the technical and economic hurdles to hardware emulation appear substantial [1].

There have been other emulation approaches, such as the development of a virtual machine architecture or emulation at the operating system level. But these approaches are not mature enough for practical use. In addition, the current emulation research efforts involve a centralized architecture with control over all peripherals seem to be counter-productive.

Now we discuss the hope. As we have evolved to a ubiquitous distributed computing environment with heterogeneous clients (see [16] for W3C activities), the level of complexity of interfaces and interactions will be far beyond the scope of current emulation efforts. The object-oriented framework of the life cycle of information fits naturally into the W3C framework that makes all digital records standard XML objects, or at least with XML preservation and indexing metadata, so that digital preservation becomes feasible. If the W3C environment can evolve stably in the long-term (indicated by computer industry's support), many features of digital preservation might be realized.

6. Security Issues of Digital Preservation

Although Internet technologies and global networking infrastructures have made information sharing much easier and less expensive, the availability of such information sharing comes at the expenses of higher risks. Information is not securely preserved in the long-term. Digital archives and storages may be broken into easily, or records lost due to human and system errors. Privacy of information can be abused. Even worse, the integrity of the systems could be compromised. Within the information flow of application domains, there are multiple exceptions of users' access control to digital records of information content. Traditional security mechanisms for access, authentication, and authorization in network domains, using login passwords, have become inadequate in most Internet-based applications. We have to develop more practical security mechanisms for access, authentication, and authorization in the so-called information domains for preserved records.

Simple examples of secure information sharing include: doctors, nurses, and patients having different access control mechanisms to patient records; teachers, parents, and students to student files and learning objects; and business and customers to electronic payments and business contracts. Obviously, some users should have a higher access control privilege under certain conditions than others. The need for efficient grouping of users and records leads to the role-based access control method. The main issue is that security mechanisms for access, authentication, and authorization must deal with the role and state of both users and information objects.

6.1 Role-Based Access Control

Traditionally security mechanisms include authentication, authorization and auditing of users into network domains. Authentication and mutual authentication is a well-established computer science area. The entities to be authenticated are typically the identity of users. Authorization of information accesses in traditional information system is typically a simple check of who has the privilege of accessing what objects. The use of roles for authentication and authorization of users matches the organizational structure more naturally with the information system, and thus can lend a more efficient implementation of the security model for digital records. Auditing is a passive way of security. However, it is often useful in deterring security threats, resolving disputes and proving integrity, and checking long-term preservation. An activity log can also provide useful information for understanding and enhancement of the archiving system.

An access control model regulates the secure access of any active entity (user) to any passive entity (digital object) in archives. All system attributes are given some security attributes, and a set of access control rules determines how a user can access a digital object, based on their security attributes.

The Role-Based Access Control (RBAC) model is developed by NIST (National Institute of Standards and Technology) [11]. It controls what information users can use, programs they can run, and modifications they can make. With role-based access control, access decisions are based on the roles that individual users have as part of an organization. Users take on certain assigned roles. The process of defining roles depends on how an organization operates, and requires very careful studies. Access rights are grouped by role name, and the use of resources is restricted to individuals authorized to assume the assigned role. The use of roles to control access will be effective for developing and enforcing organization-specific security policies, and for streamlining the security management process. In the RBAC framework, users are granted membership into roles based on their responsibilities in the organization. The operations that a user is permitted to perform are based on the user's role. User membership into roles can be revoked easily and new memberships established as job assignments dictate. Role assignments can be established when new operations are defined, and old operations can be deleted as organizational functions change and evolve. This simplifies the administration and management of responsibilities; roles can be updated in the role file without updating the responsibilities for every user on an individual basis. When a user is assigned to a role, the user can be given no more responsibilities than is necessary to perform the job. The concept of "least responsibility" requires identifying the user's job functions, determining the minimum set of responsibilities required to perform that function, and restricting the user to a domain with those responsibilities and nothing more.

6.2   Digital Encryption and Signature

Digital technology allows extremely easy modification on records. Recently due to substantial industrial support of e-commerce, digital encryption and signature technology has been developed in XML and DOM standards. For examples, the W3C has started several security initiatives on the Web: XML Key Management, XML Digital Signatures, XML Encryption, and P3P (Platform for Privacy Preferences) activities. It is of importance to consider digital preservation within the framework of encryption and signature activities.

Digital records have higher risk of being forged. Digital records are fundamentally different from paper records. Tests can be performed on paper records to determine what was written on them, who was the author, and when was the time of authorship. Changes made to paper records can be detected by testing ink, paper, and other information. These tests are accepted in many court cases of legal value. However the same cannot be said of digital records. Being a bit sequence, it can be changed without leaving a trace. Although modern file systems provide the last modified time stamp, they do not provide the information about what and where a record is modified. The digital encryption and signature prevents this problem, and thus provides the authenticity of records. They are fixity attributes for authenticity assurance. Privacy of user profiles and content information will be also addressed by digital encryption. Encryption will make the whole or a part of user profiles and content information private. A XML digital signature system provides integrity, record authenticity, and signer authentication for any information located within XML records. The XML encryption standards specify the process for encrypting information and representing the results in XML records. Both XML signature and encryption activities use XML "canonicalization" standards to produce a canonical form of original XML records. Except a few unusual cases, if two records have the same canonical form, the two records are considered logically equivalent within the given API context. A XML record is part of a set of XML records that are logically equivalent within an API context, but with varying physical representations (i.e., permitted syntactic changes). This specification describes a method for generating a physical representation, the canonical form, of a XML record that accounts for the permissible changes. Note that two records may have differing canonical forms yet still be equivalent in a given context based on API-specific equivalence rules for which no generalized XML specification could account.

Despite the promise of XML encryption and signature, the preservation of digital records, which are encrypted or digitally signed, is more complicated than those are not. First the access services software must include decryption and key management for those records. Secondly, such security measures are likely circumvented with the advance in technology. With the PKI (Public Key Infrastructure) technology, we must preserve in the long-term key recovery services, time stamping services, and CA (Certification Authority) services. For example, it is uncertain that the public or private keys for a XML record will be in the long-term maintained, even if the record is permanently preserved. Thus we have to design a preservation strategy for PKI technology if it is used in digital preservation of records.

ACKNOWLEDGEMENT

The author acknowledges generous supports from NSF, IMLS, and NHPRC. He appreciates also participation in the InterPARES project.

REFERENCES

[1] CCSDS and ISO TC20/SC13, "Reference Model for an Open Archival Information System", July 2001. Available at http://www.ccsds.org/documents/pdf/CCSDS-650.0-R-2.pdf.

[2] Chen S., "The paradox of digital preservation", *IEEE Computer* (2001).

[3] Chen S., *Digital Libraries: The Life Cycle of Information*, BE Publisher, 1998, pp. 2–6.

[4] Chen S., Rodriguez O., Choo C., Shang Y., Shi H., "Personalizing digital libraries for learners", in: *12th International Conference DEXA 2001, Munich Germany*, 2001, pp. 112–121.

[5] Dollar C.M., "Archivists and records managers in the information age", *Archivaria* **36** (1993) 37–52.

[6] Dollar C.M., *Archival Theory and Information Technologies: The Impact of Information Technologies on Archival Principles and Methods*, University of Macerata Press, Macerata, 1992.

[7] Duranti L., "Diplomatics: New uses for an old science (Part V)", *Archivaria* **32** (1991) 6–24.

[8] Garrett, J., Waters, D., "Preserving digital information", Report of the Task Force on Archiving of Digital Information, May 1996. Available at http://www.rlg.org/ArchTF/.

[9] Hedstrom M., "Descriptive practices for electronic records: Deciding what is essential and imaging what is possible", *Archivaria* **36** (1993) 53–63.

[10] InterPARES, http://www.InterPARES.org/.

[11] NIST Role-Based Access Control, http://csrc.nist.gov/rbac/.

[12] Rothenberg J., "Ensuring the longevity of digital documents", *Scientific American* **272** (1995) 42–47.

[13] Rumbaugh J., Blaha M., Premerlani W., Eddy F., Lorensen W., *Object-Oriented Modeling and Design*, Prentice Hall, 1991.

[14] Shepard, T., UPF User Requirements. Available at http://info.wgbh.org/upf/.

[15] Victorian Electronic Records Strategy Final Report, Public Record Office Victoria, 1999. Available at http://www.prov.vic.gov.au/vers/.

[16] W3Consortium, http://www.w3.org/.

Managing Historical XML Data[1]

SUDARSHAN S. CHAWATHE

Computer Science Department
University of Maryland
College Park, MD 20742
USA
chaw@cs.umd.edu
http://www.cs.umd.edu/~chaw/

Abstract

The *Extensible Markup Language* (*XML*) provides a standard, text-based serialization for hierarchically structured tagged data. An important feature of XML is that the hierarchical tag structure is controlled by the source of the data, not the standard. This feature permits each database to be presented in the form that best suits it, and greatly simplifies the task of publishing data. Consequently, XML data has proliferated in both quantity and variety. The very flexibility in structure that simplifies data publishing also complicates the task of effective storage of XML data, since traditional methods rely on the presence of a rigid structure (schema). For historical databases, older versions of the database must remain accessible as the database evolves. Efficient data retrieval in the face of such an ever-growing data store presents additional challenges. In this chapter, we describe several methods for storing historical XML data, ranging from simple software layers on top of standard relational databases to solutions tailored specifically to historical XML. We discuss methods from the research literature as well as those implemented in commercial database systems and use a running example that aids in comparing the methods.

[1] This material is based upon work supported by the National Science Foundation under grants IIS-9984296 (CAREER) and IIS-0081860 (ITR). Any opinions, findings, and conclusions or recommendations expressed in this material are those of the author(s) and do not necessarily reflect the views of the National Science Foundation.

1. Introduction

At its core, the *Extensible Markup Language (XML)* [6] is a standard, text-based
serialization of data that has application-specified hierarchical structure. A key benefit of XML is that, instead of requiring data to conform to a predetermined structure,
it permits a data source to define a structure that best suits the data. For example, a
relational data source can use an XML structure that encodes database tables while
an object database can use a deeply nested structure that reflects the nested-object
hierarchy. Document databases can use a nested tag structure that corresponds to
document markup for authors, title, dates, and such fields. What XML standardizes
is not a particular structure, but the method for expressing that structure syntactically
in serial form. There are numerous extensions to the core XML standard, some of
which elevate this simple idea to a full-fledged schema language [4,5]. However, our
emphasis in this chapter is on storing XML data, not on the specification of complex
schemas. For this purpose, the simple view of XML presented below suffices. More
detailed descriptions of XML may be found in [7,6].

An XML document consists of *text* demarcated using *tags*. Tags consist of properly nested begin-end pairs of the form <tagname>... </tagname>. Figure 1
depicts a simple XML document. Tags separate an XML document into *elements*,
which are the parts of the document between matching pairs of begin and end tags.
Elements may contain text as well as other (nested) elements. In Fig. 1, the first
products element contains three product elements, each of which contains a
price element that has textual content. An element is optionally adorned with one

```
<manufacturer>
   <name>Nikon</name>
   <products>
      <product model="900"> <price>500</price> </product>
      <product model="990"> <price>600</price> </product>
      <product model="995"> <price>700</price> </product>
   </products>
</manufacturer>
<manufacturer>
   <name>Olympus</name>
   <products>
      <product model="OM-1"> <price>300</price> </product>
      <product model="OM-2"> <price>400</price> </product>
   </products>
</manufacturer>
```

FIG. 1. Sample XML data.

or more *attribute-value* pairs, specified within the element's begin tag using the syntax `<tagname attr1=val1 attr2=val2...>`. Each of the `product` elements of Fig. 1 has a `model` attribute. The document of Fig. 1 has a uniform structure; for example, the `price` elements are identically structured (each with a `price` subelement and a `model` attribute). However, such uniformity is not required. Figure 21 depicts a similar document that has a `product` element with a more varied content.

The flexibility in structuring afforded by XML makes it an attractive data format for *semistructured data*, a term we use to refer to data whose structure is irregular, incomplete, and dynamic. At first glance, such characterization of data may seem artificial, since there is a well-developed body of work on methods for translating domain characteristics into structured database schemas (relational or object). However, there are situations in which such methods are not practical. Data integration systems, which present a unified view of data from several sources, are important sources of semistructured data. In a heterogeneous and autonomous system (e.g., a collection of bibliographic information sources on the Web), data is likely to be modeled differently by each data source. Reconciling these differences is often difficult and may lead to degenerate schemas that model data using only the low-level concepts on which all sources agree. For example, bibliographic sources may represent addresses using a variety of formats. One may use lines one through three, followed by city, state, country, and postal code. Another may skip some of these fields, while still another may represent the entire address as a single string. A simple attempt to unify these representations results in the use of the least restrictive format, which in this case is a single string. Such degenerate representations result in a loss of information. For example, if all addresses are stored as strings, there is no way to reliably search for addresses with a given postal code.

In other situations, data that is not important enough to justify the effort of a careful database design may best be treated as semistructured data. A collection of structured documents (e.g., memos, reports, forms) is often a source of valuable organizational information. However, due to the flexible structure inherent in such documents, storing the documents in a well structured database using anything other than a degenerate schema is typically not practicable. Indeed, such collections are often accessed using text search engines, which model documents as bags (or lists) of words with no further structure. Modeling such documents as semistructured data permits their structure to be recognized and queried without imposing strict schema constraints. In effect, modeling data as semistructured data permits effective use of available structure without mandating any structure. (This characteristic is often summarized by stating that structure is descriptive, not proscriptive.)

While the flexible data structuring permitted by XML makes it easy for a data source to publish its data, it complicates the task of effectively storing the resulting XML database. Traditionally, databases have stored data that has a well-defined and strict structure. Relational databases require all data to be represented in collection of tables that have a fixed number of strongly typed columns. Exceptions or changes to this structure (schema) of the database are difficult. Similarly, object databases are based on a well-defined type hierarchy to which all data must conform. Indeed, when one wishes to use a database system, one of the first tasks that must be completed is a careful design of a database schema, termed *logical database design*, that best suits the domain [51]. Logical database design is based on structuring constraints that are at odds with the laissez faire structuring inherent in XML. A naive application of standard techniques results in a degenerate relational schema that makes querying difficult. (We describe this schema in Section 2.1.) The design of effective physical storage methods (disk layout, primary and secondary indexes, etc.), termed *physical database design*, is also complicated by the lack of a fixed structure. We use the term *historical data* to refer to data that is modified in only a nondestructive manner. When such a database is modified, the old state of the database continues to remain accessible (typically using timestamps or version identifiers). While the problem of storing well-structured historical data (e.g., historical relational data) has been well studied, there is little work on the analogous problem for semistructured data and XML.

1.1 Preliminaries

Before continuing with our main discussion, we present a brief description of two XML concepts that we shall use later: DTD and XPath.

DTD. A *Document Type Definition* (*DTD*) defines a set of constraints on XML documents. Documents that satisfy the constraints imposed by a DTD are said to be *valid* with respect to that DTD (or to conform to that DTD). The constraints that a DTD may define are limited in their scope. There are two kinds of constraints. The first kind, which we call *attribute constraints*, limit the names and types of attributes that may adorn an XML element. For example, the following constraint (in the syntax specified by the XML standard) indicates that a price element may be adorned with only four attributes. The first, `currency` is of type character data (CDATA) and has a default value of USD. The second, `source` is of enumerated type (`list`, `regular`, or `sale`) and has default value `list`. The third, `taxed`, has a value `yes` and its value cannot be changed. The fourth, `effectiveDate`, is of type character data, and is required. Attributes that are not marked as required or fixed are implicitly optional.

```
<!ATTLIST price currency CDATA "USD"
                source   (list|regular|sale) list
                taxed CDATA #FIXED "yes"
                effectiveDate CDATA #REQUIRED>
```

The second kind of constraints, which we call *element constraints*, limit the contents of an element using a syntax reminiscent of regular expressions. For example, the following two element constraints indicate that a `name` element may contain only text (parsed character data, or #PCDATA in XML notation), while a `product` element contains zero or more instances of text and `price`, `product`, and `promotion` elements.

```
<!ELEMENT name (#PCDATA)>
<!ELEMENT product (price | product | promotion |
                   #PCDATA)*>
```

XPath. The *XPath* standard [11] describes a query language for selecting elements in an XML document. (We present a greatly simplified description of XPath that is sufficient for our discussion in this chapter.) Elements are selected in a navigational manner, starting at the document root. Navigational steps are demarcated using the / character in an XPath query. At each navigational step, one may choose a node related to the current node by the usual tree relationships (called axes by XPath): parent, child, ancestor, descendant, sibling, preceding, following, etc. The child axis is specified by simply naming the child, while the descendant axis is specified using //. For example, the XPath query /catalog/manufacturer/product navigates from the root by descending to catalog elements that are children of the root, then to manufacturer children of these catalog elements, and finally to the product children of the manufacturer elements. The product elements reached in this manner form the result of the XPath query (match the given expression). The child axis in XPath may also specify the order of the child among its like-named siblings. For example, `/catalog[1]/manufacturer[4]/product[2]` denotes the second product (in order of appearance in the document) of the fourth manufacturer in the first catalog.

A navigational step may be qualified by requiring the presence of certain subelements or attributes. For example, the query

```
/catalog/manufacturer[name]/product[@model]
```

indicates that only manufacturer elements that have name subelements, and product elements that have model attributes, qualify for navigation at the appropriate step. In addition to simply testing the presence of subelements and attributes, an XPath query may require them to have specific values. For example, the query

```
/catalog/manufacturer[name="Olympus"]
/product[@model="OM-1"]
```

restricts our earlier example further by requiring that the name subelements of qualifying manufacturer elements have value Olympus and, further, that qualifying product subelements have a model attribute with value OM-1.

The rest of this chapter is organized as follows. We begin by describing methods for managing (non-historical) XML data. In Section 2, we describe methods that use relational databases to store XML data. We motivate increasingly sophisticated relational encodings of XML data in Sections 2.1 through 2.4. Section 2.5 addresses the dual problem of publishing relational data as XML. In Section 3, we present a brief survey of XML support in four commercial database systems: Microsoft's SQL Server, IBM's DB2 with the XML Extender, Oracle's XML SQL Utility, and Sybase's Adaptive Server. Methods for storing XML in object database systems and native XML database systems are discussed in Sections 4 and 5, respectively. Next, we present methods for managing historical XML data. The first set of methods is based on encoding a history of changes to a database (an edit script). Section 6 introduces a simple scheme based on encoding changes to XML using XML annotations. Performance enhancements for these methods are discussed in Section 7. The second set of methods for managing historical XML data is based on using timestamped snapshots of portions of the database. Section 8 introduces some of these methods while Section 9 describes methods for the special case when the XML data has keys and satisfies some additional constraints.

2. XML in a Relational Database

Although the forgoing discussion may suggest avoiding relational databases for storing XML data, there are several advantages to using relational database systems: First, there is a well developed design theory for relational databases [51]. That is, the task of converting a conceptual model of data to physical storage structures is very well understood (and significant parts of it can be automated). Second, relational databases are backed by a well established standard, SQL, that continues to evolve to accommodate new requirements [21,33]. Third, there are mature products (both commercial and noncommercial) that implement this standard (e.g., Oracle [44] and PostgreSQL [34]). Finally, there is an array of techniques for implementing the SQL standard efficiently on computer systems ranging from laptops and main-memory machines to large multiprocessor and multi-disk installations [24,39,31]. Reconciling the strong structuring requirements of relational database systems with the flexible structuring permitted by XML requires the development and use of new techniques. We describe these techniques below, starting with the simplest ones and progressing to more sophisticated ones.

2.1 Generic Relational Representation

Perhaps the simplest method for storing XML data in a relational database is one that encodes the graph structure of XML in a standard manner by using four tables: a *Vertices* table that stores name of each element, a *Contents* table that stores the data related to each XML element, an *Attributes* table that stores the attribute name-value pairs for each element, and an *Edges* table that stores subobject and reference relationships.

For example, the relational representation of the XML fragment in Fig. 1 is depicted in Fig. 2. The key attributes of each relation are underlined in the relation's title row. The ID fields are automatically generated identifiers for the elements in the XML document. (The document root is denoted by r. We use n1 and n2 to identify the two name objects, pc1, pc2, and pc3 to identify the three Nikon products, and so on.)

This method has the advantage of generality: Any well-formed XML data can be represented in a database with this schema because the schema is essentially a relational representation of a graph. (Well-formed XML data is simply data that satisfies the syntactic conventions of the standard and properly nests its elements. This requirement is a very weak one, in contrast to validity, which requires the data to conform to a specific structure [6].) However, this method suffers from at least two drawbacks: First, the schema may be overly permissive for many applications. That

Vertices		Contents		Attributes			Edges	
ID	Name	ID	Data	ID	AttrName	AttrVal	SID	DID
r	m1	n1	Nikon	mc1	model	900	m1	n1
r	m2	n2	Olympus	mc2	model	990	m1	ps1
m1	manufacturer	pc1	500	mc3	model	995	ps1	mc1
m2	manufacturer	pc2	600	mo1	model	OM-1	ps1	mc2
n1	name	pc3	700	mo2	model	OM-2	ps1	mc3
n2	name	po1	300				mc1	pc1
ps1	products	po2	400				mc2	pc2
ps2	products						mc3	pc3
mc1	product						m2	n2
mc2	product						m2	ps2
mo1	product						ps2	mo1
mo2	product						ps2	mo2
mo3	product						mo1	po1
pc1	price						mo2	po2
pc2	price							
pc3	price							
po1	price							
po2	price							

FIG. 2. The XML fragment in Fig. 1 stored in a graph relational schema.

is, the lack of restrictions on the kind of data that may be stored may result in additional work for an application in the form of integrity constraint checking. Second, the bundling of data from different element types into the same relation makes querying cumbersome because each step in an XML path traversal becomes a join in the query over the relational representation. For example, to list Nikon products that cost less than $650 we must use a SQL query similar to the following [21]:

```
select v3
from Vertices v1, Vertices v2, Vertices v3, Vertices v4,
    Vertices v5
    Edges e1, Edges e2, Edges e3, Edges e4
    Contents c4, Contents c5
where
    e1.SID = v1.ID and v1.name = "manufacturer" and
    e1.DID = e2.SID and
    e1.SID = v2.ID and v2.name = "products" and
    e2.DID = v3.ID and v3.name = "product" and
    e3.SID = v1.ID and e3.DID = v4.ID and v4.name = "name" and
    c4.ID = v4.ID and c4.Data = "Nikon" and
```

```
e4.SID = v3.ID and e4.DID = v5.ID and v5.name = "price"
and c5.ID = v5.ID and c5.Data < 650;
```

In contrast, the equivalent query on the original XML representation, using *XPath* (introduced in Section 1) is much more direct:

```
/manufacturer[name="Nikon"]/products
/product[price<650]
```

The above XPath query may be interpreted as a traversal that starts at the document root, descends first to a manufacturer element that has a name subelement with value *Nikon* (indicated using the box brackets), then to a products element, and finally to a product element that has a price subelement with value less than 650. In the SQL query, each descent to a subobject is mapped to a join.

2.2   Alternate Relational Representation

Instead of storing element names (e.g., manufacturer, product) as attribute values in a *Vertices* relation as above, we may create a separate relation for each element type. More precisely, we create two kinds of relations. One relation of the first kind, called an *element relation*, is created for each element type that has XML attributes. One relation of the second kind, called an *subelement relation*, is created for each element type-subelement type pair. Elements with text content (e.g., price, name) are represented by their values, while elements that have subelements (e.g., manufacturer, product) are represented by a unique identifier. Figure 3 depicts a relational mapping of our running example (Fig. 1) based on this idea. Since there is only one XML element type that has attributes (product), there is only one

Manufacturers	
ID	Name
m1	Nikon
m2	Olympus

ManufProds	
ID	Products
m1	ps1
m2	ps2

ProductSets	
ProdSet	Product
ps1	pc1
ps1	pc2
ps1	pc3
ps2	po1
ps2	po2

Models	
ID	Model
pc1	900
pc2	990
pc3	995
po1	OM-1
po2	OM-2

Prices	
ID	Price
pc1	500
pc2	600
pc3	700
po1	300
po2	400

FIG. 3. Mapping each element type to a relation.

element relation, called `Models`. The relations `Manufacturers`, `ManufProds`, `ProductSets`, and `Prices` are subelement relations for the pairs manufacturer-name, manufacturer-products, products-product, and product-price, respectively. The key attributes of each relation are underlined in Fig. 3. We do not make assumptions regarding the uniqueness of manufacturer names and product prices. Therefore the ID attributes of the Manufacturers and Products relations do not constitute keys by themselves. (We discuss this topic further in Section 2.3.)

The separation of data into relations corresponding to element types results in a simpler and more intuitive SQL expression of our earlier query:

```
select p1
from Manufacturers m1, ManufProds mp1,
     ProductSets ps1, Models mo1, Prices p1
where m1.Name = "Nikon" and m1.ID = mp1.ID and
    mp1.Products = ps1.ProdSet and
    ps1.Product = mo1.ID and
    mo1.ID = p1.ID and p1.Price < 650;
```

Unlike the generic representation discussed earlier, the representation suggested by Fig. 3 is specific to the implied schema of our running example because the relation names are based on the element names and the expected element nesting. This schema specificity of the relational encoding restricts the kinds of data that it can encode. For example, the fact that `manufacturer` elements may have a `name` subelement is encoded by the `ManufNames` relation. The name element is not permitted to occur in any other context. There is no way to use this relational schema to encode XML data in which a name element occurs as a child of a product element (perhaps representing the informal name of a product).

2.3   Encoding Schema Assumptions

Intuitively, the relational schema of Fig. 3 includes some cumbersome features. For example, a product's model number and price are stored in separate relations. Indeed, all subelement relations produced by that method are binary because it makes no XML schema assumptions other than the kinds of element nesting that are permitted. (Element relations have arity one greater than the number of XML attributes adorning the corresponding XML elements.) If other schema assumptions are known to hold for the XML data of interest, they can be used to generate a better relational schema. Suppose we make the following additional schema assumptions about the domain of the XML data in our running example: (1) Every manufacturer element has a unique name subelement and a unique products subelement, (2) Every product

Manufacturers		
ID	Name	Products
m1	Nikon	ps1
m2	Olympus	ps1

ProductSets	
ProdSet	Product
ps1	pc1
ps1	pc2
ps1	pc3
ps2	po1
ps2	po2

Products		
ID	Model	Price
pc1	900	500
pc2	990	600
pc3	995	700
po1	OM-1	300
po2	OM-2	400

FIG. 4. Mapping each element type to a relation.

element has a unique model subelement and a unique price subelement. A relational schema that uses these assumptions is depicted in Fig. 4.

The query from our running example is now much simpler:

```
select p1
from Manufacturers m1, ManufProds mp1,
     ProductSets ps1, Models m1, Prices p1
where m1.Name = "Nikon" and m1.ID = mp1.ID and
     mp1.Products = ps1.ProdSet and
     ps1.Product = m1.ID and
     m1.ID = p1.ID and p1.Price < 650;
```

Let us compare the schemas suggested by Figs. 3 and 4. Following convention, key attributes are underlined in the title rows of relations. We note that there is only one relation of the five in Fig. 3 that has a nontrivial key constraint: Models's key is ID; thus, a product's model number is unique. (This constraint follows from restrictions placed on attributes by the XML standard.) The schema depicted in Fig. 4 has non-trivial key constraints on the Manufacturers and Products relations. These relational key constraints enforce the uniqueness constraints on the name and products subelements of manufacturer and, similarly, the uniqueness constraints on the model attribute and price subelement of product.

2.4   Partial Parsing

In the methods described above, each XML element is stored in a fully parsed form. That is, its content (text, subelements) and XML attributes, if any, are stored as separate relational attributes in the relational representation. The advantage of fully parsing an XML document in this manner is that subsequent relational operations on the data (selections on attribute values and element content, joins, etc.) proceed as in standard relational databases. The requirement to fully parse XML data in this manner is a manifestation of the first normal form (1NF) requirement of relational

Manufacturers

ID	Name	Products
m1	Nikon	ps1
m2	Olympus	ps1

Products

ProdSet	Product
ps1	`<product model="900"><price>500</price></product>`
ps1	`<product model="990"><price>600</price></product>`
ps1	`<product model="995"><price>700</price></product>`
ps2	`<product model="OM-1"><price>300</price></product>`
ps2	`<product model="OM-2"><price>400</price></product>`

FIG. 5. Storing partially parsed XML data.

design. However, parsing incurs substantial overheads at database population time, especially for XML data with a large number of small elements. In applications that access the data in larger units (entire documents or large parts thereof), this parsing represents unnecessary overhead. Further, although relational operations on the parsed representation are efficient, reconstruction of the original XML (or the XML version of a query result) requires substantial work. (We discuss methods for generating XML from relational databases in Section 2.5.) Therefore, in some applications, it may be advantageous to store some XML data in unparsed form (serialized XML) using the CLOB (character large object) or a similar datatype. It is often possible to speed up queries that search for terms within such CLOB data items by building text indexes on them.

Figure 5 depicts such a schema for our running example. It stores product elements (and their subelements) as unparsed XML, while the manufacturer and product set elements are parsed. The query from our running example must now use a user-defined function (UDF) *getPrice* to extract the numerical price value from the string-valued Product attribute:

```
select p1
from Manufacturers m1, Products p1
where m1.name = "Nikon" and
      m1.Products = p1.ProdSet and
      getPrice(p1.Product) < 650;
```

The disadvantage of unparsed elements is evident from this query. Since the query engine does not know the semantics of the UDF *getPrice*, query optimization suffers. For example, if the Products table has an index on the Price attribute, the query for the schema of Fig. 3 can use an index scan instead of a table scan, resulting in fewer disk accesses in general. In contrast, any query plan for the query with the UDF must scan the entire Products table. Further, the need to invoke a UDF on each tuple of a table typically results in a significant slowdown in query processing. Despite this limitation, storing partially parsed XML is often an attractive option, especially when there is a need to reconstruct XML fragments from the relational representation (Section 2.5).

The partially parsed representation scheme raises the question of deciding which elements should be parsed and which should be stored as text. One simple rule is to parse the elements in the first few levels of the XML tree, representing the rest as CLOBs. Another rule is to parse only those elements whose size (in characters) exceeds a threshold. The latter rule is helpful in limiting the overhead of parsing and reassembling XML from the relational representation.

The above methods ignore the order among siblings in the XML tree structure. For example, the relational encodings of a variant of the XML data of Fig. 1 that has the product subelements for models OM-1 and OM-2 swapped are identical to the ones suggested by Figs. 2, 3, 4, and 5. This feature is troublesome because the XML standard specifies that order is significant. For example, Fig. 1 lists product elements in order of their market introduction and losing this information is undesirable. The methods described above are easily modified to include order by adding a *cnum* attribute to each relation. For each tuple, this attribute denotes the sibling order of the element represented by that tuple. Insertions and deletions of elements require updating the cnum attribute of tuples representing all siblings that are to the right of the inserted or deleted elements.

2.5   XML Rendering of Relational Data

In our discussion above, we have focused on native XML data, that is, on data that originates as XML (or in a form very similar to XML). We contrast this situation with one in which the data originates in a relational format but must be occasionally rendered in XML form (for applications such as generating Web pages and transferring data to a remote database). In the latter situation, modeling and storing the data does not pose any new challenges, and is amenable to standard relational database design theory [51,36,41]. However, efficient rendering of such data as XML does pose some challenges. Relational databases are well suited to efficient retrieval of data in tabular format. However, an XML rendering requires that data in such a tabular format be converted to a structured and tagged format. Our presentation below is based on the ideas in [42].

Structuring may be thought of as the process of converting relational data to a nested relational form, based on grouping of the tuples by some attributes. For example, Fig. 6 suggests such a transformation of a relation with product data by grouping

Catalog		
Manufacturer	Product	Price
Olympus	OM-1	300
Nikon	990	600
Olympus	OM-2	400
Nikon	995	700
Nikon	900	500

$\longrightarrow$

Nested Catalog		
Manufacturer	Product	Price
Nikon	900	500
	990	600
	995	700
Olympus	OM-1	300
	OM-2	400

FIG. 6. Structuring relational data by grouping.

on the manufacturer. The table on the right hand side depicts two nested relations: one with the product codes and prices for Nikon, and the other with those for Olympus.

This transformation may be expressed by the following query, which uses a nested-table syntax similar to that used by Oracle [50]:

```
select C1.Manufacturer, ProdPriceTable(
    select ProdPrice(Product, Price)
    from Catalog C2
    where C2.Manufacturer = C1.Manufacturer
    order by Product)
from Catalog C1
group by Manufacturer
order by Manufacturer;
```

In the above query, the nested table listing the product-price tuples for each manufacturer is populated using the constructor `ProdPriceTable`, which takes a set of product-price tuples as its argument. The product-price tuples themselves are created using the constructor `ProdPrice` in the subquery that retrieves the tuples for each manufacturer.

The nested table on the right-hand side of Fig. 6 is naturally mapped to the XML fragment depicted in Fig. 1 by introducing nested tags that reflect the structure of the nested relations. Although this tagging operation is conceptually simple, it requires string manipulation operations for each element and attribute in the output. These operations are typically compute-intensive and sharply deteriorate query response times.

There are three implementation choices in the above framework. First, the structuring task, that is, the conversion from (flat) relations to nested relations, can occur at different points in the query plan. One extreme is to leave data in the flat relational form until the final stages of query processing, the other is to convert data to nested form as soon as it becomes available. Second, the tagging operation, that is, the conversion from nested tabular data to serialized XML, can also occur in different parts of the query plan (with the restriction that it be preceded by the structuring operation on the required data). Third, structuring and tagging operations can be performed inside the database engine (using user defined functions) or outside the database engine (using the features of a host language such as Java or C). These alternatives are discussed in [42], which also presents detailed implementation notes. That paper notes that the strategy of late structuring and late tagging works well when the query results fit in main memory, while the strategy of early structuring and late tagging works well if the results are too large for main memory. In both cases, the authors note significant benefits to performing the operations inside the database engine.

In many applications (e.g., Web page generation) the XML data published in this manner is likely to be further queried using an XML query language such as XQuery or XPath. In such cases, further performance improvements may be achieved by combining the two stages of query processing to avoid materializing XML fragments that do not appear in the final result. Techniques for pushing operations from XQuery down to the SQL level in the database engine are presented in [40].

3. XML Support in Commercial Database Systems

There is ongoing standards work on the mapping between SQL and XML (*SQL/XML*) [23,30]. The early work has focused on low-level tasks such as the mappings between SQL character sets and Unicode, SQL identifiers and XML names, SQL and XML data types, and SQL and XML values. Although such mappings are an important part of an implementation, our focus here is on mapping higher level entities, such as tables, columns, rows, elements, and attributes. Such mapping is not addressed by the current standards documents. However, there are several features in current releases of commercial database systems for specifying and implementing this mapping. These features address two main tasks: publishing relational data as XML and storage of XML data (not necessarily generated from relations) in relations. Our discussion is based on information gleaned from published descriptions of these features [15,20,38,29,28,45,46], and uses a common running example to permit easy comparison of features across systems.

3.1   Microsoft SQL Server

Publishing.   SQL Server provides three methods for publishing relational data as XML, using a *for XML* clause as an extension to SQL. The simplest method, called the *RAW mode*, produces one XML element for each tuple in the result of a SQL query. The element has empty content and one XML attribute for each relational attribute. For example, the following query on the Catalog table depicted in Fig. 6 produces the two XML elements listed below it.

```
select Product, Price
from Catalog
where Manufacturer = 'Olympus'
for XML RAW;

<row Product="OM-1" Price="300"/>
<row Product="OM-2" Price="400"/>
```

Referring back to the discussion in Section 2.5, we note that the RAW mode performs tagging, but no structuring.

The *AUTO mode* tries to produce an intuitively structured XML fragment corresponding to the result of a SQL query. Element nesting is based on the order of relations in the from clause of the query. Relational attributes in the from clause are mapped to XML attributes by default. They can be mapped to subelements instead by using the ELEMENTS qualifier after the for XML AUTO clause. The following query illustrates the use the AUTO mode on the Catalog and Ratings relations depicted in Figs. 6 and 7. The query results are depicted in Fig. 8.

```
select C.Manufacturer, C.Product, R.Source, R.Rating
from Catalog C, Ratings R
where C.Manufacturer = R.Manufacturer and
C.Product = R.Model
for XML AUTO;
```

Appending a ", ELEMENTS" to the for XML clause of the query produces the results depicted in Fig. 9.

The third method for rendering data as XML, called the *EXPLICIT mode*, provides the most flexibility in structuring the output. A query using this mode must produce a table that encodes the desired XML structure as follows: Each row of the table encodes one element. The first column of the table, named *Tag*, indicates the tag number (unique identifier per tag) of the element. The second column, named

Ratings

Source	Manufacturer	Model	Rating
PC Magazine	Olympus	OM-1	5
PhotoLife	Olympus	OM-1	4.5
PC Magazine	Nikon	990	3

FIG. 7. Data complementing the Catalog relation in Fig. 6.

```
<Catalog Manufacturer="Olympus" Product="OM-1">
   <Ratings Source="PC Magazine" Rating="5"/>
   <Ratings Source="PhotoLife" Rating="4.5"/>
</Catalog>
<Catalog Manufacturer="Nikon" Product="990">
   <Ratings Source="PC Magazine" Rating="3"/>
</Catalog>
```

FIG. 8. Query results in AUTO mode.

```
<Catalog>
   <Manufacturer>Olympus</Manufacturer>
   <Product>OM-1</Product>
   <Ratings>
      <Source>PC Magazine</Source>
      <Rating>5</Rating>
   </Ratings>
   <Ratings>
      <Source>PhotoLife</Source>
      <Rating>4.5</Rating>
   </Ratings>
</Catalog>
<Catalog>
   <Manufacturer>Nikon</Manufacturer>
   <Product>990</Product>
   <Ratings>
      <Source>PC Magazine</Source>
      <Rating>3</Rating>
   </Ratings>
</Catalog>
```

FIG. 9. Query results with the ELEMENTS option.

Parent, indicates the tag number of the element's parent. A null or 0 value in the column is used to denote an element at the top level (no parent). In addition to these two columns, the table has one column for each XML attribute of each element in the desired result. (This representation is similar to the Universal Relation [49].) In the row representing an element, all columns representing that element's attributes or those of its ancestors are populated with the appropriate values. The unused columns have null values. All columns except the first two have names of the form E!N!A, where E is an element name, N is a positive integer denoting an element's nesting depth, and A is an attribute name. Finally, the order of rows in the result table is sig-

Tag	Parent	Prod!1!Manuf	Prod!1!Model	Rev!2!Src	Rev!2!Rating
1	NULL	Olympus	OM-1	NULL	NULL
2	1	Olympus	OM-1	PC Magazine	5
2	1	Olympus	OM-1	PhotoLife	4.5
1	NULL	Nikon	990	NULL	NULL
2	1	Nikon	990	PC Magazine	3

FIG. 10. Universal relation encoding for generating the XML in Fig. 11 using SQL Server's *explicit* mode.

```
<Prod Manuf="Olympus" Model="OM-1">
    <Rev Src="PC Magazine" Rating="5"/>
    <Rev Src="PhotoLife" Rating="4.5"/>
</Prod>
<Prod Manuf="Nikon" Model="990">
    <Rev Src="PC Magazine" Rating="3"/>
</Prod>
```

FIG. 11. XML fragment encoded by the table in Fig. 10.

nificant. The rows corresponding to an element's children must immediately follow the row for the element, recursively (in a depth-first order). Continuing with our running example, Fig. 10 depicts the tabular encoding of the XML fragment depicted in Fig. 11. The tabular encoding is generated using the following query on our sample data.

```
select 1 as Tag, NULL as Parent,
    C.Manufacturer as Prod!1!Manuf, C.Product as
    Prod!1!Model,
    NULL as Rev!2!Src, NULL as Rev!2!Rating
from Catalog C
union all
select 2 as Tag, 1 as Parent,
    C.Manufacturer as Prod!1!Manuf, C.Product as
    Prod!1!Model,
    R.Source as Rev!2!Src, R.Rating as Rev!2!Rating
from Catalog C, Ratings R
where C.Manufacturer = R.Manufacturer and
    C.Product = R.Model
for XML EXPLICIT;
```

The default method described above maps each non-null column value in a row of the encoded table to an XML attribute-value pair in the element corresponding to that row. Individual column values can be mapped to subelements instead of attributes by suffixing the column name with the literal string !element (i.e., by using a column name of the form E!N!A!element). We may also make such mapping to subelements the default for all columns in the query result by using the clause for XML EXPLICIT, ELEMENTS instead of for XML EXPLICIT.

Storage. SQL Server provides two methods for storing XML documents in relations. The first is a simple encoding of the XML graph using an edges table. This method is essentially the generic relational representation of Section 2.1. The second method is similar to the alternate relational representations of Sections 2.2 and 2.3. It permits the use of a separate relation for each element type, mapping each element to a tuple in the appropriate table. The mapping is specified using XPath expressions with the help of a predefined rowset function *OpenXML*. For example, the following statement on the XML fragment depicted in Fig. 8 populates an initially empty Ratings table to yield the table depicted in Fig. 7.

```
select *
from OpenXML(@doc, '/Catalog/Ratings', 2)
with (Source varchar(30), '@Source',
      Manufacturer varchar(30), '../@Manufacturer'
      Model varchar(10), '../@Product',
      Rating number, '@Rating');
```

The OpenXML function has three parameters: The first, @doc is a handle for the source XML document. The second parameter is an XPath expression that identifies nodes in the XML document that are converted to tuples (as detailed in the with clause). The third parameter is a flag: The value 2 denotes an element-centric mode that allows access to elements other than the ones identified by the second parameter. (A flag value of 1 denotes a simpler, attribute-centric mapping.) The with clause includes the name and data type of each relational attribute. In addition, it specifies the mapping from elements to relational attributes using an XPath expression that identifies the XML node with the data for each relational attribute. The XPath expressions in the with clause are relative to the base node specified by the XPath expression in the OpenXML function call. In our example query, the base nodes are the Ratings elements, identified by the expression /Catalog/Ratings. The relative expression @Source in the with clause maps the Source (XML) attribute of a Ratings element to the Source attribute in the tuple for that element. (The Rating attribute is specified analogously.) The Manufacturer and Model attributes of the Ratings tuple are obtained from the parent of the Ratings node in the XML tree (i.e., from the containing Catalog element) using . . / to navigate up the XML tree.

3.2 DB2 XML Extender

Publishing. In order to publish relational data as XML, IBM's DB2 XML Extender [29] uses a user-specified mapping called the Data Access Definition (DAD). There are two kinds of DADs. The first, called a *SQL DAD*, maps column names in the select clause of a SQL query to element and attribute nodes in the desired XML document. The second, called a *RDB-node DAD*, maps columns of database tables, optionally qualified by predicates, directly to XML. In both kinds of DADs, the mapping to XML is specified by using an outline of the desired XML document. (This outline is similar to methods for summarizing XML data, such as data guides, representative objects, and graph schemas [25,35,2].) For each element type in the desired document, the DAD indicates the element name and the source of its text, attribute contents, and subelements (recursively).

Figure 12 depicts a SQL DAD for mapping the relational data of our running example (Figs. 1 and 7) to XML. (Here, and in Fig. 13, we omit some minor details, such as the XML prolog, for clarity.) There are two main parts of this DAD. The first is the SQL statement within the SQL_stmt element; the result of this query provides the data that is used to generate XML. The second part is the template for the output XML, within the root_node element. Suppose our goal is to generate the XML fragment depicted in Fig. 11. This fragment consists of Prod elements, with attributes Manuf and Model at the top level. Each Prod element encloses zero or more Rev elements, which have attributes Src and Rating. This outline is encoded by the DAD using the elements element_node and attribute_node, appropriately nested; both element types admit a name attribute whose value is the name of the corresponding element in the output XML. Finally, the data within these elements is specified using the column element, whose name attribute refers to columns in the output of the SQL query specified earlier.

Figure 13 depicts a RDB-node DAD that may be used to produce an XML document that is identical to that produced by the SQL DAD of Fig. 12. The DAD includes an outline of the desired XML document, specified as in the SQL DAD. There are two major differences. First, there is no SQL statement, since an RDB-node DAD maps data from database tables instead of from query results. Second, the source of data for an attribute or element is specified by listing the names of a table and a column in the underlying relational database instead of listing a column name in a SQL query. The correlation of data from multiple tables is specified using the condition element. In our example, the condition element contains the join predicate of the earlier SQL query. This predicate applies to the rest of the DAD and

```
<dad>
    <Xcollection>
        <SQL_stmt>
            select C.Manufacturer, C.Product, R.Source, R.Rating
            from Catalog C, Ratings R
            where C.Manufacturer = R.Manufacturer and
            C.Product = R.Model
        </SQL_stmt>
        <root_node>
            <element_node name="Prod">
                <attribute_node name="Manuf">
                    <column name="Manufacturer"/>
                </attribute_node>
                <attribute_node name="Model">
                    <column name="Product"/>
                </attribute_node>
                <element_node name="Rev">
                    <attribute_node name="Src">
                        <column name="Source"/>
                    </attribute_node>
                    <attribute_node name="Rating">
                        <column name="Rating"/>
                    </attribute_node>
                </element_node>
            <element_node>
        </root_node>
    </Xcollection>
</dad>
```

FIG. 12. A SQL DAD for mapping the relational data of Figs. 1 and 7 to the XML fragment of Fig. 11.

ensures that, in the output XML, each product review element (Rev) is placed within the appropriate product element (Prod).

Storage.   DB2 Extender permits simple storage of XML documents in a single column. It provides the data types XMLVARCHAR for small documents, XMLCLOB for larger documents, and XMLFile for large documents that are to be stored in a separate file outside the database system. XML data from a file is stored in a column of type XMLCLOB using a function XMLCLOBFromFile. Similar functions exist for the two other XML column types. The database designer has the option of creating one or more structured representations of the data in an XML-typed column. These structured representations, called *side tables*, are maintained automatically by the database system as data in the XML column is inserted, updated, or deleted. Indexes

```
<dad>
    <Xcollection>
        <root_node>
            <element_node name="Prod">
                <RDB_node>
                    <table name="Catalog"/>
                    <table name="Reviews"/>
                    <condition>
                        Catalog.Manufacturer = Reviews.Manufacturer
                        and
                        Catalog.Product = Reviews.Model
                    </condition>
                </RDB_node>
                <attribute_node name="Manuf">
                    <RDB_node>
                        <table name="Catalog"/>
                        <column name="Manufacturer"/>
                    </RDB_node>
                </attribute_node>
                <attribute_node name="Model">
                    <RDB_node>
                        <table name="Catalog"/>
                        <column name="Model"/>
                    </RDB_node>
                </attribute_node>
                <element_node name="Rev">
                    <attribute_node name="Src">
                        <table name="Reviews"/>
                        <column name="Source"/>
                    </attribute_node>
                    <attribute_node name="Rating">
                        <table name="Reviews"/>
                        <column name="Rating"/>
                    </attribute_node>
                </element_node>
            <element_node>
        </root_node>
    </Xcollection>
</dad>
```

FIG. 13. A RDB-node DAD for mapping the relational data of Figs. 1 and 7 to the XML fragment of Fig. 11.

```
create table Manufacturers(
   ID char(10) primary key not null,
   phone varchar(20),
   manufData XMLCLOB);

<dad>
   <dtdid>catalog.dtd</dtdid>
   <validation>yes</validation>
   <Xcolumn>
      <table name="name_side_table">
         <column name="name" type="varchar(20)"
         path="/manufacturer/name" multi_occurrence="no"/>
      </table>
      <table name="model_side_table">
         <column name="model" type="varchar(10)"
         path="/manufacturer/products/product/@model"
         multi_occurrence="yes"/>
         <column name="price" type="decimal(10,2)"
         path="/manufacturer/products/product/price"
         multi_occurrence="yes"/>
      </table>
   </Xcolumn>
<dad>
```

FIG. 14. Table and side-table DAD for storing XML fragments of our running example (Fig. 1) as XML column values separated by manufacturer.

on the side tables provide an efficient mechanism for querying XML column data when the query attributes match those in the side tables. Side tables are specified by means of a DAD that indicates the parts of the XML data that are to be mapped to the tables.

We return to the data for our running example, depicted in Fig. 1, to illustrate the use of side tables on XML columns. Suppose we decide to store the XML document by partitioning it by manufacturer, as suggested by the create table statement in Fig. 14. The Manufacturers table includes an XML column called manufData for storing the manufacturer XML element for each manufacturer, identified by an artificial key ID. The figure also depicts a DAD that defines two side-tables for the manufData XML column. It begins by indicating the Document Type Definition (DTD) governing the data stored in the column and whether validation is required. (Recall our discussion of DTDs in Section 1.) Side tables are specified within the Xcolumn element using the syntax suggested by Fig. 14. Each table element defines a side table and contains several column elements, each name_side_table

ID	name
1001	Nikon
1002	Olympus

model_side_table

ID	model	price
1001	900	500
1001	990	600
1001	995	700
1002	OM-1	300
1002	OM-2	400

FIG. 15. Side tables corresponding to the specification in Fig. 14.

of which describes the name and type of a column in the table. The path attribute defines the association of elements in the XML-typed column in the main table to column values in the side table. The boolean multi_occurrence attribute indicates whether the element or attribute identified by the path attribute may occur more than once in the XML column value. In our example, the first side table stores the names of manufacturers and the second stores model number and price data.

A side-table DAD is associated with an XML column using an enable-column command. This command also permits the specification of the primary key of the main table. The primary key column is appended to the schema of each side table, where it forms a foreign key used to associate data with the appropriate tuples in the main table. In our example, specifying the ID attribute of the Manufacturers table as the primary key results in creation of the side tables depicted in Fig. 15.

When an XML column is enabled, the database system creates a view that joins the side tables with the main table using foreign key joins. The default view definition for our example is the following:

```
create view manufacturers_view(ID, phone, name,
    model, price) as
    select M.ID, M.phone, N.name, P.model, P.price
    from Manufacturers M, name_side_table N,
        model_side_table P
    where M.ID = N.ID and M.ID = P.ID;
```

Since side tables are typically indexed, this view provides a convenient and efficient method for querying XML column data. For example, the following query returns model number and price information for products priced under $450, along with the phone number of the products' manufacturers:

```
select V.phone, V.model, V.price
from manufacturers_view V
where V.price < 450;
```

Side tables are typically used to provide convenient access to portions of the XML-typed column data that is expected to be frequently accessed. If the data required by a query is not included in a side table, it can be accessed directly. Data in an XML-typed column may be accessed (in entirety) as a `varchar` by using a type-cast function `XMLVarChar`. Portions of data in an XML column can be accessed using *extracting functions*. The function `extractVarchar(x, p)` traverses XML column x as indicated by the path expression p and returns the varchar-typed value of the element thus reached. This function is an example of a *scalar extracting function*. Similar functions are available for other scalar types, such as integers and reals. The following query illustrates the use of a scalar extracting function in our running example. The name element is extracted from the XML column `manufData` of the Manufacturer table.

```
select M.phone, extractVarchar(M.manufData,
"/manufacturer/name")
from Manufacturers M;
```

In addition to extracting individual scalars in this manner, a query may extract several scalars together using *table extracting functions*. The name of the table function corresponding to each scalar function is obtained by pluralizing the name of the scalar function. For example, consider the following query, which returns the names and phone numbers of manufacturers of products that cost less than $450. The table extracting function `extractReals` is used in the subquery to extract the set of product prices from the XML column value. The return type of this function is a unary relation with a real-valued attribute named `returnedReal`.

```
select extractVarchar(M.manufData,
             "/manufacturer/name"), M.phone
from Manufacturers M
where exists
    (select 1
    from table(extractReals(M.manufData,
    "/manufacturer/products/product/price"))
         as C
    where C.returnedReal < 450;
```

The XML Extender also supports the storage of XML data in *collection mode*. In this mode, XML data is parsed and stored in a collection of tables. The mapping from

XML documents to database tables is specified using a RDB-node DAD similar to the one in Fig. 13. When an XML collection is enabled, the database system creates the tables defined in the RDB-node DAD of that collection. In our earlier discussion of the DAD in Fig. 13, the DAD was used for publishing XML data from existing tables. In the current context, the same DAD is used to define tables for storing XML. The schema for each table is inferred using the `table` and `column` subelements of the `RDB_node` elements in the DAD. Once enabled, an XML collection is populated from the source XML document using a stored procedure. The populated tables may now be queried and modified just like any other database table. At any time, an XML rendering of the current state of the tables can be produced using the rendering method described earlier. It is often convenient to render only a part of an XML collection as an XML document. In our running example, for instance, we may wish to publish the reviews for only a subset of the manufacturers in the database. Such selective rendering is easily achieved using a SQL DAD on the XML collection. (Although the collection must be defined using a RDB DAD, data from the collection can be published using both SQL and RDB DADs.) The extender provides a stored procedure for overwriting the SQL statement part of a previously defined SQL DAD for this purpose.

3.3   Oracle XSU

Publishing.   Oracle's *XML SQL Utility* (*XSU*) builds on the object-relational features of the database engine to support XML data [28, Chap. 7]. XSU provides a simple default mapping from a table to an XML fragment. Rows in the table are mapped to `row` elements that contain one subelement for each column of the table, with the column's name as element name and the column's value as the element content. The row elements are enclosed in a rowset element that represents the table. For example, the query `select * from Catalog` on the Catalog table of our running example (Fig. 6) is mapped to the XML fragment depicted in Fig. 16.

The mapping from tables to XML fragments can be customized. A deep and domain-specific nesting of XML elements can be obtained by using an object-relational database schema in which data is nested using object references. Further, the SQL query can be modified to influence the translation to XML: Names of elements are determined by the column names in the query result. Columns whose names begin with the @ character are mapped to attributes, instead of subelements, of row elements in the generated XML. The XSU utilities also permit customization of the default names `rowset` and `row`, the format for dates, the treatment of nulls, and a few other parameters. These customizations are limited in their scope. In particular, it is not possible to specify a complex structuring of the output XML that is different from the default. When such structuring is needed, the default XML output can be post-processed using the XML transformation language XSLT [13].

```
<rowset>
    <row num="1">
        <manufacturer>Olympus</manufacturer>
        <product>OM-1</product>
        <price>300</price>
    </row>
    <row num="2">
        <manufacturer>Nikon</manufacturer>
        <product>990</product>
        <price>600</price>
    </row>
    <row num="3">
        <manufacturer>Olympus</manufacturer>
        <product>OM-2</product>
        <price>400</price>
    </row>
    <row num="4">
        <manufacturer>Nikon</manufacturer>
        <product>995</product>
        <price>700</price>
    </row>
    <row num="5">
        <manufacturer>Nikon</manufacturer>
        <product>900</product>
        <price>500</price>
    </row>
</rowset>
```

FIG. 16. XSU's default XML rendering of the Catalog table of Fig. 6.

XSU provides methods for registering XSL transformations so that they are applied automatically as needed.

Storage. Using XSU, an XML document can be parsed and stored into a database table. However, such storage is possible only if the schema of a database table precisely matches the structure of the XML document. Briefly, a table's schema matches an XML document's structure if the document can be generated by rendering a suitable instance of the table as XML, using XSU's mapping rules from tables to XML. This restriction does not cause difficulties if the XML document being loaded was generated from a relational database with compatible schema. However, for loading data that was generated natively in XML form, the requirement of schema matching is too restrictive. Minor discrepancies, such as differing attribute names, can be corrected by modifying XSU's mapping rules. However, any significant discrepancy requires a cumbersome change of the database schema.

Recent versions of Oracle include a XMLType datatype for storing XML data in unparsed form [28, Chap. 5]. In the light of the above difficulties in storing parsed XML data, such native storage is an attractive alternative. In addition to functions for converting between string and XMLType representations of XML data, there are functions for selecting and searching portions of XMLType data. The extract function allows extraction of parts of an XMLType value by using a subset of XPath, and is similar to the extracting functions used by DB2. There is also an existsNode function that is used to check existence of specific elements in an XMLType value. Let us return to the Manufacturers table of our running example, suggested by Fig. 14. Recall that it partitions the data of Fig. 1 by manufacturer, storing the information for each manufacturer in a separate tuple. This table can be created in Oracle by replacing XMLCLOB with XMLType in the query of Fig. 14. The following query uses the extract function and returns the phone numbers and names of all manufacturers:

```
select M.phone,
       M.manufData.extract("/manufacturer/name").
       getStringVal()
from Manufacturers M;
```

Unlike DB2, Oracle does not associate XMLType data with side tables. However, such data can be indexed using functional indexes on the extract or existsNode functions, permitting efficient access to parts of the XMLType data. In our running example, an index on manufacturer names may be specified as follows:

```
create index manuf_name_idx on Manufacturers(
       manufData.extract("/manufacturer/name").
       getStringVal());
```

Further, Oracle's standard text indexes can also be used for XMLType data. In addition to supporting the usual text queries, such indexes on XMLType data support context-sensitive lookup of the form *word in context*, where context is specified using a path expression. With such indexing applied to our running example, we can efficiently search for, say, manufacturers whose names contain the term *Systems*.

3.4   Sybase ASE

Sybase *Adaptive Server Enterprise* (*ASE*) supports transformations between XML and relational renderings of data by means of a tight coupling with a set of Java classes [45,46]. ASE provides three methods for storing XML in the database. In the first method, called *element storage*, XML elements are extracted from the source document and stored separately in database tables. In the second method, called *document storage*, XML documents are stored as atomic values in a single column of a table. In the third method, called *hybrid storage*, XML documents are stored as in the document storage method; however, selected elements are extracted and stored in separate columns for more efficient access.

In order to use these methods, the database designer must implement a collection of methods in a standard Java interface defined by ASE. For example, in order to manipulate XML documents such as the Ratings fragment depicted in Fig. 8, we define a class, `ReviewsXml`, as a subclass of a system-provided `JXml` class. This class defines one constructor for creating ReviewsXML objects from serialized XML and another for creating ReviewsXML objects by executing SQL queries on database tables. We also define a method `order2Sql` that generates a SQL script for populating database tables with XML data. In our example, the XML data (Fig. 8) is mapped to two tables: Catalog and Reviews (Figs. 1 and 7). Thus, this method generates a sequence of SQL statements that extract data items from the XML representation and inserts them into these tables. There are also get and set methods for each element and attribute of a ReviewsXML object, and these perform the standard actions. When there are multiple instances of an element type, individual instances are identified using their serial order in the document. Attributes are identified by reference to their elements. For example, given a ReviewsXML object `rx` generated for the data in Fig. 8, the value of the Rating attribute for the PhotoLife Ratings element is accessed as `rx.getCatalogAttribute(2, Ratings, Rating)`.

The methods of this interface may be invoked from both the host Java program by using standard Java syntax and from within SQL queries at the server by using » as the method-referencing operator. For example, if Catalog elements such as the one in our running example (Fig. 8) are stored in the second column of a table `CatalogTab(catID, catData)`, the following query lists the manufacturer, model number, and first Ratings element for each entry:

```
select R.catData»getCatalogAttribute(1, "Catalog",
       "Manufacturer"),
       R.catData»getCatalogAttribute(1, "Catalog",
           "Product"),
       R.catData»getCatalogElement(1, "Ratings")
   from CatalogTab R;
```

Above, we have used the element storage method, separating the Catalog elements into separate attributes. If we choose to use the document storage method instead, the entire XML document (all Catalog elements) is stored as a single attribute value, say, as the second column of the table `CatalogDocs(docID, docText)`. In

this storage method, individual Catalog elements are easily accessed as illustrated by
the following query.

```
select D.docText»getCatalogElement(1, "Catalog")
    D.docText»getCatalogElement(2, "Catalog")
from CatalogDocs D;
```

However, the lack of a priori knowledge of the number of Catalog elements in a
document makes it difficult to write a query equivalent to the `CatalogTab` query
above.

In order to permit efficient access to XML data based on its content, the hybrid
method uses a table with additional columns that are populated by parsing the required data from the XML columns. In motivation, these columns are similar to
the side tables used by IBM's DB2. However, in contrast to DB2's side tables, the
server does not maintain the consistency of such columns automatically. That is, the
applications that modify XML data are responsible for modifying these additional
columns should the values of their source elements change.

The above method for manipulating XML data is specifically tailored to a class
of XML documents (Catalog data in our example). If a large variety of XML documents is expected, such tailoring for each kind of document is tedious. Sybase
ASE provides an alternative method for storing XML documents that are generated by arbitrary SQL queries. Such XML documents have limited variability
in their structure. (There is no method for storing arbitrary XML documents that
are not generated by SQL statements.) The mapping between XML and the relational data produced by a SQL query is achieved using a `ResultSet` document.
This document is similar to the DAD used by DB2, but is more restricted in the
scope of mappings it may specify. Briefly, a `ResultSet` document consists of
two parts: The first part, `ResultSetMetaData`, specifies the schema of the SQL
query results. Types, names, and other properties of columns are specified as attributes of `ColumnMetaData` elements. The attribute name for each property is
identical to the name of the corresponding JDBC method [22]. The second part,
`ResultSetData`, enumerates the tuples that form the SQL query result using a
simple row-and-column delimited format. Figure 17 suggests a `ResultSet` document for the following query on the data of our running example (Figs. 1 and 7):

```
select C.Manufacturer, C.Product, R.Source, R.Rating
from Catalog C, Ratings R
where C.Manufacturer = R.Manufacturer and
C.Product = R.Model;
```

```
<ResultSet>
   <ResultSetMetaData>
      <ColumnMetaData
         getColumnName="Manufacturer"
         getColumnType="12"
         isNullable="false"
         isSigned="false"
         . . .
         />
      <ColumnMetaData
         getColumnName="Product"
         getColumnType="12"
         . . .
         />
      . . .
   </ResultSetMetaData>
   <ResultSetData>
      <Row>
         <Column name="Manufacturer">Olympus</Column>
         <Column name="Product">OM-1</Column>
         <Column name="Source">PC Magazine</Column>
         <Column name="Rating">5</Column>
      </Row>
      <Row>
         <Column name="Manufacturer">...</Column>
         . . .
      </Row>
      . . .
   </ResultSetData>
</ResultSet>
```

FIG. 17. ResultSet format for Sybase ASE.

The system provides a ResultSetXml class with constructors for instantiating it from either a SQL query or a string representation of query results. There are get and set methods for the columns of such a document; data items are identified by specifying the row number (in document order) and either the column name or the column number.

In order to query data within ResultSet documents, one option is to use the toSqlScript method to obtain a script that creates and populates a database table based on the ResultSet document. The resulting table may then be queried as needed. However, it is also possible to query the document directly as a

ResultSet object. The value of a column *cname* of row *r*can be accessed using
the getColumn(r, cname) method. Columns may also be referenced by position. Further, there are methods for quantification over column values in all rows.
Universal quantification is provided by methods of the form allString(c, op,
lit) which evaluates the predicate *v op lit* over all rows, where *v* is the value of
the *c*'th column, *op* is a comparison operator (=, <, etc.), and *lit* is a string literal.
Similar methods exist for other types, and existential quantification is provided by
methods of the form someString(c, op, lit).

Continuing with our running example, suppose ResultSet documents of
the form suggested by Fig. 17 are stored in the second column of a table
ProductData(docID, docText). The following query finds documents that
contain information about only products made by Olympus, and returns the IDs of
such documents along with the product name of the first listed product.

```
select P.docID, P.docText»getColumn(1, "Product")
from ProductData P
where P.docText»allString(1, "=", "Olympus");
```

4. XML in an Object Database

Although object database systems are not as common as relational systems, they
share many of the advantages of relational database systems in terms of design theory, standards, products, and implementation. The ODMG standard takes the place
of the SQL standard [8]. An advantage of object databases over relational databases
for XML is that the object model is closer to the native XML model.

Despite the difference between the relational and object database models, several
design decisions for storing XML in an object database are very similar to those for
storing XML in a relational database. Again, one must decide the extent to which
an XML document is parsed. At one extreme, every element and attribute may be
mapped to a distinct object. At the other, the entire XML document may be stored
as a single object. The former option corresponds to parsing every element in a relational database and the latter corresponds to storing the document as a single CLOB.

The *Document Object Model (DOM), Level 2* [27] provides a simple and general
mapping from any XML document to a set of objects. The object-subobject hierarchy reflects the nesting of the corresponding elements and attributes in the XML
document. This mapping models XML concepts such as elements, attributes, and text
using object classes such as Element, Attr, and Text, respectively. Thus, all element types (such as manufacturer and products in our running example) are mapped
to the same class of objects; the different element tags affect only the methods such
as getTagName. This mapping is essentially the object database equivalent of the

```
<!ELEMENT manufacturer (name, products)>
<!ELEMENT name (#PCDATA)>
<!ELEMENT products (product*)>
<!ELEMENT product (price | #PCDATA)>
<!ATTLIST product model CDATA #REQUIRED>
<!ELEMENT price (#PCDATA)>
```

FIG. 18. Sample DTD for data such as that in Fig. 1.

```
interface Manufacturer {
    Name name;
    Set<Product> products;
};
interface Product {
    String model;
    String price;
    String desc;
};
```

FIG. 19. An object schema corresponding to the DTD in Fig. 18.

simple relational mapping of Section 2.1, and shares the advantages and disadvantages of that mapping. Therefore, we do not discuss it further here.

Consider the DTD depicted in Fig. 18. (Recall our discussion of DTDs from Section 1.) It describes XML data such as the fragment pictured in Fig. 1. Suppose we wish to design an object schema for storing data that conforms to this DTD. Figure 19 depicts an object database schema corresponding to this DTD. (We use a syntax similar to the Object Definition Language (ODL) [8]; an overview appears in [51, Chap. 2].) This example suggests an intuitive mapping from DTDs to ODL schemas. Elements with #PCDATA content are mapped to inlined strings. (We adopt the convention of inlining objects of primitive types.)

Figure 20 suggests an object database instance corresponding to the XML data in Fig. 1. The reader may observe that the DTD in Fig. 18 admits XML documents that are less rigidly structured than the document in Fig. 1. Specifically, product elements are permitted to have text (#PCDATA) content instead of a single price sub-element as do all product elements in the XML fragment in Fig. 1. Therefore, the interface definition for Product in Fig. 19 includes a desc (description) member in addition to the price member.

In the above example, the task of mapping a DTD to an object schema was simplified by the simple and regular structure of the DTD. For more realistic DTDs, the variety of features available in content models may make translation to object schemas

Object ID	Type	Value
DB	Set<Manufacturer>	{ m1, m2}
m1	Manufacturer	{name: "Nikon"; products: ps1; }
ps1	Set<Product>	{ mc1, mc2, mc3 }
mc1	Product	{ model: "900"; price "500" }
mc2	Product	{ model: "990"; price "600" }
mc3	Product	{ model: "995"; price "700" }
m2	Manufacturer	{name: "Olympus"; products: ps2; }
ps2	Set<Product>	{ mo1, mo2 }
mo1	Product	{ model: "OM-1"; price "300" }
mo2	Product	{ model: "OM-2"; price "400" }

FIG. 20. An object database representation of the XML fragment in Fig. 1.

```
<manufacturer>
    <name>Olympus</name>
    <products>
        <product model="OM-1">
            Discontinued. Suggest <product idref="22"/> as an
            alternative at a special price <price>350</price>
            (special promotion <promotion pid="1212"><expires>
            <date day="31" month="12" year="2002"/>manager can
            extend</expires> </promotion>)
        </product>
        <product id="22" model="OM-2"> <price>400</price>
        </product>
    </products>
</manufacturer>
```

FIG. 21. Sample XML document.

more complex. For example, consider the XML fragment depicted in Fig. 21. The corresponding DTD appears in Fig. 22. The product element now has a mixed content; that is, the content consists of an arbitrary interleaving of zero or more text fragments along with the price, product (recursively), and promotion elements. In the object schema (see Fig. 23), we use a helper interface ProductContent to model this situation. A given ProductContent must have exactly one data member non-null. This constraint is externally enforced. We use a list of ProductContent objects to model the contents of a Product element because order is significant within a Product element. (For example, in Fig. 21, the text to the left of the element with idref 22 cannot be swapped with that to the right of the element.)

```
<!ELEMENT manufacturer (name, products)>
<!ELEMENT name (#PCDATA)>
<!ELEMENT products (product*)>
<!ELEMENT product (price | product | promotion | #PCDATA)*>
<!ATTLIST product model CDATA #REQUIRED>
<!ELEMENT price (#PCDATA)>
<!ATTLIST price currency "USD">
<!ELEMENT promotion (expires)>
<!ATTLIST promotion pid CDATA #REQUIRED>
<!ELEMENT expires (date, #PCDATA?)>
<!ELEMENT date EMPTY>
<!ATTLIST date day CDATA #REQUIRED
               month CDATA #REQUIRED
               year CDATA #REQUIRED>
```

FIG. 22. A DTD for document similar to the one in Fig. 21.

```
interface Manufacturer {              interface Promotion {
    Name name;                            String pid;
    Set<Product> products;                Expires exp;
};                                    };
interface Product {                   interface Expires {
    String model;                         Date date;
    List<ProductContent>;                 String comment;
interface ProductContent {            };
    Price price;                      interface Date {
    Product product;                      String day;
    Promotion promo;                      String month;
    String desc;                          String year;
};                                    };
interface Price {
    String currency;
    Decimal amount;
};
```

FIG. 23. An object schema for the DTD in Fig. 22.

5. Native XML Databases

Recently, there has been an emergence of so-called native XML database systems (e.g., Tamino [47] and Xindice [43]). These systems are designed specifically for XML and take advantage of this specialization at all levels of the system. In Xindice, XML data is stored as named documents in collections that are hierarchically organized, in a manner resembling a file system hierarchy. Examples of collections are /db/customers, /db/products/optical/cameras, and /db/products/audio. The documents within each collection are referenced using the document names. Thus, /db/products/optical/cameras/ digital refers to a document named digital in the second collection. Unqualified document names are not necessarily unique.

Xindice uses XPath as its query language, and these XPath queries operate on either a single document or all documents in a collection. For example, the query //manufacturer[country="Japan"]/address on the collection /db/products/optical/cameras asks for the addresses of Japanese camera manufacturers in that collection. Such XPath queries are evaluated over each document in a collection by first instantiating the DOM tree for the document.

Xindice permits the creation of indexes for speeding up queries that perform selections on element and attribute values. Indexes are created by specifying a pattern with the general form element-name@attribute-name. For example, the pattern manufacturer@country specifies an index on the country attribute of manufacturer elements in the collection. A wildcard in the element or attribute position of a pattern matches all elements and attributes, respectively. Thus, the pattern *@price indexes the price attribute of all elements (that have the attribute). The pattern *@* indexes all attributes of all elements and * indexes all element values. Such indexes, especially those with patterns (perhaps wildcards) that match a large number of elements or attributes have a significant storage and maintenance cost. These indexes are related to the path indexes proposed for object databases (and semistructured databases). The difference is that path indexes specify a complete path from the database entry point (typically the document root in XML) to the elements being indexed. For example, a path index on /digital-cameras/camera/manufacturer@country maps countries to the digital-camera manufacturers in that country. In contrast, an index on manufacturer@country maps countries to all manufacturers in that country. With such an indexing facility, there arises the problem of selecting an appropriate set of indexes, given statistics on the data and expected query load. This problem is similar to the index selection problem in relational and object databases and some of the cost-based methods for index selection (e.g., [1,10]) can be adapted for this purpose.

6. Historical XML as Annotated XML

A simple method for storing historical XML is one that annotates each XML element with its history of changes. These annotations can themselves be represented in XML. We use an edit model consisting of four operations on elements: insertion, deletion, update (change of content), and move. For simplicity, we do not model edit operations on attributes separately; doing so would not change the following method substantially. The edit operations describing the changes between two versions are computed using structured differencing algorithms, such as [14].

Intuitively, there is a (possibly empty) set of annotations attached to every element of the most recent version of the XML document. Ignoring all the annotations yields the current state of the XML data. We refer to this property as *snapshot transparency*. Snapshot transparency is a desirable property because it permits applications that are not concerned with historical data to operate on the current state of data without any change. Ignoring annotations is easy because they use a separate namespace (h in our examples below). Each annotation includes a timestamp or version identifier that associates it with the time or version of its effect. Annotations are attached to elements involved in an edit operation as follows: If an element is inserted, we add an insert annotation to its content by: `<h:ins ts="n"/>`, where n is the version or timestamp resulting from the insertion. If an element is deleted, we enclose the deleted element in a delete annotation: `<h:del ts="n">E</h:del>`, where E is the deleted element. It would be simpler (and more symmetric with insertion) to simply add an annotation of the form `<h:del "ts=n"/>` to the content of the deleted element. However, such a representation would not maintain snapshot transparency. By enclosing the deleted data in the delete annotation, we ensure that applications that skip the delete annotation also skip the deleted data. The representation of updates is very similar to that of deletions. An annotation that encloses the old value is used: `<h:upd ts="n">O</h:upd>`, where O is the old value. However, in contrast to deletions, updates result in the annotation being added to the content of the (updated) element. Unlike the above operations, moves refer to two locations in an XML document: the old and new positions of the element that is moved. Thus, a move operation results in two annotations. The first, called the mark, serves as a placeholder for the old position of the moved element: `<h:mrk id="i"/>`, where i is a unique identifier. Unlike the other annotations, marks do not have a timestamp attribute because the same mark may be used by multiple versions. The second annotation for a move operation is placed in the content of the moved element, and it refers to the corresponding mark: `<h:mov ts="n" mrk="i"/>`. Figure 24 depicts a DTD for these annotations. (Recall our discussion of DTDs from Section 1.)

As an example, let the XML fragment depicted in Fig. 1 be the initial version (say, version 1.0). Consider the following sequence of changes: In version 1.1, an element `<editorsChoice ref="PC Magazine"/>` is added to the content of the product element for model 990. In version 1.2, a `<phone>555-1212</phone>` element is added to the content of the manufacturer element for Nikon. (We assume that appropriate changes are made to the DTD of Fig. 21 to permit the validity of

```
<!ELEMENT ann (ins|del|upd|mov)*>    <!ATTLIST ins ts CDATA #REQUIRED>
<!ELEMENT ins EMPTY>                 <!ATTLIST del ts CDATA #REQUIRED>
<!ELEMENT del ANY>                   <!ATTLIST upd ts CDATA #REQUIRED>
<!ELEMENT upd ANY>                   <!ATTLIST mov ts CDATA #REQUIRED
<!ELEMENT mov EMPTY>                             mrk IDREF #REQUIRED>
<!ELEMENT mrk EMPTY>                 <!ATTLIST mrk id ID #REQUIRED>
```

FIG. 24. Simple DTD for historical annotations to XML.

documents with the added elements.) In version 1.3, the editorsChoice element is moved from the model 900 element to the model 995 element, and the model 900 element is deleted. Finally, in version 1.4, the price of model OM-1 is changed to 350.

The annotated XML fragment resulting from this history is depicted in Fig. 25. If elements belonging to the annotation namespace h are ignored, the annotated XML fragment yields the current version (1.4) of the data. For the editorsChoice element, the h:ins element records its insertion in version 1.1, while the h:mov element records its move from the model 990 element to the model 995 element in version 1.3 (with the help of the h:mrk annotation in the model 990 element, which is now encapsulated in a h:del annotation).

Our method uses *reverse deltas*; that is, we store the information needed to generate each version (other than the most recent) from its successor (all successors, in the case of branching versions). Despite their names, the annotations are meant to be applied in reverse. Thus, an insert annotation is applied in reverse as a delete, and vice versa. For example, the delete annotation in Fig. 25 includes the deleted data that is needed to generate version 1.2 from version 1.3. On the other hand, the insert annotation does not need to include any data, since while generating the previous version, applying the annotation in reverse requires no new data.

In the above scheme for representing historical XML, all historical information is encapsulated in annotations rendered in XML. Therefore this scheme can be used for converting any XML storage system into a historical one. For example, [9] describes a method similar to the above for storing historical information in Lore, a (non-historical) database for XML [32]. This advantage of the above method comes at the price of performance: Since the underlying storage system does not know of the special status of the annotation elements, there are no low-level facilities for efficient access to these elements for commonly performed operations. We discuss next methods for low-level storage of historical information.

If we store historical XML documents in a file system, we have the option of using methods analogous to those commonly used by version control systems such as RCS and SCCS [48,37]. There are two standard approaches: The most direct storage interpretation of the annotation-based scheme simply stores the annotations inline as

```
<manufacturer>
    <name>Nikon</name>
    <phone>555-1212<h:ins ts="1.2"/></phone>
    <products>
        <product model="900"> <price>500</price> </product>
        <h:del ts="1.3">
            <product model="990">
                <price>600</price>
                <h:mrk id="001"/>
            </product>
        </h:del>
        <product model="995">
            <price>700</price>
            <editorsChoice ref="PC Magazine">
                <h:ins ts="1.1"/>
                <h:mov ts="1.3" mrk="001"/>
            </editorsChoice>
        </product>
    </products>
</manufacturer>
<manufacturer>
    <name>Olympus</name>
    <products>
        <product model="OM-1">
            <price>350<h:upd ts="1.4"><h:oldval>300</h:oldval>
            </price>
        </product>
        <product model="OM-2"> <price>400</price> </product>
    </products>
</manufacturer>
```

FIG. 25. A historically annotated XML fragment.

suggested by Fig. 25. This method is very similar to that used by the SCCS version control system. It keeps all the information pertinent to an element in close proximity to the element. Thus, recovering the history of an element is efficient. On the other hand, this method requires a scan of the entire version data file when materializing any version. As the amount of historical information grows, fragments of data belonging to any version are scattered over the entire file, separated by a large amount of historical annotation data, resulting in ever increasing retrieval times.

The above observation leads to another simple storage scheme: one that stores all the annotations in a separate file (or a separate section of the data file). This method

```
<manufacturer>
   <name>Nikon</name>
   <phone>555-1212</phone>
   <products>
      <product model="900"> <price>500</price> </product>
      <product model="995">
         <price>700</price>
         <editorsChoice ref="PC Magazine"/>
      </product>
   </products>
</manufacturer>
<manufacturer>
   <name>Olympus</name>
   <products>
      <product model="OM-1"> <price>350</price> </product>
      <product model="OM-2"> <price>400</price> </product>
   </products>
</manufacturer>

<h:ann>
   <h:del ts="1.1">
      <h:ref>/manufacturer[1]/products[1]/product[2]
      /editorsChoice[1]</h:ref>
   </h:del>
   <h:del ts="1.2">
      <h:ref>/manufacturer[1]/phone[1]</h:ref>
   </h:del>
   <h:ins ts="1.3">
      <h:ref>
         /manufacturer[1]/products[1]/product[2]
         /editorsChoice[1]
      </h:ref>
      <h:val>
         <product model="990"> <price>600</price> </product>
      </h:val>
   </h:ins>
   <h:mov ts="1.3">
      <h:ref>
         /manufacturer[1]/products[1]/product[2]
         /editorsChoice[1]
      </h:ref>
      <h:mrk>
```

FIG. 26. The historical data of Fig. 25 with annotations stored separately, using XPath references and reverse deltas.

```
              /manufacturer[1]/products[1]/product[3]
              /editorsChoice[1]
          </h:mrk>
      </h:mov>
      <h:upd ts="1.4">
          <h:ref>/manufacturer[2]/product[1]/price[1]</h:ref>
          <h:val>300</h:val>
      </h:upd>
  </h:ann>
```

FIG. 26. — *continued from previous page*

is used by the RCS version control system, which stores the set of changes from each version to its predecessor (as determined by the Unix *diff* facility [26]) contiguously. It supports efficient retrieval of the base (most recent) version since annotations do not interleave with the data of the most recent version.

We now modify our earlier inline annotation-based scheme to store annotations at the end of the file instead of next to the elements to which they refer. To enable separate storage, we include in each annotation a logical pointer to the element to which it refers. By logical pointers, we mean references to elements in an XML document independent of the low-level storage scheme. We use XPath for specifying our pointers. (Recall the discussion of XPath in Section 1.)

Figure 26 depicts a historical XML document that uses these ideas. The first part of the document is simply the snapshot of the base (most recent) version. (It is possible to use another version as the base should such a choice be advantageous to an application.) As a result, retrieving the most recent version is very efficient. The second part of the document is a set of annotations, identified by a separate namespace (abbreviated by h in the figure). The annotations adopt a different naming convention. In the inline annotation method described earlier, annotations are named in the forward application sense (although they are reverse deltas). When the annotations are stored separately, it is more intuitive to name the annotations based on the reverse application. Thus, an insert operation generates a delete annotation, and vice versa.

As before, there are four kinds of annotations. The major change is that each annotation now includes a ref element whose content is an XPath expression that identifies the element to which the annotation refers. Since the content of annotations now contains the ref element, annotations that include data pertaining to the edit operation they represent (such as update annotation, which includes the value of the element before the update) now enclose that data in a val element to separate it from the ref element. For example, the insert annotation in Fig. 26 includes a val subelement containing the data that must be inserted at the location given by the XPath expression in the ref subelement in order to step back to the previous

```
<!ELEMENT ann (ins|del|upd|mov)*>   <!ATTLIST ins ts CDATA #REQUIRED>
<!ELEMENT ins (ref, val)>           <!ATTLIST del ts CDATA #REQUIRED>
<!ELEMENT del (ref)>                <!ATTLIST upd ts CDATA #REQUIRED>
<!ELEMENT upd (ref, val)>           <!ATTLIST mov ts CDATA #REQUIRED>
<!ELEMENT mov (ref, mrk)>
<!ELEMENT ref (#PCDATA)>
<!ELEMENT val ANY>
<!ELEMENT mrk (#PCDATA)>
```

FIG. 27. DTD for separately stored historical annotations in XML.

version (1.2). Another important difference pertains to moves. In the inline annotation method, marks (mrk elements) are placed in the document as needed to indicate
the old position of moved elements. In the separate annotation method, such inline
placement of marks is not possible. Therefore, the location is encoded by an XPath
expression within a mrk element. For example, the move annotation in Fig. 25 encodes the move operation necessary to go from version 1.3 to version 1.2. The XPath
expressions contained in the two subelements, ref and mrk, encode the target and
the source locations, respectively, of the move operation. The DTD for our modified
annotations is presented in Fig. 27.

7. Performance Enhancements for Historical Stores

By storing annotations separately from the snapshot of the current version of data,
the second method described in Section 6 (Fig. 25) is able to retrieve the current
version of an XML document with no performance penalty when compared with the
document stored in a non-historical database. However, there is no such guarantee
for the retrieval of versions other than the most recent. Recall that the representation stores reverse deltas; that is, it stores the instructions for generating each version
from the version or versions that are its immediate successors in the version sequence
or hierarchy. In the simple case of a linear version sequence, retrieving a version requires the instantiation of all versions that lie between it and the most recent version.
Each instantiation consists of applying a set of annotations to generate a new snapshot. This process may require a substantial amount of time when the recovery of
an old version is necessary. For example, experimental studies have reported a linear growth in the number of disk page accesses as the age of the desired version
increases. When deep version hierarchies are expected, it is desirable to be able to
recover an arbitrary version in time proportional to the size of the version, and independent of the size of the version hierarchy. We discuss such schemes below, loosely
following the development in [16,17,19,18].

If we are concerned only with the number of disk accesses required to retrieve a version, a simple method is to store each version separately, with a simple index mapping version numbers to disk addresses or file names. This simple solution has two disadvantages. First, it is likely to consume an inordinately large amount of disk space. Specifically, the storage required is the sum of the sizes of all version snapshots, irrespective of the similarity between versions. For example, if a single element in a 100 megabyte file is updated, the new version requires roughly an additional 100 megabytes. In contrast, our annotation based scheme described earlier requires only a few bytes of additional storage for such a version. Second, it does not support efficient access to the history (over all versions, or a range of versions) of a given element or set of elements. Such access is important for processing temporal queries.

The above solution may be regarded as one extreme in localizing the data relevant to a version: all such data is stored contiguously. The other extreme is the annotation-based solution described earlier: data pertinent to a version is, in general, scattered all over the entire version file or database. A method that choses a configurable intermediate point along this space-time trade-off axis is described in [16]. We define the *usefulness* of a page version to be the ratio of the fraction of that page's data (measured as a ratio of bytes) that is required to materialize the version. The chief idea is to maintain a *usefulness constraint*: For every page that holds data required to materialize a version, the usefulness of that page to that version must exceed a certain threshold U_t, called the *usefulness threshold* (a parameter specified at database design time). The last page for a version is excluded from this requirement, since it is, in general, only partly filled.

A scheme that stores the snapshot of each version separately satisfies the usefulness constraint trivially, since the usefulness of every page, except the last, storing a version's data is 1. However, the idea is to use as little storage as possible while maintaining the usefulness constraint. We can achieve this goal by using the following simple rule: Assume that initially all pages satisfy the usefulness constraint (as is trivially true for a historical store that contains only one version). When a page violates this constraint for some version, the situation is corrected by copying all of that version's data from this page to another page, where it is stored without intervening data from other versions, leading to a usefulness of 1. We now describe this method in more detail.

Let us begin by revisiting our running example from Fig. 26. In Fig. 28, we depict the same data rendered using forward deltas. (Recall that the data depicted in Fig. 26 uses reverse annotations.) In order to simplify our description of the layout of data on disk, we will assume that each element (proper, excluding its descendants) requires a fixed amount of disk space, and that the page-size is an integral multiple of this

```
<manufacturer>
   <name>Nikon</name>
   <products>
      <product model="900"> <price>500</price> </product>
      <product model="990"> <price>600</price> </product>
      <product model="995"> <price>700</price> </product>
   </products>
</manufacturer>
<manufacturer>
   <name>Olympus</name>
   <products>
      <product model="OM-1"> <price>300</price> </product>
      <product model="OM-2"> <price>400</price> </product>
   </products>
</manufacturer>
<h:ann>
   <h:val id="1"> <editorsChoice ref="PC Magazine"/>
   </h:val>
   <h:val id="2"> <phone>555-1212</phone> </h:val>
   <h:val id="3"> <editorsChoice ref="PC Magazine"/>
   </h:val>
   <h:val id="4"> <price>300</price> </h:val>
   <h:ins ts="1.1">
      <h:ref>/manufacturer[1]/products[1]/product[2]
      /editorsChoice[1]</h:ref>
      <h:val idref="1"/>
   </h:ins>
   <h:ins ts="1.2">
      <h:ref>/manufacturer[1]/phone[1]</h:ref>
      <h:val idref="2"/>
   </h:ins>
   <h:ins ts="1.3">
      <h:ref>/manufacturer[1]/products[1]/product[3]
       /editorsChoice[1]</h:ref>
      <h:val idref="3"/>
   </h:ins>
   <h:del ts="1.3">
      <h:ref>
         /manufacturer[1]/products[1]/product[2]
      </h:ref>
   </h:del>
```

FIG. 28. The historical data of Fig. 25 with annotations and new data stored separately, using XPath references and forward deltas.

```
<h:del ts="1.4">
    <h:ref>/manufacturer[2]/product[1]/price[1]</h:ref>
</h:del>
<h:ins ts="1.4">
    <h:ref>/manufacturer[2]/product[1]/price[1]</h:ref>
    <h:val idref="4"/>
</h:ins>
</h:ann>
```

FIG. 28. — *continued from previous page*

Page	ID	Tag	Attributes	Content	Ver.
1	m1	manufacturer		{ n1, ps1 }	1.0
	n1	name		Nikon	1.0
	ps1	products		{ mc1, mc2, mc3 }	1.0
	mc1	product	model:"900"	{ pc1 }	1.0
2	pc1	price		500	1.0
	mc2	product	model:"990"	{ pc2 }	1.0
	pc2	price		600	1.0
	mc3	product	model:"995"	{ pc3 }	1.0
3	pc3	price		700	1.0
	m2	manufacturer		{ n2, ps2 }	1.0
	n2	name		Olympus	1.0
	ps2	products		{ mo1, mo2 }	1.0
4	mo1	product	model:"OM-1"	{ po1 }	1.0
	po1	price		300	1.0
	mo2	product	model:"OM-2"	{ po2 }	1.0
	po2	price		400	1.0
5	ec1	editorsChoice	ref:"PC Magazine"		1.1
	ph1	phone		555-1212	1.2
	ec2	editorsChoice	ref:"PC Magazine"		1.3
	po3	price		350	1.4

FIG. 29. Disk representation of the data in our running example.

quantity. Thus, each page holds a constant number of elements, say, four. (We pick a small number to better illustrate the method.)

Figure 29 depicts the disk layout for the data of Fig. 28. The page numbers (disk addresses) to the left of the main table. The right of the table indicates the version at which the data to its left was written to disk. For example, the first element in page 4 was written at version 1.0, while the last element of page 4 was written at version 1.4. The table proper lists for each element its identifier (physical object identifier, typically composed of a page address and page offset) along with its tag, attributes, and content. Subelements are referenced using their element identifiers. For example, the first manufacturer element of Fig. 28 is represented as the element with identifier m1 in the table. Its content, consisting of a name element and a products element, is represented as a set of the corresponding element identifiers, n1 and ps1.

The edit scripts for each version are stored in a separate area, as suggested by Fig. 30. In the edit script for version 1.0, we use the notation ins(*) as short hand for the edit script consisting of an insert operation for each element in version 1.0. We use a simple edit model consisting of only insertion and deletion operations. Update and move operations are mapped to insertion-deletion pairs. For example, the move of the editorsChoice element from model 990 to model 995 in version 1.3 is modeled by the deletion of that element in the model 990 context and its insertion in the model 995 context. However, in this example, the deletion operation is redundant because it deletes an object that lies in a deleted subtree (the one rooted at the product element for model 990). We discuss the disk representation of edit scripts in more detail below.

The process of materializing a requested version proceeds by examining the operations in the edit script for that version in turn. Whenever there is a *gap* between consecutive edit operations, i.e., when the operations operate on non-consecutive elements, the gap is filled by making a recursive request for the missing objects from the previous version. (We assume that an element identifier is easily mapped to the sequence number of the element in document order, and that the number of elements in each version is stored with the edit script.)

For example, suppose we wish to materialize version 1.1. The edit script for this version consists of a single operation, ins(pc2,2,ec1), which inserts the element ec1. The gap of elements before ec1 is filled by making a recursive call to the previous version, 1.0. The edit script for version 1.0 consists of insert operations for each element in the version: ins(root,1,m1), ins(m1,1,n1), ins(m1,2,ps1), ..., where we use root to denote the document root. The part of this edit script that refers to objects that precede ec1 (in document order) is ins(root,1,m1), ins(m1,1,n1), ins(m1,2,ps1),

Page	Version	Edit Script	Pages Needed	Ver.
s1	1.0	ins(*)	1-5	1.0
	1.1	ins(mc2,2,ec1)	1-5	1.1
	1.2	ins(m1,2,ph1)	1-5	1.2
	1.3	ins(pc3,2,ec2), del(mc2)	1-5	1.3
	1.4	del(po1), ins(po3,2,ec2)	1-5	1.4

FIG. 30. Edit scripts for the disk representation of Fig. 29.

ins(ps1,1,mc1), ins(mc1,1,pc1), ins(ps1,2,mc2), ins(mc2, 1,pc2). By looking up all the referenced objects in the object store on disk (pages 1 and 2), the required part of version 1.0 is easily reconstructed. These objects from version 1.0 are now available for incorporation into version 1.1. Returning to the edit script for version 1.1, the insert operation can now be applied by looking up the newly inserted object, ec1, on disk (page 5). The gap between ec1 and the end of the document is filled in an analogous manner to generate the complete document for version 1.1. Figure 30 indicates the disk pages that must be accessed in order to materialize each version. The accesses include those made recursively.

The above disk layout scheme does not maintain the page usefulness constraint described earlier, and may thus result in poor performance. For example, it is easy to verify that the materialization of version 1.3 requires access to the pages 1–5. However, only two of the four objects in page two are used by the materialization process, since the objects mc2 and pc2 have been deleted and are not in version 1.3. Thus, the usefulness of page 2 to version 1.3 is 50%. Although this inefficiency seems small in this example, the situation responsible for it is likely to repeat in many instances, resulting in many more page accesses than those incurred by a scheme that stores each version contiguously on disk.

Figures 31 and 32 depict a modified disk layout that maintains the minimum usefulness constraint with a threshold of 75% (meaning at least 3 of the 4 objects per page must be useful to a version that needs the page). Let us trace the evolution of the version store. As in Fig. 29, the numbers to the right of the table in Fig. 31 denote the version at which the data to its left was entered into the version store. At version 1.0, version store consists of the first four pages in Fig. 31 and the first row in Fig. 32.

Version 1.1 adds an editorsChoice element to the product element for model 990. This delta is represented as suggested by the second row of the table in Fig. 32, and the inserted element is recorded on page 5 of the store. At this point, the usefulness of the first four pages is 100%. The last page has a usefulness of 25% but is exempt from the constraint. Therefore no further changes to the version store are necessary. The situation with version 1.2 is very similar. The insertion of the phone element results in the addition of the third row of the edit script table and the second data item on page 5 of the data store. Again, no further changes are needed because all but the last page have a usefulness of 100%.

The situation is more interesting with version 1.3. Recall that this version is generated from version 1.2 by deleting the product element for model 990 along with its subelements, except the editorsChoice element, which is moved to the content of the product element for model 995. Recall that our simple edit model maps a move operation to an insertion-deletion pair. The edit script describing this delta is noted as suggested by Fig. 32. The data for the inserted editorsChoice element is put into the partially filled page 5. A consequence of the deletion is that elements mc2

Page	ID	Tag	Attributes	Content	Ver.
1	m1	manufacturer		{ n1, ps1 }	1.0
	n1	name		Nikon	1.0
	ps1	products		{ mc1, mc2, mc3 }	1.0
	mc1	product	model:"900"	{ pc1 }	1.0
2	pc1	price		500	1.0
	mc2	product	model:"990"	{ pc2 }	1.0
	pc2	price		600	1.0
	mc3	product	model:"995"	{ pc3 }	1.0
3	pc3	price		700	1.0
	m2	manufacturer		{ n2, ps2 }	1.0
	n2	name		Olympus	1.0
	ps2	products		{ mo1, mo2 }	1.0
4	mo1	product	model:"OM-1"	{ po1 }	1.0
	po1	price		300	1.0
	mo2	product	model:"OM-2"	{ po2 }	1.0
	po2	price		400	1.0
5	ec1	editorsChoice	ref:"PC Magazine"		1.1
	ph1	phone		555-1212	1.2
	ec2	editorsChoice	ref:"PC Magazine"		1.3
	po3	price		350	1.4
6	pc2	price		600	1.3
	mc3	product	model:"995"	{ pc3 }	1.3
	ec1	editorsChoice	ref:"PC Magazine"		1.3
	ph1	phone		555-1212	1.3
7	ec2	editorsChoice	ref:"PC Magazine"		1.3
	po3	price		350	1.4

FIG. 31. Disk representation of the data in our running example with the minimum page usefulness constraint at version 1.3.

Page	Version	Edit Script	Pages Needed	Ver.
s1	1.0	ins(*)	1-4	1.0
	1.1	ins(mc2,2,ec1)	1-5	1.1
	1.2	ins(m1,2,ph1)	1-5	1.2
	1.3	ins(pc3,2,ec2), del(pc2)	1, 3-7	1.3
	1.4	del(po1), ins(po3,2,ec2)		1.4

FIG. 32. Edit scripts for the disk representation of Fig. 31.

and pc2 are not needed in order to materialize version 1.3. Thus, the usefulness of page 2 drops to 50%, which is below our threshold of 75%. To fix this situation, the useful data from pages below the usefulness threshold (pages 2 and 5) is copied to fresh pages. On page 2, the first and last elements are useful. On page 5, both the elements from prior versions are useful. These four elements are copied to the new page 6. However, another page is required to hold the editorsChoice element for the insertion operation in the script for version 1.3 in Fig. 32. Finally, the update operation that results in version 1.4 is represented by an deletion-insertion pair in the edit script and requires the addition of a price element (with the new value) to page 7. The resulting disk layout is depicted in Fig. 31.

8. Timestamp-Based Methods

Methods based on edit scripts incur the overhead of applying edit scripts in order to instantiate the desired version of the database (or a portion of the database). This overhead can be avoided trivially by storing a snapshot of each version, indexed by version identifiers (timestamps). Unfortunately, this method is typically impracticable due to the excessive storage requirements. Intuitively, we may avoid the storage overhead by avoiding repetition of elements that remain unchanged across versions. Such repetition can be avoided by attaching to each element a set of timestamps identifying the versions in which it participates. In this section, we describe methods based on this idea, following the development in [3]. In our running example, the product element for model OM-2 remains unchanged in versions 1.0 through 1.4; this fact is represented by associating the set {1.0, 1.1, 1.2, 1.3, 1.4} with the representation of this element's data (which is not repeated). In order to reduce the storage overhead of the timestamp annotations, we adopt the convention that a node that does not have an explicit timestamp annotation inherits the timestamps of its parent (recursively). Further, sequences of consecutive timestamps are represented more compactly using intervals.

Figure 33 depicts the XML version store of our running example at version 1.2. The document root is annotated with the entire range of versions seen so far. The phone element's annotation indicates that it is valid for version 1.2 only. Unannotated elements such as the products elements inherit their timestamps from the root. The annotation of the editorsChoice element indicates that it is valid for versions 1.1 and 1.2.

Let us now consider the actions necessary for checking in version 1.3 of our running example. Recall that, in this version, the product element for model 990 (and its subelements) are absent, and the editorsChoice element appears as a child of the product element for model 995. Figure 34 depicts the version store after version 1.3 is checked in. The timestamp range of the annotation on the root element now includes 1.3. The absence of the model 990 product element is encoded by its annotation, which excludes 1.3. Unannotated elements inherit their timestamps from their

```
<root>
   <h:ts>1.0-1.2</h:ts>
   <manufacturer>
      <name>Nikon</name>
      <phone> <h:ts>1.2</h:ts> 555-1212 </phone>
      <products>
         <product model="900"> <price>500</price> </product>
         <product model="990">
            <price>600</price>
            <editorsChoice ref="PC Magazine">
               <h:ts>1.1-1.2</h:ts>
            </editorsChoice>
         </product>
         <product model="995">
            <price>700</price>
         </product>
      </products>
   </manufacturer>
   <manufacturer>
      <name>Olympus</name>
      <products>
         <product model="OM-1">
            <price>300</price>
         </product>
         <product model="OM-2"> <price>400</price> </product>
      </products>
   </manufacturer>
</root>
```

FIG. 33. Timestamped version store at version 1.2.

closest ancestor. Thus, the implicit annotation for the price subelement of the model 990 product element is 1.0-1.2 (inherited from its parent) and not 1.0-1.3. There are now two editorsChoice elements. The first denotes the old position and the second denotes the new, as suggested by the timestamps.

In order to instantiate a requested version from such a timestamped version store, a single, sequential scan of the version store suffices. During this scan, the timestamp set of each element (either explicit from its annotation or implicitly derived from the timestamp set of its parent) is used to determine whether the element belongs to the requested version, in which case it is written to the output. This simple method suffers from the disadvantage of requiring a complete scan of the version store, whose size may be significantly larger than that of the requested version.

```
<root>
   <h:ts>1.0-1.3</h:ts>
   <manufacturer>
      <name>Nikon</name>
      <phone> <h:ts>1.2, 1.3</h:ts> 555-1212 </phone>
      <products>
         <product model="900"> <price>500</price> </product>
         <product model="990">
            <h:ts>1.0-1.2</h:ts>
            <price>600</price>
            <editorsChoice ref="PC Magazine>
               <h:ts>1.1-1.2</h:ts>
            </editorsChoice>
         </product>
         <product model="995">
            <editorsChoice ref="PC Magazine">
               <h:ts>1.3</h:ts>
            </editorsChoice>
            <price>700</price>
         </product>
      </products>
   </manufacturer>
   <manufacturer>
      <name>Olympus</name>
      <products>
         <product model="OM-1">
            <price>300</price>
         </product>
         <product model="OM-2"> <price>400</price> </product>
      </products>
   </manufacturer>
</root>
```

FIG. 34. Timestamped version store at version 1.3.

Elements belonging to a version may be efficiently located by using an auxiliary index structure. One example of such a structure is the *timestamp tree* described in [3]. Briefly, a timestamp tree is a binary tree that indexes the subelements of each element by their timestamps (i.e., by the versions in which they occur). There is one timestamp tree for each element in the version store. (These trees may be stored separated from the main version store, with pointers leading from each element to its timestamp tree.) Each leaf of an element's timestamp tree represents one of its subelements, and includes a pointer to that subelement along with its set of timestamps. Each interior node contains a set of timestamps that is the union of the timestamp sets of its subelements.

Since an element occurs in several versions in general, using this tree requires some care to ensure that using the index does not end up requiring more work than using the simple method. Specifically, while traversing the timestamp tree for an element e, we keep track of the number of tree nodes encountered, and fall back to the simple method if this number exceeds the number of e's subelements. With this modification, one can prove that looking up the subelements of any element that are relevant to a version requires $\max\{2\alpha - 1 + \alpha \log(k/\alpha), 2k\}$ probes, where α and k denote, respectively, the number of subelements belonging to the version of interest and the total number of subelements [3]. The set of timestamp trees for a version store can be built by performing a single sequential scan of the version store. The set of trees must be rebuilt every time there is an update to the version store (i.e., every time a new version is checked in). This extra work at version check-in time speeds up version retrieval.

9. Using Key Constraints

In the methods discussed so far, the first step in checking in a new version is a *diff* operation that compares the new version with its predecessor in order to infer the set of changes, or *delta*, between the versions. The critical task in such a diff operation is determining the identity of elements across versions. That is, we need to map elements in the older version to their instantiations in the new version (if present). Once such a mapping is available, generating the edit operations that form the delta is straightforward. The methods discussed so far make no assumptions about the data that is being stored beyond well-formedness of XML. In some instances, current and future versions of data are known to obey additional constraints. In our running example, one may reasonably assume that model numbers are unique among the products of each manufacturer. Such *key constraints* can be used to speed up the process of mapping elements in one version to those in the other. We now describe one such method, loosely following the development in [3], with some modifications. (We use a more expressive constraint language and present an alternative method for resolving unkeyed data.)

In relational databases, key constraints are specified by indicating a relation name and the set of key attributes. In effect, the relation indicates the scope in which tuples are uniquely identified by the key attributes (i.e., the scope in which distinct tuples cannot agree on all key attributes). We can specify keys in XML by mapping to XML the three main concepts used in a key constraint: relations, tuples, and key attributes.

In more detail, an XML key constraint is a 3-tuple (R, T, A), where R is an absolute XPath expression, T is a relative XPath expression, and A is a set of relative XPath expressions. Intuitively, R denotes the scope of the constraint and corresponds to relation names in traditional key constraints. The set of objects that are subject to the universal quantification implicit in a key constraint (similar to tuples in relational key constraints) is specified by T. Finally, the set of objects denoted by the XPath expressions in A corresponds to the set of key attributes in a relational key constraint. An example is (/, manufacturer, {name, phone}), which states that within the scope of the document root (indicated by the expression /), no two manufacturer elements can agree on both name and phone subelements.

Informally, an XML database satisfies a key constraint (R, T, A) if, starting at any object that matches R, the objects reachable by T-paths (paths matching the XPath expression T) are uniquely identified by their sets of A-subobjects (subobjects reachable by a path that matches some path in A). Formally, let by $o.[\![X]\!]$ denote the set of objects that are reachable from object o by a path that matches the XPath expression X. (We model the attributes of an element as special subelements that encode the attribute names and values.) Let ρ denote the document root. An XML database satisfies a key constraint (R, T, A) iff $\forall r \in \rho.[\![R]\!]$: (1) $\forall t \in r.[\![T]\!]$ and $\forall a \in A$, $t.[\![a]\!]$ exists uniquely and (2) if $t_1, t_2 \in r.[\![T]\!]$ such that $\forall a \in A, t_1.[\![a]\!] = t_2.[\![a]\!]$, then $t_1 = t_2$.

Let us establish some key constraints for our running example. (Obviously, we cannot infer constraints from a database instance. Instead, we use the running example as an exemplar and make assumptions about the application domain.) A natural constraint is the uniqueness of model numbers within the products of a manufacturer: (//manufacturer, /products/product, {@model}). We note that we permit model numbers to be shared by products from different manufacturers, although the sample instance does not contain such products. Further, we also note the distinction between this constraint and the closely related constraint (/, //manufacturer/products/product, {@model}). The latter asserts that model numbers uniquely identify products from all manufacturers (and is thus is strictly stronger than the former constraint). We may also wish to express the constraint that there is at most one product designated as the editor's choice by any magazine (or other source). In other words, in any version, there cannot be two editorsChoice elements with the same ref attribute: (/, //editorsChoice, {@ref}).

We say an element is *keyed* if it is identified by a key constraint. More precisely, an element e is keyed if the path to it from the document root matches the concatenation of the first two components of some key constraint. We say an element type is keyed if all occurrences of its instances are necessarily keyed. In other words, an element type is keyed if, for every element of that type that occurs in a document, there is a constraint such that the concatenation of the first two components of the constraint matches the path from the root to the element. Different instances of the element may match different constraints. Since we permit XPath expressions in constraints to include the closure operator (`//`), an element type can be keyed even if there is no DTD to which the document conforms. That is, the constraint language is powerful enough to express constraints on elements that can occur at arbitrary positions in an XML document. For example, consider a bibliographic database in which a `paper` element may appear in two contexts: `/bib/journal/paper` and `/bib/conference/paper`. Instances in the first context are constrained by (`/bib, journal/paper, {title, jname, volume, number}`), which states that journal papers are uniquely identified by paper titles, and the journal names, volumes, and numbers. Those in the second context are constrained by (`/bib, conference/paper, {title, name, year}`), which states that conference papers are uniquely identified by their titles, conference names, and years. The element type paper is keyed.

If all element types in the document types of interest are keyed, matching nodes across versions and, consequently, determining the delta between versions, is very simple. Elements are matched based on their key values, recursively, in a bottom up manner, so that the matches, if any, to an element's key attributes (subelements) are determined when that element is being matched. The resulting matching algorithm is similar to the differencing algorithm in [14].

It is, however, unlikely that every element type in a document type is keyed. A more likely scenario is one similar to that in our running example, in which the element types product and editorsChoice are keyed, but the other element types (e.g., price, phone) are not. In this situation, we must use something other than keys to match the unkeyed elements. One possibility is to first match the keyed elements as above and then match the fragments of the XML tree consisting of paths between (excluding) two keyed elements. Figure 35 suggests such matching of elements across versions 1.2 and 1.3 of our running example. In the figure, keyed elements are indicated by underlining their start tags. The matching of keyed elements is suggested by the superscripts on the start tags. Keyed elements with missing superscripts have no match in the other version. Once the keyed elements have been matched, the unkeyed fragments are matched using a differencing algorithm that is restricted to honor the established partial matching. For example, the *mhdiff* algorithm can accept a partial matching as input and is a suitable candidate [12]. For the data suggested by Fig. 35, the matching produced by the mhdiff algorithm is the intuitive one and it extends the partial matching by matching the semantically corresponding elements for manufacturer, name, phone, and price. The resulting delta is `mov(2,3,1)`, `del(4)`, where we use the superscripts in the figure to identify elements. The delta indicates that version 1.3 is obtained from version 1.2 by (1) moving the editorsChoice ele-

```
<manufacturer>
    <name>Nikon</name>
    <phone>555-1212</phone>
    <products>
        <product model="900">[1] <price>500</price> </product>
        <product model="990">
            <editorsChoice ref="PC Magazine"/>[2]
            <price>600</price>
        </product>
        <product model="995">[3] <price>700</price> </product>
    </products>
</manufacturer>
<manufacturer>
    <name>Olympus</name>
    <products>
        <product model="OM-1">[4] <price>300</price> </product>
        <product model="OM-2">[5] <price>400</price> </product>
        </products>
</manufacturer>

<manufacturer>
    <name>Nikon</name>
    <phone>555-1212</phone>
    <products>
        <product model="900">[1] <price>500</price> </product>
        <product model="995">[3]
            <editorsChoice ref="PC Magazine"/>[2]
            <price>700</price>
        </product>
    </products>
</manufacturer>
<manufacturer>
    <name>Olympus</name>
    <products>
        <product model="OM-1">[4] <price>300</price> </product>
        <product model="OM-2">[5] <price>400</price> </product>
        </products>
</manufacturer>
```

FIG. 35. Matching keyed elements (underlined) and unkeyed fragments from versions 1.2 and 1.3 of the running example.

ment (number 2) to the first position as child of the product element for model 995 (element 3) and (2) deleting the subtree rooted at element 4 (the product element for model 990).

We note that by using a differencing algorithm that recognizes move operations (such as the move of the editorsChoice element in our running example), the version store can store information more compactly. In our earlier description of the timestamped version store (depicted in Figs. 33 and 34), there are two identical editorsChoice elements, one for each position in which the element occurs in the document versions. Such redundancy is the result of move operations being expressed as insert-delete pairs. In contrast, when move operations are explicit, all the redundant copies of such elements can be replaced by a reference to the original. The references have their own timestamp sets (because their intervals of validity are distinct from those of the original copy to which they refer). Figure 36 depicts the version store of Fig. 34 with this change. The second editorsChoice element now has a reference to the first. In our artificially small running example, the savings, if any, are small since the editorsChoice element has empty content and only one attribute and thus does not consume much space. However, in general, moved elements are much larger. Further, there may be several redundant copies of such elements, multiplying the savings realized by using explicit move operations in the deltas.

An alternative method to cope with unkeyed elements is presented in [3]. This method provides a simpler and more efficient version check-in procedure by making four assumptions about keys. First, the XPath expressions used in key definitions must use only the child axis. That is, the expressions must consist solely of element names separated by the path separator /. In particular, the closure operator // is not permitted. Second, keys must be defined in a level-wise manner. More precisely, the second component in all key constraints is restricted to be a single path component consisting of an element name. Thus, a key constraint such as (/store, //book, {@ISBN}), which indicates that books are uniquely identified by their ISBN attribute irrespective of where they occur, is not permitted. Third, there can be no keyed nodes in the subtree rooted at a key attribute (i.e., an element that is part of some key). That is, we cannot have key constraints $(R_1, T_1, \{a_1, \ldots, a_i, \ldots, a_k\})$ and (R_2, T_2, A_2) such that $R_1/T_1/a_i$ is a proper prefix of R_2/T_2. This assumption permits the version store to store keyed elements in an order different from the document order of the elements in any given version. Fourth, every element must have an ancestor (not necessarily proper) that is keyed. As a result of this assumption, any element can either be identified by a key or has an ancestor that can be identified by a key.

The tree structure of an XML document that satisfies these assumptions consists of two parts. The first part consists of nodes involved in some key constraint as key attributes or paths to them. The second assumption implies that any node on a path

```
<root>
    <h:ts>1.0-1.3</h:ts>
    <manufacturer>
        <name>Nikon</name>
        <phone> <h:ts>1.2, 1.3</h:ts> 555-1212 </phone>
        <products>
            <product model="900"> <price>500</price> </product>
            <product model="990">
                <h:ts>1.0-1.2</h:ts>
                <price>600</price>
                <editorsChoice ref="PC Magazine id="ec1">
                    <h:ts>1.1-1.2</h:ts>
                </editorsChoice>
            </product>
            <product model="995">
                <editorsChoice idref="ec1">
                    <h:ts>1.3</h:ts>
                </editorsChoice>
                <price>700</price>
            </product>
        </products>
    </manufacturer>
    <manufacturer>
        <name>Olympus</name>
        <products>
            <product model="OM-1">
                <price>300</price>
            </product>
            <product model="OM-2"> <price>400</price> </product>
        </products>
    </manufacturer>
</root>
```

FIG. 36. Keyed, timestamped version store at version 1.3.

to a key attribute is also a key. The second part consists of the nodes below the nodes in the first part. These nodes are not involved in any key constraint; rather, they are treated as parts of the (structured) values of their nearest ancestor (which is a key attribute for some constraint). The boundary between these two parts consists of the so-called *frontier nodes*: nodes whose descendants do not contain any key attributes.

Given this document structure, checking a new version into the version store is much simpler than the check-in procedure for the general case. For the first part of a document (above the frontier nodes), every node that is encountered is keyed (by the assumptions). Therefore merging it requires only the identification of the corresponding (same key value) node, if any, in the version store followed by a suitable update of the timestamp sets. When a matching pair of nodes is found, the new timestamp is added to the timestamp set of the node in the version store. Nodes in the version store that do not have a match in the new version have a timestamp set that excludes the new version's timestamp. Nodes in the new version that are not matched to a node in the version store are inserted into the version store with the new version's timestamp forming the singleton timestamp set. For the second part of a document (below the frontier nodes) merging does not occur by individual node. Instead, the proper subtree rooted at each frontier node is treated as the (complex) value of that node. The frontier nodes are then compared by value for the purpose of merging. This method is described and analyzed in [3] to yield an $O(N \log N)$ running time, where N is the sum of the sizes of the version store and new version.

References

[1] Agrawal S., Chaudhuri S., Narasayya V.R., "Automated selection of materialized views and indexes in sql databases", in: *Proceedings of the International Conference on Very Large Data Bases (VLDB), Cairo, Egypt*, 2000, pp. 496–505.

[2] Buneman P., Davidson S., Fernandez M., Suciu D., "Adding structure to unstructured data", in: *Proceedings of the International Conference on Database Theory*, 1997.

[3] Buneman P., Khanna S., Tajima K., Tan W.-C., "Archiving scientific data", in: *Proceedings of the ACM SIGMOD International Conference on Management of Data (SIGMOD), Madison, Wisconsin*, 2002.

[4] Beech D., Lawrence S., Maloney M., Mendelsohn N., Thompson H., *XML Schema, part 1: Structures. W3C Working Draft*, May 1999. Available at http://www.w3.org/TR/1999/xmlschema-1/.

[5] Biron P., Malhotra A., *XML Schema, part 2: Datatypes. W3C Working Draft*, May 1999. Available at http://www.w3.org/TR/1999/xmlschema-2/.

[6] Bray T., Paoli J., Sperberg-McQueen C., *Extensible Markup Language (XML) 1.0. World Wide Web Consortium Recommendation*, February 1998. Available at http://www.w3.org/TR/REC-xml.

[7] Bradley N., *The XML Companion*, 2nd edn., Addison-Wesley, 2000.

[8] Cattell R., *The Object Database Standard: ODMG-93 Release 1.2*, Morgan Kaufmann Publishers, San Francisco, CA, 1996.

[9] Chawathe S., Abiteboul S., Widom J., "Managing historical semistructured data", *Theory and Practice of Object Systems* 5 (3) (1999) 143–162.

[10] Chawathe S., Chen M.-S., Yu P., "On index selection schemes for nested object hierarchies", in: *Proceedings of the International Conference on Very Large Data Bases*, 1994, pp. 331–341.

[11] Clark J., DeRose S., *XML Path Language (XPath), Version 1.0. W3C Recommendation*, November 1999. Available at http://www.w3.org/.

[12] Chawathe S., Garcia-Molina H., "Meaningful change detection in structured data", in: *Proceedings of the ACM SIGMOD International Conference on Management of Data, Tuscon, Arizona*, 1997, pp. 26–37.

[13] Clark J., *XSL Transformations (XSLT), Version 1.0. W3C Working Draft*, July 1999. Available at http://www.w3.org/TR/WD-xslt-19990709.

[14] Chawathe S., Rajaraman A., Garcia-Molina H., Widom J., "Change detection in hierarchically structured information", in: *Proceedings of the ACM SIGMOD International Conference on Management of Data, Montréal, Québec*, 1996, pp. 493–504.

[15] Chaudhuri S., Shim K., "Storage and retrieval of XML data using relational databases", in: *Tutorial Notes, International Conference on Very Large Data Bases (VLDB)*, 2001. Available at http://www.dia.uniroma3.it/~vldbproc/.

[16] Chien S.-Y., Tsotras V.J., Zaniolo C., "Version management of XML documents", in: *Proceedings of the ACM SIGMOD Workshop on the Web and Databases, Dallas, Texas*, 2000.

[17] Chien S.-Y., Tsotras V.J., Zaniolo C., "Copy-based versus edit-based version management schemes for structured documents", in: *Proceedings of the International Workshop on Research Issues in Data Engineering (RIDE), Heidelberg, Germany*, 2001, pp. 95–102.

[18] Chien S.-Y., Tsotras V.J., Zaniolo C., "Efficient management of multiversion documents by object referencing", in: *Proceedings of the International Conference on Very Large Data Bases (VLDB), Rome, Italy*, 2001, pp. 291–300.

[19] Chien S.-Y., Tsotras V.J., Zaniolo C., "XML document versioning", *SIGMOD Record* **30** (3) (2001) 46–53.

[20] Dayen I., *Storing XML in Relational Databases*, O'Reilly & Associates, June 2001. Available at http://www.xml.com/.

[21] Date C., Darwen H., *A Guide to the SQL Standard*, Addison-Wesley, Reading, MA, 1993.

[22] Ellis J., Ho L., Fisher M., *JDBC 3.0 Specification*, October 2001. Available at http://java.sun.com/.

[23] Eisenberg A., Melton J., "SQL/XML and the SQLX informal group of companies", *SIGMOD Record* **30** (3) (2001) 105–108.

[24] Garcia-Molina H., Ullman J.D., Widom J., *Database System Implementation*, Prentice-Hall, Upper Saddle River, NJ, 2000.

[25] Goldman R., Widom J., "DataGuides: Enabling query formulation and optimization in semistructured databases", in: *Proceedings of the Twenty-third International Conference on Very Large Data Bases, Athens, Greece*, 1997.

[26] Haertel M., Hayes D., Stallman R., Tower L., Eggert P., Davison W., *The GNU diff Program Texinfo System Documentation*, 1998. Available through anonymous FTP at ftp://prep.ai.mit.edu.

[27] Le Hors A., Le Hegaret P., Wood L., Nicol G., Robie J., Champion M., Byrne S., *Document Object Model (DOM) Level 2 Core Specification, Version 1.0. W3C Recommen-

dation, November 2000. Available at http://www.w3.org/TR/2000/REC-DOM-Level-2-Core-20001113.

[28] Higgins S., *Oracle9i Application Developer's Guide—XML. Release 1 (9.0.1), part number A88894-01*, June 2001. Available at http://www.oracle.com/.

[29] XML Extender administration and programming, version 7. Product information, 2000. Available at http://www.ibm.com/.

[30] Information technology—database languages—SQL—part 14: XML-related specifications (SQL/XML). Working draft of ISO/IEC JTC 1/SC32/WG3 Database Languages Working Group, June 2001. Available at http://www.sqlx.org/.

[31] Lewis P.M., Bernstein A., Kifer M., *Databases and Transaction Processing: An Application Oriented Approach*, Addison-Wesley, 2001.

[32] McHugh J., Abiteboul S., Goldman R., Quass D., Widom J., "Lore: A database management system for semistructured data", *SIGMOD Record* **26** (3) (1997) 54–66.

[33] Melton J., "An SQL3 snapshot", in: *Proceedings of the Twelfth International Conference on Data Engineering, New Orleans, Louisiana*, 1996, pp. 666–672.

[34] Momjian B., *PostgreSQL: Introduction and Concepts*, Addison-Wesley, 2001.

[35] Nestorov S., Ullman J., Wiener J., Chawathe S., "Representative objects: Concise representations of semistructured, hierarchial data", in: *Proceedings of the International Conference on Data Engineering*, 1997, pp. 79–90.

[36] Ramakrishnan R., Gehrke J., *Database Management Systems*, 3rd edn., McGraw-Hill, 2002.

[37] Rochkind M.J., "The source code control system", *IEEE Transactions on Software Engineering* **1** (4) (1975) 364–370.

[38] Selinger P., "What you should know about DB2 support for XML: A starter kit", *The IDUG Solutions Journal* **8** (1) (May 2001), International DB2 Users Group. Available at http://www.idug.org/.

[39] Stonebraker M., Hellerstein J. (Eds.), *Readings in Database Systems*, 3rd edn., Morgan Kaufmann, San Francisco, CA, 1998.

[40] Shanmugasundaram J., Kiernan J., Shekita E., Fan C., Funderburk J., "Querying XML views of relational data", in: *Proceedings of the International Conference on Very Large Data Bases (VLDB), Rome, Italy*, 2001.

[41] Silberschatz A., Korth H.F., Sudarshan S., *Database System Concepts*, 4th edn., McGraw-Hill, 2001.

[42] Shanmugasundaram J., Shekita E., Barr R., Carey M., Lindsay B., Pirahesh H., Reinwald B., "Efficiently publishing relational data as XML documents", *The VLDB Journal* **10** (2–3) (2001) 133–154.

[43] Staken K., *Xindice Users Guide 0.7*, The Apache Software Foundation, 2002. Available at http://xml.apache.org/xindice/.

[44] Sunderraman R., *Oracle8 Programming: A Primer*, Addison-Wesley, 2000.

[45] Using XML with the Sybase Adaptive Server SQL databases. Technical White Paper, 1999. Available at http://www.sybase.com/.

[46] XML technology in Sybase Adaptive Server Enterprise. Technical White Paper, 2001. Available at http://www.sybase.com/.

[47] Tamino XML server. White Paper. Software AG, October 2001. Available at http://www. softwareag.com/taminio/.

[48] Tichy W., "RCS—A system for version control", *Software—Practice and Experience* **15** (7) (1985) 637–654.

[49] Ullman J., *Principles of Database and Knowledge-Base Systems, Vol. 2*, Computer Science Press, 1989.

[50] Ullman J.D., *Object-Relational Features of Oracle. Course Notes for CS145*, October 1998. Available at http://www-db.stanford.edu/.

[51] Ullman J.D., Widom J., *A First Course in Database Systems*, 2nd edn., Prentice-Hall, Upper Saddle River, NJ, 2001.

Adding Compression to Next-Generation Text Retrieval Systems

NIVIO ZIVIANI

Department of Computer Science
Univ. Federal de Minas Gerais
Brazil

EDLENO SILVA DE MOURA

Department of Computer Science
Univ. Federal do Amazonas
Brazil

Abstract

In this chapter we present a combination of several data compression features to provide economical storage, faster indexing, and accelerated searches. We discuss recent methods for compressing the text and the index of text retrieval systems. By compressing both the complete text and the index, the total amount of space is less than half the size of the original text alone. Most surprisingly, the time required to build the index and also to answer a query is much less than if the index and text had not been compressed. This is a rare case where there is no space-time trade-off. Moreover, the text can be kept compressed all the time, allowing updates when changes occur in the compressed text.

1. Introduction

The widespread use of digital libraries, office automation systems, document data-bases, and lately the World-Wide Web has led to an explosion of textual information available online [6,45]. In [22], the Web alone was shown to have approximately 800 million static pages, containing a total of approximately 6 terabytes of plain text. A *terabyte* is a bit more than one million of million bytes, enough to store the text of a million books. In June 2002 the search engine Google [11] claims to have more than 2.5 billion static pages in its database. Text retrieval is the kernel of most Information Retrieval (IR) systems, and one of the biggest challenges to IR systems is to provide fast access to such a mass of text.

In this chapter we discuss recent techniques that permit fast direct searching on the compressed text and how the new techniques can improve the overall efficiency of IR systems. Traditionally, compression techniques have not been used in IR systems because the compressed texts did not allow fast access. However, recent text compression methods [33,50] have enabled the possibility of searching directly the compressed text *faster* than in the original text, and have also improved the amount of compression obtained. Direct access to any point in the compressed text has also become possible, and the IR system might access a given word in a compressed text without the need to decode the entire text from the beginning. The new features lead to a win–win situation that is raising renewed interest in text compression for the implementation of IR systems.

Text compression is about finding ways to represent actual text in less space. This is accomplished by substituting the symbols in the text by equivalent ones that are represented using a smaller number of bits or bytes. For large text collections, text compression appears as an attractive option for reducing costs. The gain obtained from compressing text is that it requires less storage space, it takes less time to be read from disk or transmitted over a communication link, and it takes less time to search. The price paid is the computing cost necessary to code and decode the text. This drawback, however, is becoming less and less significant as technology progresses. In the last 20 years the time to access disks kept approximately constant while processing speed increased approximately 2,000 times [37]. As time passes, investing more and more computing power in compression in exchange for less disk or network transfer times becomes a profitable option.

The savings of space obtained by a compression method is measured by the *compression ratio*, defined as the size of the compressed file as a percentage of the uncompressed file. Besides the economy of space, there are other important aspects to be considered, such as compression and decompression speed. In some situations, decompression speed is more important than compression speed. For instance, this is the case with textual databases and documentation systems in which it is common to compress the text once and to read it many times from disk. Another important characteristic of a compression method is the possibility of performing pattern matching in a compressed text without decompressing it. In this case, sequential searching can be speeded up by compressing the search key rather than decoding the compressed text being searched. As a consequence, it is possible to search faster on compressed text because fewer bytes have to be scanned.

Efficient text retrieval on large text collections requires specialized indexing techniques. An *index* is a data structure built on the text collection intended to speed up queries. A simple and popular indexing structure for text collections is the inverted file [6,45]. Inverted files are especially adequate when the pattern to be searched for is formed by simple words. This is a common type of query, for instance, when searching the Web for pages that include the words "text" and "compression". An *inverted file* is typically composed of a vector containing all the distinct words in the text collection (which is called the *vocabulary*) and a list of all document numbers in which each distinct word occurs (sometimes its frequency in each document is also stored). The largest part of the index is the lists of document numbers, for which specific compression methods have been proposed that provide very good compression ratios. In this case, both index construction time and query processing time can be significantly improved by using index compression schemes.

In the next section we review traditional and recent methods for compressing text. Following, we discuss how recent techniques permit fast direct searching on the compressed text. Next, we present compression methods for compressing the index. Later on, we show how the new techniques can improve the overall efficiency of IR systems. Next, we show how the text can be kept compressed all the time, allowing updates when changes occur in the compressed text. Finally, we discuss the trends and research issues and present a bibliographic discussion.

2. Text Compression Methods for IR Systems

One well-known coding strategy is Huffman coding [20]. The idea of Huffman coding is to compress the text by assigning shorter codes to symbols with higher frequencies. This can be achieved by assigning a unique variable-length bit encoding to each different symbol of the text. The traditional implementations of the Huffman method are character-based, i.e., adopt the characters as the symbols in the alphabet. A successful idea towards merging the requirements of compression algorithms and the needs of IR systems is to consider that the symbols to be compressed are words and not characters. Words are the atoms on which most IR systems are built. Taking words as symbols means that the table of symbols in the compression coder is exactly the vocabulary of the text, allowing a natural integration between an inverted file and a word-based Huffman compression method. Word-based Huffman methods allow random access to words within the compressed text, which is a critical issue for an IR system. Moreover, character-based Huffman methods are typically able to compress English texts to approximately 60% while word-based Huffman methods are able to reduce them to just over 25%, because the distribution of words is much more biased than the distribution of characters.

Another important family of compression methods, called Ziv–Lempel, substitutes a sequence of symbols by a pointer to a previous occurrence of that sequence. Compression is obtained because the pointers need less space than the phrase they replace. The Ziv–Lempel family can be classified in two sub-groups. The first one is derived from a method published by Ziv and Lempel in 1977 [48], which is known as LZ77. The compression methods derived from the LZ77 obtain good compression ratios for a large variety of data sources and are extremely fast on decoding. Their main drawback is that the compression is slower than the decompression. For this reason, algorithms derived from the LZ77 are the preferred choice for situations where the data is compressed once and decompressed more frequently. Examples of applications which are based on the LZ77 method are the Gzip, which is popular in UNIX operating systems, and the Winzip, which is popular in Windows operating systems.

The other subgroup of the Ziv–Lempel family is derived from a method presented by Ziv and Lempel in 1978, which is known as LZ78. In most practical applications, the compression methods based on the LZ78 obtain compression ratios slight worse than the ones obtained by methods derived form the LZ77. However, the compression and decompression processes are performed faster in LZ78 than in the LZ77. This characteristic makes the LZ78 based methods the preferred choice in applications where time is a critical factor in performance, such as data transmission operations. Two examples of applications based on LZ78 are the utility Compress, available in UNIX systems, and the compression methods used in modem data transmission, which in general use a variation of LZ78 proposed by Welch in 1984 [44], which is known as LZW.

Ziv–Lempel methods are popular for their speed, economy of memory and good performance, but they present important disadvantages in an IR environment. First, they require decoding to start at the beginning of a compressed file, which makes random access expensive. Second, they are difficult to search without decompressing. A possible advantage is that they do not need to store a table of symbols as a Huffman-based method does, but this has little importance in IR scenarios because the vocabulary of the text is needed anyway for indexing and querying purposes.

Arithmetic coding [39,46], another well-known compression method, presents similar problems. Since we here are interested in applications of compression methods that are important for IR systems, we will not present further discussions about Ziv–Lempel methods or arithmetic coding. A reader interested in more details about Ziv–Lempel methods can find it in [48,49,7]. A reader more interested in Arithmetic coding can find it in [45].

2.1   Word-Based Huffman Compression

For natural language texts used in an IR context, the most effective compression technique is word-based Huffman coding. Compression proceeds in two passes over the text. The encoder makes a first pass over the text to obtain the frequency of each different text word and then it performs the actual compression in a second pass.

The text is not only composed of words but also of the strings which appear between the words, which we will name here as separators. An efficient way to deal with words and separators is to use a model called *spaceless words* [33]. This model takes in account that most of all the separators in a natural language text are composed by a single blank space. The spaceless model takes advantage of this fact by representing the spaces implicitly in the compressed text. In this model if a word is followed by a space, just the word is encoded. If not, the word and then the separator are encoded. At decoding time, it is assumed that a space follows each word, except if the next symbol corresponds to a separator. Figure 1 presents an example of compression using Huffman coding for the spaceless words method. The set of symbols in this case is {"the", "pink", "panther", "is", ",⊔", "a"}, whose frequencies are 1, 4, 2, 1, 1, 1, respectively.

The example also shows how the codes for the symbols are organized in a *Huffman tree*. The most frequent word (in this case, "pink") receives the shortest code (in this case, "0"). The Huffman method gives the coding tree that minimizes the length of the compressed file, but many coding trees would have achieved the same

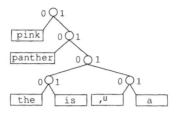

Original text: the pink panther is pink, a pink pink panther

Compressed text: 1100   0   10   1101 0 1110 1111 0 0 10

FIG. 1. Compression using Huffman coding for spaceless words.

compression. For instance, exchanging the left and right children of a node yields an alternative coding tree with the same compression ratio.

When dealing with large vocabularies, the preferred choice for most applications is the *canonical tree*. A Huffman tree is canonical when the height of the left subtree of any node is never smaller than that of the right subtree, and all leaves are in increasing order of probabilities from left to right. The tree presented in Fig. 1 is canonical. The deepest leaf at the leftmost position of the Huffman canonical tree, corresponding to one element with smallest probability, will contain only zeros, and the following codes will be in increasing order inside each level. At each change of level we shift left one bit in the counting. Table I shows the canonical codes for the example of Fig. 1.

A canonical code can be represented by an ordered sequence S of pairs (x_i, y_i), $1 \leqslant i \leqslant \ell$, where x_i represents the number of symbols at level i, y_i represents the numerical value of the first code at level i, and ℓ is the height of the tree. For the example in Fig. 1, the ordered sequence is $S = \langle (1, 0), (1, 2), (0, \infty), (4, 12) \rangle$. For instance, the fourth pair $(4, 12)$ in S corresponds to the fourth level and indicates that there are four nodes at this level and to the node most to the left is assigned a

TABLE I
CANONICAL CODE

Symbol	Probabilities	Canonical codes
the	1/10	1100
is	1/10	1101
,␣	1/10	1110
a	1/10	1111
panther	2/10	10
pink	4/10	0

code, at this level, with value 12. Since this is the fourth level, a value 12 corresponds to the codeword 1100.

One of the properties of canonical codes is that the set of codes having the same length are the binary representations of consecutive integers. Interpreted as integers, the 4-bit codes in Table I are 12, 13, 14, and 15, the 2-bit code is 2 and the 1-bit code is 0. Another interesting property is that, interpreting the code as integers, if c is the code for the first element of level l and d is the code for the last element of level m, where m is the biggest nonempty level smaller than l, then $c = 2^{(l-m)} \times (d + 1)$. In the example, the last element of level one has code 0, so the first element of level two has code $2^{(2-1)} \times (0 + 1) = 2$. As level three has no code and the last element of level two has value 2, so the first element of level four has value $2^{(4-2)} \times (2 + 1) = 12$.

In the example, if the first character read from the input stream is 0, a codeword has been identified and the corresponding symbol can be output. If this value is 1, a second bit is appended and the two bits are again interpreted as an integer and used to index the table and identify the corresponding symbol. Once we read '11' we know that the code has four bits and therefore we can read two more bits and use them as an index into the table. This fact can be exploited to enable efficient encoding and decoding with small overhead. Moreover, much less memory is required, which is especially important for large vocabularies.

The compact representation of canonical trees and its sorting properties allow more efficiency at decoding time with less memory requirement. A careful discussion about how to implement efficient coding and decoding programs using canonical trees is described in [18]. An efficient algorithm for building the Huffman tree from the symbol frequencies is described in [45], and can be done in linear time after sorting the symbol frequencies.

Decompression in Huffman trees is accomplished as follows. The stream of bits in the compressed file is traversed sequentially. The sequence of bits read is used to traverse the Huffman tree, starting at the root. Whenever a leaf node is reached, the corresponding word (which constitutes the decompressed symbol) is printed out and the tree traversal is restarted. Thus, according to the tree in Fig. 1, the presence of the code "1100" in the compressed file leads to the decompressed symbol "the".

2.2   Byte-Oriented Huffman Coding

The original method proposed by Huffman is mostly used as a binary code. In [33], the code assignment is modified such that a sequence of whole bytes is associated with each word in the text. As a result, the maximum degree of each node is now 256. This version is called *plain Huffman code* in this chapter. An alternative use of byte coding is what we call *tagged Huffman code*, where only 7 of the 8 bits of each byte are used for the code (and hence the tree has degree 128). The eighth bit is used

TABLE II
COMPARISON OF COMPRESSION TECHNIQUES ON THE WSJ TEXT COLLECTION

Method	Compression Ratio (%)	Compression Time (min)	Decompression Time (min)
Binary Huffman	27.13	8.77	3.08
Plain Huffman	30.60	8.67	1.95
Tagged Huffman	33.70	8.90	2.02
Gzip	37.53	25.43	2.68
Compress	42.94	7.60	6.78

to signal the first byte of each codeword (which, as seen later, aids the search). For example, a possible plain code for the word "blue" could be the 3-byte code "47 81 8", and a possible tagged code for the word "blue" could be "175 81 8" (where the first byte $175 = 47 + 128$). Experimental results have shown that no significant degradation of the compression ratio is experienced by using bytes instead of bits when coding the words of a vocabulary. On the other hand, decompression and searching are faster with a byte-oriented Huffman code than with a binary Huffman code, because bit shifts and masking operations are not necessary.

Table II shows the compression ratios and the compression and decompression times achieved for binary Huffman, plain Huffman, tagged Huffman, *gnu Gzip* and Unix *Compress* for the file WSJ containing the Wall Street Journal (1987, 1988, 1989), part of the TREC 3 collection [16]. The WSJ file has 250 megabytes, almost 43 million words and nearly 200,000 different words (vocabulary). As it can be seen, the compression ratio degrades only slightly by using bytes instead of bits. The increase in the compression ratio of the tagged Huffman code is approximately 3 points over that of the plain Huffman code, which comes from the extra space allocated for the tag bit in each byte. The compression time is 2–3 times faster than Gzip and only 17% slower than Compress (which achieves much worse compression ratios). Considering decompression, there is a significant improvement when using bytes instead of bits. Using bytes, both tagged and plain Huffman are more than 20% faster than Gzip and three times faster than Compress.

One important consequence of using byte Huffman coding is the possibility of performing fast direct searching on compressed text. A search algorithm is explained in the next section. The exact search can be done on the compressed text directly, using any known sequential pattern matching algorithm. The search algorithm presented allows a large number of variations of exact and approximate searching, such as phrases, ranges, complements, wild cards and arbitrary regular expressions. This technique is not only useful to speed up sequential search. As we see later, it can also be used to improve indexed schemes that combine inverted files and sequential search [35,50,45].

3. Online Search of Compressed Text

One of the most attractive properties of the Huffman method oriented to bytes rather than bits is that it can be searched exactly like any uncompressed text. When a query is submitted, the text is in compressed form and the pattern is in uncompressed form. The key idea is to compress the pattern instead of uncompressing the text. We call this technique *direct searching*.

The algorithm to find the occurrences of a single word starts by searching it in the vocabulary, where binary searching is a simple and inexpensive choice. Once the word has been found, its compressed code is obtained. Then, this compressed code is searched in the text using *any* classical string matching algorithm with no modifications. This is possible because the Huffman code uses bytes instead of bits, otherwise the method would be complicated.

A possible problem with this approach is that the compressed code for a word may appear in the compressed text even if the word does not appear in the original text. This may happen in plain Huffman codes because the concatenation of the codes of other words may contain the code sought, but it is impossible in tagged Huffman code [33]. The extra bit in the tagged Huffman code is employed to mark the starting point of each word in the compressed text, avoiding false matches during the searching process.

A common requirement of today's IR systems is flexibility in the search patterns. We call those "complex" patterns, which range from disregarding upper or lower case to searching for regular expressions and/or "approximate" searching. Approximate string searching, also called "searching allowing errors", permits at most k extra, missing or replaced characters between the pattern and its occurrence.

If the pattern is a complex word, we perform a *sequential* search in the vocabulary and collect the compressed codes of *all* the words that match the pattern. A multi-pattern search for all the codes is then conducted on the text [33]. Sequential vocabulary searching is not expensive for natural language texts because the vocabulary is small compared with the whole text (0.5% is typical for large texts). On the other hand, this sequential searching permits extra flexibility such as allowing errors.

The final setup allows a large number of variants, which forms a language originally defined for *Agrep* [47].

- Searching allowing errors (also called "approximate pattern matching"): given a query pattern and a number k, the system retrieves the occurrences of words which can be transformed into the query with up to k "errors". An error is the insertion, deletion or replacement of a character. For instance, searching "color" with $k = 1$ retrieves "colour" as well.

- Searching for classes of characters: each pattern position may match with a set of characters rather than with just one character. This allows some interesting queries:
  - range of characters (e.g., t[a-z]xt, where [a-z] means any letter between a and z);
  - arbitrary sets of characters (e.g., t[aei]xt meaning the words taxt, text and tixt);
  - complements (e.g., t[~ab]xt, where ~ab means any single character except a or b; t[~a-d]xt, where ~a-d means any single character except a, b, c or d);
  - arbitrary characters (e.g., t·xt means any character as the second character of the word);
  - case insensitive patterns (e.g., Text and text are considered as the same word).
- Searching for regular expressions (exactly or allowing errors). Some examples are:
  - unions (e.g., t(e|ai)xt means the words text and taixt);
  - arbitrary number of repetitions (e.g., t(e|ai)*xt means the words beginning with t followed by e or ai zero or more times followed by xt);
  - arbitrary number of characters in the middle of the pattern (e.g., t.*xt). It is customary to denote .* as #.
- Combining exact matching of some of their parts and approximate matching of other parts (e.g., <te>xt, with $k = 1$, meaning exact occurrence of te followed by an occurrence of xt with 1 error).
- Matching with nonuniform costs (e.g., the cost of insertions can be defined to be twice the cost of deletions).

3.1 Flexible Pattern Matching

Direct searching is very efficient but difficult to extend to handle much more complex queries, formed by phrases of complex patterns that are to be searched allowing errors and/or are defined by regular expressions. A more general approach, which works also on plain Huffman codes, uses the Huffman tree to guide the search process. To understand how this approach works we will first study the search algorithm for simple words and then show progressively how the query can be extended to phrases formed by complex patterns.

The searching algorithm for a single word starts again in the vocabulary using binary search. Once the word has been found the corresponding leaf in the Huffman

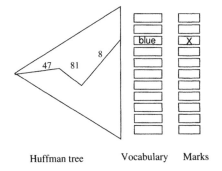

Huffman tree   Vocabulary   Marks

FIG. 2. General searching scheme for the word "blue".

tree is marked. Next, the compressed text is scanned byte by byte, and at the same time the Huffman tree is traversed downwards, as if one were decompressing the text, but without generating it. Each time a leaf of the Huffman tree is reached, one knows that a complete word has been read. If the leaf has a mark then an occurrence is reported. Be the leaf marked or not, one returns to the root of the Huffman tree and resumes the text scanning. Figure 2 illustrates the algorithm for the pattern "blue", encoded as the 3-byte 47 81 8. Each time this sequence of bytes is found in the compressed text the corresponding leaf in the Huffman tree is reached, reporting an occurrence. Complex patterns are, as before, handled by a sequential search in the vocabulary. This time we mark all the leaves corresponding to matching words.

This simple scheme can be nicely extended to handle complex phrase queries. Phrase queries are a sequence of patterns, each of which can be from a simple word to a complex regular expression allowing errors. If a phrase has ℓ elements, we set up a mask of ℓ bits for each vocabulary word (leaf of the Huffman tree). The ith bit of word x is set if x matches the ith element of the phrase query. For this sake, each element i of the phrase in turn is searched in the vocabulary and marks the ith bit of the words it matches with. Figure 3 illustrates the masks for the pattern "bl* blue is" allowing one error per word, where "bl*" means any word starting with "bl". The words "blue" and "blues" in the vocabulary match the pattern in the first and the second position. Therefore, their mask is "110" for the given pattern. The mask for the words "is" and "in" is "001", since they both match only the third position of the pattern. The mask for the word "gray" is "000", since it does not match any position of the pattern. A mask is assigned in a similar way for each work in the vocabulary.

After the preprocessing phase is performed the text is scanned as before. The state of the search is controlled by a nondeterministic automaton of $\ell + 1$ states, as shown in Fig. 3 for the pattern "bl* blue is". The automaton allows to move from

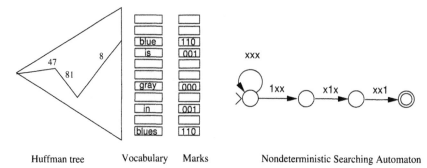

| Huffman tree | Vocabulary | Marks | Nondeterministic Searching Automaton |

FIG. 3. General searching scheme for the phrase "bl* blue is" allowing 1 error. The x in the automaton stands for 0 or 1.

state i to state $i + 1$ whenever the ith pattern of the phrase is recognized. State zero is always active and occurrences are reported whenever state ℓ is activated. The automaton is nondeterministic because at a given moment many states may be active. The bytes of the compressed text are read and the Huffman tree is traversed as before. Each time a leaf of the tree is reached its bit mask is sent to the automaton. An active state $i - 1$ will activate the state i only if the ith bit of the mask is active. Therefore, the automaton makes one transition per word of the text.

This automaton can be implemented efficiently using the Shift-Or algorithm [3]. This algorithm is able to simulate an automaton of up to $w + 1$ states (where w is the length in bits of the computer word), performing just two operations per entry. This means that it can search phrases of up to 32 or 64 words, depending on the machine. This is more than enough for common phrase searches. Longer phrases would need more machine words for the simulation, but the technique is the same.

The Shift-Or algorithm maps each state of the automaton (except the first one) to a bit of the computer word. For each new word reached in the Huffman three, each active state can activate the next one, which is simulated using a *shift* in the bit mask. Only those states that match the current text word can actually pass, which is simulated by a bit-wise *and* operation with the bit mask found in the leaf of the Huffman tree. Therefore, with one *shift* and one *and* operation per text word the search state is updated (the original algorithm uses the reverse bits for efficiency, hence the name Shift-Or).

It is simple to disregard separators in the search, so that a phrase query is found even if there are two spaces instead of one. Stopwords (articles, prepositions, etc.) can also be disregarded. The procedure is just to ignore the corresponding leaves of the Huffman tree when the search arrives to them. This ability is common on inverted files but is very rare in online search systems.

TABLE III
SEARCHING TIMES (IN SECONDS) FOR THE WSJ TEXT FILE, WITH 99% CONFIDENCE

Algorithm	$k = 0$	$k = 1$	$k = 2$	$k = 3$
Agrep	23.8 ± 0.38	117.9 ± 0.14	146.1 ± 0.13	174.6 ± 0.16
Direct Search	14.1 ± 0.18	15.0 ± 0.33	17.0 ± 0.71	22.7 ± 2.23
Automaton Search	22.1 ± 0.09	23.1 ± 0.14	24.7 ± 0.21	25.0 ± 0.49

Table III presents exact ($k = 0$) and approximate ($k = 1, 2, 3$) searching times for the WSJ file using *Agrep* [47], the direct search on tagged Huffman and the automaton search using plain Huffman. It can be seen from this table that both direct and automaton search algorithms are almost insensitive to the number of errors allowed in the pattern while Agrep is not. It also shows that both compressed search algorithms are faster than Agrep, up to 50% faster for exact searching and nearly 8 times faster for approximate searching. Notice that automaton searching permits complex phrase searching at exactly the same cost. Moreover, the automaton technique permits even more sophisticated searching, which is described below. However, automaton searching is always slower than direct searching, and should be used for complex queries as just described above.

3.2   Enhanced Searching

The Shift-Or algorithm can do much more than just searching for a simple sequence of elements. For instance, it has been enhanced to search for regular expressions, to allow errors in the matches and other flexible patterns [47,4]. This powerful type of search is the basis of the software Agrep [47].

A new handful of choices appear when we use these abilities in the word-based compressed text scenario that we have just described. Consider the automaton of Fig. 4. It can search in the compressed text for a phrase of four words allowing up to two insertions, deletions or replacements of *words*. Apart from the well known horizontal transitions that match characters, there are vertical transitions that insert new words in the pattern, diagonal transitions that replace words, and dashed diagonal transitions delete words from the pattern.

This automaton can be efficiently simulated using extensions of the Shift-Or algorithm, so we can search in the compressed text for *approximate* occurrences of the phrase. For instance, the search for "identifying potentially relevant matches" could find the occurrence of "identifying a number of relevant matches" in the text with one replacement error, assuming that the stop words "a" and "of" are disregarded as explained before. Moreover, if we allow three errors at the character level as well we could find the occurrence of "who

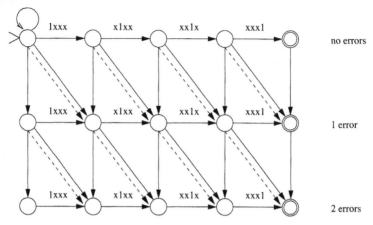

FIG. 4. A nondeterministic automaton for approximate phrase searching (4 words, 2 errors) in the compressed text. Dashed transitions flow without consuming any text input. The other unlabeled transitions accept any bit mask.

identified a number of relevant matches" in the text, since for the algorithm there is an occurrence of "identifying" in "identified".

Other efficiently implementable setups can be insensitive to the order of the words in the phrase. The same phrase query could be found in "matches considered potentially relevant were identified" with one deletion error for "considered". *Proximity searching* is also of interest in IR and can be efficiently solved. The goal is to give a phrase and find its words relatively close to each other in the text. This would permit finding out the occurrence of "identifying and tagging potentially relevant matches" in the text.

Approximate searching has traditionally operated at the character level, where it aims at recovering the correct *syntax* from typing or spelling mistakes, errors coming from optical character recognition software, misspelling of foreign names, and so on. Approximate searching at the word level, on the other hand, aims at recovering the correct *semantics* from concepts that are written with a different wording. This is quite usual in most languages and is a common factor that prevents finding the relevant documents.

This kind of search is very difficult for a sequential algorithm. Some indexed schemes permit proximity searching by operating on the list of exact word positions, but this is all. In the scheme described above, this is simple to program, elegant and extremely efficient (more than on characters). This is an exclusive feature of this compression method that opens new possibilities aimed at recovering the intended semantics, rather than the syntax, of the query. Such capability may improve the retrieval effectiveness of IR systems.

4.   Compression Methods for Inverted Indexes

An IR system normally uses an inverted index to quickly find the occurrences of the words in the text. Until now we have only considered text compression, but the index can be compressed as well. An attractive property of word-based Huffman text compression is that it integrates very well with an inverted index [35]. Since the table of Huffman symbols is precisely the vocabulary of the text, the data structures of the compressor and the index can be integrated, which reduces space and I/O overhead. At search time, the inverted index searches the patterns in the vocabulary; while if a sequential scan is necessary the online algorithm also searches the pattern in the vocabulary. Both processes can therefore be merged. We now show how text and index compression can be combined.

Three different types of inverted indices can be identified. The first one, called "full inverted index", stores the exact positions of each word in the text. All the query processing can be done using the lists and the access to the text is not necessary at all. In this case, the text can be compressed with any method, since it will only be decompressed to be presented to the user.

The second type is the "inverted file", which stores the documents where each word appears. For single word queries it is not necessary to access the text, since if a word appears in a document the whole document is retrieved. However, phrase or proximity queries cannot be solved with the information that the index stores. Two words can be in the same document but they may or may not form a phrase. For these queries the index must search directly the text of those documents where all the relevant words appear. If the text is to be compressed, an efficient compression scheme like that explained in previous sections must be used to permit fast online searching.

The third type, called "block addressing index", is presented in detail in the next section.

4.1   Block Addressing Index

Block addressing was first proposed in a system called *Glimpse* [25]. It divides the text in blocks of fixed size, which may span many documents, be part of a document or overlap with document boundaries. The index stores only the blocks where each word appears. Space is saved because there are less blocks than text positions (and hence the pointers are shorter), and also because all the occurrences of a given

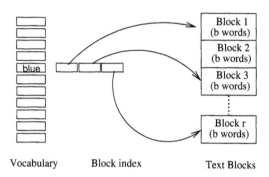

FIG. 5. A block addressing index.

word in a single text block are referenced only once. Any query must be solved using online searching because it is not known in which documents of the block the word appears. The index is used just as a device to filter out some blocks of the collection that cannot contain a match. This type of filter also needs efficiently searchable compression techniques if the text is to be kept compressed. Figure 5 illustrates a block addressing index with r blocks of b words each (i.e., $n = rb$). The figure shows the entries in the block index for the word "blue", which has occurred in the blocks 1, 3 and r.

Searching in a block addressing index is similar to searching in a full inverted index. The pattern is searched in the vocabulary and a list of blocks where the pattern appears is retrieved. However, to obtain the exact pattern positions in the text, a sequential search over the qualifying blocks becomes necessary. The index is therefore used as a filter to avoid a sequential search over some blocks, while the others need to be checked. Hence, the reduction in space requirements is obtained at the expense of higher search costs.

At this point the reader may wonder what is the advantage of pointing to artificial blocks instead of pointing to documents or files, this way following the natural divisions of the text collection. If we consider the case of simple queries (say, one word), where we are required to return only the list of matching documents, then pointing to documents is a very adequate choice. Moreover, as shown in [5], it may reduce space requirements with respect to using blocks of fixed size. Also, if we use blocks of fixed size and pack many short documents in a logical block, we will have to traverse the matching blocks (even for these simple queries) to determine which documents inside the block actually matched.

However, consider the case where we are required to deliver the exact positions which match a pattern. In this case we need to sequentially traverse the qualifying blocks or documents to find the exact positions. Moreover, in some important types of queries such as phrases or proximity queries, the index can only tell that two words appear in the same block, and we need to traverse it in order to determine if they form a phrase.

In this case, pointing to documents of different sizes is not a good idea because larger documents are searched with higher probability and searching them costs more. In fact, the expected cost of the search is directly related to the variance in the size of the pointed documents. This suggests that if the documents have different sizes it may be a good idea to (logically) partition large documents into blocks and to put small documents together, such that blocks of the same size are used.

Block addressing was analyzed in [5], where an important result is analytically proved and experimentally verified: a block addressing index may yield sub-linear space overhead and at the same time sub-linear query time. Traditional inverted indexes pointing to words or documents achieve only the second goal. It is shown in [5] that in order to obtain a space overhead of $\Theta(n^\gamma)$, it is necessary to set $b = \Theta(n^{(1-\gamma)/(1-\beta)})$, in which case the query time obtained is $O(n^\beta + n^{1-\beta+\alpha}b)$. In the formula, α is related to the query complexity: $O(n^\alpha)$ vocabulary words match the query, where $\alpha = 0$ for exact queries and $0 < \alpha < \beta$ for complex queries. The time complexity is sub-linear for $\gamma > 1 - (1 - \beta)(\beta - \alpha)$. In practice, $O(n^{0.85})$ space and query time can be obtained for exact queries.

Of course there is not an "optimal" block size but a space-time tradeoff related to b. The case $b = O(1)$ corresponds to full inverted indexes, whose space requirements are $O(n)$ and their time for a single word query is $O(n^\beta + n^{1-\beta+\alpha})$ (about $O(n^{0.5})$ for exact searching). The other extreme, $b = \Omega(n)$, means that just the vocabulary is stored, needing $O(n^\beta)$ (about $O(n^{0.5})$) space and $O(n)$ search time.

4.2   Combining Inverted Indexes and Index Compression

We show in this section how to compress inverted indexes in order to achieve significant space reduction and also allow fast access to the inverted lists. We also describe in this section a simple technique to improve the compression when using block addressing. The idea is to avoid storing the lists of words that appear in almost all the text blocks, therefore reducing the size of the index and the amount of processing in queries.

Any of the three schemes (full inverted index, inverted file, or block addressing index) can be combined with index compression. The size of an inverted index can be reduced by compressing the occurrence lists [45]. Because the list of occurrences within the inverted list is in ascending order, it can also be considered as a sequence of *gaps* between positions (be them text positions, document numbers, or block numbers). Since processing is usually done sequentially starting from the beginning of the list, the original positions can always be recomputed through sums of the gaps.

By observing that these gaps are small for frequent words and large for infrequent words, compression can be obtained by encoding small values with shorter codes. Moreover, the lists may be built already in compressed form, which in practice expands the capacity of the main memory. This improves index construction times because the critical feature in this process is the amount of main memory available. In practice, text compression plus compressed index construction can be carried out faster than just index construction on uncompressed text.

The type of index chosen influences the degree of compression that can be obtained. The more fine-grained the addressing resolution of the occurrence lists (i.e., from pointing to blocks of text to pointing to exact positions), the less compression can be achieved. This occurs because the *gaps* between consecutive numbers of the occurrence lists are larger if the addressing is finer-grained. Therefore, the reduction in space from a finer-grained to a coarser-grained is more noticeable if index compression is incorporated into the system.

Comprehensive works showing how to compress inverted indexes can be found on the literature [24,28,45] and block addressing is just a type of inverted index. All these previous works are therefore useful here. The techniques used to compress inverted indexes can be classified in parameterized and non-parameterized. Parameterized techniques, such as *Golomb* codes [14], produce different outputs depending on their parameters, so that one can adjust the coding scheme to the characteristics of the input to compress. Non-parameterized coding schemes do not need any information about the elements to be coded, so their output is fixed for each input. When using parameterized coding, the necessity of previous knowledge about the input requires two passes on the list of symbols to be coded, which can be a drawback if we are interested in good performance (in particular, the inability to generate the inverted list directly in compressed form may translate into higher I/O at indexing time). These two passes could be merged with the two passes that we need to obtain an approximation of the parameters, but decompression would be slower anyway. Further, the best parameterized coding methods produce just slight better compression ratios when compared against the best non-parameterized methods.

Our main focus when building block addressing indexes is to improve the performance. Therefore we use a non-parameterized scheme in this work. Previous studies have already shown the best non-parameterized methods that can be used in inverted index compression [28,45]. We present here four important concepts: the gaps, Unary coding, Elias-γ coding, and Elias-δ coding.

Gaps: The block numbers are assigned incrementally during the parsing of the text, the pointers in each inverted list are in ascending order. Each non-initial pointer can then be substituted by the difference (or *gap*) from the previous number of the list. Since processing is usually done sequentially starting from the beginning of the list, the original block numbers can always be recomputed through sums of

TABLE IV
SAMPLE CODES FOR INTEGERS

Integer x	Unary	Elias-γ	Elias-δ
1	0	0	0
2	10	100	1000
3	110	101	1001
4	1110	11000	10100
5	11110	11001	10101
6	111110	11010	10110
7	1111110	11011	10111
8	11111110	1110000	11000000
9	111111110	1110001	11000001
10	1111111110	1110010	11000010

the gaps. The lists are now composed by smaller integers and we can obtain better compression using an encoding that represents shorter values in fewer bits.

Unary coding: A simple scheme codes an integer x in $(x - 1)$ one-bits followed by a zero-bit and therefore is called *Unary code*. The unary codes for numbers 1 to 10 are shown in Table IV.

Elias-γ coding: Elias [10] studied other variable-length encodings for integers. Elias-γ code represents an integer x by the concatenation of two parts, a unary code for $1 + \lfloor \log x \rfloor$ followed by a code of $\lfloor \log x \rfloor$ bits corresponding to $x - 2^{\lfloor \log x \rfloor}$ in binary. The total code length is thus $1 + 2\lfloor \log x \rfloor$. Some examples are presented in Table IV.

Elias-δ coding: The other coding scheme introduced by Elias is the δ code, in which the prefix indicating the number of bits in the second part is coded in Elias-γ code rather than unary. The Elias-δ code for an integer x requires $1 + 2\lfloor \log \log 2x \rfloor + \lfloor \log x \rfloor$ bits. As Table IV shows, for small values of x, Elias-γ codes are shorter than Elias-δ codes, but this situation is reversed as x grows. We will present experiments using both methods to compress the index in this work.

In particular, these techniques can be combined with methods that allow direct access to the list at periodic intervals [45], which permits speeding up phrase and conjunctive queries between very long and very short lists. We do not use these techniques in the present work.

4.3 Improving the Index Compression

The techniques presented in the previous section were developed to compress inverted files or full inverted indexes. Special features of the block addressing indexes can be used to improve the compression without significant changes in the performance of the system.

In blocking addressing, many words can appear in more than half of the blocks. This phenomenon is not common in full inverted indexes or inverted files, but can occur frequently in block addressing indexes when large block sizes are used. In these cases, a simple idea to improve the index compression is to represent the list of non-occurrences of these more frequent words. That is, if a word occurs in more than half of the blocks then we store the block numbers where it does *not* occur. We will call these lists *complemented lists.*

An alternative form to compress those words would be to use run length compression on the gaps (which would be 1 at least half of the times). The economy of space is very similar because the length of each run of "ones" is precisely the value of the gap in the complemented list minus 1. For instance, if there are 100 blocks and the word appears in all but the 32nd and 61st, then its list of gaps is $[1, 1, \ldots, 1, 2, 1, 1, \ldots, 1, 2, 1, \ldots, 1]$. Run length compression on the list of gaps yields $\langle 1, 31 \rangle \langle 2, 1 \rangle \langle 1, 28 \rangle \langle 2, 1 \rangle \langle 1, 39 \rangle$, in the format $\langle number, repetitions \rangle$. On the other hand, the complemented list is $[32, 61]$, and the list of gaps is $[32, 29]$. Note that run length compression needs to store more information than that of the gaps in the complemented list.

A second advantage is that complemented lists can be operated upon efficiently without converting them into normal lists. We describe later how to perform Boolean operations among normal and complemented lists in time proportional to their normal or complemented representations. Depending on the operation, the result is left in normal or complemented form.

In inverted indexes it is common to not index the stopwords to save space. Since stopwords will most probably appear in all the blocks, we can index them at almost zero cost. Moreover, we need to keep them in the vocabulary for decompression purposes.

4.4 In-Memory Bucket Compression

In other compressed inverted schemes [45] the generation of the inverted list proceeds in a first step and their compression in a second step. This is not only because the compression is parametric in some cases, but also because of the way in which the lists are generated. In a first step, the text is traversed and the occurrences are generated in text order. Later, the occurrences are sorted by the word they represent. Therefore, only after this final sorting the lists are separated by words and the gaps can be generated in order to compress the lists.

As we are using a non-parameterized coding scheme, we do not need global information about the list in order to compress it. An additional decision that allows the lists to be generated in memory already in their compressed form is that we do not generate the occurrences in text order and later sort them, but we generate them already separated by word. Since we already know the vocabulary we store a separate list of occurrences of each word and each new text occurrence is added at the end of the occurrence list of the corresponding word. Therefore, the gaps are computed and stored in compressed form on the fly.

The technique of generating the occurrences in unsorted form first is sometimes preferred because of space reasons: storing a list of occurrences for each word may be a waste of space because either too many pointers have to be stored or too much empty space has to be preallocated. This is especially important because, by Zipf's Law, many words have very few occurrences. Zipf's law states that, if we order the words of a natural language text in descending order of probability then the probability of the first word is i times the probability of the ith word, for every i. Storing separate lists, on the other hand, have the advantage of avoiding the final sort, which saves time. When combining this with compression, another advantage for separate lists appears: the lists can be generated in compressed form and therefore they take less space. This improved space usage translates also into better indexing time because more text can be indexed in memory without resorting to disk. Other indexing schemes that avoid sorting the occurrences are presented in [17,27,15].

We propose now an efficient approach to store the lists of occurrences of each word that tries to adapt to the typical word frequencies. The idea is to represent the list of occurrences of each word by using a linked list where each node is a bucket of occurrences. These buckets are composed by a pointer to the next bucket of the term and by a stream of bits that represents a portion of the compressed list of this term. The next bucket pointed has the same structure and continues the stream of bits.

An important decision in this scheme is the size of the buckets. They should be large enough to compensate the extra space used by the pointer to the next bucket, and should be small enough to reduce the extra memory lost with the empty spaces on the last bucket of each term. After some experiments, we have chosen to use 8 bytes for the first bucket of each term and 16 byte buckets for the remaining buckets of each term. The reason to use a smaller first bucket is that many terms can occur just once on the whole collection. So, using a smaller first bucket saves memory in these terms.

Figure 6 shows an example with the list of the occurrences of a term t that has appeared at the blocks $[1, 5, 10, 12, 14, 20, 30]$. Using the coding scheme shown in the last section, this list is converted in the list of *gaps* $[1, 4, 5, 2, 2, 6, 10]$. Using the Elias-γ coding scheme the list of *gaps* is converted into the stream of bits

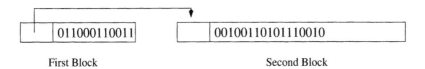

First Block   Second Block

FIG. 6. Linked list of buckets used with the in-memory compression scheme.

0110001100110010011010110010. Using a first bucket size of 32 bits and the remaining buckets with 64 bits, the buckets for this term are as shown in Fig. 6. The empty space in the two buckets is the space to represent the pointer to the next bucket in the linked list. This pointer can be represented in $\lceil \log b \rceil$ bits, where b is the number of buckets that can fit in the memory buffer. In the example of Fig. 6, these pointers were represented in 20 bits, allowing up to 2^{20} buckets in the main memory.

This in-memory bucket compression technique allows us to index large texts by making just one pass on the text to generate the index. It is general and can be applied in the construction of any kind of inverted index, such as in full inversion and inverted files. If the whole index cannot be placed in memory, we need to dump the partial list to disk and make a second pass to merge the dumps as described in [28].

4.5   Compressing Frequencies

The research presented in [38] shows that for ranked queries it may be more efficient to store document numbers sorted by frequency rather than by document number. The compression techniques have to be adapted to this new problem. For instance, since the frequencies are decreasing, gaps between frequencies can be coded. Normally, in the list of each word there are a few documents with high frequencies and many with low frequencies. This information can be used to efficiently compress the frequencies. Moreover, all the documents with the same frequency can be stored in increasing document number, so gaps between documents can be used.

5.   Integrated Approaches for IR Systems

We present in this section a combined design for block addressing index into a single approach, which includes text compression, block addressing and index compression. Figure 7 illustrates a block addressing structure, which has the following components:

Canonical Huffman Tree: the canonical Huffman tree is a small extra structure which is used to decode the text and to perform the sequential search on the blocks.

Vocabulary: the vocabulary of the collection is useful both as the symbol table of the Huffman coding in use and as the inverted index vocabulary.

Compressed Block Index: for each vocabulary word we have a list of the blocks where the word appears. The list is in increasing block number and is compressed using the techniques of Section 4. Despite that separators are kept in the vocabulary for decompression purposes, there are no list of occurrences for them in the index. Another common choice in inverted indexes is to filter the words using

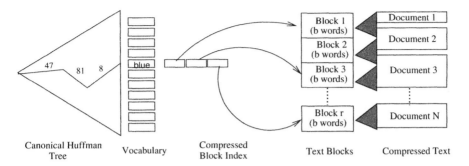

FIG. 7. The structure of our index.

techniques such as map letters to lowercase and apply stemming [6]. This choice may be done by not constructing lists of occurrences for these lists, as it is done with the separators. Figure 7 presents the block list for the word "blue".

Text Blocks: the text blocks form a logical layer over the natural document structure of the collection, so that the documents are not physically split or concatenated. This is implemented as a list of the documents of the collection, so that the position of a document in that list is a sort of identifier. We also keep a list of the r blocks used. All the blocks have the same number of words and span a continuous range in the list of document identifiers, not necessarily matching the document boundaries. For each block we store the identifier of the last document that it spans in the list, and the offset of the last byte in that document that belongs to the block.

Compressed Text: each original document in the collection is compressed using a single canonical Huffman coding for the whole collection.

The space of this index is analyzed in [5], where it is shown that the vocabulary takes $O(n^\beta)$ space and the occurrences take $O(rb^\beta)$ space, since, by Heaps' Law, each new block has $O(b^\beta)$ different words, and one reference for each of them exists in the lists of occurrences. The lists of blocks and documents are negligible in size. On the other hand, the occurrences are compressed now, which reduces their space by a factor independent of n (and therefore the space is still $O(rb^\beta)$). As shown in [5], the β value for small blocks is larger than its asymptotic value, but it converges very close to it for relatively small blocks.

5.1   Index Construction

The index can be efficiently built if we notice that many processes can be merged in a single pass over the text. The Huffman compression needs two passes over the text, and in the same two passes we are able to build the index. The index construction process has three steps.

Step 1

The first step corresponds to finding all the global information of interest. This step has the following main components: determine the set of documents to index and the number of blocks to use; compute the vocabulary of the whole collection and the frequencies of each word; and determine which lists will be represented by their complement. This requires a simple linear pass over the text, and the memory required is that of storing the vocabulary as the list of documents can be output to disk as they are found. At the end of this pass, we have computed the list of documents and the vocabulary of the text with its frequencies. At the end we also know the total number of words in the collection and therefore, we can define the number of blocks r.

Next, we need to collect two different frequency parameters. The first one is the number of times that each word occurs and the second one is the number of blocks in which each word occurs. The first one is needed by the Huffman algorithm, while the second one is used to determine whether the list of the word will be stored in simple or complemented form. These statistics are also useful for relevance ranking. While the number of times that a word occurs is easy to compute, the number of blocks requires a little care: we store for each word the last block where it appeared and the number of blocks where it already appeared. We know which is the current block because we increment it each time b new words are read. Hence, for each occurrence of a word we check whether it already appeared in the current block or not. In the second case, we increment the number of blocks where it appeared and update the last block where the word was seen.

Finally, before moving to the next step we run the Huffman algorithm on the vocabulary and build the canonical Huffman tree (see Section 2.1). We replace the frequency information of each vocabulary word by the compressed code it has been assigned. The tree itself can immediately be swapped out to disk, although it is very small anyway. On the other hand, any data structure used to build the vocabulary, i.e., to efficiently find the words, should be kept in memory as it will be of help in the second step. The vocabulary can be stored in memory by using a hash table or a trie in order to provide $O(1)$ average or worst-case access time, respectively.

Step 2

The second step does the heavier part. Each text document of the collection is compressed, in the order dictated by the list of documents. Each word or separator of the text is searched in the vocabulary and its Huffman code is output to the compressed document. When we finish with a document, the compressed version replaces the original one.

At the same time, we construct the lists of occurrences. Each time a word is found and we output its compressed code, we add an entry to its list of occurrences, which is represented as shown in Section 4.4. Of course the entry is not added if it has already appeared in that block, so we store for each word the last block it appeared in. Recall also that the inverse process is done for words whose occurrence list is to be stored in complemented form: if a word appears in a block and the previous block it appeared is neither the current nor the previous one, then we add to its list all the block interval between the current block and its last occurrence (all the last non occurrences of its word).

The current block number is incremented each time b new words are processed. At this time, we add a new entry to the list of blocks pointing to the current document being processed and store the number of bytes already written in the compressed version of the document. This list can be sent to disk as it is generated and will be used to map a block number to the physical position of the block in the collection.

At the end, the list of occurrences is sent to disk in its compressed form. Separately, we save the vocabulary on disk with pointers to the place where the list of occurrences of each word starts in the document of the occurrences.

The problem with the above scheme is that, despite that the index needs little space, we may not be able to store all the occurrence lists in memory at construction time. This is the only problematic structure, as the rest either is small enough or it can be buffered. The occurrences, on the other hand, cannot be sent to disk as they are generated because all the final entries of the first list should come before those of the second list. The solution chosen is that each time the memory is filled we store all the occurrences computed up to now on disk and free their space in memory, starting again with an empty list.

Step 3

At the end of Step 2, we will have a set of partial occurrence lists which have to be merged in the order given by the words they correspond to. All the lists of each word are concatenated in the order they were generated. So some auxiliary information has to be stored with the partial lists to help identify the word they belong to: a word identifier and the length of the list is enough.

Analysis

Collecting the vocabulary of the text can be done in linear time provided adequate data structures are used (e.g., a trie of the words to guarantee worst case linear time or a hash table for average linear time). Huffman construction can be done in linear expected time if the words follow some statistical rules widely accepted in text retrieval, as shown in [34]. The other processes of the first step are also of linear time and negligible in practice.

The second step is also linear if we use the discussed data structures to find the text words in the vocabulary. The compressed codes output total less space than the text itself (so they take also linear time) and adding the block numbers to the end of the lists of occurrences is also constant time per text word.

What is not linear is the third step that merges the lists. If we have $O(M)$ memory available for index construction, then $O(n/M)$ partial occurrence lists will be generated and will have to be merged. By using heapsort, the total merge takes $O(n \log(n/M))$ time. This third step can be avoided by resorting to virtual memory, but writing partial lists to disk and merging them is much faster in practice. It is interesting to see that the merge phase will commonly not be needed because we use in-memory compression and block indexes tend to be small. For example, using a machine with 100 megabytes of RAM and a 500 words block length (a small block size), we are able to index a collection size close to 1 gigabytes without needing Step 3.

5.2 Query Searching

We describe now the search process using the index presented in the previous section, which can be divided in three steps. We first explain the search of a single element and then show how to search phrases.

Step 1

The first step of the search is to find the query pattern in the vocabulary, be it a single word, a regular expression, exactly or allowing errors. The data structures used at indexing time can be kept to speed up this search, or we can resort to sequential or binary search to save space. Note, however, that the words cannot be simultaneously sorted alphabetically and in the order required by the canonical Huffman tree, so at least an extra indirection array is required. This is done exactly as explained in Section 3. At the end, we have a list of words that match the query, and we have built the binary masks for each of them (in case of phrase searching).

Step 2

This is where we take advantage of the block information, which cannot be done in simple sequential searching. The query pattern has been matched to a set of vocabulary words (just one if we search for a single word). We take the list of blocks where each of the words occur and merge all them into a single list, which is ordered by increasing block number. None of the blocks excluded from this final list can contain an occurrence of the query element.

Since the lists to merge are in compressed form we decompress them on the fly at the same time we merge them. For each new list element to read, we decode the bits of the compressed representation of the gap and add that gap to the last element of the list that has already been processed.

The other technique we used to reduce the size of the lists is the complementation of long lists. The operation on complemented lists can be done very fast, in time proportional to the complemented list. If two complemented lists ℓ_1^c and ℓ_2^c have to be merged, the complemented result is $(\ell_1 \cup \ell_2)^c = \ell_1^c \cap \ell_2^c$, i.e., we intersect their complements and have the complement of the result. Similarly, if they have to be intersected we apply $(\ell_1 \cap \ell_2)^c = \ell_1^c \cup \ell_2^c$. If ℓ_1 is complemented and ℓ_2 is not, then we proceed by set difference: $(\ell_1 \cup \ell_2)^c = \ell_1^c - \ell_2$ and $\ell_1 \cap \ell_2 = \ell_2 - \ell_1^c$.

Step 3

The final step is the sequential search on the blocks, to find the exact documents and positions where the query occurs. Only the blocks that are mentioned in the list of occurrences of the matched words need to be searched. The block structure is used to determine which portions of which documents are to be sequentially traversed.

The search algorithm is exactly the same as for sequential searching without index. However, we have a new choice with respect to the multi-pattern Boyer-Moore search. In the sequential setup, all the compressed codes of the matching words are simultaneously searched, since there is no information of where each different word appears. It is clear that the search performance degrades as the number of patterns to search grows.

With the index we have more information. We know in which block each vocabulary word matched. Imagine that the query matched words w_1 and w_2. While w_1 appears in blocks b_1 and b_2, w_2 appears in blocks b_2 and b_3. There is no need to search w_2 in b_1 or w_1 in b_3. On the other hand, b_2 has to be searched for both words. We can therefore make a different (and hopefully faster) search in each text block. The price is that we need a different preprocessing for each block, which could be counterproductive if the blocks are very small. This idea is mentioned in [5], but not tested.

Phrase search

A query may not be just a pattern but a sequence of patterns, each one being a word, a regular expression, etc. The main idea to search phrases is to take the *intersection* of the occurrence lists of the involved blocks. This is because all the elements of the phrase must appear in the same block (we consider block boundaries shortly). We proceed as before with each pattern of the phrase: the list of occurrences of each pattern is obtained by making the union of all the list of the vocabulary words that match the pattern. Once we have the list for each pattern of the phrase, we intersect all the lists, and perform the sequential search only on the blocks where all the patterns appear at the same time. Unlike the case of simple elements, we may search blocks that have no occurrences of the complete query.

A natural question at this point is how can we avoid losing phrases that lie at block boundaries, since the intersection method will fail. This can be solved by letting consecutive blocks *overlap* in a few words. At indexing time we determine that we will allow searching phrases of at most ℓ words. Therefore, if a block ends at the ith word of a document, the next one does not start at word $i + 1$ but at $i + 2 - \ell$. This causes a very small overhead and solves elegantly the problem, since every phrase of ℓ words or less appears completely inside a block. The main problem is that we limit at indexing time the longest phrase that can be searched. For words longer than ℓ we can modify the list intersection process, so that two contiguous blocks are verified if the first words of a phrase appears in the first block and the last words in the second block. This, however, is much more expensive.

Another solution is to slightly relax the rule that the blocks are exactly b words long and move block boundaries a little to make them match with the end of a sentence (i.e., a separator containing a period). In this case no phrase can cross the block boundaries and there is no need to make blocks overlap or to limit beforehand the length ℓ of the phrases to search. On the other hand, parsing the text is a bit more complicated.

Even more sophisticated searching, such as proximity search, can be accommodated in a very similar way. Proximity search corresponds to a sequence of ℓ words that must appear in correct order in an interval of ℓ' text words. Only the sequential searching changes, and the block boundaries are made overlap in $\ell' - 1$ words. Techniques to search diverse sophisticated patterns can be found in [33].

Analysis

We now analyze the performance of the search process. The first step (vocabulary search) has already been analyzed in Section 3: a phrase of j elements takes $O(jn^\beta)$ or $O(jkn^\beta)$ time depending on the complexity of the search.

The second step is the merging and/or intersection of lists. First consider one-word queries, which is analyzed in [5]. Since each word has an occurrence list of $O(n^{1-\beta})$ average length, the cost to merge the lists is $O(n^{1-\beta+\alpha} \log n)$. The cost to intersect the lists of a phrase of j such patterns is $O(jn^{1-\beta+\alpha} \log n)$, because since the lists are stored in compressed form we need to traverse all of them. Recall, however, that very long lists are compressed by representing their complement and these representations can be efficiently handled.

However, the cost of the first and second steps is negligible compared to that of the third step. Since we know already the search cost on a text of a given size, what remains to be determined is the percentage of text that has to be traversed when a block index is used. First we consider one-word patterns. Since a block of b words has $O(b^\beta)$ different words, and $O(n^\alpha)$ random words out of $O(n^\beta)$ vocabulary words are selected by the search, the probability that the block gets a selected word and hence is searched is $O(b^\beta n^{\alpha-\beta})$. Since there are r blocks and the cost to traverse them is $O(b)$, we have that the total search cost is $O(brb^\beta n^{\alpha-\beta}) = O(n^{1-\beta+\alpha}b^\beta)$. When b tends to 1 the cost approaches that of full inverted files [2].

However, phrase searching is much better. Using Zipf's Law, the shortest list among 2 or more random words has constant length, as shown in [2]. This means that on average we will search $O(1)$ blocks for phrase searching, which is $O(b)$ time. The cost to intersect the lists is similar to that of the union, because they are sequentially processed.

To summarize, the total search cost is $O(n^\beta + n^{1-\beta+\alpha}b^\beta)$ for single patterns and $O(n^\beta + n^{1-\beta+\alpha} + b)$ for phrases. We have considered k and j as constants to simplify the final complexity.

6. Updating the Text Collection

An important issue regarding text databases is how to update the index when changes occur. Inverted indices normally handle those modifications by building differential inverted indices on the new or modified texts and then merging periodically the main and the differential index. When using compression, however, a new problem appears because the *frequencies* of the words change too, and therefore the current assignment of compressed codes to them may not be optimal anymore. Even worse, new words may appear which have no compressed code. The naive solution of recompressing the whole database according to the new frequencies is too expensive, and the problem of finding the cheapest modification to the current Huffman tree has not been yet solved.

Fortunately, simple heuristics work well. At construction time, a special empty word with frequency zero is added to the vocabulary. The code that this empty word receives is called the *escape* code and is used to signal new words that appear. When new text is added, the existing words use their current code, and new words are codified as the escape code followed by the new words in plain form. Only at long periods the database is recompressed to recover optimality. If the text already compressed is reasonably large, the current code assignments are likely to remain optimal, and the number of new words added pose negligible overheads. For instance, experiments have shown a degradation of only 1% in the compression ratio after adding 190 megabytes to a text database of 10 megabytes. The search algorithms have also to be adapted if these new words are to be searched.

7. Final Remarks

7.1 Trends and Research Issues

For effective operation in an IR environment a compression method should satisfy the following requirements: good compression ratio, fast coding, fast decoding, and direct searching without the need to decompress the text. A good compression ratio saves space in secondary storage and reduces communication costs. Fast coding reduces processing overhead due to the introduction of compression into the system. Sometimes, fast decoding is more important than fast coding, as it happens in documentation systems in which a document is compressed once and decompressed many times from disk. Fast random access allows efficient processing of multiple queries submitted by the users of the information system. Fast sequential search reduces query times in many types of indices.

We have shown compression techniques that satisfy all these goals. The compressed text *plus* a compressed inverted index built on it take no more than 40% of the original text size *without* any index. Index construction, *including* the text compression, proceeds *faster* than the indexing of the uncompressed text, and needs less space. Any search scheme, be it based on the index, on sequential searching, or on a combination of both, proceeds *faster* than on the uncompressed text and allows more flexible searching. Moreover, the text can be kept compressed *during all times*, being decompressed only to be displayed to the user. Such combination of features is unbeaten in efficiency and flexibility, and permits transparent integration into not only traditional text databases but also, for example, Web servers and compressed file systems, with the additional benefit of providing searchability [35,50].

The most adequate indexing technique in practice is the inverted file. The main trends in indexing and searching textual databases are influenced by the following aspects. Searching is becoming more complex. As textual databases grow and become error-prone, enhanced query facilities are required, such as allowing errors in the text. At the same time, text collections are becoming huge, thus imposing more demanding requirements at all levels. With the speed of processors and the relative slowness of disks, it is better to keep the texts compressed, because reading less text from disk and decompressing it in main memory pays off. Also, techniques such as block addressing trade space for processor time. Considering the aspects just mentioned we might say that compression is becoming a very important issue for next generation text retrieval systems.

7.2 Bibliographic Discussion

Regarding text compression, several books are available. Most of the topics discussed here are covered in more detail by Witten, Moffat and Bell [45]. They also present implementations of text compression methods, such as Huffman and arithmetic coding. Bell, Cleary and Witten [7] cover statistical and dictionary methods, laying particular stress on adaptive methods as well as theoretical aspects of compression, with estimates on the entropy of several natural languages. Storer [41] covers the main compression techniques, with emphasis on dictionary methods. Moffat and Turpin [29] covers compression and coding algorithms.

Huffman coding was originally presented in [20]. Adaptive versions of Huffman coding appear in [13,21,42]. Word-based compression is considered in [9,26,19,8]. Canonical codes were first presented in [40]. Many properties of the canonical codes are mentioned in [18]. Byte Huffman coding was proposed in [32]. Sequential searching on byte Huffman compressed text is described in [32,31,50].

Sequential searching on Ziv–Lempel compressed data is presented in [12,1]. More recently, implementations of sequential searching on Ziv–Lempel compressed text are presented in [36].

A variety of compression methods for inverted lists are studied in [30]. The most effective compression methods for inverted lists are based on the sequence of gaps between document numbers, as considered in [8] and in [28]. Their results are based on run-length encodings proposed by Elias [10] and Golomb [14]. A comprehensive study of inverted file compression can be found in [45]. More recently Vo and Moffat [43] have presented algorithms to process the index with no need to fully decode the compressed index.

A detailed explanation of a full inverted index and its construction and querying can be found in [2]. This work also includes an analysis of the algorithms on inverted lists that take into consideration the distribution of words in natural language texts. An in-place construction of inverted files is described in [28].

The idea of block addressing inverted indexes was first presented in [25]. This work presented a system called Glimpse, which also first explored the idea of performing complex pattern matching using the vocabulary of the index. Block addressing indexes are analyzed in [5], where some performance improvements are proposed. One variant for block addressing that indexes sequences instead of words has been implemented in a system called Grampse, described in [23].

REFERENCES

[1] Amir A., Benson G., Farach M., "Let sleeping files lie: pattern matching in z-compressed files", *Journal of Computer and Systems Sciences* **52** (2) (1996) 299–307.

[2] Araújo M.D., Navarro G., Ziviani N., "Large text searching allowing errors", in: Baeza-Yates R. (Ed.), *Proc. of the 4th South American Workshop on String Processing, Carleton University Press International Informatics Series*, Vol. 8, 1997, pp. 2–20.

[3] Baeza-Yates R., Gonnet G., "A new approach to text searching", *Comm. of the ACM* **35** (10) (1992) 74–82.

[4] Baeza-Yates R., Navarro G., "Faster approximate string matching", *Algorithmica* **23** (2) (1999) 127–158.

[5] Baeza-Yates R., Navarro G., "Block-addressing indices for approximate text retrieval", *Journal of the American Society for Information Science (JASIS)* **51** (1) (2000) 69–82.

[6] Baeza-Yates R., Ribeiro-Neto B., *Modern Information Retrieval*, Addison-Wesley, 1999.

[7] Bell T., Cleary J., Witten I., *Text Compression*, Prentice Hall, New Jersey, 1990.

[8] Bell T.C., Moffat A., Nevill-Manning C., Witten I.H., Zobel J., "Data compression in full-text retrieval systems", *Journal of the American Society for Information Science* **44** (1993) 508–531.

[9] Bentley J., Sleator D., Tarjan R., Wei V., "A locally adaptive data compression scheme", *Communications of the ACM* **29** (1986) 320–330.

[10] Elias P., "Universal codeword sets and representations of the integers", *IEEE Transactions on Information Theory* **IT-21** (1975) 194–203.

[11] Google Search Engine, http://www.google.com.

[12] Farach M., Thorup M., "String matching in Lempel–Ziv compressed strings", in: *Proc. 27th ACM Annual Symposium on the Theory of Computing*, 1995, pp. 703–712.

[13] Gallager R.G., "Variations on a theme by Huffman", *IEEE Transactions on Information Theory* **24** (1978) 668–674.

[14] Golomb S.W., "Run-length encodings", *IEEE Transactions on Information Theory* **IT-12** (3) (1966) 399–401.

[15] Harman D., Fox E., Baeza-Yates R., Lee W., *Inverted Files*, Prentice-Hall, 1992, pp. 28–43.

[16] Harman D.K., "Overview of the third text retrieval conference", in: *Proc. Third Text REtrieval Conference (TREC-3)*, Gaithersburg, Maryland, 1995, pp. 1–19. National Institute of Standards and Technology Special Publication.

[17] Hawking D., "Scalable text retrieval for large digital libraries", in: Peters C., Thanos C. (Eds.), *Proc. of the 1st European Conference on Digital Libraries, Pisa, Italy, September 1997*, in: *Lecture Notes in Computer Science*, Vol. 1234, Springer-Verlag, 1997, pp. 127–146.

[18] Hirschberg D.S., Lelewer D.A., "Efficient decoding of prefix codes", *Communications of the ACM* **33** (4) (1990).

[19] Horspool R.N., Cormack G.V., "Constructing word-based text compression algorithms", in: *Proc. of IEEE Second Data Compression Conference*, 1992, pp. 62–81.

[20] Huffman D., "A method for the construction of minimum-redundancy codes", in: *Proc. of the Institute of Electrical and Radio Engineers*, Vol. 40, 1952, pp. 1090–1101.

[21] Knuth D.E., "Dynamic Huffman coding", *Journal of Algorithms* **6** (1985) 163–180.

[22] Lawrence S., Giles C.L., "Accessibility of information on the web", *Nature* **400** (8) (1999) 107–109.

[23] Lehtinen O., Sutinen E., Tarhio J., "Experiments on block indexing", in: *Proc. of the 3th South American Workshop on String Processing (WSP'96)*, Carleton University Press, 1996, pp. 183–193.

[24] Linoff G., Stanfill C., "Compression of indexes with full positional information in very large text databases", in: *Proc. of the International ACM SIGIR Conference on Research and Development in Information Retrieval (SIGIR'93)*, 1993, pp. 88–95.

[25] Manber U., Wu S., "GLIMPSE: A tool to search through entire file systems", in: *Proc. USENIX Technical Conference*, USENIX Association, Berkeley, CA, USA, 1994, pp. 23–32.

[26] Moffat A., "Word-based text compression", *Software Practice and Experience* **19** (2) (1989) 185–198.

[27] Moffat A., "Economical inversion of large text files", *Computing Systems (USENIX Assoc. Journal)* **5** (2) (1992) 125–139.

[28] Moffat A., Bell T.A.H., "In-situ generation of compressed inverted files", *Journal of the American Society for Information Science* **46** (7) (1995) 537–550.

[29] Moffat A., Turpin A., *Compression and Coding Algorithms*, Kluwer Academic Publishers, 2002.

[30] Moffat A., Zobel J., "Parameterized compression for sparse bitmaps", in: *Proc. of the ACM-SIGIR International Conference on Research and Development in Information Retrieval*, 1992, pp. 274–285.

[31] Moura E., Navarro G., Ziviani N., Baeza-Yates R., "Direct pattern matching on compressed text", in: *Proc. of the 5th Symposium on String Processing and Information Retrieval (SPIRE'98)*, IEEE CS Press, 1998, pp. 90–95. Available at ftp://ftp.dcc.uchile.cl/pub/users/gnavarro/spire98.3.ps.gz.

[32] Moura E., Navarro G., Ziviani N., Baeza-Yates R., "Fast searching on compressed text allowing errors", in: *Proc. of the 21st International ACM SIGIR Conference on Research and Development in Information Retrieval*, 1998, pp. 298–306.

[33] Moura E., Navarro G., Ziviani N., Baeza-Yates R., "Fast and flexible word searching on compressed text", *ACM Transactions on Information Systems* **18** (2) (2000) 113–139.

[34] Moura E.S., Navarro G., Ziviani N., "Linear time sorting of skewed distributions", in: *Proc. 6th String Processing and Information Retrieval Symposium (SPIRE'99)*, Cancun, Mexico, IEEE Computer Society, 1999, pp. 135–140.

[35] Navarro G., Moura E., Neubert M., Ziviani N., Baeza-Yates R., "Adding compression to block addressing inverted indexes", *Information Retrieval* **3** (1) (2000) 49–77.

[36] Navarro G., Raffinot M., "A bit-parallel approach to suffix automata: Fast extended string matching", in: *Proc. of the 9th Symposium on Combinatorial Pattern Matching (CPM'98)*, in: *Lecture Notes in Computer Science*, Vol. 1448, Springer-Verlag, 1998, pp. 14–33.

[37] Patterson D.A., Hennessy J.L., *Computer Architecture: A Quantitative Approach*, 2nd edn., Morgan Kaufmann Publishers, 1995.

[38] Persin M., "Document filtering for fast ranking", in: *Proc. of the 17th International ACM SIGIR Conference on Research and Development in Information Retrieval*, Springer-Verlag, 1994, pp. 339–348.

[39] Rissanen J., Langdon G.G., "Arithmetic coding", *IBM Journal of Research and Development* **23** (1979) 149–162.

[40] Schwartz E.S., Kallick B., "Generating a canonical prefix encoding", *Communications of the ACM* **7** (1964) 166–169.

[41] Storer J.A., *Data Compression: Methods and Theory*, Computer Science Press, 1988.

[42] Vitter J.S., "Algorithm 673: Dynamic Huffman coding", *ACM Transactions on Mathematical Software* **15** (1989) 158–167.

[43] Vo A.N., Moffat A., "Compressed inverted files with reduced decoding overhead", in: *Proc. of the ACM-SIGIR International Conference on Research and Development in Information Retrieval*, 1998, pp. 290–297.

[44] Welch T.A., "A technique for high-performance data compression", *IEEE Computer* **17** (6) (1984) 8–19.

[45] Witten I., Moffat A., Bell T., *Managing Gigabytes*, 2nd edn., Morgan Kaufmann Publishers, 1999.

[46] Witten I.H., Neal R., Cleary J.G., "Arithmetic coding for data compression", *Communications of the ACM* **30** (6) (1987) 520–541.

[47] Wu S., Manber U., "Fast text searching allowing errors", *Comm. of the ACM* **35** (10) (1992) 83–91.

[48] Ziv J., Lempel A., "A universal algorithm for sequential data compression", *IEEE Transactions on Information Theory* **23** (3) (1977) 337–343.

[49] Ziv J., Lempel A., "Compression of individual sequences via variable-rate coding", *IEEE Transactions on Information Theory* **24** (5) (1978) 530–536.

[50] Ziviani N., Moura E., Navarro G., Baeza-Yates R., "Compression: A key for next-generation text retrieval systems", *IEEE Computer* **33** (11) (2000) 37–44.

Are Scripting Languages Any Good?
A Validation of Perl, Python, Rexx,
and Tcl against C, C++, and Java

LUTZ PRECHELT

Fakultät für Informatik
Universität Karlsruhe
76128 Karlsruhe
Germany
prechelt@computer.org
http://wwwipd.ira.uka.de/~prechelt/

Abstract

Four scripting languages are introduced shortly and their theoretical and pur-
ported characteristics are discussed and related to three more conventional programming languages. Then the comparison is extended to an objective empirical
one using 80 implementations of the same set of requirements, created by 74
different programmers. The limitations of the empirical data are laid out and
discussed and then the 80 implementations are compared for several properties,
such as run time, memory consumption, source text length, comment density,
program structure, reliability, and the amount of effort required for writing them.
The results indicate that, for the given programming problem, "scripting languages" (Perl, Python, Rexx, Tcl) are more productive than conventional languages. In terms of run time and memory consumption, they often turn out better than Java and not much worse than C or C++. In general, the differences
between languages tend to be smaller than the typical differences due to different programmers within the same language.

ADVANCES IN COMPUTERS, VOL. 57
ISSN: 0065-2458

205

1. On Scripting Languages

Historically, the state of the programming practice has continually moved towards ever higher-level languages; for instance there is a mainstream that started with machine code and then progressed first to assembler, then to Fortran and Cobol, then to C and Pascal, then to C++, and then to Java.

Whenever the next step on this ladder was about to occur, the new candidate mainstream language was initially accused of not being practical. The accusations always claimed an unacceptable lack of runtime and memory efficiency and sometimes also that the language was too complicated for programmers. However, the following happened in each case: After a while (when compilers and runtime systems had matured, computers had gotten still faster, and programmers had had some time to learn the languages and related design methods and programming styles) it turned out that the runtime and memory efficiency problems were neither as big nor as relevant as had been believed and that the higher language level had rather beneficial effects on programmer efficiency. Consequently, the older mainstream representatives have slowly but surely started to go out of business—at least since the advent of C++.

This chapter attempts to evaluate whether or in what respect scripting languages represent the next step on this ladder and how far they have progressed towards refuting the usual counterarguments. The evaluation will ground in an empirical comparison of 80 separate implementations of the same specification (each written in either of 4 scripting languages or 3 "conventional" languages) and relate the empirical results to claims made by advocates or opponents of each scripting language and to a theoretical analysis of language properties to be plausibly expected.

1.1 What Is a Scripting Language?

What makes a language a scripting language, anyway? And what is the opposite of a scripting language? There are at least two possible perspectives from which these questions can be answered: Either in terms of features of the language or in terms of its purpose and use.

The protagonists of the most successful scripting languages are mostly rather pragmatic folks and do not care much about the answers at all. Larry Wall: "*A script is what you give the actors. A program is what you give the audience.*" When forced to answer, they mostly relate to language features and say

- Scripting languages usually lack an explicit compilation step and perhaps even provide an interactive interpreter dialog mode.
- Scripting languages are a blend of those features that make a programmer productive and attempt to leave out everything else.
- In particular, they tend to have automatic memory management and powerful operations tightly built in (rather than relying on libraries), and
- they tend not to have strong typing rules and access rules that restrict the programmer from doing certain things.

The more philosophical approach to scripting languages proposes a dichotomy between scripting languages (also called systems integration languages or glue languages) on the one hand and systems programming languages on the other. Their difference is claimed first and foremost to be a difference of purpose and any differences in language characteristics to be mere consequences of that. The most prominent representative of this school of thought is John Ousterhout, the creator of Tcl. In [18] he describes

- Scripting languages aren't intended for writing applications from scratch; they are intended primarily for plugging together components (which are usually written in systems programming languages).
- Scripting languages are often used to extend the features of components but they are rarely used for complex algorithms and data structures.
- In order to simplify the task of connecting components, scripting languages tend to be typeless.
- Applications for scripting languages are generally smaller than applications for system programming languages, and the performance of a scripting application tends to be dominated by the performance of the components.

As we will see in the language descriptions below, each of the scripting languages mixes and weighs these ideas rather differently.

However, if we view scripting languages as the potential next step on the ladder of ever higher-level languages described in the introduction, their most striking feature is certainly the by-and-large lack of static typing: Whereas previous languages introduced more and more elaborate mechanisms for statically declaring types, data structures, and access rules to be checked before the program is executed, scripting languages use hardly any type declarations and consequently do type checking only at run time; they also check fewer aspects.

1.2 Language Comparisons: State of the Practice

The scientific and engineering literature provides many comparisons of programming languages—in different ways and with different restrictions:

Some comparisons are purely theoretical discussions of certain language constructs. The many examples range from Dijkstra's famous letter "Go To statement considered harmful" [6] to comprehensive surveys of many languages [4,19]. These are non-quantitative and usually partly speculative. Some such works are more or less pure opinion-pieces. There is also plenty of such discussion about scripting languages, though most of it does not claim to be scientific.

Some comparisons are benchmarks comparing a single implementation of a certain program in either language for expressiveness or resource consumption, etc.; an example is [11]. Such comparisons are useful, but extremely narrow and hence always slightly dubious: Is each of the implementations adequate? Or could it have been done much better in the given language? Furthermore, the programs compared in this manner are sometimes extremely small and simple.

Some are narrow controlled experiments, e.g., [7,15], often focusing on either a single language construct, e.g., [14, p. 227], or a whole notational style, e.g., [14, p. 121], [22].

Some are empirical comparisons based on several and larger programs, e.g., [9]. They discuss for instance defect rates or productivity figures. The problem of these comparisons is lack of homogeneity: Each language is represented by different programs and it is unclear what fraction of the differences (or lack of differences) originates from the languages as such and what fraction is due to different programmer backgrounds, different software processes, different application domains, different design structures, etc.

1.3 The Structure of This Study

The present work provides both subjective/speculative and objective information comparing 4 popular scripting languages (namely Perl, Python, Rexx, and Tcl) to one another and to 3 popular representatives of the last few generations of high-level mainstream languages (namely C, C++, and Java).

It has the following features:

- The comparison grounds in objective information gathered in a large empirical study. The speculative discussion is guided and limited by the results obtained empirically.

- In the empirical study, the same program (i.e., an implementation of the same set of requirements) is considered for each language. Hence, the comparison is narrow but homogeneous.

- For each language, we analyze not a single implementation of the program but a number of separate implementations by different programmers. Such a group-wise comparison has two advantages. First, it smoothes out the differences between individual programmers (which threaten the validity of any comparison based on just one implementation per language). Second, it allows to assess and compare the *variability* of program properties induced by the different languages.

- Several different aspects are investigated, such as program length, amount of commenting, run time efficiency, memory consumption, and reliability.

The chapter has the following structure. It will initially introduce the individual scripting languages: Their most salient properties, their likely strengths and weaknesses. Then we will look at the programming task underlying the empirical data and what it can plausibly tell us about other applications of the languages. The next section describes the origin of the program implementations and discusses the validity that we can expect from their comparison. Each subsequent section then compares one attribute of the programs across the language groups and relates the findings to the claims stated in the language description, explaining any contradictions where possible.

2. The Languages

This chapter assumes the reader is at least roughly familiar with some or all of C, C++, and Java. Consequently, these will be described only briefly. However, each of the scripting languages is introduced in a little more detail, including a small program example that illustrates a few of the basic characteristics; see Fig. 1 for the description.

Most of the material in each description is taken or derived from various kinds of language documentation and from statements made by third parties (often including proponents of other scripting languages).

2.1 C, C++, Java

C is a small, relatively low-level high-level language that became immensely popular during the 1980s with the widespread adoption of Unix operating systems, which are traditionally written largely in C. The terse syntax of C has once looked rather

```
obtain filename fn from first command line argument;
open the file named fn as filehandle f for reading;
for each line in f:
  read next line from f into variable s;
  remove all '-' characters from s;
  remove all '"' characters from s;
  print s to standard output;
end;
```

FIG. 1. Example program in pseudocode: Print the contents of a file with all dashes and doublequotes removed. All three subtasks (reading file, printing to standard output, removing certain characters from many strings) also occur in the programming task used in the empirical study.

strange, but has now become so mainstream that it appears almost canonical—C++, Java, Perl and many other languages borrow heavily from C's syntax. Since C does hardly impose any overhead on the programmer (in terms of memory and runtime), one can write extremely efficient programs in C. The lack of certain high-level language features plus the presence of easily misused features such as the preprocessor make the design soundness and maintainability of a C program highly dependent on the knowledge and discipline of the programmer.

C++, which became popular starting around 1990 and has undergone two major revisions and extensions since then, is more or less a superset of C, adding object-oriented language features (classes and inheritance) plus many other extensions such as template types, operator overloading, an exception mechanism, and others. It retains most of the strengths and weaknesses of C, except that it is much larger and more powerful—which makes it perhaps even more reliant on well-trained programmers. Like C programs, well-written C++ programs can be very efficient and have good access to low-level features of the machine.

Java is also an object-oriented language that resembles C, but compared to C++ it is much smaller: It attempts to leave out many constructs that are difficult to control—but also lacks some that are quite useful. Java provides no access to low-level pointers, memory management is automatic (garbage collection) and the language enforces full type-safety (e.g., for safe execution in a "sandbox" on other people's computers). The language Java is tightly bundled with a rather large standardized library that promotes many good design practices. Java is usually not compiled into machine code but rather into a machine-independent and rather high-level "byte-code", which is then further compiled usually at load time ("just-in-time compiler", JIT). Java's characteristics support writing clean and well-designed programs, but make obtaining highly efficient code more difficult for both the programmer and the compiler than C and C++ do.

2.2   Perl

Version 1 of Perl came out in December 1987 and at that time, the name was meant to be an acronym meaning "Practical Extraction and Report Language", where the term "practical" is explained as *"The language is intended to be practical (easy to use, efficient, complete) rather than beautiful (tiny, elegant, minimal)."* This ambition includes lots of built-in support for reading text files, scanning and massaging strings, and formatting text output. However, Perl quickly grew way beyond that by incorporating direct access to many of Unix's system calls and thus became what may be the most powerful language for system administration tasks on Unix systems. The language became highly popular with Version 4 released in March 1991. The current major version, 5, was first released October 1994 and "introduced everything else, including the ability to introduce everything else" [10]. In particular, it introduced object-oriented programming features.

Perl is a very powerful language (a quote from the Perl documentation: *"The three principal virtues of a programmer are Laziness, Impatience, and Hubris."*), which has a number of interesting consequences. For instance, most things, even at the level of individual statements, can be expressed in more than one manner in Perl. This is also the semi-official Perl motto *"There's more than one way to do it"*, also known as TMTOWTDI (often pronounced Tim Towdy). For instance, there are different constructs and styles that minimize either the time for writing a program, the time to run it, the amount of memory required by it, or the time to understand it. Following the motto, Perl has a rather large core language and a large library of built-in operations. Both are very well thought-out, but the extremely pragmatic approach of Perl's design makes it rather odd in places (another quote from the documentation: *"Perl actually stands for "Pathologically Eclectic Rubbish Lister", but don't tell anyone I said that."*). In fact however, the potential uglyness of any aspect of Perl has carefully been balanced with the power that can be derived from it. Nevertheless, Perl makes it relatively easy to shoot oneself in the foot or to produce programs that are very short but also very difficult to understand. For this reason, somewhat like for C++, writing good Perl programs depends more strongly on the knowledge and discipline of the programmer than in most other languages.

See the small example program in Fig. 2, which illustrates a few aspects of the terse syntax and powerful constructs found in Perl. The alternative version of the same program (shown in Fig. 3) shows one of the many constructs for writing supershort programs and represents one example of TMTOWTDI.

The best starting points for tons of further information on Perl, including lists of books and articles, are http://www.perl.org/ and http://www.perl.com/. A fairly comprehensive introduction is [24].

```
open(F, $ARGV[0]);
while ($s = <F>) {    # read next line, terminating at eof
   $s =~ s/-|"//g;    # in s replace - or " by nothing, globally
   print $s;
}
```

FIG. 2. Example program in Perl, normal style. <F> means reading the next line from a text file; s/pattern1/pattern2/ is a general regular-expression pattern replacement operator.

```
#!/bin/perl -p
s/-|"//g;
```

FIG. 3. Example program in Perl, minimalistic style. Execution option -p provides implicit iteration over all lines of each file provided as a command line argument plus implicit printing of the results.

2.3 Python

Python (the name derives from the old British TV comedy show Monty Python's Flying Circus) first became publicly available in 1991. The self-description says *"Python is an interpreted, interactive, object-oriented programming language that combines remarkable power with very clear syntax."*

This statement is in fact modest, because it is not only the syntax that is clear about Python but rather all of the language's concepts. Python is defined in such a way as to minimize the potential confusion of a programmer trying to learn it and also the strain on his or her memory. Most language constructs are nicely orthogonal so that no special rules are required for describing what happens if one combines them. Python resembles Java in that most of the many built-in features are not actually part of the language itself, but rather reside in many separate modules to be used (or ignored) explicitly and individually, which makes incremental learning of the language somewhat easier.

As a result of this design, Python programs cannot be quite as short as minimalistic Perl programs, but on the average Python programs are easier to read.

The small example program in Fig. 4 illustrates some of these points: Although it is effectively only three statements long, it accesses three different modules from the standard library. The module approach allows, for instance, to choose between three different kinds of regular expressions (from the modules regexp, regex, and re).

The best starting point for tons of further information on Python, including lists of books and articles, is http://www.python.org/. A fairly comprehensive introduction is [16].

```
import sys, fileinput, re
for s in fileinput.input(sys.argv[1]):  # iterate line-by-line
    s = re.sub("-|\"", "", s)  # replace - or " by nothing in s
    print s,                     # comma avoids additional newline
```

FIG. 4. Example program in Python. Only indentation is required to indicate block structure.

2.4 Rexx

All other scripting languages discussed here either started in an academic setting (Tcl) or were initially the work of a single individual (Perl, Python). In contrast, Rexx is a creation of IBM. It was historically available on various mainframe operating systems and consists of a system-independent core language plus system-specific extensions. It has now also been ported to other systems, in particular Windows and Unix systems (AIX, Linux) and at least one open source implementation is available (Regina).

Rexx is probably the least interesting of the languages discussed here in several respects: It is not as widely available on mainstream platforms as are the other languages; its user community is neither as large nor as dynamic; it has neither the conceptual and syntactical cleanliness of Python or Tcl, nor the extreme power and versatility of Perl. Here is the (somewhat dull) description of Rexx given on its homepage http://www.ibm.com/software/ad/rexx/: "IBM REXX is a powerful procedural programming language that lets you easily write programs and algorithms that are clear and structured. It includes features that make it easy to manipulate the most common symbolic objects, such as words, numbers, and names."

Due to the smaller user community, there are also only 4 Rexx programs in our empirical study which makes for too small a dataset for properly judging Rexx's behavior. Therefore we will limit the discussion of Rexx to a few words here and there.

2.5 Tcl

Tcl (Tool Command Language, pronounced "tickle") was invented by John Ousterhout, then at the University of California in Berkeley, and was first released in 1989. Since then it has had quite a lively career leading to its current major version 8: Ousterhout (and Tcl) left Berkeley and went to Sun in 1994, the Tcl Consortium took over Tcl in 1997, but was abandoned in 1999. Meanwhile in 1998, Ousterhout had founded Scriptics, which developed the commercial TclPro tools, but still kept the basic Tcl language implementation free and open source. In 2000, Scriptics renamed

```
set f [open [lindex $argv 0]]
while {1} {
   gets $f s
   if {[eof $f]} break
   regsub -all -- {[-\"]} $s {} s; # replace all - and"in s by
   puts $s                       #    nothing, giving s
}
```

FIG. 5. Example program in Tcl. Section enclosed in square brackets denote command substitution and are replaced at run time by the result of executing what is inside. Braces are strong quotes, forming one long word as-is to be evaluated later.

itself to Ajuba Solutions and later merged with Interwoven, which made TclPro open source software, too. Then ActiveState took over its development and made it commercial again, but basic Tcl is still free (also being maintained by ActiveState now as of early 2002).

Tcl has by far the smallest core language of all contestants; it basically consists of a general comment, command, and block syntax and evaluation semantics but has no actual language primitives whatsoever. Even constructs as fundamental as if-then-else or variable assignment are not part of the core language but rather take the form of built-in library operations called command words. See Fig. 5 for the Tcl version of our small example program.

The Tcl core is so small that its syntax and semantics are quite precisely described by only 11 paragraphs of text. The Tcl distribution is complemented by a large built-in library of such command words covering most of the large base functionality that one might expect from a scripting language. This approach is both curse and glory at the same time.

On the positive side, since almost everything in Tcl is an extension, Tcl makes for a good meta-language, allowing extensions of essentially every kind and in every direction. Consequently, a number of special-purpose languages built on top of Tcl exist, e.g., tclX for Unix system calls and many other extensions, Expect for adding automation to interactive user interfaces, Incr Tcl for object-oriented programming, etc.

Furthermore, since almost everything in Tcl is an extension anyway, Tcl smoothly allows for two-way embedding with other programs: Say, you have written a large program system in C++, then you can embed it with Tcl, provide simple adapter wrappers for all relevant functions, and then call all these functions from Tcl scripts as if they were built into Tcl. It also works the other way round: Your system can call Tcl scripts to simplify some of its own tasks. In particular, this is an easy way for adding a clean, powerful, standard-based interactive command language to a system and is why Tcl calls itself the Tool Command Language.

On the negative side, many program constructs are necessarily awkward and inconvenient. For instance, even integer arithmetic and infix notation are available only through a command word (called "expr") so that one has to write, e.g., `[expr $i+1]` rather than just `$i+1`.

Furthermore, Tcl is inefficient by design. In Tcl, everything is a String—and that includes the program text itself, even while it is running. Consequently, a Tcl interpreter has a hard time avoiding doing certain things over and over in a loop that yield the same results over and over. For instance, it may convert the fixed string "1234" into the integer number 1234 each time this value is passed to a function as an argument.

The best starting point for lots of further information on Tcl, including lists of books and articles, is http://www.scriptics.com/ (now also known as http://tcl. activestate.com).

3.   Overview of the Empirical Study

This section describes the programming task solved by the participants of the empirical study and the number and origin of the programs (which come from two fairly different sources). It then discusses the validity of the study: To what degree must we expect that differences in programmer ability and other factors have distorted the results? Finally, it explains the statistical evaluation approach and format of the graphs used in the subsequent results parts of this chapter.

3.1   Short Overview

The programming task was a program called *phonecode* that maps telephone numbers into strings of words according to a German dictionary supplied as an input file and a fixed digit-to-character encoding. It will be described in Section 3.2.

The programs analyzed in this report come from two different sources. The Java, C, and C++ programs were produced by paid student subjects in the course of a controlled experiment, the others were produced by a broad variety of subjects under unobserved conditions after a public call for volunteers sent to Usenet newsgroups and were submitted by Email. Find some more details in Sections 3.3 and 3.4. Section 3.5 discusses the number of programs from each language that were collected for the study

In a study of this kind, there are always concerns with respect to the validity of the comparison. In our case, we find that the conditions of the study probably put the script language groups at some advantage compared to the non-script groups with respect to the following criteria: possibly slightly higher average programmer capability, more flexible work conditions, better up-front information about evaluation criteria and about specific task difficulties, a better program testbed. Fortunately, all of these differences can be expected to be only modest, though. They should make us ignore small differences between the groups' performance when discussing the results and focus on major differences only. Section 3.6 provides a thorough discussion of these issues.

3.2 The Programming Task 'Phonecode'

The programs analyzed in this study represent solutions of the following task.

We want to encode telephone numbers as words to make them easier to remember. Given the following mapping from letters to digits

E	J N Q	R W X	D S Y	F T	A M	C I V	B K U	L O P	G H Z
e	j n q	r w x	d s y	f t	a m	c i v	b k u	l o p	g h z
0	1	2	3	4	5	6	7	8	9

and given a dictionary like this

```
Bo"
da
Doubletten-Konkatenations-Form
je
mir
Mix
Mixer
Name
neu
o"d
so
su"ss
superkalifragilistisch
Tor
```

and given a list of "telephone numbers" like this

```
5624-82
0721/608-4067
10/783--5
/378027586-4259686346369
```

```
1078-913-5
381482
```

write a program that encodes the phone numbers into all possible sequences of words
according to the mapping like this

```
5624-82: mir Tor
5624-82: Mix Tor
10/783--5: je Bo" da
10/783--5: neu o"d 5
/378027586-4259686346369: superkalifragilistisch
381482: so 1 Tor
```

Building the encoding sequentially left-to-right, a single digit from the original number may be placed at a point where no matching word is available.

The character mapping is fixed and can be coded right into the program.

The dictionary is supplied as a text file and should be read into memory (maximum size 75000 words). Words may contain dashes and double quotes (signifying
umlaut characters) which are to be ignored for the encoding. A word may be up to
50 characters long.

The phone numbers are supplied as a text file of unlimited size and must be read
and processed line by line. Phone numbers may contain dashes and slashes which
are to be ignored for the encoding. A phone number may be up to 50 characters long.

The output encodings must be printed exactly as shown (except for their order
within each number's block). Nothing at all is printed for numbers that cannot be
encoded.

For details on the task and how it was communicated to the participants, see Appendix A.

3.3 Origin of the C, C++, and Java Programs

All C, C++, and Java programs were produced in 1997/1998 during a controlled
experiment that compared the behavior of programmers with and without previous
PSP (Personal Software Process [12]) training. All of the subjects were Computer
Science master students. They chose their programming language freely. A few
participants of the experiment used languages other than C, C++, or Java, such as
Modula-2 and Sather-K. The subjects were told that their main goal should be producing a correct (defect-free) program. A high degree of correctness was ensured
by an acceptance test. The sample of programs used here comprises only those that
passed the acceptance test. Several subjects decided to give up after zero, one, or
several failed attempts at passing this test.

Detailed information about the subjects, the experimental procedure, etc. can be found in [21].

For brevity, I will often call these three languages *non-script languages* and the corresponding programs *non-scripts*.

3.4 Origin of the Perl, Python, Rexx, and Tcl Programs

The Perl, Python, Rexx, and Tcl programs were all submitted in late 1999 by volunteers after I had posted a "Call for Programs" on several Usenet newsgroups (comp.lang.perl.misc, de.comp.lang.perl.misc, comp.lang.rexx, comp.lang.tcl, comp. lang.tcl.announce, comp.lang.python, comp.lang.python.announce) and one mailing list (called "Fun with Perl", fwp@technofile.org).

For four weeks after that call, the requirements description and test data were posted on a website for viewing and download. The participants were told to develop the program, test it, and submit it by email. There was no registration and I have no way of knowing how many participants started to write the program but gave up.

Detailed information about the submission procedure can be found in Section 3.2.

3.5 Number of Programs

As shown in Table I, the set of programs analyzed in this study contains between 4 and 24 programs per language, 80 programs overall. Note that the sample covers

TABLE I

FOR EACH NON-SCRIPT PROGRAMMING LANGUAGE: NUMBER OF PROGRAMS ORIGINALLY PREPARED (PROGS), NUMBER OF SUBJECTS THAT VOLUNTARILY PARTICIPATED A SECOND TIME ONE YEAR LATER (SECOND), NUMBER OF PROGRAMS THAT DID NOT PASS THE ACCEPTANCE TEST (UNUSABLE), AND FINAL NUMBER OF PROGRAMS USED IN THE STUDY (TOTAL). FOR EACH SCRIPT PROGRAMMING LANGUAGE: NUMBER OF PROGRAMS SUBMITTED (PROGS), NUMBER OF PROGRAMS THAT ARE RESUBMISSIONS (SECOND), NUMBER OF PROGRAMS THAT COULD NOT BE RUN AT ALL (UNUSABLE), AND FINAL NUMBER OF PROGRAMS USED IN THE STUDY (TOTAL)

language	progs	second	unusable	total
C	8	0	3	5
C++	14	0	3	11
Java	26	2	2	24
Perl	14	2	1	13
Python	13	1	0	13
Rexx	5	1	1	4
Tcl	11	0	1	10
Total	91	6	11	80

80 different programs but only 74 different authors, as six of them submitted two versions—two of these in a different language (namely Java) than the first.

As many as 91 programs were actually collected, but 11 of them had to be discarded for the evaluation because they did not work properly.

Furthermore, the results for C and Rexx will be based on only 5 or 4 programs, respectively, and are thus rather coarse estimates of reality. Given the large amount of variation between individual programs even within the same language, statistically significant results can rarely be obtained with such a small number of data points. We will hence often disregard these languages in the discussion as they would contribute more confusion than information.

For all of the other languages there are 10 or more programs, which is a broad-enough base for reasonably precise results.

3.6   Validity: Are These Programs Comparable?

The rather different conditions under which these programs were produced raise an important question: Is it sensible and fair to compare these programs to one another or would such a comparison say more about the circumstances than it would say about the programs? Put differently: Is our comparison valid? (More precisely: internally valid) The following subsections discuss problems that threaten the validity. The most important threats usually occur between the language groups script and non-script; a few caveats when comparing one particular script language to another or one non-script language to another also exist and will be discussed where necessary.

3.6.1   Programmer Capabilities

The average capabilities of the programmers may differ from one language to the other.

It is plausible that the Call for Programs has attracted only fairly competent programmers and hence the script programs may reflect higher average programmer capabilities than the non-script programs. However, two observations make me estimate this difference to be small. First, with some exceptions, the students who created the non-script programs were also quite capable and experienced with a median programming experience of 8 years (see [21]). Second, some of the script programmers have described themselves as follows:

– *"Most of the time was spent learning the language not solving the problem."*

– *"Things I learned: [...] Use a language you really know."*

– *"First real application in Python."*

- *"It was only my 4th or 5th Python script."*
- *"I'm not a programmer but a system administrator."*
- *"I'm a social scientist."*
- *"I am a VLSI designer (not a programmer) and my algorithms/coding-style may reflect this."*
- *"This is my first Tcl prog. I'm average intelligence, but tend to work hard."*
- *"Insight: Think before you code. [...] A lot of time was lost on testing and optimising the bad approach."*

Taken together, I expect that the script and non-script programmer populations are roughly comparable—at least if we ignore the worst few from the non-script group, because their would-be counterparts in the script group have probably given up and not submitted a program at all. We should keep this in mind for the interpretation of the results below.

Within the language groups, some modest differences between languages also occurred: In the non-script group, the Java programmers tend to be less experienced than the C and C++ programmers for two reasons. First, most of the noticeably most capable subjects chose C or C++, and second, nobody could have many years of Java experience at the time, because the experiment was conducted in 1997 and 1998, when Java was only about three years old.

Within the script group, my personal impression is that the Perl subjects tended to be more capable than the others. The reasons may be that the Perl language appears to irradiate a strange attraction to highly capable programming fans and that the "fun with Perl" mailing list on which I posted the call for programs appears to reach a particularly high fraction of such persons.

3.6.2 Work Time Reporting Accuracy

Even if the capabilities of the programmers are comparable, the work times reported by the script programmers may be inaccurate.

In contrast to the non-script programs from the controlled experiment, for which we know the real programming time accurately, nothing kept the script programmers from heavily "rounding down" the working times they reported when they submitted their program. Some of them also reported they had had to estimate their time, as either they did not keep track of it during the actual programming work or they were mixing too much with other tasks (*"many breaks to change diapers, watch the X-files, etc."*). In particular, some apparently read the requirements days before they actually started implementing the solution as is illustrated by the following quotes:

- *"Design: In my subconscious for a few days."*

– "*The total time does not include the two weeks between reading the require-ments and starting to design/code/test, during which my subconscious may have already worked on the solution.*"

– "*The actual time spent pondering the design is a bit indeterminate, as I was often doing other things (eating cheese on toast, peering through the snow, etc).*"

Nevertheless, there is evidence (described in Section 8) that at least on the average the work times reported are reasonably accurate for the script group, too: The old rule of thumb, saying the number of lines written per hour is independent of the language, holds fairly well across all languages.

3.6.3 Different Task and Different Work Conditions

The requirements statement, materials provided, work conditions, and submission procedure were different for the script versus non-script group.

The requirements statement given to both the non-script and the script program-mers said that correctness was the most important aspect for their task and also that the algorithms must be designed such that they always consider only a fraction of the words from the dictionary when trying to encode the next digit. However, the announcement posted for the script programmers (although not the requirements de-scription) also made a broader assignment, mentioning programming effort, program length, program readability/modularization/maintainability, elegance of the solution, memory consumption, and run time consumption as criteria on which the programs might be judged.

This focus difference may have directed somewhat more energy towards produc-ing an efficient program in the script group compared to the non-script group. On the other hand, two things will have dampened this difference. First, the script group participants were explicitly told "*Please do not over-optimize your program. Deliver your first reasonable solution*". Second, in the non-script group highly inefficient programs were filtered out and sent back for optimization in the acceptance test, be-cause the test imposed both a time and memory limit[1] not present in the submission procedure of the script group.

There was another difference regarding the acceptance test and reliability mea-surement procedures: Both groups were given a small dictionary (test.w, 23 words) and a small file of inputs (test.t) and correct outputs (test.out) for program develop-ment and initial testing, plus a large dictionary (woerter2, 73113 words). The accep-tance test for the non-script group was then performed using a randomly created input file (different each time) and a medium-large dictionary of 20946 words. A failed

---

[1] 64 MB total, 30 seconds maximum per output plus 5 minutes for loading on a 143 MHz Sparc Ultra I.

acceptance test cost a deduction of 10 Deutschmarks from the overall compensation paid for successful participation in the experiment, which was 50 Deutschmarks (about 30 US Dollars).

In contrast, the script group was given both the input file z1000.in and the corresponding correct outputs z1000.out that are used for reliability measurement in this report and could perform as many tests on these data as they pleased.

Possessing these data is arguably an advantage for the script group with respect to the work time required. Note, however, that the acceptance test in the non-script group automatically flagged and reported any mistakes separately while the script group had to perform the comparison of correct output and actual output themselves. The web page mentioned that the Unix utilities sort and diff could be used for automating this comparison.

A more serious problem is probably the different working regime: As mentioned above, many of the script group participants thought about the solution for several days before actually producing it, whereas the non-script participants all started to work on the solution right after reading the requirements. This is probably an advantage for the script group. On the other hand, for more than two thirds of the non-script group one or several longer work breaks (for the night or even for several days) occurred as well.

Summing up we might say that the tasks of the two groups are reasonably similar, but any specific comparison must clearly be taken with a grain of salt. There was probably some advantage for the script group with respect to work conditions: some of them used unmeasured thinking time before the actual implementation work. Hence, only severe results differences should be relied upon.

3.6.4 Handling a Misunderstood Requirement

There was one important statement in the requirements that about one third of all programmers in both groups misunderstood at first (see Section A.3), resulting in an incorrect program. Since many these programmers were not able to resolve the problem themselves, help was required. This help was provided to the non-script programmers as follows: When they failed an acceptance test due to this problem, the respective sentence in the requirements was pointed out to them with the advice of reading it extremely carefully. If they still did not find the problem and approached the experimenter for further help, the misunderstanding was explained to them. All of these programmers were then able to resolve the problem. Actually correcting this mistake in a faulty program was usually trivial.

For the script programmers, no such interaction was possible, hence the requirements description posted on the web contained a pointer to a "hint", with the direction to first re-read the requirements carefully and open the hint only if the problem could not be resolved otherwise. The exact wording and organization is shown in Appendix A below.

The easier access to the hint may have produced an advantage (with respect to work time) for the script-group, but it is hard to say whether or to which extent this has happened. On the other hand, a few members of the script group have reported having had a hard time understanding the actual formulation of the hint. My personal impression based on my observations of the non-script group and on the feedback I have received from participants of the script group is that the typical work time penalty for misunderstanding this requirement was similar in the script and non-script group.

3.6.5 Other Issues

The non-script programmers had a further slight disadvantage, because they were forced to work on a computer that was not their own. However, they did not complain that this was a major problem for them. The script programmers used their own machine and programming environment.

The Rexx programs may experience a small distortion because the platform on which they were evaluated (a Rexx implementation called "Regina") is not the platform on which they were originally developed. Similarly, the Java programs were evaluated using a much newer version of the JDK (Java Development Kit) than the one they were originally developed with. These context changes are probably not of major importance, though.

3.6.6 Summary

Overall, it is probably fair to say that

- due to the design of the data collection, the data for the script groups will reflect several relevant (although modest) a priori advantages compared to the data for the non-script groups and

- there are likely to be some modest differences in the average programmer capability between any two of the languages.

Due to these threats to validity, we should discount small differences between any of the languages, as these might be based on weaknesses of the data. Large differences, however, are likely to be valid.

3.7   Evaluation Conditions

The programs were evaluated using the same dictionary woerter2 as given to the participants. Three different input files were used: z1000 contains 1000 non-empty

TABLE II

COMPILERS AND INTERPRETERS USED FOR THE VARIOUS LANGUAGES. NOTE ON JAVA
PLATFORM: THE JAVA EVALUATION USES THE JDK 1.2.2 HOTSPOT REFERENCE VERSION (THAT
IS, A NOT PERFORMANCE-TUNED VERSION). HOWEVER, TO AVOID UNFAIR DISADVANTAGES
COMPARED TO THE OTHER LANGUAGES, THE JAVA RUN TIME MEASUREMENTS WILL REFLECT
TWO MODIFICATIONS WHERE APPROPRIATE: FIRST, THE JDK 1.2.1 SOLARIS PRODUCTION
VERSION (WITH JIT) MAY BE USED, BECAUSE FOR SHORT-RUNNING PROGRAMS THE TUNED JIT
IS FASTER THAN THE UNTUNED HOTSPOT COMPILER. SECOND, SOME PROGRAMS ARE
MEASURED BASED ON A SPECIAL VERSION OF THE JAVA.UTIL.VECTOR DYNAMIC ARRAY CLASS
NOT ENFORCING SYNCHRONIZATION. THIS IS SIMILAR TO JAVA.UTIL.ARRAYLIST IN JDK 1.2,
BUT NO SUCH THING WAS AVAILABLE IN JDK 1.1 WITH WHICH THOSE PROGRAMS WERE
WRITTEN

language	compiler or execution platform
C	GNU gcc 2.7.2
C++	GNU g++ 2.7.2
Java	Sun JDK 1.2.1/1.2.2
Perl	perl 5.005_02
Python	python 1.5.2
Rexx	Regina 0.08g
Tcl	tcl 8.2.2

random phone numbers, m1000 contains 1000 arbitrary random phone numbers
(with empty ones allowed), and z0 contains no phone number at all (for measuring
dictionary load time alone).

Extremely slow programs were stopped after a timeout of 2 minutes per output
plus 20 minutes for loading the dictionary—however, three quarters of all programs
finished the whole z1000 run with 262 outputs in less than 2 minutes.

All programs were executed on a 300 MHz Sun Ultra-II workstation with 256 MB
memory, running under SunOS 5.7 (Solaris 7); the compilers and interpreters are
listed in Table II.

3.8 External Validity: To What Degree Can These Results Be Generalized?

Even if the results discussed below are nicely valid as they stand, there is still
the question whether they are also relevant: Will similar differences between the
languages be observed in many practical situations? When and where can the results
be generalized to other circumstances, that is, how much external validity do they
exhibit?

3.8.1 Stability of Results Over Time

The results regarding execution time and memory consumption depend not only on the language and the capabilities of the programmer, but also on the quality of the compiler or interpreter and the runtime system used.

In this respect it should be noted that while the translation and execution technology for C and C++ is rather mature, a lot of progress is still possible for the other languages—most strongly probably for Java and Tcl, whose design requires rather complex optimization technology for producing optimal efficiency. And indeed the language communities of all of these languages are working busily on improving the implementations—most strongly certainly for Java, but also quite actively for Python and Perl, perhaps a little less for Tcl and Rexx.

Therefore, in those cases where Java or the script languages impose an execution time or memory penalty compared to C or C++, this penalty can be expected to shrink over time.

3.8.2 Generalizability of Results to Other Programming Tasks

Little can be inferred directly from the results of the study that reliably applies to very different programming tasks, e.g., requiring much larger programs, involving a lot of numerical computations, handling much larger amounts of data or much coarser-grained data, having an interactive user interface, etc.

However, the class of programs represented by the phonecode task is rather large and common, especially in an area for which script languages are often used, namely transcribing text files from one format into another, perhaps including some semantic processing underways. If these transcriptions are such that the rules are not fixed in the program, but rather also rely on some kind of mapping instructions or vocabulary described by a run-time data set, then such programs often resemble the phonecode task fairly well. A frequent example of such programs could be the conversion from one XML-based specification language into another that has similar expressive power but different constructs.

At least for this class of programs, we can expect to find results similar to this study when comparing these languages.

3.9 Evaluation Tools: Data Plots and Statistical Methods

The plots and statistical methods used in the evaluation are described in some detail in [21]; we only give a short description here.

The main evaluation tool will be the multiple boxplot display, see, for example, Fig. 7 on page 229. Each of the "lines" represents one subset of data, as named on the left. Each small circle stands for one individual data value. The rest of the plot provides visual aids for the comparison of two or more such subsets of data. The shaded box indicates the range of the middle half of the data, that is, from the first quartile (25% quantile) to the third quartile (75% quantile). The "whiskers" to the left and right of the box indicate the bottom and top 10% of the data, respectively. The fat dot within the box is the median (50% quantile). The "M" and the dashed line around it indicate the arithmetic mean and plus/minus one standard error of the mean.

Many interesting observations can easily be made directly in these plots. For quantifying some of them, I will also sometimes provide the results of statistical significance tests: Medians are compared using the Wilcoxon Rank Sum Test (Mann–Whitney U-Test) and in a few cases means will be compared using the t-Test. All tests are performed one-sided and all test results will be reported as p-values, that is, the probability that the observed differences between the samples are only due to random variations and either no difference between the underlying populations does indeed exist or there is even a difference in the opposite direction.

At some points I will also provide confidence intervals, either on the differences in means or on the differences in logarithms of means (that is, on the ratios of means). These confidence intervals are computed by Bootstrapping. They will be chosen such that they are open-ended, that is, their upper end is at infinity. Bootstrapping is described in more detail in [8].

Note that due to the caveats described in Section 3.6 all of these quantitative statistical inference results can merely indicate trends; they should not be considered precise evidence.

For explicitly describing the variability within one group of values we will use the *bad/good ratio*: Imagine the data be split in an upper and a lower half, then the bad/good ratio is the median of the upper half divided by the median of the lower half. In the boxplot, this is just the value at the right edge of the box divided by the value at the left edge. In contrast to a variability measure such as the standard deviation, the bad/good ratio is robust against the few extremely high values that occur in our data set.

4.   Results for Execution Time

4.1   Total Run Time: z1000 Data Set

4.1.1   Results

The global overview of the program run times on the z1000 input file is shown in Fig. 6. Except for C++, Java and Rexx, at least three quarters of the programs run

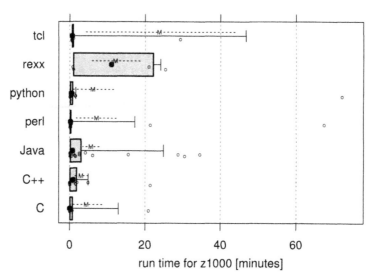

FIG. 6. Program run time on the z1000 data set. Three programs were timed out with no output after about 21 minutes. One Tcl program took 202 minutes. The bad/good ratios range from 1.5 for Tcl up to 27 for C++.

in less than one minute. The most important lesson to learn from this plot is that in all languages there are a few programs that are not just slower than the others but rather are immensely much slower. Put differently: With respect to execution time, an incompetent programmer can shoot him or herself in the foot quite badly in any language.

In order to see and discriminate all of the data points at once, we can use a logarithmic plot as shown in Fig. 7. We can make several interesting observations:

- The typical (i.e., median) run time for Tcl is not significantly longer than that for Java (one-sided Wilcoxon test $p = 0.21$) or even for C++ ($p = 0.30$).

- Don't be confused by the median for C++. Since the distance to the next larger and smaller points is rather large, it is unstable. The Wilcoxon test, which takes the whole sample into account, confirms that the C++ median in fact tends to be smaller than the Java median ($p = 0.18$).

- The median run times of Python are smaller than those of Rexx ($p = 0.024$), and Tcl ($p = 0.047$). The median run times of Perl are also smaller than those of Rexx ($p = 0.018$), and Tcl ($p = 0.002$).

- Except for two very slow programs, Tcl and Perl run times tend to have a smaller variability than the run times for the other languages. For example, a one-sided

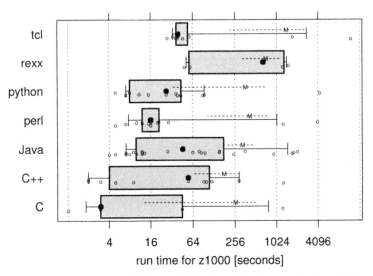

FIG. 7. Program run time on the z1000 data set. Equivalent to Fig. 6, except that the axis is logarithmic and indicates seconds instead of minutes.

bootstrap test for differences in interquartile range of logarithmic run times (i.e., differences in box width in Fig. 7) between Perl and Python indicates $p = 0.15$.

Remember to interpret the plots for C and Rexx with care, because they have only few points.[2]

If we aggregate the languages into only three groups, as shown in Fig. 8, we find that the run time advantage of C/C++ is not statistically significant: Compared to Scripts, the C/C++ advantage is accidental with probability $p = 0.15$ for the median and with $p = 0.11$ for the log mean (via t-test). Compared to Java, the C/C++ advantage is accidental with $p = 0.074$ for the median and $p = 0.12$ for the log mean.

The larger samples of this aggregate grouping allow for computing reasonable confidence intervals for the differences. A bootstrap-estimated confidence interval for the log run time means difference (that is, the run time ratio) indicates that with 80% confidence a script will run at least 1.29 times as long as a C/C++ program (but with higher log run time variability, $p = 0.11$). A Java program must be expected to

---

[2] Regarding the performance of Rexx, participant Ian Collier pointed out that the otherwise high performance Regina interpreter suffers from its fixed hashtable size for the phonecode problem, because the default size of 256 is too small. Increasing this value to 8192 (which requires recompiling Regina) reduced the run time of Collier's Rexx program from 53 seconds down to 12. Further increasing the value would probably reduce the run time still more, because a hash table for 70000 elements should best have more than 70000 entries.

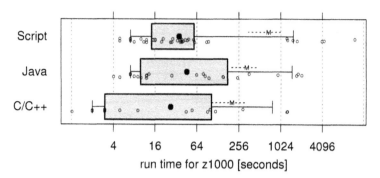

FIG. 8. Program run time on the z1000 data set on logarithmic axis; just like Fig. 7, except that the samples for several languages are aggregated into larger groups. The bad/good ratios are 4.1 for script, 18 for Java and 35 for C/C++.

run at least 1.22 times as long as a C/C++ program. There is no significant difference between average Java and Script run times.

4.1.2 Discussion

- The run time penalty of a script relative to a C or C++ program is a lot smaller for the phonecode problem than probably most of us would have expected. There are two reasons for this. First, scripts can generally be quite efficient if their most sensible implementation can make heavy use of powerful built-in operations, because these operations are written in lower-level languages and have usually been thoroughly optimized. Second, as we can see in the plots, each of the non-script program groups can be distinguished quite clearly into an efficient and an inefficient subgroup. No such effect is present for Perl, Python, or Tcl. As we will see in Section 9, the reason for this lies in the program design: While the scripts more or less all use the same basic algorithm design, the non-script programs use either of two designs that are radically different in terms of execution time.

- The slower execution of Tcl compared to Perl and Python corroborates the speculative statement from the language introduction that the design of Tcl makes it hard to obtain efficient implementations.

- The smaller variance in execution time (as described by the bad/good ratio) for the script languages in general and for Perl and Python in particular can be considered an advantage of the script languages: They appear to be less dependent on the programmer for obtaining reasonable performance than are the non-script languages. This may be quite important in practice. The point here is one of risk: Yes, a well-optimized C or C++ program is likely to be faster than any script, but is there a high-enough probability that you really get one?

- Given Perl's TMTOWTDI principle, the smaller bad/good ratio of Perl compared to Python is a surprise. Thinking of a good reason why the bad/good ratio of Tcl should be so much smaller than that of Python is also difficult. Perhaps both these facts are indications that the Perl and Tcl programmers were somewhat better trained in their language than some of the Python programmers.

Summing up, the script programs are not only much faster than expected, compared to the non-script programs, they also exhibit better predictability of the execution time where different programmers are concerned.

4.2   Run Time for Initialization Phase Only: z0 Data Set

4.2.1   Results

We can repeat the same analysis for the case where the program only reads, and stores the dictionary; almost all programs also reverse-encode the words as telephone numbers in this phase to accelerate further execution. Figure 9 shows the corresponding run time.

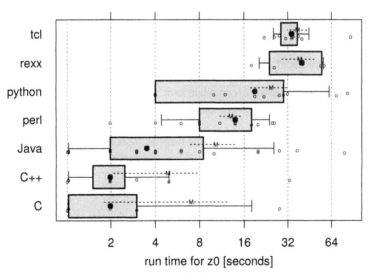

FIG. 9. Program run time for loading and preprocessing the dictionary only (z0 data set). Note the logarithmic axis. The bad/good ratios range from 1.3 for Tcl up to 7.5 for Python.

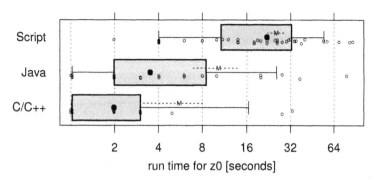

FIG. 10. Program run time for loading and preprocessing the dictionary only (z0 data set); just like Fig. 7, except that the samples for several languages are aggregated into larger groups. The bad/good ratio is about 3 for Script and C/C++ and 4.3 for Java.

We find that C and C++ are clearly faster in this situation than all other programs. The fastest script languages are again Perl and Python. Rexx and Tcl are again slower than these but now Java is faster.

For the aggregate grouping (Fig. 10) we find that, compared to a C/C++ program, a Java program will run at least 1.3 times as long and a script will run at least 5.5 times as long (at the 80% confidence level). Compared to a Java program, a script will run at least 3.2 times as long.

4.2.2 Discussion

These results are obviously somewhat more of the kind that one might have expected: All scripting languages are slower than Java and Java is slower than both C and C++.

No explanation, however, will be given here, as there are three very different components in the run time for this phase and I performed no analysis trying to decompose them:

- Reading the dictionary file.
- Converting each word into the corresponding bare telephone number. (As we will see in Section 9, the eventually slower non-script programs were the fastest here, as they converted the first letter of each word only.)
- Storing the words in a data structure that allows to retrieve them quickly based on the corresponding phone number.

4.3   Run Time for Search Phase Only

4.3.1   Results

Finally, we may subtract this run time for the loading phase (z0 data set) from the total run time (z1000 data set) and thus obtain the run time for the actual search phase only. Note that these are time differences from two separate program runs. Due to the measurement granularity, a few zero times result. These were rounded up to one second. Figure 11 shows the corresponding run times.

We find that very fast programs occur in all languages except for Rexx and Tcl and very slow programs occur in all languages without exception. More specifically:

- The median run time for Tcl is longer than that for Python ($p = 0.10$), Perl ($p = 0.012$), and C ($p = 0.099$), but shorter than that of Rexx ($p = 0.052$).

- The median run times of Python are smaller than those of Rexx ($p = 0.007$), and Tcl ($p = 0.10$). They even tend to be smaller than those of Java ($p = 0.13$).

- The median run times of Perl are smaller than those of Rexx ($p = 0.018$), Tcl ($p = 0.012$), and even Java ($p = 0.043$).

- Although it doesn't look like that, the median of C++ is not significantly different from any of the others (two-sided tests yield $0.26 < p < 0.92$).

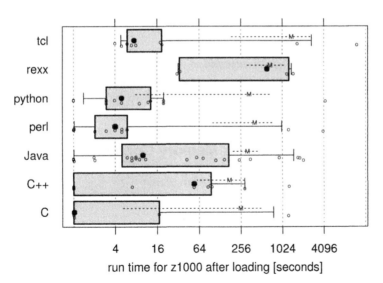

FIG. 11. Program run time for the search phase only. Computed as time for z1000 data set minus time for z0 data set. Note the logarithmic axis. The bad/good ratios range from 2.9 for Perl up to over 50 for C++ (in fact 95, but unreliable due to the imprecise lower bound).

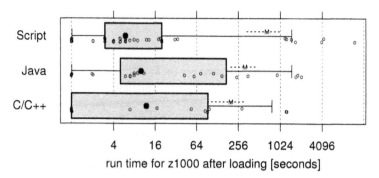

FIG. 12. Program run time for the search phase only. Computed as time for z1000 data set minus time for z0 data set. This is just like Fig. 11, except that the samples for several languages are aggregated into larger groups. The bad/good ratio is about 7 for Script, 34 for Java, and over 50 for C/C++ (in fact 95, but unreliable due to the estimated lower bound).

The aggregated comparison in Fig. 12 indicates no significant differences between any of the groups, neither for the pairs of medians ($p > 0.14$) nor for the pairs of means ($p > 0.20$).

However, a bootstrap test for differences of the box widths indicates that with 80% confidence the run time variability of the Scripts is smaller than that of Java by a factor of at least 2.1 and smaller than that of C/C++ by a factor of at least 3.4.

4.3.2   Discussion

Some people may be quite surprised at this, but given the right kind of work to do, the average script may be just as fast as the average non-script. What may even be more important in practice is the fact that, just as for the overall run time, the variability of script run times is so much smaller.

5.   Results for Memory Consumption

How much memory is required by the programs?

5.1   Results

Figure 13 shows the total process size at the end of the program execution for the z1000 input file.

Several observations are interesting:

- The most memory-efficient programs are clearly the smaller ones from the C and C++ groups.

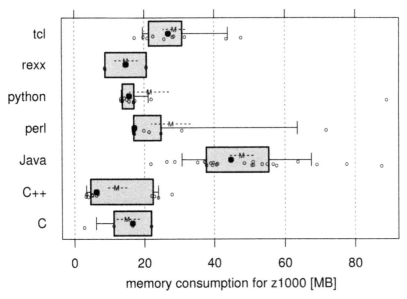

Fig. 13. Amount of memory required by the program, including the interpreter or run time system, the program itself, and all static and dynamic data structures. The bad/good ratios range from 1.2 for Python up to 4.9 for C++.

- The least memory-efficient programs are clearly the Java programs.
- Except for Tcl, only few of the scripts consume more memory than the worse half of the C and C++ programs.
- Tcl scripts typically require clearly more memory than other scripts.
- Python scripts typically require less memory than both Perl and Tcl scripts.
- Especially for Python, but also for Perl and Tcl, the relative variability in memory consumption tends to be much smaller than for C and in particular C++.
- A few (but only a few) of the scripts have a horribly high memory consumption compared to the others.
- On the average (see Fig. 14) and with a confidence of 80%, the Java programs consume at least 32 MB (or 297%) more memory than the C/C++ programs and at least 20 MB (or 98%) more memory than the script programs. The script programs consume only at least 9 MB (or 85%) more than the C/C++ programs.

Summing up, the memory consumption of Java is typically more than twice as high as that of scripts, and scripts are not necessarily worse than a program written in C or C++, although they do beat the most parsimonious C or C++ programs.

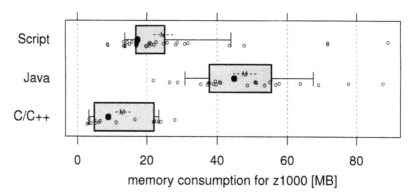

FIG. 14. Like Fig. 13, except that the languages are aggregated into groups. The bad/good ratios are 1.5 for Script and for Java and 4.5 for C/C++.

5.2   Discussion

We can conclude

- Neither scripts nor Java programs can beat a memory-efficient C or C++ program. This is partially due to the much lower level (and hence more controlled) memory management in these languages and partially due to the simpler data structure for one of the two major program designs used in the non-script languages (as described in Section 9). As we will see in Section 10.1, the latter point involves a time/memory tradeoff.

- Just like for run time, the variability in memory consumption from one programmer to the next tends to be substantially smaller in the script languages compared to the non-script languages, which may help reduce risk in software development.

- The very high memory consumption of the Java programs, where even the best ones are worse than most scripts, probably has two main reasons. For one, the improvements in the Java execution platforms have so far focused on execution time. However, garbage collection mechanisms (as present in Java) usually involve strong time/memory tradeoffs. Java run time systems can probably be made a lot more memory-efficient than they are today with only a small run time penalty. Second, at the time when these programs were written, Java was still quite young and a memory-conscious programming style was not yet widely known.

Summing up, for the phonecode problem one cannot generally speak of a memory penalty due to using script languages.

6. Results for Program Length and Amount of Commenting

How long are the programs?
How much commenting do they contain?

6.1 Results

Figure 15 shows the number of lines containing anything that contributes to the semantics of the program in each of the program source files, e.g., a statement, a declaration, or at least a delimiter such as a closing brace (end-of-block marker).

We see that non-scripts are typically two to three times as long as scripts. Even the longest scripts are shorter than the average non-script and even the shortest non-scripts are longer than the average script. Furthermore, the variability of program length for the scripts, at least for Perl and Python, is also smaller than for the non-scripts.

At the same time, scripts tend to contain a significantly higher density of comments (Fig. 16), with the non-scripts averaging a median of 22% as many comment

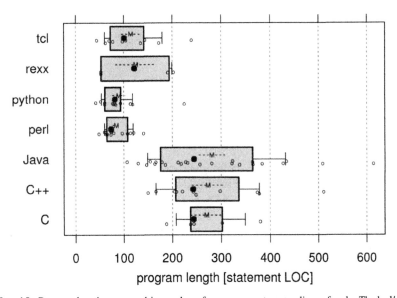

FIG. 15. Program length, measured in number of non-comment source lines of code. The bad/good ratios range from 1.3 for C up to 2.1 for Java and 3.7 for Rexx.

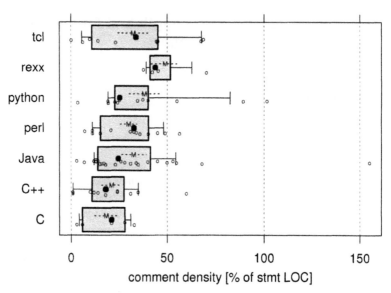

FIG. 16. Percentage of comment lines plus commented statement lines, relative to the number of statement lines. The bad/good ratios range from 1.3 for Rexx up to 4.2 for Tcl.

lines or commented lines as statement lines and the scripts averaging 34% ($p = 0.020$ when we compare the language groups rather than individual languages).

6.2 Discussion

These results are quite spectacular. Scripts are not just shorter than "real" programs, they are very much shorter. Looking into the program source texts, one finds three reasons for that: First, the lack of declarations in the scripts; second, the generally more powerful (and thus compact) constructs for everyday operations such as opening and reading files (see the program examples in Section 2); and finally a different algorithm structure, which we will discuss further below in Section 9.

Many people believe that scripts tend to be less readable than non-scripts. Looking at some fixed amount of program source code, this may well be true: Scripts typically have more program logic packed into the same number of lines and will hence often appear more convoluted. However, the above results show that there are two effects that may result in an overall readability that is as good or even better than that or non-scripts. First, the much lower amount of program text in a script makes it much easier to have a complete overview of a program. Second, it may be that the denser logic in scripts provokes higher efforts at commenting the program, further reducing any readability penalty of script languages, if such a thing exists. However, we should take into account that the higher density of commenting may at least in part be due to the different programmer populations in the two major language groups.

7.   Results for Program Reliability

Do the programs conform to the requirements specification?
How reliable are they?

7.1   Results for "Standard" Inputs

Each of the programs in this data set processes correctly the simple example dictionary and phone number input file that was given (including a file containing the expected outputs) to all participants for their program development.

However, with the large dictionary woerter2 and the partially quite strange and unexpected "phone numbers" in the larger input files, not all programs behaved entirely correctly. The percentage of outputs correct is plotted in Fig. 17.

5 programs (1 C, 1 C++, 1 Perl) produced no correct outputs at all, either because they were unable to load the large dictionary or because they were timed out during

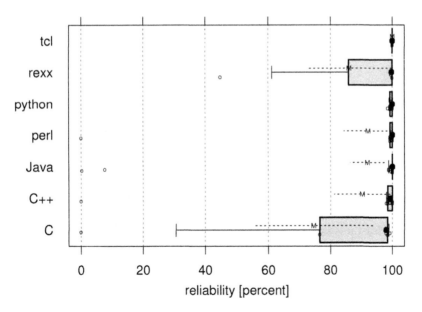

FIG. 17.   Program output reliability in percent for the z1000 input file.

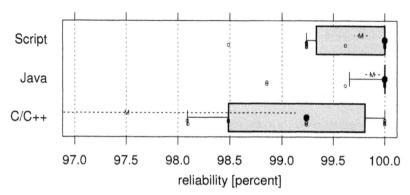

F<small>IG</small>. 18. Program output reliability in percent (except for those programs with reliability below 50 percent), with languages aggregated into groups.

the load phase. 2 Java programs failed with near-zero reliability for other reasons and 1 Rexx program produced many of its outputs with incorrect formatting, resulting in a reliability of 45 percent. The only language with all flawless programs is Tcl.

If we ignore the above-mentioned highly faulty programs and compare the rest (that is, all programs with reliability over 50 percent, hence excluding 13% of the C/C++ programs, 8% of the Java programs, and 5% of the script programs; Fig. 18) by language group, we find that C/C++ programs are on average less reliable than both the Java and the script programs ($p < 0.0004$ for the median, $p < 0.04$ for the mean).

7.2 Discussion

These latter differences all depend on just a few programs showing one or the other out of a small set of different behaviors and should hence not be over-generalized.

On the other hand, since these differences show exactly the same trend as the fractions of highly faulty programs mentioned above, there is some evidence that this ordering of reliability among the language groups in the present experiment may be real.

Remember, though, that the reliability advantage of the scripts may be due to the better test data available to the script programmers.

But at least it is fair to say there is no evidence in this data suggesting that script programs may be less reliable than non-scripts.

7.3 Results for "Surprising" Inputs

It is very instructive to compare the behavior on the more evil-minded input file m1000, again disregarding the programs already known as faulty as described above.

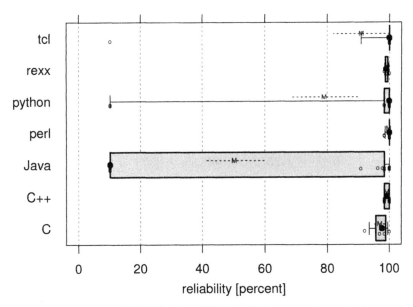

FIG. 19. Program output reliability for the m1000 input file in percent (except for those programs whose z1000 reliability was below 50 percent), with languages aggregated into groups.

The m1000 input set also contains phone numbers whose length and content is random, but in contrast to z1000 it even allows for phone numbers that do not contain any digits at all, only dashes and slashes. Such a phone number always has a correct encoding, namely an empty one, but one does not usually think of such inputs when reading the requirements. Hence the m1000 input file tests the robustness of the programs. The results are shown in Figs. 19 and 20.

Most programs cope with this situation well, but half of the Java programs and 4 of the script programs (1 Tcl and 3 Python) crash when they encounter the first empty phone number (which happens after 10% of the outputs), usually due to an illegal string subscript or array subscript. The languages that do not perform array subscript checking may still produce an incorrect output for the empty phone numbers but at least survive the mistake and then continue to function properly. Note that the huge size of the box for the Java data in Fig. 20 is quite arbitrary; it completely depends on the position of the first empty telephone number within the input file.

Except for this phenomenon, there are no large differences. 13 of the other programs (1 C, 5 C++, 4 Java, 2 Perl, 2 Python, 1 Rexx) fail exactly on the three empty phone numbers, but work allright otherwise, resulting in a reliability of 98.4%.

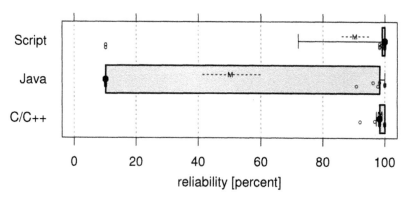

FIG. 20. Program output reliability for the m1000 input file in percent (except for those programs whose z1000 reliability was below 50 percent), with languages aggregated into groups.

7.4 Discussion

Summing up, it appears warranted to say that the scripts are not less reliable than the non-scripts.

The only salient reliability difference in the given situation is not between scripts and non-scripts but rather between languages that perform array subscript checking and those that do not—in our particular measurement, the latter are at an advantage, but the same problems exist in these programs and are of course comparatively harder to find and fix.

8. Results for Programmer Work Time

How long have the programmers taken to design, write, and test the program?

8.1 Results

Figures 21 and 22 show the total work time as reported by the script programmers and measured for the non-script programmers.

As we see, scripts (total median 3.1 hours) take only about one third of the time required for the non-scripts (total median 10.0 hours). Note, however, that the meaning of the measurements is not exactly the same: First, non-script times always include the time required for reading the requirements (typically around 15 minutes), whereas many of the script participants apparently did not count that time. Second, some of the script participants estimated (rather than measured) their work time. Third, we do not know whether all script participants were honest in their work time reporting. Fourth, and most importantly, all of the non-script participants started

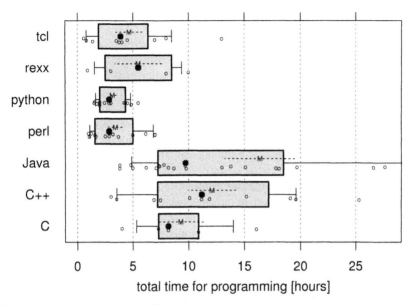

FIG. 21. Total working time for realizing the program. Script group: times as measured and reported by the programmers. Non-script group: times as measured by the experimenter. The bad/good ratios range from 1.5 for C up to 3.2 for Perl. Three Java work times at 40, 49, and 63 hours are not shown.

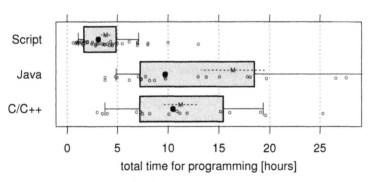

FIG. 22. Like Fig. 21, except that the languages are aggregated into larger groups. The bad/good ratio is 3.0 for Script, 2.6 for Java, and 2.1 for C/C++.

working on the solution immediately after reading the requirements, whereas some of the script participants started only days later but did not include the time in which they were thinking, perhaps subconsciously, about the program design in the meantime (see the quotes in Section 3.6 above).

8.2   Discussion

Even if we subtract a substantial discount from the times of the non-script programmers, these results are fairly spectacular: Scripts with the same functionality
are written and tested in half the time of corresponding non-scripts. For the class of
problems, to which these results can be generalized (which we cannot characterize
based on this study, but which certainly is not small) and maintenance issues left
aside (which we do not investigate empirically here; but see Sections 6.2 and 9), this
implies a large improvement in programming productivity by replacing non-script
languages by script languages—a trend one can already observe frequently in practice.

The scripting literature and folklore features a number of case studies where programs previously written in a non-script language were rewritten in a script language
in only a fraction of the time. Even if one is willing to fully believe the numbers
given, they do not mean very much: Usually, the first implementation of a program
involves a lot of work for determining and refining the requirements and if the reim-
plementation is done by the same programmer, program design is also performed a
lot quicker the second time around.

The present study provides data that is more realistic and also provides a comparison of not just individual cases, but of a statistical average for a substantial number
of cases. No programmer in the sample has performed a re-implementation in a different language. But is the data credible?

8.3   Validation

Fortunately, there is a way how we can check two things at once, namely the
correctness of the work time reporting *and* the equivalence of the programmer capabilities in the script versus the non-script group. Note that both of these possible
problems, if present, will tend to bias the script group work times downwards: we
would expect cheaters to fake their time to be smaller, not larger, and we expect to
see more capable programmers (rather than less capable ones) in the script group
compared to the non-script group if the average programmer capabilities are any
different.

This check relies on an old rule of thumb, which says that programmer productivity measured in lines of code per hour (LOC/hour) is roughly independent of the
programming language: With a few extreme exceptions such as APL or Assembler,
the time required for coding and testing a program will often be determined by the
amount of functionality that can be expressed per line, but the time required per line
will be roughly constant.

This rule is mostly an empirical one, but it can be explained by cognitive psychology: Once a programmer is reasonably fluent in a programming language, one

statement or line of code is the most important unit of thinking (at least during coding and debugging phases). If that is dominant, though, the capacity limit of short term memory—7 units plus or minus two—suggests that the effort required for constructing a program that is much longer than 7 lines may be roughly proportional to its number of lines, because the time required for correctly creating and handling one unit is constant and independent of the amount of information represented by the unit [17,23].

Actually, two widely used effort estimation methods explicitly assume the productivity in lines of code per hour is independent of programming language:

The first is Barry Boehm's CoCoMo [3]. This popular software estimation model uses software size measured in LOC as an input and predicts both cost and schedule. Various so-called *cost drivers* allow adjusting the estimate according to, for instance, the level of domain experience, the level of programming language experience, the required program reliability etc. However, the level of programming language used is not one of these cost drivers, because, as Boehm writes, *"It was found [...] that the amount of effort per source statement was highly independent of language level."* [3, p. 477]. He also cites independent research suggesting the same conclusion, in particular a study from IBM by Walston and Felix [25].

The second is Capers Jones' *language list* for the Function Point [1] method. Function Points are a software size metric that depends solely on program functionality and is hence independent of programming language [2]. Jones publishes a list [5] of programming languages, which indicates the value of LOC/FP for each language (the number of lines typically required to implement one function point) and also its so-called *language level* LL, a productivity factor indicating the number of function points that can be realized per time unit T with this language: $LL = FP/T$. T depends on the capabilities of the programmers etc. In this list, LL is exactly inversely proportional to LOC/FP; concretely $LL \times LOC/FP = 320$, which is just a different way of saying that the productivity of any language is a fixed 320 LOC per fixed time unit T. Independent studies confirming language productivity differences with respect to function points per time have also been published, e.g., [13]. Table III provides the relevant excerpt from the language table and Fig. 23 relates this data to the actual productivity observed in the present study.

So let us accept the statement "the number of lines written per hour is independent of programming language" as a rule of thumb for this study. The validation of our work time data based on this rule is plotted in Fig. 24. Judging from the productivity range of Java, all data points except maybe for the top three of Tcl and the top one of Perl are quite believable. In particular, except for Python, all medians are in the range 22 to 31. The variability between programmers is also similar across the languages. Hence, the LOC productivity plot lends a lot of credibility to the reported times:

TABLE III

EXCERPT FROM CAPERS JONES' PROGRAMMING LANGUAGE TABLE FOR THE LANGUAGES USED
IN THIS STUDY. LL IS THE LANGUAGE LEVEL AND LOC/FP IS THE NUMBER OF LINES OF CODE
REQUIRED PER FUNCTION POINT. SEE THE MAIN TEXT FOR AN EXPLANATION

language	LL	LOC/FP
C	3.5	91
C++	6	53
Java	6	53
Perl	15	21
Python	–	–
Rexx	7	46
Tcl	5	64

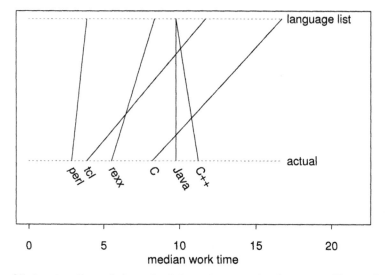

FIG. 23. Actual median work times of each language compared to those we would expect from the
relative productivity as given in Capers Jones' programming language list [5], normalized such that the
Java work times are exactly as predicted. We find that the language list underestimates the productivity of
C and Tcl for this problem. For the phonecode problem, C is almost as well-suited as C++ at least given
the approaches used by most participants, in contrast to the language levels indicated by Jones. For Tcl,
the given language level of 5 may be a typo which should read "15" instead. For the other languages, the
prediction of the table is reasonably accurate.

Only four productivity values overall are outside the (reliable) range found in the
experiment for the non-script programs.

None of the median differences are clearly statistically significant, the closest being Java versus C, Perl, Python, or Tcl where $0.07 \leqslant p \leqslant 0.10$.

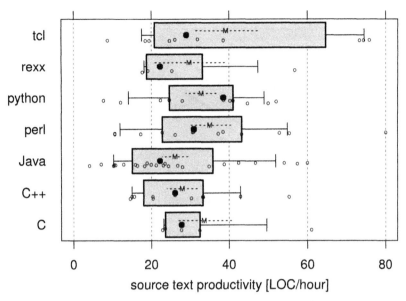

FIG. 24. Source text productivity in non-comment lines of code per total work hour. The bad/good ratios range from 1.4 for C up to 3.1 for Tcl.

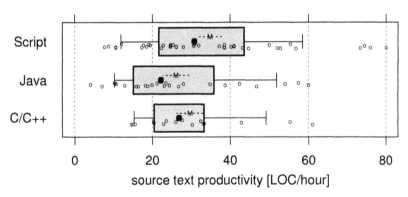

FIG. 25. Like Fig. 24, except that the languages are aggregated into groups. The bad/good ratio is 2.0 for Script, 2.4 for Java, and 1.6 for C/C++.

Even in the aggregated view (Fig. 25) with its much larger groups, the difference between C/C++ and scripts is not significant ($p = 0.22$), only the difference between Java and scripts is ($p = 0.031$), the difference being at least 5.2 LOC/hour (with 80% confidence).

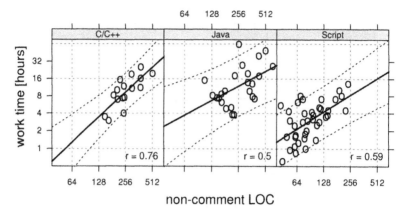

FIG. 26. The same data as in Fig. 25, except that the program lengths and work times are shown separately. The lines are a standard least squares regression line and its 90% prediction interval. Note the logarithmic axes. r is the correlation coefficient of the logarithmic data.

This comparison lends a lot of credibility to the work time comparison shown above. The times reported for script programming are probably only modestly too optimistic, if any, so that a work time advantage for the script languages of about factor two holds.

Figure 26 shows the same data as a two-dimensional plot including a regression line that could be used for (logarithmically) predicting work time from expected size. The higher productivity of the script languages shows up as a trend line lying lower in the plot. The C/C++ line is steeper than the others, which in this logarithmic plot shows non-linear increase of effort: programs that are twice as long take more than twice as much work time. This is probably due to the fact that the best C/C++ programmers not only were more productive but also wrote more compact code.

9.   Discussion of Program Structure

If one considers the program designs (i.e., algorithms and data structures) typically chosen in the various languages, there is a striking difference.

9.1   Results for Scripts

Most of the programmers in the script group used the associative arrays provided by their language and stored the dictionary words to be retrieved by their number encodings. The search algorithm simply attempts to retrieve from this array, using

```
sub encode {
  my $phonenumber = shift;  # retrieve argument
  my @results = &encodeByWords($phonenumber);
  return if @results && !defined $results[0];  #antibacktrack
  return @results if @results;
  return $phonenumber if length $phonenumber == 1;
  my $first = substr $phonenumber,0,1;
  @results = &encodeByWords(substr $phonenumber,1);
  return unless defined $results[0];
  return map {"$first $_"} @results; #prepend $first everywhere
}
sub encodeByWords {
  my $phonenumber = shift;  # retrieve argument
  my @results, $hasword, $head;  # make variables local
  for my $len (1..length($phonenumber)-1) {  # for increasing prefixes
    next unless exists $words{$head = substr $phonenumber,0,$len};
    $hasword++;  #word found for prefix substring
    my @found=&encode(substr $phonenumber,$len);  # encode rest
    for my $tail (@found) {  # concatenate each head with each tail
      push @results, map {"$_ $tail"} @{$words{$head}};
    }
  }
  # end recursion: encode by just one word, if possible:
  push @results, @{$words{$phonenumber}}if exists $words{$phonenumber};
  return undef if $hasword && !@results; # no complete encoding found?
  return @results;  # else: return all encodings thus found
}
```

FIG. 27. Example Perl search routine from program s149103, the third-fastest-written, fastest-running, and shortest Perl script. Identifiers and comments have been changed to maximize readability. words is the associative array that is indexed by digit strings (partial phone numbers) and contains as values lists of words matching these partial numbers.

prefixes of increasing length of the remaining rest of the current phone number as the key. Any match found leads to a new partial solution to be completed later. See three rather different implementations of this algorithm in Figs. 27, 28, and 29.

These programs were selected from their respective group according to the following criteria: Short (so the code can be displayed on one page), efficient (in terms of execution time), and written in a short time (and hence hopefully by a rather competent programmer).

9.2 Discussion

The Tcl script has arguably the simplest and most straightforward formulation of the algorithm. However, this clarity comes at the price of a rather broad call interface

```
def encode(phonenumber, digitAllowed=1):
  results = []
  for i in range(1, len(phonenumber)+1): # for increasing substrings
    s1 = phonenumber[:i]                  # split number into two parts
    s2 = phonenumber[i:]
    if words.has_key(s1):                 # first part has an encoding
        digitAllowed = 0  # no single digit needed or allowed
        if s2:       # second part is not empty, try to encode it
            for m in encode(s2):
                for w in words[s1]:
                    # combine encodings for first and second part
                    results.append("%s %s" % (w, m))
        else:        # remainder is empty, first part is result
            results.extend(words[s1])
  if digitAllowed:
    # no results found starting here   AND
    # we also did not insert a digit just before
    if phonenumber[1:]:  # match the rest
        for m in encode(phonenumber[1:], 0):
            # combine first digit with further encodings found
            results.append("%s %s" % (phonenumber[0], m))
    else:
        # last character matches itself.
        results.append(phonenumber[0])
  return results
```

FIG. 28. Example Python search routine from program s149205, the fastest-written and fastest-running, but only fifth shortest Python script. This script fails and crashes on empty phone numbers. Identifiers and comments have been changed to maximize readability. words is the associative array that is indexed by digit strings (partial phone numbers) and contains as values lists of words matching these partial numbers.

(with four parameters) and printing of the results from within the search routine (which is no good modularization). Furthermore, the Tcl script takes 9 times as long for execution as the Python and Perl scripts.

The Python version avoids all three of these drawbacks and is still very easy to understand. However, it fails to handle phone numbers with no digits correctly.

The Perl program, in comparison, is fairly convoluted and hard-to-understand, but is both correct and efficient.

I have not attempted to verify whether the programming styles represented by these three somewhat arbitrarily selected programs are in any way typical among the scripts of each language group (though many people may expect they are). However, please note that the styles are by no means preferred or triggered—let alone enforced—by particular features of the respective language. Quite on the contrary:

```
proc encode {phonestring phonenumber resultwords wasdigit} {
  if {![string length $phonenumber]} {  # nothing more to encode
    puts "$phonestring: [join $resultwords { }]"  # print $resultwords
    found return
  }
  set found 0
  for {set i 0} {$i<[string length $phonenumber]} {incr i} {
    set subnumber [string range $phonenumber 0 $i] # pick number prefix
    set subwords {}; catch {set subwords $::words($subnumber)} # find
    words foreach subword $subwords {  # for each word found for prefix
      encode $phonestring [string range $phonenumber [expr $i+1] end] \
            [concat $resultwords [list $subword]] 0 # encode remainder
      set found 1
    }
  }
  if {!$found && !$wasdigit} {  # insert one digit, encode the rest
    encode $phonestring [string range $phonenumber 1 end] \
          [concat $resultwords [string range $phonenumber 0 0]] 1
  }
}
```

FIG. 29. Example Tcl search routine from program s149407, the fastest-written, seventh-fastest-running, and shortest Tcl script. Identifiers and comments have been changed to maximize readability. words is the associative array that is indexed by digit strings (partial phone numbers) and contains as values lists of words matching these partial numbers.

Each of the variants can straightforwardly be translated into each of the other two languages without changing its structure.

9.3 Results for Non-Scripts

In contrast, essentially all of the non-script programmers chose either of the following solutions. In the simple case, they simply store the whole dictionary in an array, usually in both the original character form and the corresponding phone number representation. They then select and test one tenth of the whole dictionary for each digit of the phone number to be encoded, using only the first digit as a key to constrain the search space. This leads to a simple, but inefficient solution.

The more elaborate case uses a 10-ary tree in which each node represents a certain digit, nodes at height n representing the nth character of a word. A word is stored at a node if the path from the root to this node represents the number encoding of the word. This is the most efficient solution, but it requires a comparatively large number of statements to implement the tree construction. In Java, the large resulting number of objects also leads to a high memory consumption due to the severe per-object memory overhead incurred by current implementations of the language.

9.4   Global Discussion

In light of these results, the shorter program length of the script programs can be explained by the fact that most of the actual search is done simply by the hashing algorithm used internally by the associative arrays. In contrast, the non-script programs with their array or tree implementations require most of these mundane elementary steps of the search process to be coded explicitly by the programmer. This is further pronounced by the effort (or lack of it) for data structure declarations.

The larger variation in execution time and in memory consumption that was found for the non-scripts can be explained by the two very different dictionary lookup mechanisms employed within each of these groups (one being memory-conservative but having effort linear in the number of words, the other requiring larger administrative memory overhead but providing logarithmic access time).

It is an interesting observation that despite the existence of hash table implementations in both the Java and the C++ class libraries none of the non-script programmers used them (but rather implemented a tree solution by hand), whereas for almost all of the script programmers the hash tables built into the language were the obvious choice.

10.   Testing Two Common Rules of Thumb

Having so many different implementations of the same requirements allows for a nice test of two common rules of thumb in programming:

- The time/memory tradeoff: To make a program run faster, one will often need to use more memory.

- The elegance-is-efficient rule: A shorter (in terms of lines of code) solution to the same problem will often also run faster than a longer one.

10.1   The Run Time Versus Memory Consumption Tradeoff

The time/memory tradeoff is a frequent effect in algorithm design: An algorithm can often be made asymptotically faster if it is allowed to use an asymptotically larger data structure.

Similar effects may also occur on a more tactical level in programming, e.g., by precomputing and storing certain results rather than recomputing them each time they are required, or by storing data in a more uniform manner rather than in the most compact way.

Can a time/memory tradeoff be found in the programs of our study for one or several languages?

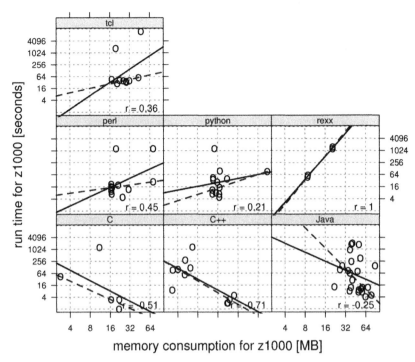

FIG. 30. Memory consumption versus program run time. The thick line is a least squares regression trend line; the dashed line is a least absolute distance trend line. *r* denotes the correlation (computed on the logarithms of the values). Note the logarithmic axes.

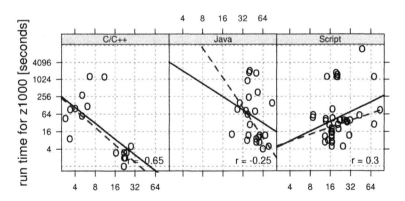

FIG. 31. The same data as in Fig. 30, by language group. Note the logarithmic axes.

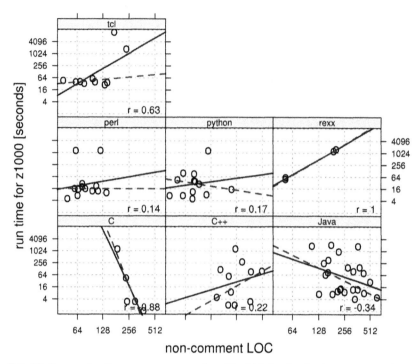

FIG. 32. Program length versus program run time. The thick line is a least squares regression trend line; the dashed line is a least absolute distance trend line. Note the logarithmic axes.

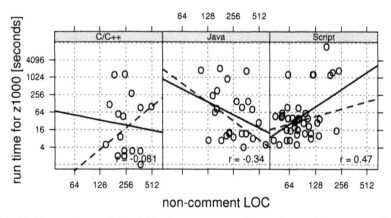

FIG. 33. The same data as in Fig. 32, by language group. r denotes the correlation (computed on the logarithms of the values). Note the logarithmic axes.

The time/memory tradeoff is shown for the individual languages in Fig. 30 and for the language groups in Fig. 31.

Apparently, the rule is quite correct for all three non-script languages: The faster running C and C++ programs require quite clearly more memory than the slower ones. A similar effect appears to be present for Java, though much more blurred because Java gives more opportunities for memory inefficiency at a tactical level.

The reason in all three cases is the design dichotomy described above between programs using the simpler group-by-first-character-only approach on the one hand and programs implementing the full 10-ary search tree on the other hand.

For the script languages, the opposite rule tends to be true: Those programs that use more memory actually tend to be slower (rather than faster) than the others, because given the associative array design of the scripts, additional memory does not contribute to algorithmic efficiency, but rather represents tactical inefficiency only.

10.2 Are Shorter Programs Also More Efficient?

The data for the elegance-is-efficient rule is shown for the individual languages in Fig. 32 and for the language groups in Fig. 33. The evidence for this rule is rather mixed: For the phonecode problem, a somewhat longer program appears to be required for full efficiency in both C and Java—in opposition to the rule; see also Section 9. In contrast, for some strange reason the rule appears to hold for C++, at least for the data we have here. For the individual script languages, program length appears to have rather little influence on run time, if we discount the Rexx programs (where there are only 4 programs from 3 different programmers) and the two extremely slow Tcl programs. However, if we consider all script programs together as in Fig. 33, there is quite some evidence that the rule may be correct: with 90% confidence, the correlation is larger than 0.25.

11. Metrics for Predicting Programmer Performance

In practical software engineering situations it would often be very useful if one could predict an unknown programmer's performance in advance, in particular the time required to complete a task and various quality attributes of the resulting program such as those investigated in this study.

The large number of directly comparable data points in this study allows for testing several possible approaches to such predictions.

11.1   Results for Objective Metrics

The non-script programmers were asked several questions about their previous programming experience, as described in detail in [21]. Examples are number of years of programming experience, total amount of program code written, size of largest program ever written, etc.

None of these questions had any substantial predictive value for any aspect of programmer performance in the experiment, so I will not delve into this data at all.

11.2   Results for Programmer Self-Rating

In contrast, the script programmers (but unfortunately not the non-script programmers) were asked the following question:

```
# Overall I tend to rate myself as follows compared to all other
# programmers
# (replace one dot by an X)
# among the upper 10 percent      .
# upper 11 to 25 percent          .
# upper 25 to 40 percent          .
# upper 40 to 60 percent          .
# lower 25 to 40 percent          .
# lower 11 to 25 percent          .
# lower 10 percent                .
```

On this scale, the programmers of as many as 14 of the scripts (35%) rated themselves among the upper 10 percent and those of another 15 (37.5%) among the top 10 to 25. The programmers of only 9 scripts (22.5%) rated themselves lower than that and 2 (5%) gave no answer. Across languages, there are no large self-rating differences: If we compare the sets of self-ratings per language to one another, using a Wilcoxon Rank Sum Test with normal approximation for ties, no significant difference is found for any of the language pairs ($0.58 < p < 0.94$).

As for correlations of self-rating and actual performance, I found that higher self-ratings tend to be somewhat associated with lower run time (as illustrated in Fig. 34; the rank correlation is -0.33) and also with shorter work time for producing the program (Fig. 35; the rank correlation is -0.30).

No clear association was found for memory consumption, program length, comment length, comment density, or program reliability.

Summing up, to predict how good a programmer will perform compared to others, it may be the best to just ask him or herself for an opinion of his or her general capabilities. This is not to be confused with direct personal estimates of, say, expected effort for one particular task.

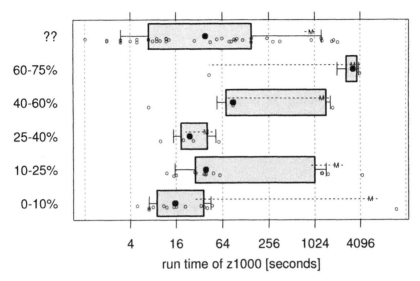

FIG. 34. Relationship between self-rating and program efficiency: higher self-rating is correlated with faster programs. The uppermost boxplot represents all non-script programs. Note the logarithmic axis.

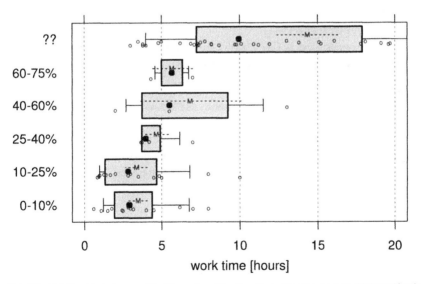

FIG. 35. Relationship between self-rating and working time for writing the program: higher self-rating is correlated with shorter work time. The uppermost boxplot represents the non-script programs.

12. Conclusions

The following statements summarize the findings of the comparative analysis of 80 implementations of the phonecode program in 7 different languages:

- Designing and writing the program in Perl, Python, Rexx, or Tcl takes only about half as much time as writing it in C, C++, or Java and the resulting program is only half as long.
- No clear differences in program reliability between the language groups were observed.
- The typical memory consumption of a script program is about twice that of a C or C++ program. For Java it is another factor of two higher.
- For the initialization phase of the phonecode program (reading the 1 MB dictionary file and creating the 70k-entry internal data structure), the C and C++ programs have a strong run time advantage of about factor 3 to 4 compared to Java and about 5 to 10 compared to the script languages.
- For the main phase of the phonecode program (search through the internal data structure), the advantage in run time of C or C++ versus Java is only about factor 2 and the script programs even tend to be faster than the Java programs.
- Within the script languages, Python and in particular Perl are faster than Rexx and Tcl for both phases.
- For all program aspects investigated, the performance variability due to different programmers (as described by the bad/good ratios) tends to be larger than the variability due to different languages.

Due to the large number of implementations and broad range of programmers investigated, these results, when taken with a grain of salt, are probably reliable despite the validity threats discussed in Section 3.6. We can expect to find similar results for most members of the frequent class of programs that performs sequential transcoding of input records into output records based on some kind of translation vocabulary. Generalizing the results to very different application domains, however, would be haphazard.

It is likely that for many other problems the results for the script group of languages would not be quite as good as they are. However, I would like to emphasize that the phonecode problem was not chosen so as to make the script group of languages look good—it was originally developed as a non-trivial, yet well-defined benchmark for programmers' ability of writing reliable programs.

I conclude the following:

- The so-called "scripting languages" Perl, Python, Rexx, and Tcl can be preferable alternatives to "conventional" languages such as C or C++ even for tasks that need to handle fair amounts of computation and data. Their relative run time and memory consumption overhead will often be acceptable and they may offer significant advantages with respect to programmer productivity—at least for small programs like the phonecode problem.

- Within the group of scripting languages, Tcl has the caveat of substantially longer minimum execution time compared to Perl and Python. Perl may have the caveat of requiring more disciplined programmers for obtaining readable programs compared to Tcl and Python.

- Interpersonal variability, that is, the capability and behavior differences between programmers using the same language, tends to account for more differences between programs than a change of the programming language.

12.1 Further Reading

If you are interested in further information about how scripting languages compare to one another or to conventional languages, you can find some statements from the point of view of the Python people on http://www.python.org/doc/essays/comparisons.html; from the point of view of the Perl people on http://www.perl.com/language/versus/; and from the point of view of the Tcl people on http://www.scriptics.com/advocacy/. A wealth of comparisons written by others is collected on the Python website on http://www.python.org/doc/Comparisons.html.

If you want to learn how to write efficient programs in scripting languages, a very useful short article is http://www.python.org/doc/essays/list2str.html. It was written for Python, but most of its lessons apply to other script languages as well. Some of the language books such as [24] for Perl and [16] for Python also contain sections on writing efficient programs.

ACKNOWLEDGEMENTS

I thank all participants who submitted a program for this study. Without you, the unusually broad coverage could not have been obtained.

Appendix A: Specification of the Phonecode Programming Problem

The problem solved by the participants of this study (i.e., the authors of the programs investigated here) was called *phonecode*.

The exact problem description given to the subjects in the non-script group is printed in the appendix of [21]. The following subsections reproduce the description given on the web page for the participants of the script group. It is equivalent with respect to the functional requirements of the program, but had to be different with respect to the submission procedure etc.

Underlined parts of the text were hyperlinks in the original web page.

A.1 The Procedure Description

(First few paragraphs left out)

The purpose of this website is collecting many implementations of this same program in scripting languages for comparing these languages with each other and with the ones mentioned above. The languages in question are

- *Perl*
- *Python*
- *Rexx*
- *Tcl*

The properties of interest for the comparison are

- *programming effort*
- *program length*
- *program readability/modularization/maintainability*
- *elegance of the solution*
- *memory consumption*
- *run time consumption*
- *correctness/robustness*

Interested?

If you are interested in participating in this study, please create your own implementation of the Phonecode program (as described below) and send it to me by email.

*I will collect programs **until December 18, 1999**. After that date, I will evaluate all programs and send you the results.*

*The **effort** involved in implementing phonecode depends on how many mistakes you make underways. In the previous experiment, very good programmers typically finished in about 3 to 4 hours, average ones typically take about 6 to 12 hours.*

If anything went badly wrong, it took much longer, of course; the original experiment saw times over 20 hours for about 10 percent of the participants. On the other hand, the problem should be much easier to do in a scripting language compared to Java/C/C++, so you can expect much less effort than indicated above.

Still interested?

Great! The procedure is as follows:

1. *Read the task description for the "phonecode" benchmark. This describes what the program should do.*
2. *Download*

   - *the small test dictionary test.w,*
   - *the small test input file test.t,*
   - *the corresponding correct results test.out,*
   - *the real dictionary woerter2,*
   - *a 1000-input file z1000.t,*
   - *the corresponding correct results z1000.out,*
   - *or all of the above together in a single zip file.*

3. *Fetch this program header, fill it in, convert it to the appropriate comment syntax for your language, and use it as the basis of your program file.*
4. *Implement the program, using only a single file.*

   (Make sure you measure the time you take separately for design, coding and testing/debugging.) Once running, test it using test.w, test.t, test.out only, until it works for this data. Then and only then start testing it using woerter2, z1000.t, z1000.out.

   This restriction is necessary because a similar ordering was imposed on the subjects of the original experiment as well—however, it is not helpful to use the large data earlier, anyway.
5. *A note on testing:*

   - *Make sure your program works correctly. When fed with woerter2 and z1000.t it must produce the contents of z1000.out (except for the ordering of the outputs). To compare your actual output to z1000.out, sort both and compare line by line (using diff, for example).*
   - *If you find any differences, but are convinced that your program is correct and z1000.out is wrong with respect to the task description, then re-read the task description very carefully. Many people misunderstand one particular point.*

(I absolutely guarantee that z1000.out is appropriate for the given re-quirements.)

If (and only if!) you still don't find your problem after re-reading the requirements very carefully, then read this <u>hint</u>.

6. *Submit your program by email to <u>prechelt@ira.uka.de</u>, using* **Subject: phone-code submission** *and preferably inserting your program as plain text (but watch out so that your email software does not insert additional line breaks!)*

7. **Thank you!**

Constraints

- *Please make sure your program runs on Perl 5.003, Python 1.5.2, Tcl 8.0.2, or Rexx as of Regina 0.08g, respectively. It will be executed on a Solaris platform (SunOS 5.7), running on a Sun Ultra-II, but should be platform-independent.*

- *Please use only a single source program file, not several files, and give that file the name phonecode.xx (where xx is whatever suffix is common for your programming language).*

- *Please do not over-optimize your program. Deliver your first reasonable solution.*

- *Please be honest with the work time that you report; there is no point in cheating.*

- *Please design and implement the solution alone. If you cooperate with somebody else, the comparison will be distorted.*

A.2 Task Requirements Description

Consider the following mapping from letters to digits:

E	J N Q	R W X	D S Y	F T	A M	C I V	B K U	L O P	G H Z
e	j n q	r w x	d s y	f t	a m	c i v	b k u	l o p	g h z
0	1	2	3	4	5	6	7	8	9

We want to use this mapping for encoding telephone numbers by words, so that it becomes easier to remember the numbers.

Functional requirements

Your task is writing a program that finds, for a given phone number, all possible encodings by words, and prints them. A phone number is an arbitrary(!) string of dashes (−), slashes (/) and digits. The dashes and slashes will not be encoded. The words are taken from a dictionary which is given as an alphabetically sorted ASCII file (one word per line).

Only exactly each encoding that is possible from this dictionary and that matches the phone number exactly shall be printed. Thus, possibly nothing is printed at all. The words in the dictionary contain letters (capital or small, but the difference is ignored in the sorting), dashes (−) and double quotes ("). For the encoding only the letters are used, but the words must be printed in exactly the form given in the dictionary. Leading non-letters do not occur in the dictionary.

Encodings of phone numbers can consist of a single word or of multiple words separated by spaces. The encodings are built word by word from left to right. If and only if at a particular point no word at all from the dictionary can be inserted, a single digit from the phone number can be copied to the encoding instead. Two subsequent digits are never allowed, though. To put it differently: In a partial encoding that currently covers k digits, digit k + 1 is encoded by itself if and only if, first, digit k was not encoded by a digit and, second, there is no word in the dictionary that can be used in the encoding starting at digit k + 1.

Your program must work on a series of phone numbers; for each encoding that it finds, it must print the phone number followed by a colon, a single(!) space, and the encoding on one line; trailing spaces are not allowed.

All remaining ambiguities in this specification will be resolved by the following **example**. *(Still remaining ambiguities are intended degrees of freedom.)*

Dictionary (in file `test.w`*):*

```
an
blau
Bo"
Boot
bo"s
da
Fee
fern
Fest
fort
je
jemand
mir
Mix
Mixer
Name
neu
```

```
o"d
Ort
so
Tor
Torf
Wasser
```

Phone number list (in file `test.t`*):*

```
112
5624-82
4824
0721/608-4067
10/783--5
1078-913-5
381482
04824
```

Program start command:

```
phonecode test.w test.t
```

Corresponding correct program output (on screen):

```
5624-82: mir Tor
5624-82: Mix Tor
4824: Torf
4824: fort
4824: Tor 4
10/783--5: neu o"d 5
10/783--5: je bo"s 5
10/783--5: je Bo" da
381482: so 1 Tor
04824: 0 Torf
04824: 0 fort
04824: 0 Tor 4
```

Any other output would be wrong (except for different ordering of the lines).
   Wrong outputs for the above example would be, e.g.,
     `562482: Mix Tor`, *because the formatting of the phone number is incorrect,*
     `10/783--5: je bos 5`, *because the formatting of the second word is incorrect,*
     `4824: 4 Ort`, *because in place of the first digit the words* `Torf`, `fort`, `Tor` *could be used,*

1078-913-5: je Bo" 9 1 da, *since there are two subsequent digits in the encoding,*

04824: 0 Tor, *because the encoding does not cover the whole phone number, and*

5624-82: mir Torf, *because the encoding is longer than the phone number.*

The above data are available to you in the files test.w *(dictionary),* test.t *(telephone numbers) and* test.out *(program output).*

Quantitative requirements

Length of the individual words in the dictionary: 50 characters maximum.
Number of words in the dictionary: 75000 maximum
Length of the phone numbers: 50 characters maximum.
Number of entries in the phone number file: unlimited.

Quality requirements

Work as carefully as you would as a professional software engineer and deliver a correspondingly high grade program. Specifically, thoroughly comment your source code (design ideas etc.).

The focus during program construction shall be on correctness. *Generate exactly the right output format right from the start. Do not generate additional output. I will automatically test your program with hundreds of thousands of phone numbers and it should not make a single mistake, if possible—in particular it must not crash. Take yourself as much time as is required to ensure correctness.*

Your program must be run time efficient in so far that it analyzes only a very small fraction of all dictionary entries in each word appending step. *It should also be memory efficient in that it does not use 75000 times 50 bytes for storing the dictionary if that contains many much shorter words. The dictionary must be read into main memory entirely, but you must not do the same with the phone number file, as that may be arbitrarily large.*

Your program need not be robust against incorrect formats of the dictionary file or the phone number file.

A.3 The Hint

The "hint" referred to in the procedure description shown in Section A.1 actually refers to a file containing only the following:

Hint

Please do not read this hint during preparation.

*Read it only if you **really** cannot find out what is wrong with your program and why its output does not conform to z1000.out although you think the program must be correct.*

If, and only if, you are in that situation now, read the actual hint.
The link refers to the following file:

Hint

If your program finds a superset of the encodings shown in z1000.out, you have probably met the following pitfall.

Many people first misunderstand the requirements with respect to the insertion of digits as follows. They insert a digit even if they have inserted a word at some point, but could then not complete the encoding up to the end of the phone number. That is, they use backtracking.

This is incorrect. Encodings must be built step-by-step strictly from left to right; the decision whether to insert a digit or not is made at some point and, once made, must never be changed.

Sorry for the confusion. The original test had this ambiguity and to be able to compare the new work times with the old ones, the spec must remain as is. If you ran into this problem, please report the time you spent finding and repairing; put the number of minutes in the 'special events' section of the program header comment. Thanks a lot!

Appendix B: Raw Data

Below you find the most important variables from the raw data set analyzed in this report. The meaning of the variables is (left to right): subject ID (person), programming language (lang), run time for z1000 input file in minutes (z1000t), run time for z0 input file in minutes (z0t), memory consumption at end of run for z1000 input file in kilobytes (z1000mem), program length in statement lines of code (LOC), output reliability for z1000 input file in percent (z1000rel), output reliability for m1000 input file in percent (m1000rel), total subject work time in hours (work), subject's answer to the capability question "I consider myself to be among the top X percent of all programmers" (caps).

person	lang	z1000t	z0t	z1000mem	LOC	z1000rel	m1000rel	work	caps
s018	C	0.017	0.017	22432	380	98.10	96.8	16.10	??
s030	C	0.050	0.033	16968	244	76.47	92.1	4.00	??
s036	C	20.900	0.000	11440	188	0.00	89.5	8.20	??
s066	C	0.750	0.467	2952	237	98.48	100.0	7.30	??
s078	C	0.050	0.050	22496	302	99.24	98.4	10.90	??

s015	C++	0.050	0.050	24616	374	99.24	100.0	11.20	??
s020	C++	1.983	0.550	6384	166	98.48	98.4	3.00	??
s021	C++	4.867	0.017	5312	298	100.00	98.4	19.10	??
s025	C++	0.083	0.083	28568	150	99.24	98.4	3.50	??
s027	C++	1.533	0.000	3472	378	98.09	100.0	25.30	??
s033	C++	0.033	0.033	23336	205	99.24	98.4	10.10	??
s034	C++	21.400	0.033	6864	249	0.00	1.1	7.50	??
s042	C++	0.033	0.033	22680	243	100.00	100.0	11.90	??
s051	C++	0.150	0.033	3448	221	100.00	98.4	15.20	??
s090	C++	1.667	0.033	4152	511	98.48	100.0	19.60	??
s096	C++	0.917	0.017	5240	209	100.00	100.0	6.90	??
s017	Java	0.633	0.433	41952	509	100.00	10.2	48.90	??
s023	Java	2.633	0.650	89664	384	7.60	98.4	7.10	??
s037	Java	0.283	0.100	59088	364	100.00	10.2	13.00	??
s040	Java	0.317	0.283	56376	212	100.00	98.4	5.00	??
s043	Java	2.200	2.017	36136	164	98.85	90.9	8.70	??
s047	Java	6.467	0.117	54872	166	100.00	10.1	6.20	??
s050	Java	0.200	0.167	58024	186	100.00	10.2	4.80	??
s053	Java	0.267	0.100	52376	257	99.62	10.2	63.20	??
s054	Java	1.700	0.717	27088	324	100.00	10.2	13.80	??
s056	Java	0.350	0.067	22328	232	100.00	100.0	18.10	??
s057	Java	0.467	0.000	38104	434	100.00	10.2	17.80	??
s059	Java	4.150	0.050	40384	147	100.00	10.2	7.40	??
s060	Java	3.783	0.100	29432	281	98.85	96.3	27.60	??
s062	Java	16.800	0.067	38368	218	100.00	10.2	3.80	??
s063	Java	1.333	0.450	38672	155	100.00	100.0	7.30	??
s065	Java	1.467	0.117	49704	427	100.00	97.9	39.70	??
s068	Java	31.200	0.050	40584	107	100.00	10.2	15.10	??
s072	Java	30.100	0.067	52272	365	100.00	100.0	7.80	??
s081	Java	0.200	0.150	79544	614	100.00	10.2	26.60	??
s084	Java	0.150	0.133	65240	338	100.00	100.0	9.70	??
s087	Java	0.267	0.083	39896	322	100.00	100.0	19.70	??
s093	Java	37.100	0.050	41632	179	100.00	10.2	9.80	??
s099	Java	0.267	0.217	70696	228	100.00	98.4	3.80	??
s102	Java	0.167	0.150	51968	130	0.18	6.6	8.20	??
s149101	perl	0.267	0.183	17344	60	99.24	100.0	1.08	0-10%
s149102	perl	21.400	0.417	73440	62	0.00	0.0	1.67	10-25%
s149103	perl	0.083	0.067	25408	49	100.00	100.0	1.58	NA
s149105	perl	0.200	0.100	31536	97	100.00	100.0	3.17	0-10%
s149106	perl	0.117	0.033	17480	65	99.24	100.0	6.17	0-10%
s149107	perl	0.350	0.333	17232	108	100.00	100.0	2.50	0-10%
s149108	perl	0.483	0.433	73448	74	100.00	100.0	2.83	10-25%
s149109	perl	0.167	0.133	17312	141	100.00	100.0	3.67	25-40%
s149110	perl	0.200	0.133	17232	114	99.24	100.0	5.00	10-25%
s149111	perl	0.267	0.233	17224	80	100.00	100.0	1.00	10-25%
s149112	perl	0.250	0.233	17576	66	100.00	98.4	1.25	10-25%
s149113	perl	67.500	0.300	20320	121	100.00	0.0	7.00	60-75%
s149114	perl	0.333	0.233	21896	74	99.24	98.4	7.00	25-40%

```
s149201  python    0.650 0.317 22608   82  99.24  100.0    2.00 10-25%
s149202  python    1.583 1.367 17784   61  99.24   98.4    1.58    NA
s149203  python    0.183 0.167 13664   79 100.00  100.0    1.77  0-10%
s149204  python    0.117 0.067 13632   60 100.00  100.0    2.43  0-10%
s149205  python    0.083 0.067 17336   78 100.00   10.2    1.50  0-10%
s149206  python    0.117 0.067 17320   42 100.00  100.0    5.50 40-60%
s149207  python    0.133 0.067 15312  114 100.00  100.0    2.83  0-10%
s149208  python    0.450 0.367 16024   94  99.24   98.4    4.20 25-40%
s149209  python   72.300 0.500 14632  119 100.00    0.0    4.83 10-25%
s149210  python    0.250 0.200 17480  225 100.00   10.2    4.50  0-10%
s149211  python    1.483 1.150 91120   82  98.48   10.2    2.00 40-60%
s149212  python    0.617 0.467 14048   84  99.24  100.0    3.00  0-10%
s149213  python    0.733 0.533 14000   52  99.24  100.0    4.32 60-75%
s149301    rexx    0.817 0.300  8968   53 100.00   98.4    0.93 10-25%
s149302    rexx   25.400 0.900 21152  203  44.75   46.6    8.00 10-25%
s149303    rexx   21.000 0.950 21144  191  99.62   98.9   10.00 10-25%
s149304    rexx    1.000 0.433  9048   53 100.00  100.0    3.00 10-25%
s149401     tcl    0.650 0.567 32400   62 100.00  100.0    0.83 10-25%
s149402     tcl    0.567 0.433 29272   78 100.00  100.0    4.00  0-10%
s149403     tcl    0.617 0.517 28880  144 100.00  100.0    4.50 10-25%
s149405     tcl    0.967 0.667 44536   98 100.00  100.0    3.75 25-40%
s149406     tcl    0.650 0.583 26352  105 100.00  100.0    1.38 10-25%
s149407     tcl    0.783 0.467 17672   44 100.00  100.0    0.60  0-10%
s149408     tcl  202.800 0.633 48840  173 100.00  100.0    7.00  0-10%
s149409     tcl    0.683 0.567 23192   70 100.00  100.0    8.00  0-10%
s149410     tcl   29.400 1.433 20296  240 100.00   10.2   13.00 40-60%
s149411     tcl    0.467 0.367 21448  135 100.00  100.0    3.50 10-25%
```

The reliability values of 98% and higher for z1000rel occur due to some very subtle I/O issues when the programs are executed in the test harness (where output is to a pipe rather than to a terminal). These programs should be considered correct.

The reliability values of 98% and higher for m1000rel occur due to two very minor ambiguities in the task specification (see the Appendix of [20]). These programs should be considered correct.

REFERENCES

[1] Albrecht A.J., Gaffney J.E. Jr, "Software function, source lines of code, and develop-ment effort prediction: A software science validation", *IEEE Transactions on Software Engineering* **SE-9** (6) (1983) 639–648.

[2] Behrens C.A., "Measuring the productivity of computer systems development activities with function points", *IEEE Transactions on Software Engineering* **SE-9** (6) (1983) 648–652.

[3] Boehm B.W., *Software Engineering Economics*, Prentice Hall, Englewood Cliffs, NJ, 1981.

[4] Briot J.-P., Guerraoui R., Löhr K.-P., "Concurrency and distribution in object-oriented programming", *ACM Computing Surveys* **30** (3) (1998) 291–329.

[5] Capers Jones, Software Productivity Research, Programming languages table, version 7. Available at http://www.spr.com/library/0langtbl.htm, 1996 (as of Feb. 2000).

[6] Dijkstra E.W., "Go To statement considered harmful", *Communications of the ACM* **11** (3) (1968) 147–148.

[7] Ebrahimi A., "Novice programmer errors: Language constructs and plan composition", *Intl. J. of Human-Computer Studies* **41** (1994) 457–480.

[8] Efron B., Tibshirani R., *An Introduction to the Bootstrap*, in: *Monographs on Statistics and Applied Probability*, Vol. 57, Chapman and Hall, New York, London, 1993.

[9] Hatton L., "Does OO sync with how we think?", *IEEE Software* **15** (3) (1998) 46–54.

[10] Hietaniemi J., *perlhist: The Perl history records*, Unix Manual Page, 1999.

[11] Hudak P., Jones M.P., Haskell vs. Ada vs. C++ vs. awk vs. . . . an experiment in software prototyping productivity. Technical report, Yale University, Dept. of CS, New Haven, CT, July 1994.

[12] Humphrey W.S., *A Discipline for Software Engineering, SEI Series in Software Engineering*, Addison-Wesley, Reading, MA, 1995.

[13] Klepper R., Bock D., "Third and fourth generation language productivity differences", *Communications of the ACM* **38** (9) (1995) 69–79.

[14] Koenemann-Belliveau J., Mohrer T.G., Robertson S.P. (Eds.), *Empirical Studies of Programmers: Fourth Workshop, New Brunswick, NJ*, Ablex Publishing Corp, 1991.

[15] Lewis J.A., Henry S.M., Kafura D.G., Schulman R.S., "On the relationship between the object-oriented paradigm and software reuse: An empirical investigation", *J. of Object-Oriented Programming* (1992).

[16] Lutz M., *Programming Python*, O'Reilly and Associates, 2001.

[17] Miller G.A., "The magic number seven, plus or minus two", *The Psychological Review* **63** (2) (1956) 81–97.

[18] Ousterhout J.K., "Scripting: Higher-level programming for the 21st century", *IEEE Computer* **31** (3) (1998) 23–30.

[19] Philippsen M., Imperative concurrent object-oriented languages. Technical Report TR-95/50, International Computer Science Institute, University of California, Berkeley, CA, August 1995.

[20] Prechelt L., An empirical comparison of C, C++, Java, Perl, Python, Rexx, and Tcl for a search/string-processing program. Technical Report 2000-5, Fakultät für Informatik, Universität Karlsruhe, Germany, March 2000. ftp.ira.uka.de.

[21] Prechelt L., Unger B., A controlled experiment on the effects of PSP training: Detailed description and evaluation. Technical Report 1/1999, Fakultät für Informatik, Universität Karlsruhe, Germany, March 1999. Available at ftp.ira.uka.de.

[22] Scanlan D.A., "Structured flowcharts outperform pseudocode: An experimental comparison", *IEEE Software* **6** (2) (1989) 8–36.

[23] Shiffrin R.M., Nosofsky R.M., "Seven plus or minus two: A commentary on capacity limiations", *Psychological Review* **101** (2) (1994) 357–361.

[24] Wall L., Christiansen T., Orwant J., *Programming Perl*, O'Reilly and Associates, 2000.

[25] Walston C.E., Felix C.P., "A method of programming measurement and estimation", *IBM Systems Journal* **16** (1) (1977) 54–73.

Issues and Approaches for Developing Learner-Centered Technology

CHRIS QUINTANA, JOSEPH KRAJCIK, AND
ELLIOT SOLOWAY

Center for Highly Interactive Computing in Education
University of Michigan
2200 Bonisteel Blvd., 3102 IST Building
Ann Arbor, MI 48109
USA

Abstract

As computing technology has evolved, there has been significant research and a range of approaches exploring the use of computers for learning. Traditionally, the prevalent approach when developing software has been a user-centered approach that focuses on software usability to help experts in some practice effectively engage in their work. However, in recent years, researchers have come to understand that a different approach—a learner-centered approach—is needed to design tools that help novices in some practice do and learn the work involved in that practice. Rather than solely focusing on the conceptual gulfs that lie between tool users and their tools, learner-centered tools primarily focus on addressing the conceptual gulf between a learner's novice expertise in some practice and the expertise of an expert in that practice. In this chapter, we discuss some major approaches that have been considered for learner-centered technologies by describing software based on behaviorist, information processing, and social constructivist approaches. Expanding on the latter two approaches, we will focus on two types of learner-centered software. We will look at intelligent tutoring systems and how they oversee a learner's work to provide assistance when learners encounter problems as they are working on certain tasks. We will also look at scaffolded software that incorporates specific functionalities and user interface features to support learners as they use the tool to engage in new activity. For each type of software, we will discuss the issues, approaches, and trade-offs involved in designing, implementing, and evaluating the software given its learner-centered focus. Finally, we will consider emerging wireless, handheld technologies, to discuss the new kinds of functionalities offered by these technologies, their possible impact on learning, and the challenges that developers face in creating educationally effective software given the constraints of these technologies.

1.   Introduction

With the advent of computer technology and its increasing use in more aspects of society, there has been continual interest and effort in using computers for learning and education. Even at the beginning of the computer age, visionaries like Bush [16] envisioned the notion of linked collections of information and tools like the hypothetical "Memex" which would help us store, link, and retrieve scientific knowledge, freeing us to explore more creative and intellectual endeavors. Since then, there have been many other efforts and ideas for learning technologies: ideas about creating large scale "thinking machines" in the 1950s and 1960s, the 1970s vision of personal "Dynabooks" that could provide people with a portable, dynamic medium to address information access and learning needs [33], and more recent efforts during the personal computer and Internet "revolutions" to support learning activities.

With these explorations have come the recognition that the design of learning technologies involves different issues than those for typical software design. As personal computers started becoming more powerful and prevalent, much of the human-computer interaction (HCI) and software design research focused on the design of usable computer tools. This user-centered design approach [41] focused on designing tools that people could use to engage in activity with which they were largely familiar with. Helping this audience of computer users complete their activities easily and efficiently was the prime objective. However, there are also new and significant HCI and software design issues other than usability that need to be addressed when developing learning technologies. We now see that there are new implications for the design, implementation, and evaluation of software that helps people learn new activity that they are *not* familiar with. In this case, simply focusing on tool ease-of-use is not enough. Instead, we need a more *learner-centered* approach to software development that takes the unique needs of learners into consideration [66]. Certainly we cannot ignore usability issues, but we also have to consider the design of tools that support learners engaging in new processes and activity, making sense of new content and information, and articulating new ideas, information, and arguments to peers and teachers.

In this chapter, we will review current and emerging approaches to learning technologies and the issues involved with developing these technologies. We will begin with a review of the learner-centered design approach to software, summarizing its goals and the differences from the more traditional user-centered design approach. We will then describe the prevailing approaches to educational software, noting the different learning theories that underlie the software design and different issues about the design, implementation, and evaluation of these educational software approaches given the different learning theories and contexts where the software is used. Finally, we will end by taking a brief look into emerging technologies (e.g., wireless and handheld technologies) that are being explored for educational purposes. We will consider the characteristics of these technologies, and how these characteristics afford new kinds of educational activities.

2. Computers and Learning: Background on Learner-Centered Technology

At the outset, one might think that software development is the same whether designing for usability or designing for learning. Certainly at a high level, there are similarities in the overall software design processes. However, when considering the design of learner-centered versus user-centered software, there are different issues to address in terms of the target audience and the overall goals for the resulting software. Because of these different issues, we need a specific design approach and paradigm for developing learner-centered software. In previous work, we have articulated a definition for learner-centered design (LCD) and the differences between LCD and the more traditional user-centered design (UCD) approach [46,50]. Here we will summarize these differences to provide a base for the subsequent discussion and to articulate the conceptual goals for learner-centered software.

The traditional focus for UCD is on developing usable tools for some prototypical person with pre-existing expertise in some *practice*. By a practice, we mean the tools, tasks, knowledge, products, etc. that are involved in some domain, such as, for example, the practice of scientific inquiry. Because there is an implicit assumption that these computer users have some motivation and expertise about the practices they want to engage in, the primary design consideration involves designing tools that are easy to use and that allow the computer users to complete their work as easily and efficiently as possible. Thus the overriding goal for developers involves reducing the conceptual distance between the user and the tool, i.e., the user-centered "gulfs" of execution and evaluation (Fig. 1) described by [41]. By understanding how people generally use tools to do their work (using what is called in [41] a "theory of action"), designers can reduce these gulfs by making the execution of actions on the tool more straightforward and evaluation of the state of the tool more understandable. In the end, the more designers can reduce the gulfs of execution and evaluation, the more usable the resulting tool.

However, if we review the user-centered design approach, we see that many of the UCD assumptions about the different goals, characteristics, and needs that users have cannot be made when considering learners [66]. While UCD assumes prototypical users that know the practices they are engaging in, learners do not have the same underlying expertise and intrinsic motivation. Given the fact that learners have an underdeveloped or naïve model of the practice they are trying to engage in, they need tools that will support them to do and learn new practices and activities. Thus

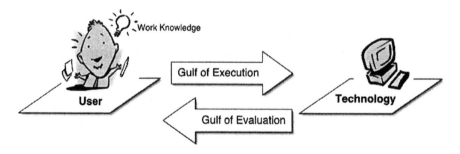

FIG. 1. Conceptual gulfs for user-centered design.

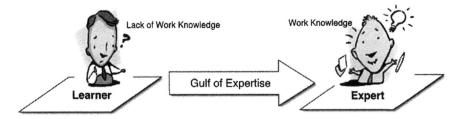

FIG. 2. Conceptual gulf for learner-centered design.

learners (e.g., science students) need more than just usable tools. Learners need tools that help them participate in a practice to gain the expertise and understanding that experts in that practice (e.g., expert scientists) already possess.

Therefore, rather than solely addressing the conceptual gulfs lying between the user and a tool, the primary focus of LCD is on addressing a conceptual "gulf of expertise" (Fig. 2) that lies between the learner and the expertise needed to become a full participant in the new practice the learner is trying to learn [46,50]. Where the primary conceptual goal for UCD is to reduce the gulfs of execution and evaluation, the primary conceptual goal for LCD is to reduce the gulf of expertise. Good learner-centered tools should help learners cross the gulf of expertise by offering the necessary guidance and support to mindfully engage in the new activity, allowing them to develop and gain more expertise in the activity.

Over the years, there have been different approaches and different kinds of software developed to support learning. Some of the major approaches to educational software are described in [49], each stemming from different underlying theories of learning: the behaviorist approach, the information processing approach, and the social constructivist approach. We will now summarize these approaches to give us a base for discussing the issues involved with designing, implementing and evaluating different kinds of educational software.

2.1 Software Based on the Behaviorist Approach

The behaviorist approach is predominately influenced by the work of B.F. Skinner, who advocated an approach where learning essentially involves "programming" a person's behavior through conditioning that rewards "correct" behavior or punishes "incorrect" behavior. Educational software based on the behaviorist approach attempts to shape or condition the learner's behavior in this manner. Early behaviorist software took the form of "teaching machines" that attempted to follow Skinnerian thinking. Subsequent software (sometimes referred to as computer-based training or computer-aided instruction) inspired by the behaviorist approach emphasizes immediate feedback to learners and constant measurement of progress to inform learners whether they are working correctly or not [4].

The basic approach for behaviorist software involves having students perform tasks or answer questions from some target domain. The software will be supplied with the answers or the appropriate courses of action to shape the learner's behavior with positive feedback for correct answers and negative feedback for incorrect answers. As learners work, the software monitors their progress and follows some pre-programmed rubric that defines whether the learner has successfully learned enough to proceed to the next work task. The software's feedback is based on scripts programmed in the software and triggered by a particular answer. The software strictly compares the learner's response with the pre-programmed answers to give feedback and does not have any mechanisms to consider the learner's knowledge and needs [6]. There is not necessarily any "intelligence" or other dynamic mechanisms involved in the software's feedback. Thus behaviorist software transitions a learner across the gulf of expertise through this positive and negative reinforcement, which attempts to steer the learner in educationally appropriate directions. The intent is that the learners will begin to learn the correct course of action based on the feedback from this conditioning approach. If the learner's behavior continues to be correct as they use the software, then it is assumed they are learning the new material and are continuing forward across the gulf of expertise.

Most contemporary examples of behaviorist software include many educational games, "flash-card" software, etc. Behaviorist software must be developed for activities that are well-defined and have specifically defined answers. Behaviorist software can be useful for such activities because it is easy to specify the learner's tasks and determine whether learners have answered correctly or incorrectly. However, such software can be difficult to develop for more exploratory, wide-ranging work that may not have such clear-cut answers. Thus the behaviorist approach is no longer significantly found in current educational software research and practices (other than some educational games) [4]. As such, we will not significantly discuss issues pertaining to behaviorist software in the remainder of this chapter, but we must include behaviorist software as an important early example of educational software.

2.2   Software Based on the Information Processing Approach

The second major approach for educational software is the information processing approach. Where the behaviorist approach simply considers externally visible human behavior, the information processing approach considers models of cognition, positing that "certain aspects of human cognition involve knowledge that is represented symbolically" [3]. Cognition involves representing knowledge symbolically and using specific rules to manipulate those representations and generate new inferences and knowledge. Because human cognition can be externally represented in some symbolic fashion, the knowledge needed to engage in some practice can be codified and cognitive processes can be represented in software as computer simulations that describe how people engage in problem-solving activity. The conceptual model is that the mind is a set of processors and symbolic rules are processed in those processors. The interaction between people and computers is considered to be a flow of symbolically represented information between the two sets of processors—the computer's processors and the mind's processors—that manipulate rule sets for cognition [18].

The software most commonly associated with the information processing approach includes *intelligent tutoring systems* (*ITSs*) that observe learners as they engage in new activity and provide assistance to support learners when they appear to have problems with the activity. Intelligent tutoring systems thus can reason about the target activity learners are engaging in, the current state of the learner's knowledge of that activity, and decide about making instructional interventions [22]. Thus software based on the information processing approach attempts to transition learners across the gulf of expertise by overseeing learners as they attempt new activity and providing support when learners appear to be working incorrectly or when they reach an impasse.

The original intent of tutoring systems was to provide individualized instruction where learners worked one-to-one with the system. This approach was inspired by the oft-cited work of Bloom [10], who noted that students receiving individualized instruction perform better than students who received more traditional classroom instruction. Because of this individualized nature, many tutoring systems have been used in skill training or industrial settings, although there have been recent efforts to integrate ITSs more fully into classroom contexts and curriculum. Broadly speaking, tutoring systems work by modeling the activities and interventions of a human teacher or other expert, which is how the tutoring systems provide the individualized instruction. While many tutors are somewhat decontextualized, there have also been attempts to incorporate aspects of the domain or context in which the ITS is being used (e.g., tutors that are more simulation based and incorporate a real-world setting in the tutor) [6]. The key feature that distinguishes ITSs is its role as an "overseer" to look at the learner's work and convey appropriate guidance.

Research into the information processing approach and ITSs has been ongoing for the last three decades, resulting in a range of ITS examples in different domains. Early systems focused on very specific and small domains, such as the SCHOLAR system for high-school geometry [17] and the MYCIN expert system for medical diagnoses [61]. As the field began to broaden, larger tutoring systems were developed.

There were different tutors to help teach different aspects of computer programming, such as the LISP tutor [5], and PROUST [32]. Smithtown was a tutor that allowed guided, student-built simulations to learn about economics [62]. More recent examples include goal-based scenario systems that allow learners to participate in very contextualized scenarios from different domains (e.g., medical training, sales training) to give them experience in participating in that domain [59]. There is now also a range of different tutors for doing geometry and algebra proofs [22] and physics [29].

2.3   Software Based on the Social Constructivist Approach

The final approach for educational software involves the social constructivist perspective of learning. Social constructivism is a perspective that is increasingly becoming the basis for many current educational approaches [63]. There are two aspects to the social constructivist perspective that describe how people learn:

- *The social aspect*: It is stated in [15] that "knowledge is ... in part a product of the activity, context, and culture in which it is developed and used". Knowledge is contextualized, meaning that learners must build their knowledge within a community of peers and experts. Thus gaining expertise involves participating in a social context, preferably one that reflects the context of some professional culture in order for learners to understand the practices, languages, tools, and values of the culture.

- *The constructivist aspect*: Learning is not a simple, passive process involving the transfer of information from expert to novice. Rather, learning and understanding involve active, generative processes where learners must cognitively manipulate the material they are learning in order to construct cognitive links from the new material they are learning to their own prior knowledge [43,44].

Because constructivism is a "theory of knowing" and not a "theory of teaching", there is no one specific constructivist pedagogical approach [14]. However, there have been recent efforts to incorporate social constructivist tenets into classroom contexts, such as the project-based science approach [12]. In considering the social constructivist approach for classrooms, the important social constructivist tenets that impact learners are summarized in [63]. Specifically learners need to:

- Engage in mindful work to *actively construct* their own knowledge.
- Be *situated* with social and intellectual support to see how knowledge is used in the practice they are learning.
- Be exposed to the *community* (or culture) of the practice.
- Engage in *discourse* with other members of the community of practice.

In short, the social constructivist perspective states that learners need to be immersed in and actively participate in representative activity from the new practice they are learning so they can begin to function as members of that community of practice. However, since learners are novices in the practice, they need significant structure and support to help them engage in the new practice. This structure or support is called *scaffolding*. From an educational perspective, scaffolding strategies can be described as support strategies used by a teacher to help students carry out previously inaccessible cognitive activities. Such strategies include coaching, advising, critiquing, etc. [21,70]. For example, teachers might decompose a complex activity into more manageable pieces so that students can begin working on the complex activity.

Technology can also scaffold students. Software-based scaffolding can be similarly defined as the design and incorporation of software features and tools that implement specific support strategies allowing learners to do inaccessible cognitive activities. Software-based scaffolding can be defined to provide different dimensions of support, such as process support, management and organizational support, content support, etc. [47,55]. For example, software developers can incorporate different kinds of "process maps" in software to realize the teacher's strategy of decomposing complex activities into manageable pieces, such as visualizing the activities involved in system modeling [39] (Fig. 3a) and science investigations [47] (Fig. 3b). By making different aspects of a new practice accessible to novice learners, scaffolded software can help provide the structure and support framework with which learners can see the culture and language of the practice and engage in different activities from that practice.

The social constructivist approach considers an overall social system: the learning context (e.g., the classroom including teachers and other students), the curriculum,

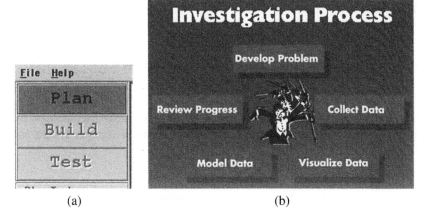

(a)   (b)

FIG. 3. Process map scaffolds for system modeling (a) and science inquiry (b).

and the technology, all of which may include scaffolding as a supportive framework allowing the novice learner to mindfully engage in and learn a new practice. Developing scaffolded software tools is one part of this overall system that software developers focus on. Scaffolded software focuses on supporting more open-ended, wide-ranging work practices by incorporating scaffolding features in tools. These scaffolds help learners cross the gulf of expertise by structuring and making visible important aspects of a practice, which help learners engage in components of the new practice, many times with collaborators, in some context.

There is a range of different scaffolded software projects, especially in the area of science inquiry and other practices that are open-ended and exploratory. For example, scaffolded tools have been developed to support different individual science activities: Model-It supports systems dynamics modeling [39], WorldWatcher supports visualization [25], and Artemis supports on-line research [69]. Other scaffolded software supports larger processes rather than specific activities. The Knowledge Integration Environment (KIE) [64] and its successor, the Web-based Integrated Science Environment (WISE) [35] helps students integrate evidence to develop and restructure their understanding of complex scientific ideas. The Biology Guided Inquiry Learning Environment (BGuILE) [56] helps students engage in biology investigations by incorporating domain-specific strategies and expert knowledge implicitly in the user interface and associated curriculum. Symphony [47] is another system that explored process scaffolding strategies to help students engage in complex processes like a full scientific investigation.

Given this overview of the different approaches to educational software, we will now look at the issues involved with developing tools based on the information processing and social constructivist approaches, the two prevailing educational software approaches found today. For each approach, we will specifically look at the issues involved with designing, implementing, and evaluating the software and articulate the tradeoffs of the different approaches.

3. Design Issues and Approaches for Educational Software

If we look at software development in general, there is a high-level, iterative cycle with different activities that software developers need to perform to design, build, and understand the effectiveness of the software [38]:

Design Phase

- Understanding the underlying tasks and activities that the software should support (i.e., the activity that the software user will be doing).

- Understanding the context in which the software will be used (e.g., will the software be used in an office or work setting, in a public-school classroom setting, etc.).
- Understanding the audience that will be using the software.
- Defining the requirements for the software given the previous analyses.

Implementation Phase

- Developing the software to address the specified requirements.

Evaluation Phase

- Evaluating the software to determine the tradeoffs and successes in terms of addressing the specified requirements and noting new requirements that may have arisen throughout the software testing.

So whether designing user-centered or learner-centered software, developers engage in the same high-level design cycle. However, the specific differences that arise stem from the different foci for UCD and LCD and the different goals for learner-centered software. First, the software development differences between UCD and LCD involve the specifics for the software design goals, the software use context and audience, and the software requirements. As we saw in the introductory material, the goals and requirements for user-centered tools primarily involve tool usability to help experts in some practice easily do their work, whereas the goals and requirements for learner-centered tools involve learning new work. These differences impact the kinds of analyses and development activity needed in different steps of the development cycle.

Second, aside from the differences between UCD and LCD, there are also additional differences in the development approaches for the different kinds of learner-centered software. Intelligent tutoring systems attempt to codify different types of knowledge to assist and train learners in a one-to-one fashion. Scaffolded software attempts to incorporate different types of support strategies in software in a wider learning context by learners either working alone or collaboratively to perform more open-ended activities. We will now begin reviewing the major activities for the different kinds of educational software by considering the design aspect of ITSs and scaffolded software.

3.1   Designing Intelligent Tutoring Systems

Because intelligent tutoring systems monitor the learner's work and intervene to help the learner when necessary, the central approach for designing ITSs is to represent expertise and other information about some given practice, represent a learner's knowledge state about that practice, and represent a range of instructional approaches to help a learner perform a progression of activities from the practice. Thus designing intelligent tutoring systems mainly involves conceptualizing the different components (or modules) that represent these different sets of knowledge. The traditional models that need to be represented in a tutoring system include the following [6,42, 71]:

- *Domain Knowledge Model*: This represents the "domain expertise" or the material about the practice that the tutor will be presenting. Designing this model involves representing the domain material in a manner that the tutor can use it.

- *Student Model*: This represents the knowledge that a student has about the target domain. The student model allows for individualized instruction because different student models can be developed for different students. Additionally, the student model allows the system to track a student's progress by allowing the system to observe the student's current knowledge about the domain they are learning.

- *Expert Model*: This represents the knowledge that an expert has about the domain. The expert model provides the system with a mechanism for tracking the student's progress by comparing the difference between what an expert knows and does and what the student knows and does. In a sense, this difference could provide a description for the current "gulf of expertise". This comparison allows the system to evaluate when the student is taking incorrect courses of action.

- *Pedagogical (or Instructional) Model*: This represents a model of instructional strategies and methods describing how the domain material will be taught to the student. The pedagogical model is responsible for selecting how and when domain topics will be presented given the student's current knowledge state, what kind of feedback and explanations to give the student, and when to move to more complex problems as the student gains more expertise.

- *Tutoring System Communications/User Interface Model*: This represents the user interface between the student and the tutor. The communications module is not necessarily a knowledge-based module in the sense of the previous modules. Rather, the communications module tackles the typical problems found in user interface design: how should material be presented to students, how do students communicate with the tutor, etc.

Given the structure of an ITS and the different components that it uses, the overall design process for an ITS corresponds to the development of the different system modules. The main design efforts involve gathering the information needed for each module and then using different techniques from artificial intelligence and cognitive science research to codify this knowledge in a manner that can be used and manipulated in the software.

3.1.1   Representing Expert and Domain Knowledge

The domain knowledge model and expert model are similar in nature since they both essentially specify knowledge that comprises some domain. From a design standpoint, the two models may be combined [71] or may be separated [6]. Regardless, domain knowledge needs to be represented in order to specify task models and a model of the target domain for the ITS. Therefore, software developers need to perform thorough task analysis to gain an understanding of the underlying material being taught by the tutor. There are also other kinds of analysis, such as *cognitive task analysis* [34] that can be used to gain an understanding about how experts might perform the relevant activity.

Once software developers have performed these analyses, they need to determine a way to codify and represent the expert and domain knowledge in the computer. One approach would be to use a rule-based representation for procedural knowledge and for teaching specific skills. An example is the GOMS approach describing procedural knowledge [18,31]. The GOMS approach represents activity in terms of a person's *goals*, the *operations* and *methods* that are carried out to meet those goals, and the *selection rules* used to select between the different operations and methods. The GOMS approach is useful because the analysis techniques for understanding the task models result in a representation for the procedural knowledge needed to perform the task. One drawback of this approach, however, is that it can become very complex to represent large domains or non-procedural tasks.

A more wide-ranging cognitive theory is the ACT* theory (and subsequent family of theories) [3]. We summarize the ACT* (or adaptive control of thought) theory as a unified theory of the nature, acquisition, and use of human knowledge. The fundamental assumption behind ACT* is that knowledge begins as declarative information, or different pieces of information that are associatively linked together. New inferences (i.e., new production rules) from existing declarative knowledge are then made to create procedural knowledge. The different ways in which production rules are created describe different kinds of learning in the ACT* model. Production rules can be broadened to encompass other areas (i.e., learning by generalization), narrowed to apply to a smaller number of areas (i.e., learning by discrimination), and applied more often resulting in material that has been learned "better" (i.e., learning by strengthening). Thus the ACT* theory provides a comprehensive theory that can be used to represent declarative knowledge, procedural knowledge, and models for learning.

3.1.2 Specifying Student Models

Aside from representing the expert knowledge and information used in the domain, designers also need to represent the student model in a way that allows the system to understand the student's knowledge as compared to an expert's knowledge. The knowledge representation approaches we just discussed can certainly be used to represent the student model. However, other techniques need to be explored because of the fact that the student model may change as the student gains expertise in the target domain, and since the relationship between the student and expert model is what drives the interventions and support provided by the ITS. Two common techniques for representing information about the student are describe and summarized in [6]: Bayesian networks and overlay models.

Bayesian networks are common techniques used for probabilistic reasoning. A Bayesian network consist of nodes representing a certain piece of knowledge and a measure describing the probability that the student has a good understanding about that piece of knowledge. As the student progresses through the material being presented by the ITS, their courses of action can trigger a mathematical readjustment of the different probability measures to update the representation of what the student now knows. The Bayesian network can now change to reflect the changes in the student's knowledge. Thus a Bayesian network serves as a probabilistic measure of the student's knowledge state at any given time.

A second technique for representing student models is the use of *overlay models*. Here, the representation of the student's knowledge is considered to be a subset of the expert's knowledge. Thus the ITS is directed to present material to the student in such a way that the student's knowledge will "grow" to fill and match the expert's knowledge model. Conceptually, this approach makes sense, but representing the student's model as a strict subset of the expert model may not be an accurate approach. One extension to the overlay model is to consider where the student and expert models intersect, since the intersection would represent their shared knowledge. Given the shared knowledge, the ITS can then present material to move the student's "unshared" knowledge into the "shared" knowledge collection.

Bayesian networks and overlay models describe how the student model should be represented. There is one other technique related to the student model that involves tracking student actions to try and understand the student's reasoning. This technique can offer more insight into the student's knowledge state. An ITS can also represent and monitor the student's sequence of actions in order to infer the student's current knowledge and understanding [42]. The actions taken by the student can then be compared with expert actions or actions recorded in the domain knowledge, such as, for example, procedural knowledge representations for how to complete some task. By comparing the student actions and expert actions, the ITS can then be directed to take a certain course of action if the student's actions were incorrect. The ITS can also review the student's actions and attempt to explain where the student's reasoning may have been faulty and to help the student understand their incorrect work.

3.1.3 Specifying Pedagogical Models

The final knowledge-based model that software developers have to consider is the pedagogical model that dictates how an ITS should select and present material to the student based on the student's current knowledge state and characteristics. In other words, instructional knowledge also needs to be encoded into the pedagogical model, which can involve the same kinds of knowledge representation schemes discussed earlier. Throughout the history of ITSs, different approaches and strategies have been explored, from more omniscient approaches where student errors are instantly corrected by the tutor to more exploratory approaches where students can "explain" their work by communicating their plans and actions to the system, which can then offer advice and other information [71]. There are also other issues to consider when designing the pedagogical module. The pedagogical module needs to be programmed with the necessary knowledge needed to determine different pedagogical issues like selecting the following [6,71]:

- The appropriate teaching strategies to use (e.g., using the Socratic method versus a more direct testing method) and appropriate topics to present to students.

- The best types of problems to generate for students and the best times to generate those problems throughout the tutoring session.

- The appropriate types of feedback (e.g., explanations, coaching, critiquing, etc.) and the best times to display such feedback.

3.1.4 Design Tradeoffs for Intelligent Tutoring Systems

Given the main design tasks of designing the knowledge-based modules, different tradeoffs arise for ITS designers. One difficulty for ITS design can occur if the underlying work being taught by the tutor is relatively unstructured and complex. Since good task models need to be represented in the domain knowledge module and expert module, if the underlying activity is too difficult to formalize, then developing these modules could be problematic. Many ITSs have supported practices where rather specific task models can be outlined and represented, such as mathematical practices involving algebraic or geometric proofs. But underlying work that is more open-ended and creative can pose problems for ITS design. Similarly, if developers are using a rule-based knowledge representation scheme, developing an ITS for a large, complex domain can result in a rule base that can quickly become too big and expensive for a useful ITS.

Another area of potential difficulty for ITS design is in the development of the student model. As we have seen, the success of a tutor depends on whether it can determine how a given student is making progress and when the student needs assistance. However, there are two areas of difficulty that arise when developing the student model. First, it may be difficult to gather enough information about a student to develop an accurate student model, resulting in a tutor that offers inappropriate guidance [6]. Second, when considering learning contexts such as school classrooms, addressing the diversity of the learner audience can be complex. Thus it may be necessary to develop different "student profiles" for the student model, which can add complexity to the design task.

Similarly, there are other design tradeoffs related to the pedagogical module and the appropriate selection of instructional strategies. Beck et al. [6] discuss the problems ITSs can have in representing and selecting high-level strategies (or meta-strategies) for instruction. An example of a meta-strategy would be to use the Socratic method of teaching. While this is certainly a viable strategy used by many teachers, it can be difficult giving the ITS enough information to determine when to use such a strategy. Another area of difficulty involves representing meta-strategies in the tutor. Continuing with this example, the Socratic method requires common-sense knowledge that can be difficult to represent [6]. Using common sense can certainly be a big part of learning and education, but while there have been attempts in artificial intelligence research to represent common-sense knowledge and reasoning, doing so can add significant complexity to the ITS.

The complexity that can arise in formulating the different modules and in addressing certain domains and learners audiences may limit successful uses of ITSs at certain times. However, the knowledge-based approach used for intelligent tutoring systems is a viable approach that has had many successes in teaching material in many domains. Given this overview of ITS design approaches and tradeoffs, we now move to a corresponding overview for the design of scaffolded tools for learners.

3.2   Designing Scaffolded Software

While scaffolded software and intelligent tutoring systems share the same overall goal of supporting novice learners, scaffolded software takes a different approach than ITSs. Rather than taking the "knowledge-based" approach, scaffolded software incorporates support strategies in the user interface design, in the conceptual design of the software and in the inclusion of tools that afford the doing of educationally viable activities. Scaffolded software does not have a prescribed modular structure like ITSs. For ITSs, analysis of the learner, expert, and practice are necessary to define the knowledge that must be codified in its modules. For scaffolded software, these analyses serve to inform the design of the software, but the design tasks are freer and not as well defined as with ITS. Designing scaffolded software involves understanding the learner, learning context, and expert work practices, not to represent the knowledge, but rather to understand the kind of software design decisions that must be made to support learners. We can summarize the iterative, high-level steps for designing scaffolded tools as follows [37,50]:

- *Understand the Learning Objectives.* Developers need to understand the educational goals for the learners. These learning objectives will subsequently inform the kinds of target practices and activities that learners will need to engage in to meet their goals (e.g., learning air quality investigations to study ozone pollution in the local community).

- *Understand and Analyze the Learning Context.* Developers need to fully understand the context in which the learning will take place (e.g., a middle-school classroom, a distance learning class, etc.) to understand the overall system in which the software will be situated. This would include defining the target learner audience, the teachers that will be involved, the software and other supporting materials that will be used by the learners, etc.

- *Understand the Underlying Practice.* Developers need to understand the overall practice that learners need to engage in to meet the learning objectives identified earlier. This is necessary so that developers can see the kinds of activities they need to support with the software (e.g., understanding what kind of work is involved with scientific inquiry and air quality investigations).

- *Identify the Learner Support Needs.* Once the learning objectives, context, and practice have all been analyzed, developers need to determine the kinds of support the target learner audience will need to do the work. By understanding what kind of work learners will be engaging in, the characteristics of the learners, and the support inherent in the learning context, developers can articulate the kinds of support learners will need to engage in the practice.

- *Design the Scaffolding Features.* The final design step involves designing the actual scaffolding features for the software to address the learner support needs identified previously. The learner needs identify areas where learners need support to do the work, so developers must determine the scaffolds that can support learners to mindfully engage in that work.

Thus we see that the overall approach for designing scaffolded software involves gaining enough information about the learning context, the learner audience, and the target work practice to inform developers and help them design appropriate scaffolds in the software to support learners with the different aspects of the overall practice they are engaging in. We now discuss these different design phases in broader detail.

3.2.1 Understanding the Learner Audience, Objectives, and Context

Software developers need to understand the specific audience of learners that will be using the software and the particular learning objectives defined for those learners. Understanding the audience is especially important for learner-centered design because of the diversity of learners that we mentioned earlier. Simply outlining a general characterization of the learner audience (e.g., sixth-grade students or university undergraduates) is not enough. Even within, for example, a sixth-grade classroom, there are still other characteristics of and differences between those learners that the software developers need to be aware of, such as differences in gender, developmental level, learning style, etc., all of which influence the kind of educational support that a teacher and the software should provide. Note that developers of ITSs and scaffolded software need to understand the learner audience, but for different reasons. Developers of ITSs need to understand the learner's knowledge state in order to represent that knowledge in the tutoring system. But developers of scaffolded software need to understand the wide range of learner characteristics and goals because those characteristics will help shape the design of the scaffolds later in the development cycle.

Aside from understanding the learner audience, developers also need to understand the learning context to see where the scaffolded software will be used and how different components in the system (e.g., tools, teachers, curriculum, etc.) will each provide different supports and constraints for the learners. For example, the learning context may be middle-school classrooms where students work collaboratively, or it can be an undergraduate student working alone at home on some web-based courses. It is vitally important for developers to understand this overall context so they can understand what kinds of learning support—if any—will be provided by the rest of the system, which in turn, informs the kind of support that the software should provide. For example, the classroom-centered design approach notes the importance of taking into consideration the contributions and roles of teachers and other non-technological tools in the classroom environment when developing scaffolded software [36]. Understanding the different educational resources and social interactions that are present in the learning context will affect the manner in which the scaffolded software should be designed. Overall, software development has seen a greater emphasis placed on understanding context in recent years, as can be seen in the contextual design approach, which aims to study how work is performed in its "native environment" [8]. The importance of context should certainly not be lost on developers of scaffolded software.

3.2.2   Analyzing the Underlying Domain of Practice

After understanding the overall learning goals and context for the software, developers need to understand the practices that learners will have to engage in to meet their learning objectives. One of the tenets of the social constructivist approach involves active construction of new knowledge, which can occur when learners actively engage in some practice. For example, one way for learners to gain more expertise into scientific practices would be to actively engage in those practices by carrying out substantive science investigations. Thus in order to develop scaffolded software supporting new practices like science inquiry, developers need to develop a richer understanding of those practices.

Understanding the underlying tasks being supported by software is a common part of the general software development process. However, there are distinctions between the different approaches. In user-centered design, developers must understand the prototypical task set that experts do in order to develop tools that make those tasks easy to do. For ITS development, developers need to understand the underlying domain knowledge in order to represent that knowledge in the tutoring system. For scaffolded software development, developers need a detailed understanding of the underlying practice in order to identify possible breakdowns for learners and to design the subsequent scaffolding features that address those breakdowns. Thus developers need to understand the full set of components that comprise the practice (e.g., the tools, activities, information, etc., needed to do the work) and the relationships between these components and other participants and components in the overall learning context [50]. Furthermore, developers need to understand the tacit knowledge that experts use to do the work, not so much to create a knowledge-based module, but to use the expert knowledge and strategies to inform the subsequent design of the scaffolds.

There are different methods that can be used to fully understand the different components that comprise a practice. Task analysis methods used in ITS development can certainly be used to understand specific procedural sequences that comprise different activities (e.g., using the GOMS method to outline procedural knowledge) and other expert knowledge about doing activities (e.g., using the cognitive task analysis method). However, developers also need other methods to understand the full set of components in the practice. For example, the contextual design method [8] can help developers define different models of the work involved in a practice (e.g., science inquiry practices), such as:

- Models that define how the work flows through the context in which it is being performed (e.g., what is the work flow for a science investigation).
- The culture and policies of the work environment (e.g., what is the culture of a science laboratory and the scientific community).

- The way artifacts (e.g., graphs in science inquiry) are produced and utilized throughout the work practice.

Another representation for analyzing a practice is the *process space* model [28] and the corresponding process space analysis method [47,50]. The process space model explicitly describes the different components that comprise a complex work practice:

- The *roles* or responsibilities undertaken by the work participants (e.g., the responsibilities of the different members of a science laboratory).
- The *activities* carried out by the different roles (e.g., the different activities of a science investigation, such as planning, data collection, visualization, etc.).
- The *services* or tools used to perform the activities (e.g., science tools such as visualization tools, data probes, notebooks, etc.).
- The *artifacts* produced in the activities (or used to mediate other activities) (e.g., scientific artifacts such as graphs, models, plans, research notes, etc.).
- The underlying *information* needed to perform the different activities (i.e., procedural information, such as the process for visualizing pollution data; content information, such as information about ozone pollution, etc.).

Using such a representation can make different components of the practice explicit, giving developers a wider understanding of the work that learners will need to engage in.

3.2.3   Identifying Learner Support Needs

The next design phase involves defining what is difficult and complex for novice learners attempting to engage in the identified work. This phase should articulate an initial set of learner support needs (or "learner needs") that essentially serve as the learner-centered software requirements. The learner needs describe the areas where learners will encounter difficulty or roadblocks in the work and thus they define the specific kinds of scaffolding features and strategies that need to be designed into the software to support learners.

The central approach for defining the learner needs involves comparing the different characteristics of the target learner audience with the results of the previous analyses of the learning objectives, learning context, and the practices learners will engage in. By doing this comparison, developers can begin to outline where learners will encounter *breakdowns* in terms of doing the underlying work. As we can see, this is a general approach and the reality is that current approaches for outlining learner needs are still more deductive than methodological [46]. Basically, software developers need to consult with educational researchers and teachers who understand the nature of learners and other pedagogical issues to see where learners will have difficulty doing the work. Consulting the educational literature is vital to see different descriptions of the kinds of difficulty learners at different developmental levels face when engaging in complex new activities. This information coupled with the different analyses of the target learners and practices can help outline an initial set of learner needs that developers can use as a guide for the initial set of scaffolding features for the software.

With more work on developing scaffolded software, researchers are beginning to articulate more general descriptions of different learner needs. For example, we can consider a general set of learner needs from the perspective of the process space components [47]:

- *Service Needs*: Learners may need explicit services to perform work activity that experts can do with less computational support. For example, learners may need additional tools for planning a science investigation than expert scientists may use.

- *Information Needs*: Learners need access to information experts use in their work, such as information that explains different aspects of the work practices, explains how to perform different work activities, and helps describe possible activity spaces in the overall work practice.

- *Activity Needs*: Learners need explicit representations of activities that may be implicit when experts with well-specified, internalized work models perform the work (e.g., learners may need to see the same space of possible science activities in the software that expert scientists have already internalized).

- *Management Needs*: Learners need to manage the different artifacts (e.g., graphs, models, plans, research notes, etc.) they create and the different activities they have performed throughout their work so that they can avoid distractions (e.g., moving from their work to the file system to find some artifact) and focus on the salient parts of their work.

These needs are taken from a "work component" perspective, but we can also outline learner needs with respect to the salient cognitive activities involved in complex practices. For example, in complex work like science inquiry, we can say learners have the following support needs [53,55]:

- *Process Management Needs*: Learners need support to navigate through their different work processes and activities (e.g., support for navigating the processes and sub-processes involved in science inquiry).

- *Sense Making Needs*: Learners need support to analyze and make sense of their work products (e.g., make sense of their graphs or scientific models) to gain insight and drive the direction of their work.

- *Articulation and Reflection Needs*: Learners need support to reflect on and express an understanding of their work to themselves, their teachers, and their peers via explanations and descriptions of the material they analyzed (e.g., articulating the question they want to investigate or the argument they have made to answer their question).

As more descriptions of learner needs arise from different perspectives, developers can begin to combine descriptions in different ways to develop a more specific, well-defined set of learner needs for their given context. Defining more detailed sets of learner needs is important because it gives developers a more detailed set of software requirements to address when designing and implementing the scaffolds for the software.

3.2.4 Addressing Learner Needs with Software-Based Scaffolding

Once the initial set of learner needs have been defined, the final design phase involves designing the scaffolds for the software to address the learner needs. Where the final design phases for ITS development involved representing the knowledge for the different system modules, the final design phases for scaffolded software involve making the design decisions for the user interface and the software itself to provide the necessary support that learners need to engage in their work. Design decisions can be described as having two different aspects, a conceptual aspect and a physical aspect that actually realizes the conceptual aspect in the software [45]. Developers have to make both of these decisions in terms of the software-based scaffolding and articulate the following design information [50]:

- *Conceptual Scaffold Design*: Determining the conceptual scaffolding strategies that will address each of the different learner needs.
- *Physical Scaffold Design*: Determining the method to physically implement each given conceptual scaffolding strategy in the software.

This conceptual/physical design distinction is not inherent to learner-centered design. For example, user-centered design would consider the conceptual strategies and physical implementations that make tools easier to use. The differences occur in the focus of the strategies. For scaffolded software, the key distinction is that design decisions occur with respect to making complex work doable by novices in such a way that those novices begin to develop an understanding of the work.

While the general notion of scaffolding is understood, clearly articulating software-based scaffolds and their representations in software is an ongoing effort. For example, from an educational perspective, we can "see" scaffolding when we see a teacher coaching a student. But from a software perspective, the question that arises about software is: What parts of the software include a scaffold? If a pull-down menu is used to physically implement a conceptual scaffolding strategy, then are all pull-down menus scaffolds? The more correct answer would be that the manner in which that pull-down menu was used in that given context provided the scaffolding for the learner. So we can see that scaffolding design decisions need to be clearly articulated along different dimensions to not only describe software features, but also to describe why and how they serve as scaffolds.

One analogous method for articulating design decisions comes from the field of architecture and Christopher Alexander's work on design patterns and pattern languages [2]. Patterns serve as a representational mechanism to guide architects by fully describing architectural constructs along with their motivation, rationale, context, and resulting behavior. The use of patterns is also becoming popular in software design [7,60] and the pattern representation can be used to articulate scaffolding information. The analogy for scaffolded software would be that the job of the software developers is to give expression to the software patterns that permit learners to carry out new activities in a educationally-viable manner. The scaffolding patterns should communicate the motivation, rationale, context, results, tradeoffs, etc. for the scaffolding strategy and its physical implementation. Figure 4 illustrates our definition of software-based scaffolds and Figs. 5 and 6 illustrate some scaffolding examples [53].

Note that the use of software patterns is not restricted to learner-centered design or the design of scaffolded software. Many researchers in user interface design and software engineering are exploring the use of patterns to specifically articulate design decisions and to facilitate sharing those designs with other developers. The pattern approach certainly does lend itself to describing scaffolded software, especially given the importance of the learner characteristics, the learning context and objectives, etc. to inform the learner needs and, in turn, the design of the scaffolds. When developers design scaffolds to address the learner needs, they need to be cognizant of all of this information and communicate it to describe their designs, not just to other software developers, but also to educators and curriculum designers who would like to understand what kind of educational supports are present in the software.

We have described the form and characteristics of the scaffolding features, but that leaves the question: how do developers design the scaffolds needed to address the learner needs? The design task is open-ended and as with any design task, it requires the skill and savvy of a good designer. Again, there is no firm methodological approach to designing scaffolds. The previous design phases we discussed give developers the necessary background information to constrain and define the central design problem: designing scaffolds to support an initial set of learner needs in a given context. The pattern representation describes the kinds of information

A software-based scaffold is a potentially "fadeable" physical realization of a conceptual scaffolding strategy that addresses a given learner need to support learners so that they can "mindfully" engage in some previously inaccessible cognitive activity from the practice they are engaging in.

- "Fadeable" means that the physical realization of the software learners have the ability to be removed from the software after learners have demonstrated that they no longer need the support from the scaffold. A scaffold can fade as directed by a teacher, a learner, or the software itself [30].

- "Mindful" means that scaffolds should support learners in doing the task, without making the task too easy to do or the learner may not learn the task. Just as good teachers guide students without giving them the answers, software-based scaffolds should provide enough structure to make the task accessible to learners, but still problematize the task enough so that learners still think about the task they are doing [55].

A scaffolding pattern should describe a given software-based scaffold by articulating the following information:

- The context in which it is being used (i.e., the learning context, the learner characteristics, etc.).

- The specific learner need it is addressing.

- The conceptual scaffolding strategies used to address the learner need.

- Examples of the physical realizations used to implement each conceptual scaffolding strategy in software (e.g., tangible user interface features, the incorporation of a specific tool to specifically support salient learner activity, or some intrinsic design feature in the software).

- A discussion about how the physical software feature was used, its success, its tradeoffs, and possible ramifications if the feature were not implemented.

FIG. 4. Definition for software-based scaffolding.

needed to articulate the specific decisions behind the scaffold. Developers can then get input from the educational literature, from teachers and curriculum designers, and perhaps even from other educational software projects to not only understand the conceptual scaffolding strategies, but also the physical implementations for the scaffolds.

3.2.5 Design Tradeoffs for Scaffolded Software

If we consider the primary tradeoffs for designing scaffolded software, one area to look at would be the relative open-endedness of the design task. Looking back at ITS design, we saw that the design tasks were more well-defined because the basic structure of an ITS is well-defined. (This is not to say that ITS design is simple, but the system has specific parts to design.) But the structure of scaffolded software is not as specific and straightforward and the design phase is more akin to the more open-ended task of user interface design. As such, while we can articulate the different design phases for scaffolded software, we still need more specific method-

---

Scaffold: Visualize Complex Tasks by Using Ordered and Unordered Task Decompositions

Context: Complex practices like science inquiry involves a range of different tasks and activities that need to be completed to converge on an answer to the driving question being investigated.

Learner Need: Since learners lack the process knowledge that experts have about the work, learners may have difficulty simply in progressing through the different activities and keeping track of where they are in the "big picture" of the overall work practice.

Conceptual Scaffolding Strategy: Designers can support learners by explicitly visualizing tasks and activities in different ways to help learners along through the work [27]. Designers can explicitly represent tasks and activities in two ways:

- Visualize unordered activity spaces that display the space of possibilities that learners can select from without necessarily describing specific activity choices for them.

- Visualize more ordered task decompositions to provide a work-oriented structure for learners so they can see the constituent steps that must be accomplished for different activities.

Physical Scaffold Implementation: For example, Model-It uses an activity palette to visually convey the high-level tasks involved in system modeling (i.e., planning, building, and testing models) and access the tools needed for the selected task [39].

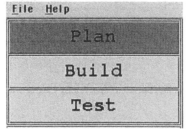

FIG. 5. Process management scaffold example.

ologies for those phases. For example, as we noted, there are no specific methodologies for determining the learner support needs or for designing the corresponding scaffolds. There are many avenues for guidance and background information, but it still takes a range of perspectives and information—computational, educational, and pedagogical—to complete these design phases. Furthermore, the nature of software-based scaffolding can be murky and take on an "I know it when I see it" quality. While recent work has served to define software-based scaffolding in a more specific manner, we need more work to articulate clear descriptions and examples for software-based scaffolding. There are ongoing research efforts to do so with the hope of articulating a more specific scaffolding framework and examples for other developers and educators to use and consult [53].

In the end, many of the complexities inherent to the development of scaffolded software arise from what we said at the beginning of this section: software in a social constructivist setting can be part of an overall system that involves learners, teach-

The main process map in Symphony visually describes the space of possible science inquiry activities in a science investigation to help learners decompose their investigations into more manageable components [47]. The process map shows learners the space of possible science activities, but learners still need to determine the specific activities to add to their plan throughout the investigation.

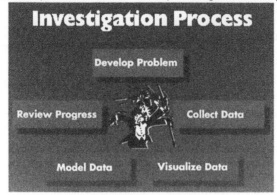

Other examples of this scaffold can be found in the KIE list of inquiry activities [64] and the Artemis task sequences found in certain parts of the software [69].

FIG. 5. — *continued from previous page*

Scaffold: Use Representations that Can Be Inspected By Learners to Reveal Important Properties of Underlying Data

Context: Complex work like the work of science inquiry involves generating, analyzing, and understanding different artifacts that rely on complex representations, such as a variety of graphs, diagrams, visualizations, and other formalisms. For example, learning science involves learning to see patterns in data, learning to test ideas against the data, and requires mapping between the phenomenon under study and the representation of characteristics of the phenomenon in data.

Learner Need: However, many of the representations that experts use and understand can be too abstract or difficult for learners to understand. Furthermore, the phenomenon may be dynamic, changing over time, and require careful examination at particular points. Therefore, learners need additional support to examine and make sense of data.

Conceptual Scaffolding Strategy: Learners need ways of simply viewing and probing complex data in ways that help them understand different aspects of the data. By giving learners "inspectable" visual representations of data, students can view and query a representation of the same data in different ways to try and develop a better understanding of the data itself.

Physical Scaffold Implementation: For example, inspectable data are an important component of the WorldWatcher environment, which uses scientific visualizations to help learners examine atmospheric sciences phenomenon [25]. WorldWatcher uses intuitive representations, color, to show value on a variable such as surface temperature. Looking for patterns in color (e.g., hotter colors near the equator) allows students to look for relationships between variables (e.g., the relationship of temperature to latitude). The representation is also inspectable to reveal specific values for any selected point, including contextual information such as political boundaries, and the name of a city or country.

FIG. 6. Sense making scaffold example.

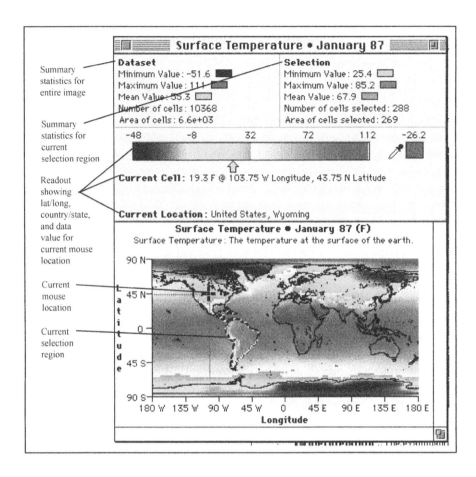

FIG. 6. — *continued from previous page*

ers, the classroom context (or other learning context), curriculum, etc. Designing any component of such a system is complicated because of the complex relationships between the different parts of the system. In this sense, the design of scaffolded software has the same difficulties that arise when designing software for an overarching work context—the same difficulties that led to recent insights that understanding the use context is important to the software design. The difficulties for developing software that is part of an overall system remain to be addressed by new generations of analysis and design approaches.

4. Implementation Issues to Aid Learner-Centered Software Developers

We have discussed many different examples of both ITSs and scaffolded tools that support many different practices and subject areas. Many of these software examples have been developed in research settings, and thus were built "from scratch" to explore new ideas and approaches. However, for educational technology to have a wider impact, developers need to have different tools and frameworks to reduce development time and cost and facilitate the development of learner-centered software. Such rapid-development tools and approaches are especially needed because given the different learning contexts and objectives, different subject areas, and the diversity of the learner audience, developing "one size fits all" tools is not a viable approach. In this section, we will review different approaches for developers— authoring tools, object libraries, and software infrastructures—that have arisen to address this implementation problem for both ITSs and scaffolded software.

4.1 Authoring Tools for Intelligent Tutoring Systems

One prevalent approach for developing ITSs is the use of an *authoring tool* or development environment to assemble an ITS. Developers of ITSs can benefit greatly from authoring tools given estimates that one hour of instruction time from an ITS can require 100–200 hours of development time [1,6]. Beck et al. [6] describe two major approaches for ITS authoring tools: tools to help developers build augmented "courseware" and tools to help developers represent knowledge for tutoring system modules.

The first category of authoring tools provides simpler development "shells" that educators can use to author learning environments for their students. These types of authoring tools offer a simpler approach to ITSs aimed at specific domains using a smaller number of instructional interactions. Rather than specifying the rules for knowledge bases, these tools allow developers to create simpler systems that specify certain scenarios and allowable courses of action in some domain. For example, the REDEEM system allows "authors to create adaptive learning environments by taking existing computer-based material as a domain model and then overlaying their teaching expertise" around the domain material to create different ITSs tailored to individual students [1]. Specifically, REDEEM allows the system author to specify the course-related material they want students to observe and work with, the teaching strategies to use for the specific system being built, and a description of the students using the system. In order to specify this information, REDEEM contains three different components used for each authoring task:

- *Courseware catalogs*: REDEEM allows developers to select the domain material they want students to work with. The domain material could be prepackaged modules created by some other authoring system (e.g., Hypercard, ToolBook, etc.), web-based material, or any other kind of material that has been separated into conceptual pages.

- *ITS authoring tools*: After the developer has selected the content, they can use the authoring tools to set up the teaching strategies for the specific target learner audience. Developers begin by defining sections of pages from the selected content and setting different characteristics about the material in the different sections, such as the difficulty level of the material, whether the material is new or familiar to the students, the level of specificity, etc. Developers then specify different teaching strategies from a pre-selected list of strategies and pedagogical approaches (e.g., level of teaching versus testing, amount of hints and other feedback to provide, times to test students, etc.). Developers then specify different categories of learners (e.g., level of literacy, learning styles, etc.) Doing this allows developers to specify different sets of teaching strategies for different students and associate teaching strategies with student categories.

- *An ITS shell*: Finally, developers input the teaching strategies and student information to the shell, which then regulates the delivery of the material to the target learners. The shell uses several pre-programmed rules, the teaching strategy/student information, and a simple overlay model to monitor the student work and determine when to present the different sections of the specified course material.

Other similar approaches include the RAPIDS II system for developing simulation-based tutoring systems [68], and INDIE [24], an authoring tool for developing goal-based scenarios (GBSs) aimed at helping learners work in domains involving different diagnosis tasks. GBSs are simulated "worlds" (e.g., a hospital) that represent specific scenarios for learners (e.g., diagnosing an unknown illness in a patient) where they learn certain objectives (e.g., making correct diagnoses) under the guidance of coaches and other tutors. INDIE, for example, allows developers to build and customize the scenarios and the user interface of the system by describing the consequences of different possible student actions in the scenario. Given the different student actions, the GBS displays different results and triggers different events that the learners must now contend with. Thus, the INDIE system basically combines a "storyboarding" approach along with intelligent tutoring support and tools for assembling different knowledge-based components (i.e., the coaches and critics) within different scenarios to guide learners in a realistic representation of the learning context.

The second category of authoring tools facilitates ITS development by helping developers represent domain information and teaching strategies in the system. This class of authoring tools provides more flexibility and results in more powerful systems because it allows developers to customize some of the knowledge bases and rule-based representations needed by the tutor (e.g., fostering the development of expert systems or other modules used in the system). One example of this type of authoring environment is the Eon system [40]. Eon contains a rich set of tools that allows developers to author all the basic components of an ITS: the domain model, the teaching strategies, the student model, and the user interface for the learning environment. The general authoring process using Eon thus includes several steps for building a full ITS:

- *Authoring the Domain Model*: Eon represents the domain model as a semantic network that links different "topics" involved in the learning objectives. Developers can construct the domain model by mapping out the different topics and the relationships between those topics to create "topic ontologies" and "topic networks".

- *Authoring the Learning Environment*: Eon allows developers to create the user interface; objects (or "widgets") in the user interface that students interact with; different kinds of properties, permissible interactions, and actions for the widgets; and content areas where different information and content can be displayed and interacted with.

- *Connecting Topics to Contents*: After the learning environment interface has been created, developers can next link the different content objects they created for the interface with specific domain content (i.e., different topics) and other tutor feedback that may be presented.

- *Authoring the Student Model*: Eon uses an overlay model for the student model to allow the system to track student work and determine the student's current knowledge state (e.g., student knowledge, misconceptions and other deficiencies in their current knowledge state). Eon provides developers with editors to help develop different rules to tailor the student model for a given target audience.

- *Authoring the Teaching Model*: Finally, Eon provides tools to allow developers to represent teaching strategies and meta-strategies that describe the different kinds of teacher interventions, actions, and feedback that can be made given certain student actions and the current knowledge state in the student model.

Thus systems like Eon allow for richer tutoring systems to be developed by providing a wider set of tools to author the different components of an ITS.

4.2 Software Libraries and Infrastructures for Developing Scaffolded Tools

Aside from ITS authoring tools, there are also approaches aimed at facilitating the development of scaffolded software, such as component libraries and software infrastructures to help developers assemble different kinds of individual scaffolded tools and integrated scaffolded software environments.

The first approach involves the use of component libraries that developers use to create new educational tools. Two examples of this approach are the Educational Software Components of Tomorrow (or ESCOT) project (http://www.escot.org) and the E-Slate project (http://e-slate.cti.gr/). ESCOT is a community of educators and tool developers that have worked to create a library of reusable, interoperable components for middle school mathematics [23]. The ESCOT project has created a library of mathematical components—spreadsheets, calculators, graphing calculators—and a technical infrastructure that allows developers to download and connect these components together to create new tools that students can use within some curriculum to explore mathematical concepts.

The E-Slate project is similar, described as an "exploratory learning environment that builds on a component-based approach of software development to fulfill some core requirements stemming from the educational domain" [9]. E-Slate includes a range of components, core services, and an API that allows developers to create "microworlds", or environments where learners can create different interactions between objects in some simulated world and explore the world by making different simulations in that world. For example, developers can set up a microworld where students fly airplanes over different maps to help students learn about geographic space and scale. Developers can set up such microworlds for learners to explore new concepts in the following manner [9]:

- *Set Up Microworld Objects*: Developers can take different components from the component library and place them in a window representing the microworld being constructed. There are many different types of components that can be used in a world representing physical objects (e.g., airplanes), representations (e.g., geographic maps, graphs), abstract representations (e.g., vectors). The different components also have property lists representing the characteristics of the components that can also be modified.

- *Connect Microworld Objects*: Components in the microworld can be connected to each other via "plugs" and "inter-component synapses" that define "transactions" between components specifying different actions and results to be taken by the components. For example, in a physics simulation, an airplane component can be connected to a vector component, which will show the speed of the airplane during a simulation. E-Slate also contains a scripting language, event handlers, and other editors that allow for more specific actions and connections to be defined by developers if necessary.

- *Using the Microworld.* The microworld itself is also now a program that can be shared and run by other E-Slate users. Once the microworlds are built, learners can use the microworld to run different simulations and explore different scenarios about the subject matter in the domain.

Another more expansive approach to aid developers of scaffolded software involves using software infrastructures to develop more complex integrated environments that support learners engaging in new practices. One example is the Symphony2 infrastructure for developing *scaffolded work environments* (or *SWEets*) for learners [54]. A SWEet is an environment that integrates a set of different learner-centered tools into a single environment that includes overarching process scaffolding and management support to help learners engage in the different aspects of a complex work practice [52].

The Symphony2 infrastructure provides software developers with core services aimed at supporting learners with many of the important cognitive activities found in complex practices. Symphony2 also has extensible facilities to allow developers to integrate different Java-based and web-based tools together and incorporate scaffolding features to assemble SWEets that learners can use to engage in different practices (e.g., science inquiry, financial analysis, etc.). The goal is to create a flexible infrastructure for developers to incorporate general core services along with specific tool sets and scaffolding features in a way that different SWEets can be developed for a range of learner audiences and practices. More specifically, the Symphony2 infrastructure includes [54]:

- *Core services to support learners.* Previous work has identified areas where learners need support across domains: support for planning and monitoring their work, support for synthesizing their work results into a coherent argument addressing the questions they are investigating, and support for managing the range of artifacts created throughout the process. Therefore, Symphony2 includes core planning, synthesis, and artifact management services that are available for developers to incorporate into any SWEet developed with the infrastructure.

- *Extensible functionality.* Once a target work practice has been identified, Symphony2 allows developers to integrate specific tools (or services) for learners into the SWEet they are building. The mechanism for integrating services is a "Project Manager" module. Services to be included in a SWEet register with the Project Manger through a software interface that describes the service, the specific activity it supports, and other information. Once registered, the services can be launched from the SWEet as needed. Thus different services can be "swapped" in and out of a SWEet by developers to address different learner audiences and different practices. (Note that core services are also "swappable" in this fashion so developers can incorporate core services for different situations, such as a planning service for 4th graders versus a planning service for 9th graders.)

- *Extensible scaffolding.* Symphony2 employs a model of "activity workspaces" representing the different activities in a practice. For example, for a science inquiry SWEet, developers might create activity workspaces for data visualization, modeling, data collection, etc. Developers can customize the different activity workspaces with different scaffolding features by using XML-based specification files. For example, developers can create different specification files to incorporate scaffolds like textual prompts and checklists in an activity workspace to help learners engage in the activity. Such scaffolding features are separate from other scaffolding features that may be incorporated in the service used for that activity (e.g., a visualization tool may have scaffolds different than the additional scaffolds added to the visualization workspace where the tool will be used). This ability gives developers the opportunity to develop more customized scaffolding features for activities that the service developers may not have originally envisioned when they created the service.

4.3   Tradeoffs for Developer Tools

The different tools and infrastructures described here certainly help software developers implement different kinds of ITSs and scaffolded software. While these approaches facilitate the development of learner-centered tools, there are still tradeoffs to consider for software developers.

The tradeoffs for ITS authoring tools involve the ease-of-authoring versus the richness of the resulting system. Developers can implement effective systems by avoiding the full sets of knowledge bases and instead integrating smaller amounts of knowledge and knowledge-based components with other tools. Using systems like REDEEM helps developers quickly implement effective systems for learners. However, since developers do not directly create the different ITS modules (other than the pre-packaged options developers are presented with), the resulting software may be more restricted and less powerful than other ITSs. The GBS approach is another example of "scaled-back" systems where smaller coaches, critics, and other expert systems are integrated with simulations to help learners engage in simulated tasks under the intelligent guidance. While these systems may not have all the conceptual components of full-fledged ITSs, they can still be quite effective [59].

More complex and effective tutoring systems require large knowledge bases for the different models in the system. However, even with the assistance of authoring tools, specifying the rules for the knowledge bases is a complex task, especially when considering the different kinds of knowledge—expert, student, instructional—that need to be incorporated into a ITS. The advantage of tools like Eon is that since the knowledge bases themselves can be created and modified, more powerful systems can be developed and customized. However, this also leads to a drawback: the authoring process is more complex than that used for constructing simple kinds of courseware-based tutoring systems (such as those created with REDEEM), especially for complex domain or learning situations where large rule-based knowledge bases are needed.

For developers of scaffolded software, the main tradeoff is that while component libraries and software infrastructures let developers implement software that learners can use to explore new concepts and practices, there is no inherent support for developing scaffolding features. ESCOT and E-Slate facilitate the creation of learner-oriented tools that allow learners to engage in cognitive and problem-solving activities from different domains. For example, instead of using a complex tool like Mathematica that assumes more mathematical expertise, developers could integrate different components to create a range of tools aimed at learners that allow them to participate in different mathematical activities. The ability to create new tools in a straightforward manner addresses some of the complexity that developers face when constructing new tools, freeing developers to consider designing additional scaffolding features for the tools they create.

However, despite the fact that developers can implement tools aimed at learners, developers are still responsible for engaging in the process we outlined for developing scaffolding features and deciding on scaffolds used to augment the tools and simulations they create. The Symphony2 infrastructure does give developers different APIs and specification abilities to produce specific software environments that can contain different scaffolding features, but there are no facilities in the infrastructure to help developers design new scaffolding features. Thus while approaches like ESCOT, E-Slate, and Symphony2 help developers assemble different components and existing scaffolding features to build scaffolded tools for learners, more developer support is needed to help them design new scaffolding features for their software projects.

5. Evaluation Issues for Determining the Effectiveness of Learner-Centered Software

After software—either intelligent tutoring systems or scaffolded software—has been designed, implemented, and used by the target learner audience, the final aspect of the development cycle involves evaluating the software. From a user-centered design perspective, the evaluation phase usually involves assessing the tool's usability and ease-of-use (or lack thereof). However, from a learner-centered perspective, evaluation also involves determining how well the software supports learners to do and learn new activities and practices. Salomon et al. [58] described two important evaluation aspects of educational technologies that need to be considered for evaluation:

- The "effects with" the software are the changes in how learners engage in some new activity as they use different features in the software. Here, evaluation involves analyzing how learners interact with different individual parts of the educational software.

- The "effects of" the software are the changes in the learner's understanding of the new practice or domain after learners have used the software (i.e., the "cognitive residue"). Here, evaluation involves analyzing the effectiveness of the educational software as a whole.

Therefore, in order to start understanding the quality of the software, developers need to understand the "local" effects of the software (i.e., how do novice learners engage in new activity with the software?) and the "global" effects of the software (i.e., what have they learned as a result of using the software?) [50].

Despite having this evaluation distinction, evaluating educational software is not as straightforward as it may initially seem. The "effects of/with" distinction broadly guides the kinds of observations to make when evaluating the software, but it does not define the specific methods that can be used to evaluate the software. Additionally, differences in the learning contexts and the basic approaches to educational software result in different tradeoffs for educational software evaluation.

5.1 Evaluating the "Effects of" Educational Software

The "effects of" aspect of educational software evaluation seems like a more obvious and straightforward aspect to consider. The main piece of information for the software developers to gain concerns the overall educational utility of the software. In this case, developers can address questions about the observed results on the learners after using the software, looking at whether learners learned the material supported by the software and the extent of the learning or the size of the learning gains that may or may not have occurred.

Many traditional evaluation methods can be used to perform "effects of" evaluation. One approach that could be used would be to compare the growth in domain knowledge of individual learners. For example, a pre/post test approach would look at the learner's knowledge before and after using the software:

- *Pre-testing*: Learners would be given a pre-test about the target domain or practice before using the software to measure their current domain knowledge.
- *Post-testing*: After using the software for some period of time, learners would be given a post-test to measure their domain knowledge after the software use (or at different intervals throughout the software use). The key here is to look at the learning gains that were made throughout the time in which they used the software.

Another approach for evaluating educational software would be to use more traditional controlled studies to gauge learning given the presence of the software. In this case, controlled studies could compare learners who used the software over some time versus a control group of learners who did not use the software over the same period of time. With such controlled studies, other factors in the learning context aside from the software—curricular material, teacher involvement, etc.—would have to be held constant in order to make valid comparisons between the study group and the control group. Controlled studies could involve making control and study groups from a single population and looking at some benchmark (e.g., test scores) from the two groups. Another controlled study approach could also involve comparing learner performance on some benchmark to the same benchmark results from similar students in previous years. Regardless of the technique, the key here is to compare the resulting domain knowledge of the software users to non-software users in order to make some generalizations about the effectiveness of the software.

5.2   Evaluating the "Effects with" Educational Software

While evaluating the "effects of" the software is important, developers also need additional information about how the software was used and what individual features of the software were successful and unsuccessful. "Effects with" evaluation is meant to give developers a more detailed look at software use. "Effects with" evaluation methods are not as straightforward and prevalent as the traditional control group studies for "effects of" evaluation. "Effects with" evaluation can require a more observational approach to look at learner actions and how the learner is interacting with different parts of the software to do the new activity being supported by the software. Developers of both ITSs and scaffolded software can thus look at how learners work with the software in different ways to gather evaluation information.

With ITSs, one possibility for "effects with" evaluation would be to look at a learner's work and knowledge states throughout the time that the learner used the system. Developers could review activity traces or other records of student work (e.g., videotapes of the student activity) at the point that the tutor intervened with assistance for the learner to try and see:

- Why the learner may have needed assistance.
- What kind of assistance the system provided.
- What actions the learner took after being given the assistance.

This information can help developers see whether the tutoring system is responding appropriately to inform possible modifications to the expert/domain knowledge modules. More importantly, developers can see whether the system is presenting appropriate instructional strategies and feedback. Developers can also consider the user interface for the ITS to look at the form of the tutor's feedback and identify cases where perhaps appropriate feedback was given by the tutor, but the form in which the feedback was presented in the user interface may have not been effective.

There is also work on how to conduct "effects with" evaluations for scaffolded software. With scaffolded software, developers want to look at how learners are working with the scaffolds in the software since those scaffolds were designed to support learners in doing the different aspects of a new practice. Since scaffolds are intended to meet certain learner support needs, developers need to consider whether different scaffolds supported the learner at the point where they were used. The approach here could involve observing learners when they interact with a scaffold to see their subsequent course of action in completing the activity being supported by that scaffold. One method for doing such an "effects with" evaluation method involves different benchmarks to judge both the usability of the scaffold feature along with how well learners did the supported activity given the scaffolding support [50, 51]. Thus, the evaluation method involves observing every use of a scaffold, and evaluating the scaffold use along different criteria [48]:

Criteria focusing more on scaffold usability:

- *Accessibility*: Was the scaffolding feature accessible to learners or were learners not able to see or find the scaffold?
- *Use*: Did learners use an accessible scaffold or did they ignore the scaffold?
- *Efficiency* (1): Were learners able to use the scaffold in a fairly efficient manner or was the scaffold too cumbersome to use?

Criteria focusing more on how learners did the supported task with the scaffold:

- *Efficiency* (2): Did learners do the task being supported by the scaffold in a very efficient manner, with some struggle, or with enough struggle that they could not do the task well?
- *Accuracy*: Did learners do the task being supported by the scaffold accurately or incorrectly?

- *Progression*: Did learners do the task being supported by the scaffold in a strictly linear fashion (which many times is the sign of more novice-like thinking) or in a more opportunistic, nonlinear fashion (which many times is the sign of more expert-like thinking).

- *Reflectiveness*: Did learners show any signs of reflecting on the task (e.g., discussion or debate about the task with peers, signs of thinking about the task before starting it, etc.) being supported by the scaffold or did they simply dive in to try and complete the task without many signs of reflection?

The qualitative information resulting from these criteria can then be compiled in different ways for the different scaffolds. Different methods could then be used for assessing these qualitative results in a more quantitative fashion [19] to give a measure about how learners used the different scaffolds to do their work and how their use of the scaffolds may have changed over time.

5.3   Tradeoffs in Educational Software Evaluation

While there are different methods that can be used for educational software evaluation, it can still be a complex endeavor to fully judge the effectiveness of educational software. Certainly the "effects of/with" distinction covers large ground to give developers different shades of information about the software. However, combining the different results for a bigger evaluation picture can be difficult because we still lack a way of relating the "effects of" and the "effects with" information. In other words, while we have the local and global observations about the software, how can we describe the contributions of the individual "effects with" results and observations to the "effects of" understanding gained by the software? Perhaps in some situations developers may have enough information about the software's effectiveness without having to unpack the role of the individual software features. But in most cases, developers might want to understand the impact of a particular tutor intervention or scaffolding feature to the overall changes in the learner's expertise. One approach to doing this could involve developing systems where different features or instructional strategies could be turned on or off. By doing so, different combinations of features could be used and then compared to the overall results of software use to try and correlate which features had a bigger impact of the overall learning. The drawback to this approach would be develop such a customizable piece of software. It would be doable (especially given some of the authoring tools and software infrastructures we outlined earlier), but it could be a complex problem for a comprehensive piece of software.

There is a larger problem to address when it comes to evaluating educational software and that is how to factor in the learning context to the overall equation. That is, even if the software is shown to have led to learning gains, how can we be sure that it was the software that led to those gains? We mentioned that one approach to answering this question would be controlled studies that keep other non-software variables constant. This could certainly be seen as a viable option when considering many ITSs, especially given their focus on individualized, one-to-one instruction. By strictly adhering to this view, we could see how other variables could be kept constant, looking at the ITS-learner pair so that the effectiveness of the ITS itself could be evaluated.

However, this solution is not so clear-cut when the learning context comes into play. Consider scaffolded software, which many times is part of an overall system where other components—teacher, peers, curriculum—can also provide scaffolding for learners. In this case, controlled studies become difficult and less viable because we now have a multivariate situation where it is difficult to hold "other variables" constant (e.g., the teacher, the classroom, peer interactions, etc.) [11]. In fact, it would go against the social constructivist view to hold many of these factors constant since the view describes the importance of different social interactions to learning. Additionally, the support provided by scaffolded software can help teachers develop more complex lessons with additional tasks and content. In this case, a controlled study becomes difficult given the fact that a control group (i.e., the group without the software) cannot attempt the same lessons that the study group does. Even previous ITS work noted that while there were several ITSs used on a one-to-one basis outside of a classroom that had favorable results, once the testing moved into the classroom, evaluation became more difficult, especially when ITSs had to be integrated with traditional school curricula [71]. Furthermore, there are ethical issues to consider when attempting controlled studies in the classroom. For example, if a certain system is used in a classroom, it becomes difficult guaranteeing that no harm will come to students, i.e., the control group who did not get to use ultimately successful software or the study group who had to use ultimately unsuccessful software.

6. The Current and Future State of Learner-Centered Technology

Having reviewed the different kinds of educational software approaches, we now conclude this chapter by considering future directions for educational software. We will also take a look at emerging technologies on the horizon and how these technologies may be developed into new devices that are advantageous for learning.

6.1   Current Directions: Exploiting the Successes of Different Learner-Centered Software

We have looked at different kinds of software for learning, each taking an approach towards supporting learners based on different underlying perspectives on learning. Each class of software poses its own set of challenges and tradeoffs for developing and evaluating the software. Many times, the discussion about the different kinds of educational software focuses on which class of software is more successful and advantageous for education. But given the different underlying approaches and different intended contexts for the software, there is probably no single "best" solution for learning. Perhaps the question we should be asking is how we could best exploit and combine the strengths of the support strategies used by the different kinds of software to provide more comprehensive support for learners. Each class of educational software can actually play a different role in supporting learners:

- Behaviorist software tries to shape learner behavior through positive and negative feedback. This could be considered "post hoc" support for developing software that sees the learner's answer and then notifies them of the results and the consequences (e.g., rewards or punishment).

- Intelligent tutoring systems try to oversee learners as they work and provide individualized assistance when the system decides that they need help. This could be considered "as needed" support for developing software that watches learners as they work and intervenes with help as needed.

- Scaffolded software uses embedded scaffolding features to support learners in those parts of the tasks where breakdowns may occur. This could be considered "a priori" support where developers try to determine areas where learners may encounter problems and develop software with scaffolding features that learners can use to avoid those possible breakdowns.

Within each class of software, there are certainly still many open questions and issues to address for development. But future work on learner-centered software should also focus on combining these techniques given the different kinds of support they each provide. For example, we could say that the kind of feedback provided by an ITS could be considered a form of scaffolding given the scaffolding definition that we gave earlier. So one approach to consider would be to use different ITS techniques to embed intelligent support within scaffolded software for additional learner support. Goal-based scenario software is an example where tutors and critics are combined with a user interface that incorporates other kinds of scaffolding features to guide learners through their tasks (e.g., using task lists to outline the composition of a complex activity) and to contextualize the activity (e.g., using video clips from other doctors in a medical diagnosis scenario). Other approaches even involve some resurrected behaviorist techniques. There are some behavioral approaches to tutorial systems that combine aspects of behaviorist software (e.g., noting whether learners have worked correctly or incorrectly) and intelligent tutors (e.g., describing why the learner's course of action was successful or problematic) [26].

Therefore, as we continue to work on improving the individual classes of educational software, we should also be cognizant on exploring advantageous combinations of support for learners. Each class of software has its tradeoffs, and only by exploiting the successful elements of each can we continue to expand the use of technology to support learners.

6.2   Future Directions: New Technologies for Learners

Throughout this chapter, we have been discussing various issues pertaining to the development of learner-centered software. But in reality, our discussion has centered on learner-centered *desktop computer* software. Whether we discussed intelligent tutoring systems or scaffolded software, the common thread between these two categories of software was that they run on desktop computers. One motivation for learner-centered software was to harness the growing power of computers (i.e., desktop computers) to support learning. However, there are new emerging technologies, specifically, wireless networking and handheld computers (e.g., Palm OS and Pocket PC devices) that are being explored for their possible uses in educational settings.

One central motivation for exploring wireless, handheld computers for education is that the increasing capabilities and decreasing prices of these devices now make them an attractive option for providing a larger learner audience with computer technology [65]. While computer access has improved greatly over the years, the fact is that many learners, especially in schools, still do not have individual access to computers. The lack of individual access can be a problem for certain software approaches, like some ITSs. Wireless, handheld computers open the door for learners to each have a networked device to use in a variety of learning contexts: in classrooms, at home, in libraries, or out in the field. With this greater access and portability, teachers can now explore new kinds of educational activities [65,67].

Research into the educational applications of wireless handhelds is still in its infancy, but there is a growing amount of work into this topic. Much of the current research involves identifying the unique characteristics and the space of educational activities for wireless, handheld devices. As new research continues to uncover unique characteristics and affordances for these devices, software developers and educators can consider new kinds of educational tools. For example, in our research work in Michigan schools, we have begun distributing handheld computers to middle school students to see what they can do with handheld-based software and what they enjoy about the handhelds. From our initial observations, we have begun contrasting hand-held and desktop computers to identify characteristics of the handheld computers from the perspective of the learners using them. For example, Bobrowsky et al. [13] have identified some characteristics of handheld computers and how they can impact learners:

- *Accessibility*: Because learners can each have a wireless handheld computer with them at all times, they can now have access to software tools and informa-tion anytime and anyplace. Thus, learners can now bring the technology with them to a variety of learning contexts rather than having to go to the technol-ogy (e.g., having to postpone certain learning activities until students go to their school computer lab).

- *Immediacy*: Similarly, the handheld, and possibly the network connection, are omnipresent in the sense that they are always on and available. With typical computers, there can be long boot times and network connection times that can distract learners from their work. When learners are trying to focus on their learning activities, they can seamlessly continue with their work without the distracting wait for the computer and network to come on.

- *Convergence*: Because of their pen-based input, many handhelds can now ac-commodate most of the work usually done with pen and paper. Coupling famil-iar pen-based activities with the other media types on the computer can allow learners to easily use and intermix a wider range of media types and information together. This convergence of different media types and natural textual capabil-ities can give learners the ability to express themselves in richer, more complex ways.

- *Permanence*: Between the networking capability offered by wireless handhelds and the "syncing" functionality of most handhelds, learners can easily save all the work the do on their handhelds to a server or desktop computer for later access, review, and modification. This can save time in classrooms over the typ-ical computer backup approach where students would have to navigate the file system and find the specific files they want to save to disk, a tedious procedure that many learners might bypass.

- *Collaborative Affordances*: The "beaming" capabilities on handhelds provide a natural and simple way of transferring information to others. This capability can allow for more social and collaborative interactions, allowing learners to work together on different parts of larger projects (e.g., different teams gathering sci-ence data to investigate a complex question) and then aggregate their different results to discuss and explore some conclusions for their project.

So we can see different kinds of interesting characteristics for wireless handhelds that software developers and educators can consider to explore new kinds of tools for learners. Handhelds can provide more ubiquitous access to educational tools and information, and a more natural, seamless device to focus more on their learning activities and less on the technology. Thus handhelds can fit more naturally into a range of learning contexts than desktop computers, or even laptop computers might.

Other research into the educational uses of wireless, handheld computers is attempting to define specific affordances of these devices that are favorable for learning. Roschelle and Pea [57] consider devices they term "wireless, Internet learning devices" (or WILDs), looking at their possible classroom use to define an initial set of application-level affordances for WILDs:

- *Augmenting physical space with information exchanges*: Because of the size and available access of WILD's to learners, the physical space of the learning environment (e.g., the classroom) can now be easily augmented with the technology to allow previously abstracted activities to be enacted in a more concrete manner. For example, with desktop computers, students could use modeling tools to set up an abstract representation of a disease simulation to study how disease spreads. With handhelds, students can engage in *participatory simulations* where the students themselves engage in a more concrete disease simulation, by "meeting" other students and using their handhelds to beam information to other students' handhelds about the possible spread of a disease in the classroom [20]. This can provide learners with a more tangible learning activity over more abstract experiences.

- *Leveraging two distinct kinds of topological space*: Similarly, handhelds allow learners to use and connect two kinds of information: *typological* information, which is more language-based and categorical in nature (e.g., information on their handheld about disease characteristics) and *topological* information, which is more spatially based, visual, and varying in nature (e.g., the location of a student in relation to other students participating in a participatory disease simulation). This ability provides students with multiple representations of information and can support different kinds of reasoning, allowing learners to explore more complex concepts in a more understandable fashion.

- *Aggregating coherently across all students participating individually*: Since handhelds can easily aggregate different pieces of information (e.g., beaming information from different handhelds to a single source), a variety of learners can now contribute information to a single representation, allowing for more collaborative activities. Furthermore, teachers can be supported with the ability to easily see the work of different students (e.g., students can all beam their work to the teacher), thus allowing teachers to gauge the learning progress of all their students in a classroom setting.

- *Conducting classroom performances*: Because all students can now be outfitted with computational tools, teachers in classrooms can now engage in different, more interactive learning activities for their students. This would not be the case for students that have to share desktop computers, especially when students are 2, 3, or even 4 to a computer.

- *Act become artifact*: With learners using handhelds in some learning context, developers and educators now have the ability to track the different actions that learners do with their handhelds in ways that would be more difficult if learners were using desktop computers. This ability allows teachers to view workflow and discourse patterns as their students work and communicate with each other so they can see if they need to modify the learning activities, intervene with some of the students, etc.

Again, the affordances of wireless handheld computers help uncover new kind of educational activities that learners can engage in and new functionalities for teachers to monitor their students, tailor their learning activities, and set up new kinds of interactive educational experiences in the classroom. In many respects, the advent of wireless, handheld devices continue to realize many of the earlier visions of educational technology [33]. However, there are still many challenges for software developers if the educational potential of wireless handhelds is to be met. Certainly, a starting point for developers would be to port existing desktop tools over to handheld computers to give learners a more portable tool set. This is a reasonable and useful activity, and there are aspects of ITSs and scaffolded software that can be written for handheld devices. More importantly, developers need to fully exploit the unique capabilities of wireless handheld devices to explore novel educational uses for these devices. But in order to do this, software developers need to address different challenges for designing, implementing, and evaluating learner-centered software for handhelds, especially when trying to incorporate aspects of the different software approaches we have discussed in this chapter:

- While the power of handheld computers is increasing, they still have less power than desktop computers. Thus, how can elements of tutoring systems, many of which are computationally expensive, be incorporated into handheld computers?

- Given the smaller screen and alternate methods of input, what kind of human–computer interaction/user interface design issues need to be addressed to develop useful, scaffolded interfaces? How can many of the current scaffolding features that are effective on desktop computers be effectively scaled down for handheld computers? What kind of new scaffolding implementations are necessary for handheld computers?

- How can handheld and desktop computers be integrated and used together to develop an overall system that exploits the advantages of each platform? Can learners use both handheld devices and desktop computers when appropriate in an effective manner?

- If technology is now pervasive to the extent that learners can use handheld devices anytime and anyplace, what new kinds of software evaluation approaches are needed to observe learners and gain a full picture about how learners are working with these technologies? How can different evaluation strategies (e.g., log files, videotaped observations of learners, etc.) be used for the different learning contexts where learners are using handhelds?

This summary describes some of the issues that need to be addressed by researchers in software, user interface design, and education, not only to foster the development of educational technology, but also to inform software development in general. With wireless, handheld devices becoming more popular, the software development community as a whole will have to address many of the computational, user interface, programming, and evaluation questions that arise with these new technologies.

7. Concluding Remarks

In this chapter, we have summarized some general approaches to educational software and we have looked at the work and tradeoffs involved in designing, implementing, and evaluating different types of learner-centered software. We have also looked at new technologies that are emerging and how they might impact learning by affording new kinds of exciting learning activities. But whether the software is desktop-based or handheld-based, we have shown that there is a range of techniques and approaches that educational software developers can draw from to embed effective support for learners in software. With these different approaches and types of learning support, developers can not only consider the specific kinds of software we have discussed here, but also new kinds of software that take advantage of different support techniques for developing new examples of educational software.

There are also different issues for software developers and researchers to explore for the future development of educational software. We have outlined different tradeoffs and issues for developing the different classes of educational software and we have seen that there are still open questions that must be explored to continue facilitating learner-centered software development. But there are also other avenues to explore that can shed light on improving software-based support for learners. For example, the work of game designers could be explored to look at techniques for motivating learners and for creating new kinds of support for learners. (Note that we do not mean to simply look at the design of educational games, but game design in general.) In a sense, there is much learning that occurs in games, as players learn the rules of the game and the game world, the rationale for the different objects and actions in the game world, information that they need to gain to proceed through the game world, etc. Essentially, these are all elements of a practice (i.e., roles, tools, tasks, information, etc.), so what kinds of game techniques can be used to support learners engaging in a new practice? Furthermore, good game designers have mastered the tasks of keeping players motivated because if the game is too easy or too hard, players will stop playing. This is analogous to the "structure/problematize" task we mentioned earlier for software scaffolding [55]. If software support makes activities too easy for learners, or if support is weak and the supported activities are still too hard for learners, then learning will not occur. So can we glean any "motivational support" from game designers to help learners stay in the optimal zone for learning?

Another area of support to explore can be found from the worlds of graphic design and information visualization. Much of the support that software can provide involves presenting learners with different kinds of information about the activities they are working on (e.g., content information, tutor feedback, visual representations about the activities they can perform, etc.). Effectively presenting this information to different learner audiences is a key support feature for software. Developers can turn to graphic designers and research on information visualization to see how to effectively present information to different learners, especially to present the complex and possibly abstract information learners will encounter when they are trying to engage in new kinds of work. Additionally, graphic design and information visualization can also be key when designing software on handheld devices to effectively present information to learners on devices where screen space is at a premium.

In the end, we see that developing software for learning is truly an interdisciplinary enterprise where multiple lines of research need to converge for effective learner-centered software. As with most complex software development efforts, the challenge for development teams is to be cognizant of not just software and user interface design expertise, but also expertise in learning and developmental theory, classroom and curricular issues, teacher development, along with the different research areas we have just outlined. Only then can effective educational software be developed. While there have been some failures and unrealistic expectations over the years, there are also many successes in educational software. By focusing the unique needs of learners and learning contexts, and by employing the expertise of researchers in different educational and technical areas, we feel that there are still many examples to come that show how technology can positively impact learning in a variety of fields.

ACKNOWLEDGEMENTS

This material is based on work supported by the National Science Foundation under Grant Nos. REC-99-80055 and ITR 00-85946. Any opinions, findings, and conclusions or recommendations expressed in this material are those of the authors and do not necessarily reflect those of the National Science Foundation.

REFERENCES

[1] Ainsworth S.E., Grimshaw S.K., Underwood D.J., "Teachers as designers: Using RE-DEEM to create ITSs for the classroom", *Computers and Education* **33** (2/3) (1999) 171–188.

[2] Alexander C., Ishikawa S., Silverstein M., *A Pattern Language: Towns, Buildings, Construction*, Oxford University Press, 1977.

[3] Anderson J.R., *The Architecture of Cognition*, Harvard University Press, Cambridge, MA, 1983.

[4] Anderson J.R., Reder L.M., Simon H., "Radical constructivism and cognitive psychology", in: Ravitch D. (Ed.), *Brookings Papers on Educational Policy 1998*, Brookings Institute Press, Washington D.C., 1998.

[5] Anderson J.R., Reiser B., "The LISP tutor", *Byte* **10** (1986) 159–175.

[6] Beck J., Stern M., Haugsjaa E., "Applications of AI in education", *ACM Crossroads* **3** (1996) 11–15.

[7] Berczuk S., "Finding solutions through pattern languages", *IEEE Computer* **27** (1994).

[8] Beyer H., Holtzblatt K., *Contextual Design: A Customer-Centered Approach to Systems Design*, Morgan Kaufmann Publishers, 2002.

[9] Birbilis G., Koutlis M., Kyrimis K., Tsironis G., Vasilou G., "E-Slate: A software architectural style for end-user programming", in: *Proceedings of ICSE 2000: 22nd International Conference on Software Engineering, Limerick, Ireland*, 2000.

[10] Bloom B.S., "The 2 Sigma problem: The search for methods of group instruction as effective as one-to-one tutoring", *Educational Researcher* **13** (6) (1984) 4–16.

[11] Blumenfeld P.C., Fishman B., Krajcik J., Marx R.W., Soloway E., "Creating usable innovations in systemic reform: Scaling up technology-embedded project-based science in urban schools", *Educational Psychologist* **35** (3) (2000) 149–164.

[12] Blumenfeld P.C., Soloway E., Marx R., Krajcik J.S., Guzdial M., Palincsar A., "Motivating project-based learning", *Educational Psychologist* **26** (3 & 4) (1991) 369–398.

[13] Bobrowsky W., Curtis M., Luchini K., Quintana C., Soloway E., "Exploring the affordances of handheld computers: Helping teachers engage in best practice", in: *ICLS 2002: International Conference of the Learning Sciences, Seattle, WA*, 2002.

[14] Bransford J.D., Brown A.L., Cocking R.R. (Eds.), *How People Learn: Brain, Mind, Experience, and School (Expanded Edition)*, National Academy Press, 2000.

[15] Brown J.S., Collins A., Duguid P., "Situated cognition and the culture of learning", *Educational Researcher* **18** (1989) 32–42.

[16] Bush V., "As we may think", *The Atlantic Monthly* **176** (1945) 101–108.

[17] Carbonell J.R., *Mixed-Initiative Man–Computer Instructional Dialogs (Technical Report)*, Bolt Beranek and Newman, Cambridge, MA, 1970.

[18] Card S.K., Moran T.P., Newell A., *The Psychology of Human–Computer Interaction*, Lawrence Erlbaum Associates, Hillsdale, NJ, 1983.

[19] Chi M., "Quantifying qualitative analyses of verbal data: A practical guide", *Journal of the Learning Sciences* **6** (3) (1997) 271–315.

[20] Colella V., Borovoy R., Resnick M., "Participatory simulations: Using computational objects to learn about dynamic systems", in: *Human Factors in Computing Systems: CHI '98 Conference Proceedings, Los Angeles, CA*, 1998.

[21] Collins A., Brown J.S., Newman S.E., "Cognitive apprenticeship: Teaching the crafts of reading, writing, and mathematics", in: Resnick L.B. (Ed.), *Knowing, Learning, and Instruction: Essays in Honor of Robert Glaser*, Lawrence Erlbaum Associates, 1989.

[22] Corbett A.T., Koedinger K.R., Hadley W.H., "Cognitive tutors: From the research classroom to all classrooms", in: Goodman P.S. (Ed.), *Technology Enhanced Learning: Opportunities for Change*, Lawrence Erlbaum Associates, Mahwah, NJ, 2001.

[23] DiGiano C., Roschelle J., "Rapid-assembly componentware for education", in: *Proceedings of the International Workshop on Advanced Learning Technologies at Palmerston North, New Zealand*, 2000.

[24] Dobson W.D., Riesbeck C.K., "Tools for incremental development of educational software interfaces", in: *Human Factors in Computing Systems: CHI '98 Conference Proceedings, Los Angeles, CA*, 1998.

[25] Edelson D.C., Gordin D.N., Pea R.D., "Addressing the challenges of inquiry-based learning through technology and curriculum design", *Journal of the Learning Sciences* **8** (3/4) (1999).

[26] Emurian H.H., Durham A.G., "Computer-based tutoring systems: A behavioral approach", in: Jacko J., Sears A. (Eds.), *Handbook of Human–Computer Interaction*, Lawrence Erlbaum Associates, 2002. To appear.

[27] Favorin M., Kuutti K., "Supporting learning at work by making work activities visible through information technology", *Machine-Mediated Learning* **5** (2) (1996) 109–118.

[28] Fitzpatrick G., Welsh J., "Process support: Inflexible imposition or chaotic composition", *Interacting with Computers* **7** (2) (1995).

[29] Gertner A., VanLehn K., "Andes: A coached problem solving environment for physics", in: *ITS 2000: Proceedings of the Fifth International Conference on Intelligent Tutoring Systems, Montreal, Canada*, 2000.

[30] Jackson S.L., Krajcik J., Soloway E., "The design of guided learning-adaptable scaffolding in interactive learning environments", in: *Human Factors in Computing Systems: CHI '98 Conference Proceedings, Los Angeles*, 1998.

[31] John B.E., Kieras D.E., "The GOMS family of user interface analysis techniques: Comparison and contrast", *ACM Transactions in Computer–Human Interaction* **3** (4) (1996) 320–351.

[32] Johnson L., Soloway E., "Intention-based diagnosis of programming errors", in: *Proceedings of the Fourth National Conference on Artificial Intelligence, Austin, TX*, 1984.

[33] Kay A., Goldberg A., "Personal dynamic media", *IEEE Computer* **10** (1977) 31–41.

[34] Lesgold A., *Guide to Cognitive Task Analysis*, University of Pittsburgh Learning Research and Development Center, Pittsburgh, PA, 1986.

[35] Linn M.C., Slotta J.D., "WISE science", *Educational Leadership* **58** (2) (2000).

[36] Loh B., Radinsky J., Russell E., Gomez L.M., Reiser B.J., Edelson D.C., "The progress portfolio: Designing reflective tools for a classroom context", in: *Human Factors in Computing Systems: CHI '98 Conference Proceedings, Los Angeles*, 1998.

[37] Luchini K., Oehler P., Quintana C., "An engineering process for constructing scaffolded work environments to support student inquiry: A case study in history", in: *ICALT 2001: IEEE Conference on Advanced Learning Technologies, Madison, WI*, 2001.

[38] Mayhew D.J., *The Usability Engineering Lifecycle*, Morgan Kaufmann Publishers, 1999.

[39] Metcalf S.J., Krajcik J., Soloway E., "Model-It: A design retrospective", in: Jacobson M.J., Kozma R.B. (Eds.), *Innovations in Science and Mathematics Education*, Lawrence Erlbaum Associates, Mahwah, NJ, 2000, pp. 77–115.

[40] Murray T., "Having it all, maybe: Design tradeoffs in ITS authoring tools", in: *Proceedings of the Third International Conference on Intelligent Tutoring Systems, Montreal, Canada*, 1996.

[41] Norman D.A., "Cognitive engineering", in: Norman D.A., Draper S.W. (Eds.), *User Centered System Design*, Lawrence Erlbaum Associates, 1986.

[42] Ong J., Ramachandran S., "Intelligent tutoring systems: The what and the how", in: *Learning Circuits*, 2000. Available at http://www.learningcircuits.org/feb2000/ong.html.

[43] Papert S., *The Children's Machine: Rethinking School in the Age of the Computer*, Basic Books, New York, 1993.

[44] Piaget J., *The Construction of Reality in the Child*, Basic Books, 1954.

[45] Preece J., Rogers Y., Sharp H., Benyon D., *Human–Computer Interaction*, Addison-Wesley, 1994.

[46] Quintana C., Carra A., Krajcik J., Soloway E., "Learner-centered design: Reflections and new directions", in: Carroll J.M. (Ed.), *Human–Computer Interaction in the New Millennium*, ACM Press, New York, 2001, pp. 605–626.

[47] Quintana C., Eng J., Carra A., Wu H., Soloway E., "Symphony: A case study in extending learner-centered design through process-space analysis", in: *Human Factors in Computing Systems: CHI '99 Conference Proceedings, Pittsburgh*, 1999.

[48] Quintana C., Fretz E., Krajcik J., Soloway E., "Evaluation criteria for scaffolding in learner-centered tools", in: *Human Factors in Computing Systems: CHI 2000 Extended Abstracts, The Hague, The Netherlands*, 2000.

[49] Quintana C., Krajcik J., Norris C., Soloway E., "A framework for understanding the development of educational software", in: Jacko J., Sears A. (Eds.), *Handbook of Human-Computer Interaction*, 2002. To appear.

[50] Quintana C., Krajcik J., Soloway E., "Exploring a description and methodology for learner-centered design", in: Heineke W., Blasi L. (Eds.), in: *Methods of Evaluating Educational Technology*, Vol. 1, Information Age Publishing, Greenwich, CT, 2001.

[51] Quintana C., Krajcik J., Soloway E., "Issues and methods for evaluating learner-centered scaffolding", in: *ICALT 2001: IEEE International Conference on Advanced Learning Technologies, Madison, WI*, 2001.

[52] Quintana C., Krajcik J., Soloway E., "Scaffolding design guidelines for learner-centered software environments", in: *Annual Meeting of the American Educational Research Association, New Orleans, LA*, 2002.

[53] Quintana C., Reiser B., Davis E.A., Krajcik J., Golan R., Kyza E., Edelson D.C., Soloway E., "Evolving a scaffolding design framework for designing educational software", in: *ICLS 2002: International Conference of the Learning Sciences, Seattle, WA*, 2002.

[54] Quintana C., Wells C., Soloway E., "The Symphony2 software infrastructure for constructing scaffolded work environments", in: *SEA 2002: 6th IASTED International Conference on Software Engineering and Applications, Cambridge, MA*, 2002.

[55] Reiser B.J., "Why scaffolding should sometimes make tasks more difficult for learners", in: *Proceedings of CSCL 2002, Boulder, CO*, 2002.

[56] Reiser B.J., Tabak I., Sandoval W.A., Smith B.K., Steinmuller F., Leone A.J., "BGuILE: strategic and conceptual scaffolds for scientific inquiry in biology classrooms", in: Carver S.M., Klahr D. (Eds.), *Cognition and Instruction: Twenty-Five Years of Progress*, Lawrence Erlbaum Associates, 2001, pp. 263–305.

[57] Roschelle J., Pea R.D., "A walk on the WILD side: How wireless handhelds may change CSCL", in: *Proceedings of CSCL 2002, Boulder, CO*, 2002.

[58] Salomon G., Perkins D.N., Globerson T., "Partners in cognition: Extending human intelligence with intelligent technologies", *Educational Researcher* (April 1991).

[59] Schank R.C., Cleary C., *Engines for Education*, Lawrence Erlbaum Associates, Hillsdale, NJ, 1995.

[60] Schmidt D.C., "Using design patterns to develop reusable object-oriented communication software", *Communications of the ACM* 38 (1995) 65–74.

[61] Shortliffe E.H., "Consultation systems for physicians: The role of artificial intelligence techniques", in: Webber B.L., Nilsson N.J. (Eds.), *Readings in Artificial Intelligence*, Tioga Publishing Company, Palo Alto, CA, 1981, pp. 323–333.

[62] Shute V., Bonar J., "Intelligent tutoring systems for scientific inquiry", in: *Proceedings of the Cognitive Science Society*, 1986.

[63] Singer J., Marx R., Krajcik J., Clay Chambers J., "Constructing extended inquiry projects: Curriculum materials for science education reform", *Educational Psychologist* 35 (3) (2000) 165–178.

[64] Slotta J.D., Linn M.C., "The knowledge integration environment: Helping students use the internet effectively", in: Jacobson M.J., Kozma R.B. (Eds.), *Innovations in Science and Mathematics Education: Advanced Designs for Technologies of Learning*, Lawrence Erlbaum Associates, Mahwah, New Jersey, 2000, pp. 193–226.

[65] Soloway E., Grant W., Tinker R., Roschelle J., Mills M., Resnick M., Berg R., Eisenberg M., "Science in the palms of their hands", *Communications of the ACM* 42 (1999) 21–27.

[66] Soloway E., Guzdial M., Hay K.E., "Learner-centered design: The challenge for HCI in the 21st century", *Interactions* 1 (1994) 36–48.

[67] Soloway E., Norris C., Blumenfeld P., Fishman B., Krajcik J., Marx R., "Log on education: Handheld devices are ready-at-hand", *Communications of the ACM* 44 (2001) 15–20.

[68] Towne D., Munro A., "Supporting diverse instructional strategies in a simulation-oriented training environment", in: Regian J., Shute V. (Eds.), *Cognitive Approaches to Automated Instruction*, Lawrence Erlbaum Associates, Hillsdale, NJ, 1992.

[69] Wallace R., Soloway E., Krajcik J., Bos N., Hoffman J., Hunter H.E., Kiskis D., Klann E., Peters G., Richardson D., Ronen O., "ARTEMIS: Learner-centered design of an information seeking environment for K-12 education", in: *Human Factors in Computing Systems: CHI '98 Conference Proceedings, Los Angeles*, 1998.

[70] Wood D., Bruner J.S., Ross G., "The role of tutoring in problem-solving", *Journal of Child Psychology and Psychiatry* **17** (1975) 89–100.

[71] Woolf B.P., "AI in education", in: Shapiro S.C. (Ed.), *Encyclopedia of Artificial Intelligence*, Wiley & Sons, 1992, pp. 434–444.

Personalizing Interactions with Information Systems

SAVERIO PERUGINI AND NAREN RAMAKRISHNAN

Department of Computer Science
Virginia Tech.
Blacksburg, VA 24061
USA
sperugin@cs.vt.edu
naren@cs.vt.edu

Abstract

Personalization constitutes the mechanisms and technologies necessary to customize information access to the end-user. It can be defined as the automatic adjustment of information content, structure, and presentation tailored to the individual. In this chapter, we study personalization from the viewpoint of personalizing *interaction*. The survey covers mechanisms for information-finding on the web, advanced information retrieval systems, dialog-based applications, and mobile access paradigms. Specific emphasis is placed on studying how users interact with an information system and how the system can encourage and foster interaction. This helps bring out the role of the personalization system as a facilitator which reconciles the user's mental model with the underlying information system's organization. Three tiers of personalization systems are presented, paying careful attention to interaction considerations. These tiers show how progressive levels of sophistication in interaction can be achieved. The chapter also surveys systems support technologies and niche application domains.

1. Introduction

Personalization entails customizing information access, structure, and presentation to the end-user. While the roots of personalization can be traced back to information filtering [8] and recommender systems [94], the web has propelled personalization into a highly studied and legitimate research area. The explosion of online content and the advent of ubiquitous computing devices and information appliances [14] have made personalization critical to the success of Internet applications. Personalization is achieved in information systems which afford complex, compelling, and user-adapted interactions. Studying how users interact with information systems and understanding the frustrations they experience provides ample motivation for personalization.

1.1   Why Personalize?

We begin with the quintessential information access paradigm on the web - browsing. Bush is regarded as the godfather of browsing as we know it today [20]. In browsing, two distinct roles are seen. "The role of the author was to create the hypertext and the role of the user/reader was to browse through it. Thus, the reader was faced with the task of understanding the author's mental model of the hypertext documents in order to navigate the collection of linked nodes (hyperbase) effectively" [9].

Pre-defined, hardwired browsing interfaces in information systems have been succinctly characterized with phrases such as 'static hypertext' [9], 'strong authoring' [9], and 'one-size-fits-all' [19,25]. Such a rigid model assumes that the author's viewpoint is correct. The resulting mental mismatch problem has been identified as a legitimate research issue in [17,101]. The goal of personalization technologies is to help overcome this mismatch. Essentially the same issue arises in other information access paradigms, and a variety of delivery mechanisms.

1.2   Approaches to Personalized Interaction

Operationally, the word 'personalization' is broad and open to many interpretations. For instance, we can aim for a naturalness in interaction, interestingness of content, quality of web pages, or speed of access. Many surveys of personalization focus on technical distinctions of how information is tailored to end-users and the level at which it is targeted. Business schools have adopted terms such as 'real time,' 'one-to-one,' and 'check-box' personalization. Therefore, there are truly 'personalized views of personalization' [87]. For instance, the articles in the *Communications of the ACM* August 2000 special issue on personalization range from topics such as natural language dialogs, to web site restructuring, to manually customizable portals.

In this survey, we approach personalization from the viewpoint of personalizing *interaction*. Interaction with an information system is thus the common thread among all systems surveyed in this chapter. Distinctions are only made when they reveal differences among interaction paradigms. For instance, Amazon's recommender system might make better recommendations of books than another bookseller's but if they possess the same interaction paradigm, they are considered equivalent for our purposes. In fact, many personalization solutions do not even explicitly recognize the issue of interaction with an user; needless to say they are not surveyed here. Distinctions such as *content-based* and *collaborative*—very popular in the recommender systems community—thus do not find place in this chapter.

We posit that surveying personalization according to interactions of users [60] is a more holistic approach to studying this subject. To the best of our knowledge, this survey is the first to employ this approach. The reader should keep in mind that we use the term *personalization* synonymously with personalized interaction.

1.3   Organization of This Survey

Three main approaches to personalizing interaction are outlined (see Fig. 1). The first approach is the terminal case where the system provides no support for maintaining interaction and the onus of personalization is shifted to the user. As shown in Fig. 1(a), the system effectively behaves as a functional engine mapping users' specification aspects into results. It doesn't recognize the fact that information access occurs in the context of an interaction.

Writing SQL queries in a database context is an example of a functional modeling. Although the user might interactively explore the database through a sequence of such queries, the system *per se* does not provide any support for interaction. We refer to these approaches as template-based and survey a sample of systems as they

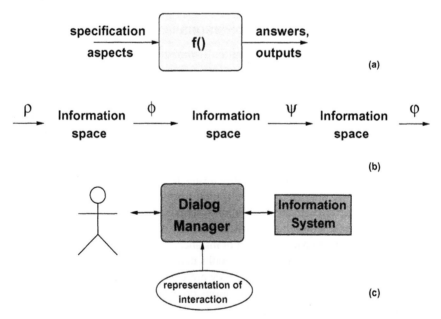

FIG. 1. Three approaches to personalized interaction surveyed in this chapter: (a) templates for personalization, (b) operators for personalization, and (c) representing and reasoning about interaction.

relate to information access on the web. We pay particular attention to systems that combine distinct modalities of information-seeking and which are especially relevant to the primary Internet access paradigms today.

Systems in the next tier provide a set of basic primitives for sustaining interaction. As shown in Fig. 1(b), these primitives are typically in the form of operators that successively transform an information space. The user is encouraged to apply these operators in a form that is suitable to his information-seeking activity. We say that such systems recognize and encourage interaction.

The third tier of systems are truly novel in that they explicitly represent and capture interaction. As Fig. 1(c) shows, interaction here resembles more a dialog between the user and the information system. A natural dialog is one where both parties interact to achieve the desired information-seeking goals. Systems in this tier are characterized by their representations, whose expressiveness and capabilities directly relate to the quality of personalized interaction. They are most capable of reconciling the mental mismatch issue introduced earlier.

1.4   Reader's Guide

The survey paints a picture of how personalization is conducted in each of the three tiers by showcasing a number of research projects. Section 2 describes templates for personalization. Section 3 introduces systems which afford expressive operators for personalization. Section 4 discusses representing and reasoning about interaction. A few novel research projects are elaborated upon here. It should be remarked that the relative lengths of these sections do not reflect our view on their relative importance. They are more a reflection of the popularities of the template and operator-based approaches and the nascency of the representational approach. Project descriptions in each tier are also not meant to be exhaustive. In Section 5 we describe systems support tools and technologies that help achieve personalization. In Section 6 we describe a few niche domains that have witnessed significant investments in personalization. Section 7 concludes this chapter with some observations about the future.

2.   Templates for Personalized Interaction

It can be argued that being able to set the background color for a desktop screen is a rudimentary form of personalization. Here, the goals of personalization have become so over-specified that the responsibility of achieving the personalization is shifted to the user, who must specify the settings.

A typical form of over-specification involves templates that are meant to be customized by the user. Another involves providing an expressive web query language, not unlike SQL. Their salient feature is a 'one-shot' [19,66] style of personalization. This section surveys such approaches. Specifically, we start from a database perspective and describe the WSQ/DSQ project and probabilistic relational algebra. We next discuss web queries as templates and the use of templates for constructing personal information spaces.

2.1 WSQ/DSQ

The WSQ/DSQ (pronounced 'wisk-disk') project [41] at Stanford University attempts to bridge the gap between structured relational databases (DBs) and the unstructured web in support of an information retrieval request. WSQ (Web-Supported Queries) incorporates web search results into SQL queries over a database to enrich an answer. On the other hand, DSQ (Database-Supported (Web) Queries), its complement, leverages DB relations to enhance and explain web search results.

For the purposes of this chapter, it is sufficient to focus on the WSQ component. WSQ leverages web search results to provide a richer set of input parameters for a query against original relational data sources. In other words, the output of one query (the web search) is provided as input, along with the extant DB relations, to a master SQL query. In WSQ the primary mode of information-seeking is thus an SQL query and the secondary mode is web search.

The essential idea behind WSQ is to permit users to make references to web search requests within a traditional SQL query. A user writes a query that makes reference to a web search engine (WSQ/DSQ uses AltaVista and Google) and search terms, obtains an answer—a new relation, and proceeds to the next independent query that may (e.g., join the resulting relation with itself) or may not involve the resulting relation. A typical WSQ query is shown in Fig. 2. Interaction in WSQ is hence limited to issuing a query and obtaining an answer. This is referred to as a one-shot interac-

```
SELECT Name, Count
FROM States, WebCount
WHERE Name = T1
ORDER BY Count Desc
```

FIG. 2. A WSQ query to rank states by how often they appear on the web (from [41]). This query has traditional SQL semantics. States and WebCount are relations. The schema of States is States(Name, Population, Capital). The WebCount relation, whose schema is WebCount(SearchExp, T1, T2, ..., TN, Count), is populated by the results of a web search request. T1, T2, ..., TN are values for parameters in SearchExp. Notice that all aspects of information-seeking necessary to determine an answer are provided in one stroke.

tion [19] or a one-shot task [66]. Furthermore, traditional query processing cannot proceed until all attribute values initially populated with calls to a particular web search engine are replaced with corresponding URL answers.

Thus, interaction in WSQ is best modeled as a template for personalization. The order of the two information-seeking interactions in WSQ are determined *a priori* at query-creation time. This design of over-specification means that information-seeking parameters are provided in one stroke.

In fairness to the designers, the design in WSQ/DSQ is commensurate with the targeted applications (i.e., answering questions regarding comparisons or frequencies of items on the web, e.g., "Rank all countries in North America by how often they are mentioned by name on the web."). Nonetheless, WSQ is an interesting research project to study with respect to personalization and combining aspects of information-seeking. We view it as a limiting case of a personalization system.

2.2   Probabilistic Relational Algebra

In [37], Fuhr and Rölleke approach the problem of integrating aspects of information-seeking from a different angle. Specifically, the designers weave canonical IR parameters (e.g., weights, rankings, and probabilities) into a DBMS in order to enhance and improve retrieval.

Integration here is motivated by the fact that database management systems (DBMSs) lack a clean method to incorporate IR parameters. For instance, DBMSs do not adequately address vagueness, imprecision, and uncertainty which IR systems are designed for. DBMSs are however strongly grounded in theory and relations afford expressive query languages (QLs). IR systems, on the other hand, incorporate parameters well but have problems incorporating ground facts. In addition, there is limited expression in IR QLs that is currently addressed with ad hoc methods.

In order to weave standard IR parameters into a DBMS, Fuhr and Rölleke generalize traditional relational algebra, where probabilities are either 0 or 1, to the continuous range $[0\ldots 1]$. Incorporating probabilities into tuples of DB relations is relatively straightforward. Ensuring that these probabilities are correctly propagated in an answer (after possibly complex joins or other operations) is difficult, due to uncertainty about the independence/dependence of tuples at query formulation time. Additional data could be modeled in relations to make such constraints explicit. With large DBs, however, such constraints and annotations embedded into relations may approach exponential levels.

Due to the explicit requirement to specify all information-seeking aspects at query formulation time, we classify Fuhr and Rölleke's work as a template for personalization. The system they developed does not allow users to specify parameters over time or leave parameters residual. Information-seeking sessions of this system resemble interaction with WSQ, with minor adaptations, e.g., instead of specifying which search engine to employ, the user indicates a probability threshold or an index weight.

2.3 Web Query Languages

Search Interfaces: Precursors to Web QLs

In order to combat cognitive frustrations experienced in browsing, many sites provide within-site search interfaces. We present three common user interface designs here. Figure 3 (top) illustrates part of a book search tool available at Amazon.com. This type of search interface is typical and requires a user to associate search terms with categorical information (e.g., author, title, and publisher). The goal of such search interfaces is to avoid enumerating multiple browsing paths to terminal information (in this case, a book webpage). An alternative design, shown in Fig. 3 (bottom), is called a 'power-search' and has gained popularity in many e-commerce sites. A power-search more closely resembles a web query language. In other words, such tools include a small language for communicating inputs involving multiple query fields (possibly combined via ANDs or ORs). The power-search of Amazon.com shown in Fig. 3 (bottom) still requires a user to specify categorical information, however. From a user perspective, a less restrictive interface is a free-form text box (Fig. 4) that does not require categorical information. In such a design, users' query terms are matched against all attributes of an information nugget (e.g., webpage, book, or movie). The search facilities involved in the interfaces outlined above do not employ expressive QLs.

The systems presented below provide users with a sophisticated QL. Through the invocation of a query, such systems combine aspects of information-seeking with reconstruction properties of an information space.

Restructuring Semistructured Data

The semistructured data [1,36] and XML communities have embraced the idea of building, restructuring, and managing information spaces (e.g., web sites) with adaptations of traditional SELECT-FROM-WHERE queries. In this context, new and personalized information spaces may be constructed from DB relations, structured files, or semistructured data (e.g., XML). In addition, extant information spaces, such as web sites, may be restructured via a declarative query. This latter application is more interesting to study for our purposes.

For example, consider a researcher who disseminates his publications on his webpage via a research area browsing dichotomy. The original data may be stored in

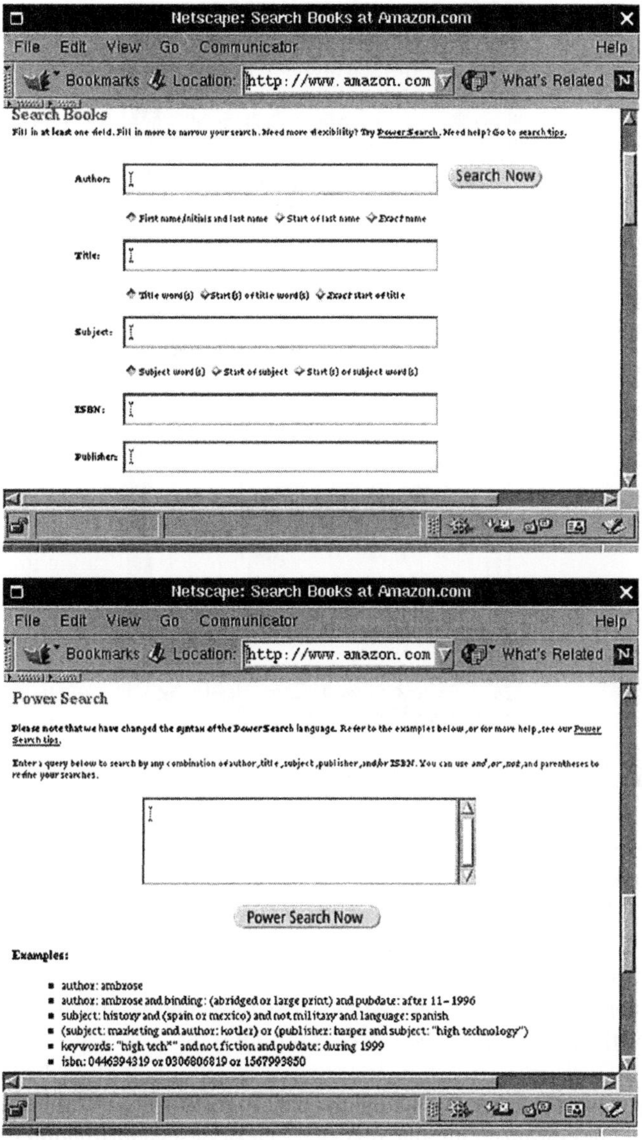

FIG. 3. (top) A book search interface at Amazon.com. This interface contains multiple category-labeled text-fields, expecting input to belong to a category. Such a design attempts to hide hyperlink enumeration in web sites. (bottom) A power-search facility at Amazon.com that allows multiple query terms from different categories, but still requires categorical information.

FIG. 4. A search facility of Amazon.com that allows the entry of free-form text.

XML files (see top side of Fig. 5). If this researcher desires to restructure the hierarchical presentation with respect to year, he could write a semistructured data query (see Fig. 6). The output of the query is another XML file containing the publications of the researcher ordered by year of publication (see bottom side of Fig. 5). We use the StruQL query language [35,34] to illustrate the query example in Fig. 6, but there exist a number of other semistructured and XML QLs such as Araneus, Florid, Lorel, WebOQL, WIRM, YAT, XSL/XSLT, and XML-QL [36].

   A query to restructure an information space actually mixes two distinct modalities of information-seeking. Typically, the data to restructure is a subset of an information space and retrieved via the WHERE clause of a semistructured data query. The WHERE clause thus serves as a match operator. Once data is bound to variables in a WHERE clause, manipulation of those variables within the CONSTRUCT clause of a query (the LINK clause in the case of StruQL) restructures the space. Thus, reconstruction activities take place following a retrieval or match operation.

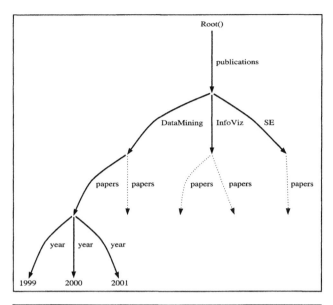

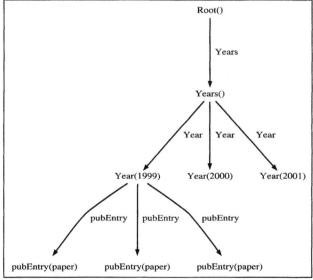

FIG. 5. (top) Directed graph model of XML input to the StruQL query shown in Fig. 6. The publications are ordered by research area. (bottom) Directed graph model of XML output from the StruQL query shown in Fig. 6. Notice that publications are now ordered by year. Such XML data sources can be easily converted into a set of browsable webpages with tools such as XSL/XSLT [24,110].

```
{ WHERE root in publications.xml,
        root -> "publications".
        ("DataMining" | "InfoViz" | "SE")."paper" -> paper,
        paper -> attribute -> attributeValue

  COLLECT Root(), pubEntry(paper)

  /* group by year */
  { WHERE attribute = "year",
          attributeValue -> "PCDATA" -> yearValue
    COLLECT Years(), Year(yearValue)
    LINK Root() -> "Years" -> Years(),
    Years() -> "Year" -> Year(yearValue),
    Year(yearValue) -> "pubEntry" -> pubEntry(paper),
    Year(yearValue) -> "year" -> yearValue
  }
}
```

FIG. 6. An StruQL query [35]. Notice that enough parameters have been specified in order to produce a reconstructed answer.

These operations are performed by the information system at query execution time. Analogous to WSQ [41], user intervention is unnecessary to realize the mixture of aspects of information-seeking. Systems supporting reconstruction via querying are best classified as templates for personalization, because users specify all aspects of information-seeking at query formulation time.

2.4 Personal Information Spaces

Yahoo! provides many tools, e.g., My Yahoo!, Yahoo! Companion, and Inside Yahoo! Search, for managing one's personal information space [70]. My Yahoo! [70], a manually customizable web portal, has been freely available since 1996. With My Yahoo! users may customize the content and layout of a personalized webpage. See Fig. 7 for the content template for personalization of My Yahoo!. Interaction here entails filling in pre-defined templates and is referred to as check-box personalization.

There are many such sites which provide templates for creating My sites. These types of templates are simply an abstraction of a personal webpage with infrastructure provided by a third party (e.g., Yahoo!). After exploring these tools for personal use, we conclude that their usefulness is limited by the absence of interactivity and interaction.

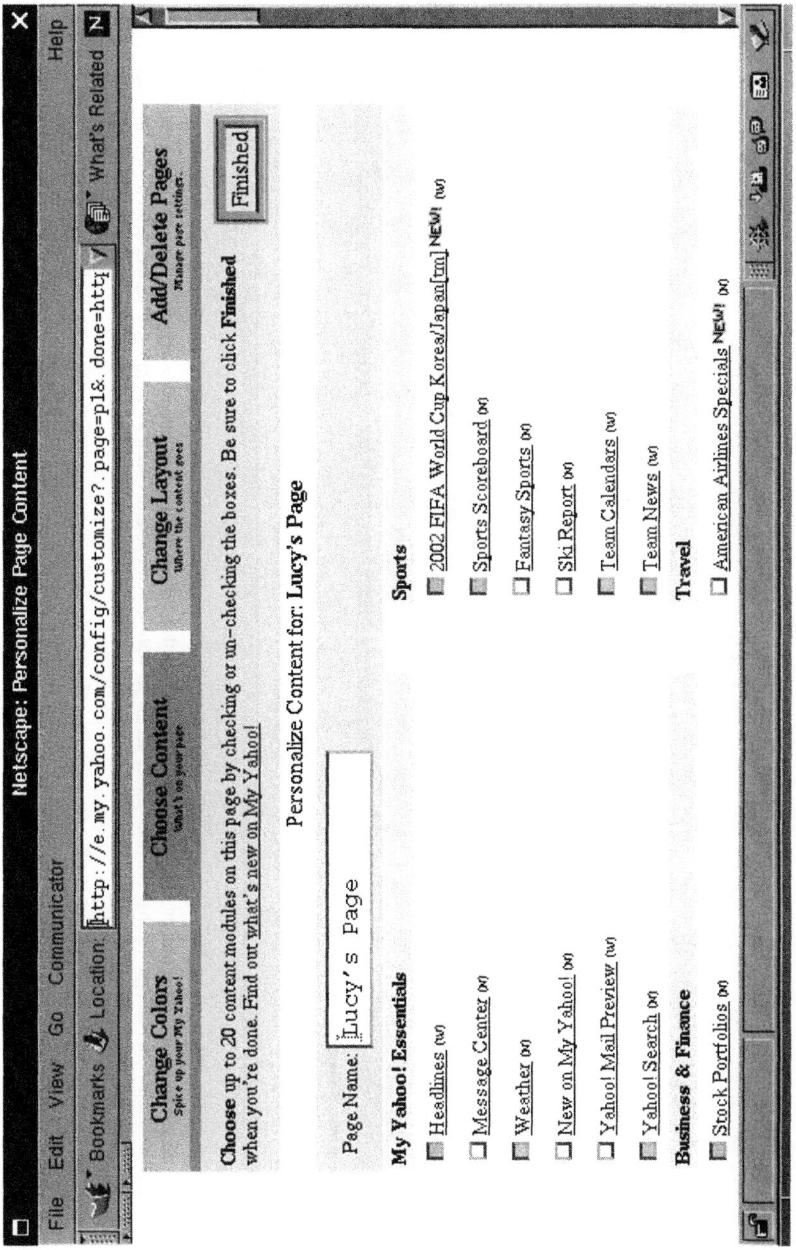

FIG. 7. The content template for personalization of My Yahoo!. In this form webpage, users select desired content within categories to appear on a My Yahoo! personalized webpage. Users may similarly customize layout and color in a personalized webpage.

FIG. 8. Static browser toolbar plugins: (top) The Yahoo! toolbar called Yahoo! Companion provides ubiquitous access to bookmarks, email, and web search. (bottom) The Google toolbar provides direct access to web search operators such as within site search, search term highlighting, and word-find.

Nevertheless, one of the main attractions to My sites is the ease with which they permit users to manage centralized bookmarks. Personal user bookmarks provide fertile ground for collaborative filtering [105] if bookmarks may be shared. The Siteseer system [90] mines overlap in bookmark folders to deliver personal recommendations of webpages to users. In addition to serendipitous webpage recommendation, users who interact with many computer systems and clients on a daily basis need central access to bookmarks.

Therefore, beyond providing templates for personalization, many of the My site providers, including Yahoo! and Google, implement web browser toolbars. The main goals of these toolbars are to provide ubiquitous access to bookmarks (stored in the My page), email, and web search. See Fig. 8 for examples of popular embedded toolbars for web browsers. Interacting with a toolbar template for personalization is useful, but again limited. These toolbars are static and only provide direct access to stored information. A toolbar that facilitates a dialogue between a user and browser is a vision for truly personal interaction.

3. Operators for Personalized Interaction

Recently, supporting the seamless integration, combination, and composition of many atomic operators by the end-user in compelling ways has become popular [86]. In this section we analyze a number of systems and projects which provide this functionality.

3.1 Search and Results Refinement

Many search systems provide users with operators to refine searches and improve search results. Typically, such operators are iteratively invoked during the course of an information-seeking session. Some operators such as relevance feedback are broad and directed toward helping users focus an initially imprecise query. Other operators, such as the 'search with results' functionality provided in many web search engines, are focused to reduce a results space. Some systems provide a hybrid of the two with a clustering operator. Users may cluster to prune results or cluster an original information space to facilitate query formulation. We expound on all three operators below.

3.1.1 Relevance Feedback

Relevance feedback is concerned with addressing the mental mismatch issue in query formulation. Namely, the vocabulary which a user employs to specify an information-seeking goal may not match the terms in the system representing the desired information. This should not come as a surprise, since information-seeking itself is ultimately concerned with resolving a problem for which existing knowledge is inadequate [13]. This problem has been identified by many in the information systems community.

> "The major problem in interaction for naive users is therefore the large semantic gap between the user model (concepts) and the system model (words)". [96]

Some systems provide static functionality supporting mnemonics to address this problem. Other researchers however contend that interaction is an ideal vehicle by which to formalize an information-seeking goal.

> "...the essence of 'interactive retrieval' lies in the constant adjustment between 'answer evaluation' and the 'command formulation' tasks to achieve user satisfaction". [25]

In the mid-1960s, Rocchio developed an interactive technique for tackling this problem called 'relevance feedback' [88]. Relevance feedback entails iteratively ranking search results by the user in order to correctly reformulate an information-seeking query. This helps to distinguish relevant results from irrelevant results and aids in query refinement. The process terminates when the user is satisfied that the query is ideal. Since the problem of finding the correct words for a successful search is still endemic to information systems today, much research has been conducted on interaction styles for relevance feedback. Belkin contends that information foragers would rather take a laissez-faire approach (i.e., uncontrolled term suggestion) toward query reformulation than explicit relevance feedback [13]. We direct the interested reader to [21,46] for treatment of relevance feedback in the context of recommendation and personalization. Relevance feedback has also been employed as a technique to model user interests [67].

3.1.2 Web Search

While visions for future web search engines include dynamically directing users with computed links [43], currently refinement operators are employed to provide aspects of personalization. Another results refinement operator, quite complementary to relevance feedback, is 'search-within.' While relevance feedback addresses a broader problem, a correctly formulated query is implicit in search-within. The operator simply reduces search to the scope of a particular information space, typically results. Search-within operators are predominantly seen in web search engines such as Google, HotBot, and Lycos. Figure 9 (top) shows Google's interface design for searching within results. On the other hand, web taxonomies such as LookSmart and Yahoo! provide search capabilities at every step while drilling-down categories in a

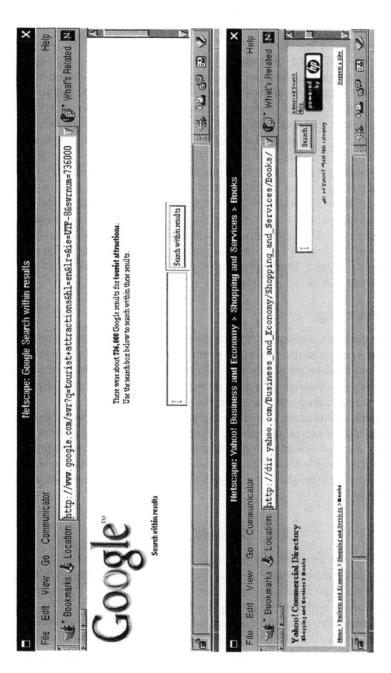

FIG. 9. (top) Free form query interface for the search-within results operation in Google. (bottom) The interface to Yahoo!'s search-within category. Designs such as these provide a simple form of integrating personalization and browsing.

hierarchical fashion. The interface design of Yahoo!'s free form categorical search is shown in the bottom of Fig. 9.

Such search functionality integrates browsing and personalization; to support a truly interactive experience, however, search-within operators should be closed and applicable at any point in the information-seeking session. The search-within results operators available in Google, HotBot, and Lycos are closed. The search-within category operator, such as that seen in Yahoo! and LookSmart, is however not closed. For example, if a user initiates a search while browsing a category hierarchy in Yahoo!, interaction via hierarchical browsing is disrupted and the user is returned a flat list of results without further search or hierarchical browsing capabilities.

Lastly, integrating modes of information-seeking is seen at other levels in Yahoo!. Since Yahoo! provides a suite of specialized pages (e.g., travel pages at http://travel.yahoo.com, movie pages at http://movies.yahoo.com, and maps at http://maps.yahoo.com), designers envision personalizing searches according to the category of the request [70]. For example, if one searches for 'Mission Impossible,' Inside Yahoo! Search can direct one to the appropriate page within http://movies.yahoo.com.

3.1.3 Clustering

Clustering elegantly reduces information overload and prevents users from sifting through many similar results. Results clustering can aid answer examination while initial clustering familiarizes a user with an information space. In many search engines, including AltaVista and Google, clustering of results is done by default so users do not see more than two pages from the same site.

Search-within functionality and clustering capabilities are just two of the many operators available in web search engines. Others include similarity and 'from links' searches. We omit discussion of these here and refer the interested reader to Search Engine Watch at http://www.seachenginewatch.com for details and comparisons. A cursory look at implementation details and structural differences in search engines is given in [106].

3.2   Scatter/Gather

We present the Scatter/Gather project [26] as an example of a system that provides operators for personalized interaction. The two interactive information-seeking operations being integrated are scattering (clustering) and gathering (browsing). We begin our discussion with some motivation for the work in [26].

A large number of research projects have addressed the use of document clustering algorithms to improve information retrieval. Due to accuracy constraints however, such algorithms have poor, quadratic, run-time complexities. Therefore, these algorithms have not been widely accepted by the IR community. The Scatter/Gather project employs document clustering for different objectives. Instead of attempting to improve information retrieval via clustering, it aims to enrich browsing experiences via clustering. Clustering facilitates the formulation of an information-seeking goal by the user. Clustering in the context of Scatter/Gather is more sophisticated than the clustering for web search results described above. For instance, it entails more than collapsing webpages from the same site.

Interaction with the Scatter/Gather system is as follows. Essentially, a one-time, offline clustering of a document corpus is performed. This initial step is expensive. Afterwards, clustering is done in an online, iterative, and interactive fashion. Clustering is the scattering component of Scatter/Gather. Clusters are described to users via terms and succinct summaries. Thus, in addition to employing clustering algorithms, Scatter/Gather makes use of summarization algorithms. These algorithms essentially consider the central words of a cluster (i.e., those which appear most frequently in the group as a whole). After an initial scatter, a user selects clusters which she wishes to explore further. This step comprises the gather phase. After gathering clusters, the documents of those selected clusters are merged and re-clustered. Then, the scatter phase resumes. This interactive and iterative process continues until a user has honed in on a desired set of documents. The interleaving of scattering and gathering operations drives the information exploration process. During this process, themes of the corpus are extracted and presented to the user. One advantage of this approach is that no browsing hierarchy is hardwired *a priori*. Rather, a hierarchy is created quite naturally, on-the-fly, via clustering. Interaction with Scatter/Gather is illustrated in Fig. 10.

The interactive nature of the personalization operators available in Scatter/Gather leads us to categorize the project here. Modes of information-seeking in Scatter/Gather follow a strict, ordered sequence dictated by operation semantics. Interaction begins with a gather operation and proceeds in a scatter, gather, scatter, gather fashion. One cannot arbitrary intermix these operations. Two scatter operations in succession produce the same set of clusters. Furthermore, gathering does not make sense if it is not immediately followed by a scatter. While these two modes of information-seeking may be specified and performed over time, they are complementary and dependent on each other. Neither have semantics in isolation because no hardwired hierarchical schema is in place from the onset.

3.3   Dynamic Taxonomies

Another project closely related to Scatter/Gather is Dynamic Taxonomies [96]. The motivation here is personalizing a taxonomy with set theoretic operations (e.g., union and intersection). In this context a dynamic taxonomy is a model of an

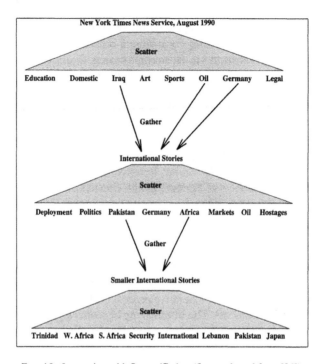

FIG. 10. Interaction with Scatter/Gather (figure adapted from [26]).

information space which can be browsed and simplified by set theoretic operations. A user may drill-down a taxonomy to arrive at an interesting node. At this point in the interaction the user may continue to browse or perform a 'zoom' operation.

The adaptation, reduction, and dynamic nature of a taxonomy via the zoom operation is computed by 'extensional inference.' The zoom can reveal relationships in the original taxonomy that even the designer may be unaware of. One caveat to this approach is that the original taxonomy must be multidimensional (i.e., an atomic data item may be classified under more than one concept).

Interaction with a dynamic taxonomy, and adaptation and reduction of it proceed as follows. Consider the multidimensional taxonomy shown on the left-top side of Fig. 11. The zoom operation begins with extensional inference. When a particular concept is selected (D in the case of Fig. 11), all the data atoms under this concept are computed. Performing a zoom on concept D of the taxonomy shown on the left-top side of Fig. 11 infers the intensional relationships illustrated with dotted arcs in the right of Fig. 11. As is shown, the zoom operation reduces the taxonomy to all the data items (i.e., concept nodes and atomic nodes) classified directly under the node

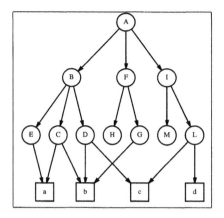

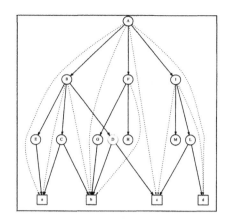

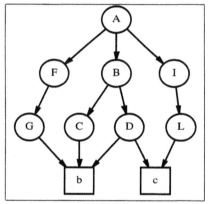

FIG. 11. Illustration of the zoom operation in Dynamic Taxonomies. (left-top) A multidimensional dynamic taxonomy. (right) Extensional inference of all concepts related to node D. (left-bottom) The reduced taxonomy after a zoom operation on concept D. Adapted from Figs. 6 and 7 of [96].

that the zoom was performed on (in this case, node D). In addition, the taxonomy retains the other nodes and paths that lead to the atomic nodes classified under the zoomed node. All nodes which do not lead to those atomic data items are pruned from the taxonomy yielding a reduced taxonomy or a conceptual summary (see left-bottom side of Fig. 11). The zoom operator is closed.

With multidimensional taxonomies it is easy to see that a conjunction of the sets of ancestor nodes of the corresponding atomic objects under which a zoom is performed thins an information space. Furthermore, multidimensional taxonomies yield all set theoretic operations applicable and useful (of which intersection is the most powerful). If the information base is restricted to monodimensional taxonomies, conjunctions result in null sets yielding set union as the only applicable operator. Union operations do not simplify the taxonomy, but rather expand it and thus do not reduce information overload.

The two modes of information-seeking mixed in Dynamic Taxonomies are browsing and zooming (also referred to as taxonomic retrieval in [96]). While decision points at which to browse or zoom are determined by the user, there is an ordering on such activities dictated by operation semantics. For instance, two zoom operations in succession yield the same taxonomy present prior to the second zoom operation. On the other hand, performing the second zoom operation on a different node transforms the taxonomy. The new node being zoomed upon must however be arrived at via browsing. It is clear that the zoom operation is subservient to browsing. Browsing operations, however, can be performed independently of zooming.

Since browsing and zooming are performed interactively and subject to constraints, the interaction model of Dynamic Taxonomies is similar to that of Scatter/Gather [26]. In other words, in both systems, the application of available operators for personalization is constrained. It is interesting to note that Sacco does not explicitly allude to this interaction constraint in [96].

A byproduct of Sacco's approach is that dynamic taxonomies can be nicely integrated with other retrieval methods (e.g., IR and DB queries). For example, Sacco states that "extensional inference can be applied to any subset of the information base, no matter how generated, and thus guarantees a tight, symmetric coupling with other retrieval methods" [96]. Such integration and associated distinctions do not alter our classification of Dynamic Taxonomies as affording operators for personalization. In conclusion, Dynamic Taxonomies is simply a set theoretic model to realize combinations of information-seeking activities. In the following systems we investigate, no constraints exist on the composition or application of available operators for personalization.

3.4   RABBIT

RABBIT is a novel information system that was well ahead of its time (circa 1984). Many of the ideas motivating RABBIT are related to a number of the papers and systems we analyze in this section. There seems to have been a gap in the literature addressing the pertinent issues (mental mismatch and combinations of interaction operators) from the time that RABBIT was published up until nearly 1995.

Essentially, RABBIT provides a unique interface to a DB. Browsing an information space is the main interaction motif. While affording compelling browsing experiences, the interface is based on the paradigm of 'retrieval by reformulation' [111]. Retrieval by reformulation allows a user to incrementally specify and formalize an information-seeking goal. Specifically, a user may interleave six closed transformation operators (called critiques) with browsing. The idea is to iteratively refine a query following an operation based on how the system responds to the previous operation. A user query is implicit in the interaction with the RABBIT system. RABBIT distinguishes itself from other IR systems by exploiting partial information. Therefore RABBIT is useful to novices in a particular domain. Specifically, RABBIT assumes that a user knows more about the generic structure of the information space than RABBIT does. RABBIT however knows more about the particulars. The six critique operators available in RABBIT—require, prohibit, alternatives, describe, specialize, and predicate—are expounded in [111].

The most interesting aspect of the RABBIT system is that its reformulation operators (i.e., the critiques) may be specified and invoked at arbitrary points in the interaction. Thus, in contrast to the personalization operators available in Scatter/Gather and Dynamic Taxonomies, RABBIT's operators may be applied in an unbiased fashion. An early interactive information retrieval system similar to RABBIT, which embraces the idea of integrating operators such as browsing and searching, is presented in [31].

The systems we present below also exhibit personalization operator independence. After a long absence from the information systems literature (over 10 years after RABBIT appeared), approaching mental model mismatches from an operation combination perspective resurfaced in [72]. This work, which motivates the need for personalization operator integration, is discussed next.

3.5 DataWeb

In 1995 researchers from IBM Almaden and the Ohio State University wrote a visionary paper outlining the issues surrounding the mental mismatch problem between the designer and users of an information system [72]. In addition to identifying and expounding on a legitimate cognitive problem, the authors identify approaches to solving the problem. Without using the phrase explicitly, the authors discuss aspects of mixed-initiative interaction [45], in the context of the interface and browsing taxonomies of Yahoo!, as chief among possible approaches.

Mixed-initiative interaction is a flexible dialogue strategy between participants where the parties can take turns at any time to change and steer the flow of interaction. It is easily observed in human conversations. For instance, the following conversation between a travel agent and a traveler illustrates a facet of mixed-initiative called unsolicited reporting [3].

Conversation

1 Agent: Where would you like to travel today, Sir?
2 Traveler: New York.
3 Agent: Do you have a particular airline in mind?

4 Traveler: Not really, but I want to sit in a first class, aisle seat.
5 Agent: Very well.
6 Traveler: I also need a vegetarian meal please.
7 Agent: Sure.
(conversation continues)

The above conversation begins by the agent having the initiative (line 1), and the traveler responding to this initiative (line 2). In line 4, however, the traveler specifies seat preferences out-of-turn and hence takes the initiative. Notice that even though the traveler does not answer the agent's question about airline, the conversation progresses smoothly. Such an interaction where the two parties can mix initiative in arbitrary ways is referred to as a mixed-initiative interaction.

Mixed-initiative interaction with the envisioned DataWeb system [72] is as follows. A user may initially enter a keyword query. The ensuing navigation and summarization of an answer is used to refine the initial and possibly imprecise query. Thus, querying and navigation activities are weaved to facilitate query refinement. One can browse (drill-down or roll-up) or query to attain a different hierarchy at any point while interacting with the DataWeb system. Transition from one operation to another is seamless. While in this context queries induce hierarchies, there are also an initial set of pre-existing hierarchies available as exemplars for a user to browse prior to querying. Similar functionality exists in RABBIT where a user can browse pre-cached hierarchies to exploit 'find one' [111] search techniques. Thus, a user may begin an information-seeking activity in the DataWeb system with a query or browse an extant hierarchy. As can be seen, DataWeb is a highly interactive system.

The authors make it clear that a user may invoke the available information-seeking operators on demand. There is no pre-determined ordering on the operations. For these reasons and the interactive nature of the outlined system, we view DataWeb as a system affording operators for personalization. The authors partially recognize that no constraints exist on the application of their information-seeking operators.

3.6 Web Browser Command Shells

The UNIX operating system typically comes bundled with many useful, focused, and atomic software development tools such as cat, grep, and sed. While these tools have merit in isolation, a large part of the success of the UNIX operating system can be attributed to the command shell which supports the composition and communication of such powerful tools via pipes. Such composition supports user interaction in creating a compelling and truly personal experience with the system while developing software. In other words, the design of tools in UNIX has been carved up at a comfortable and personable level of granularity. Furthermore the communication mechanism, which is provided by the shell, allows end-users to become programmers on-the-fly. A similar approach to personalization is advocated in [99]. The ideas presented here are motivated in [86].

Interaction with a web browser also entails invoking atomic functions (e.g., clicking on a hyperlink). Furthermore, many popular web browsers integrate access to other tools through fancy user interfaces. For example, many web browsers today provide one-click access to an email application. What web browser vendors are yet to provide is a communication mechanism to support the composition of these atomic web tools. Consider the following scenario of interaction to motivate this idea.

> Lucy launches her favorite web browser. The browser opens to her startpage—the homepage of CNN.com. The headline highlights the summer heat wave on the west coast and reminds Lucy of her trip to the Grand Canyon next week. This reminder compels Lucy to open her mail utility from within the browser, to retrieve an email sent to her last week regarding heat precautions. Upon opening the mail client, Lucy uses the find command in the browser to retrieve the message. After locating it, she opens the mail message and immediately begins clicking on the URLs provided therein. These clicks spawn page loads in her browser. After a series of mouse clicks on URLs, page loads, and invocations of the find utility of the browser (to scan the page), Lucy realizes she has found a webpage of interest. She next prints the webpage so she can take it with her on the trip. Lucy closes her browser and terminates the information-seeking session.

From the above scenario of interaction it is clear that the browser has provided easy and central access to all the tools needed to complete the information-seeking interaction (i.e., email, http requests, find, and print). Interaction with the browser is however discrete and discontinuous in the information-seeking episode. Although Lucy knows what she is looking for from the start, she has to go through a series of individual painstaking tasks. Providing a mechanism within the browser to coordinate the communication between these autonomous tasks on demand would permit a user to create truly personal interactions. It is the interleaving of these autonomous commands that is currently done by manual invocation, and which would benefit from personalization.

3.6.1 LAPIS: Engaging Your Browser

Many of these ideas were first introduced in [66] and implemented in a browser shell called LAPIS (Lightweight Architecture for Processing Information Structure). The capabilities of LAPIS include a pattern language, a scripting language, and the ability to invoke external programs. Extensions to this research include providing support in an interface for a user to create a script 'by example' (also called 'automation by demonstration') and enriching captured context such as browsing history.

With the advent of the XML suite of technologies, we expect such approaches to become more feasible and subsequently gain widespread acceptance. While toolbars such as LAPIS are a step in the direction toward engaging a browser in a dialogue, high levels of sophistication are not seen. We surmise that more research on representing and reasoning about user interaction in information systems will aid future systems [60]. The following system employs elaborate data modeling to facilitate combinations of information-seeking activities.

3.7 AKIRA

The AKIRA project [57] at the University of Pennsylvania has a theme similar to that of WSQ. The project attempts to incorporate data on the web into a canonical DB query. Instead of simply dealing with web search results as URLs and associated frequencies, the AKIRA project models webpage content. Modeling webpage content gives users the freedom to be expressive in queries. Within-webpage modeling can also affect the granularity of answers. The model employed to capture the webpage data in AKIRA is object-oriented. The information-seeking operators which are mixed in an interactive manner are browsing, querying, and output restructuring. While we classified WSQ and web query languages as templates for personalization, we view AKIRA as providing operators for personal interaction. Information-seeking sessions with AKIRA are interactive and no constraints exist on the order in which operators may be invoked.

A user interacts with the AKIRA system as follows. After he poses a query (see Fig. 12) and receives an answer, the user may browse the resulting pages or write another query to restructure the output. Furthermore, points at which these information-seeking activities are engaged may be mixed in any order. User interaction with AKIRA is similar to that with RABBIT. As opposed to RABBIT however, querying (including output restructuring) and browsing are the only two valid information-seeking operations available in AKIRA.

```
SELECT  y.URL
FROM    x in Fragment, y in Fragment
WHERE   x.URL = ''http://www.yahoo.com/headlines/tech/''
        x.HREF = y
        y.CONTENT = ''*Microsoft*'';;
```

FIG. 12. An AKIRA query. The semantics of this query are to (i) locate and fragment the specified webpage, (ii) load each webpage that the specified webpage references, and (iii) search all collected fragments for the text 'Microsoft.' This query is a modified version of one presented in [57].

3.8   Complete Answer Aggregates

Meuss and Schulz's complete answer aggregates [71] are tree based data structures used to facilitate the integration of browsing, querying and reformulation in an information-seeking session. Meuss and Schulz define a complete answer aggregate as "a complete and nonredundant view on all the possible target nodes, for each of the query variables, and on all links between these candidates that contribute to some answer" [71]. The approach of complete answer aggregates is based on sets, relations, and tree theory.

Interaction with the system proceeds as follows. A user writes a tree structured query, whose answers map tree query nodes to DB nodes. Since the number of answers to a tree query may be exponential and thus possibly lead to information overload, a method by which to summarize and compact the answer is required. The solution adopted is factorization, which not only compacts the answer, but also arranges relevant data elements of the answer in context. Such qualification was also the primary motivation for Dynamic Taxonomies [96]. A terse but expandable answer is preferred over a long, flat, and monolithic list of hits.

Aspects of information-seeking are supported by information previews (e.g., counters) to facilitate decisions on whether to construct and issue another query, drill-down, or reformulate. Reformulation here is considered as a special case of querying. Meuss and Schulz provide two closed reformulation operations: node rank by counter values and compaction by attribute values [71]. Surprisingly, the two useful operations on answer aggregates do not directly correspond to any of the six critique operations in RABBIT [111]. The main idea is that an initial tree query will present a useful starting point for active exploration of an answer space. Meuss and Schulz contend that such exploration facilitates 'interactive knowledge discovery and hypothesis testing' [71]. Subsequent browsing and reformulation is employed to refine/enhance an initial, possibly under specified query.

Connections from complete answer aggregates to Dynamic Taxonomies [96] and RABBIT [111] is seen in that all three projects model an information resource and provide canned, closed operations (including browsing) on that resource to transform, simplify, and personalize it. The zoom operation is available in Dynamic Taxonomies. In RABBIT, available operators are reformulations. Closure preservation in complete answer aggregates fosters both an exploratory style of browsing and seamless integration with further query type activities (reformulations). This browsing style is similar to that in OLAP systems [42].

It is clear that the operators here (i.e., the specification of attribute values to collapse by and the specification of counter values to rank by) are independent of each other and need not arrive in an ordered or predetermined fashion. Furthermore, although not explicitly mentioned by the authors, we believe that another tree query may be written against a complete answer aggregate (at a different time in the interaction). Such interaction exemplifies the interleaving of information foraging activities with browsing. While the authors do not explicitly address this aspect of their approach, they do stress the exploratory nature of complete answer aggregates. At different points in time, different aggregates may be viewed via certain attributes. Since the available operations may be specified in an unbiased fashion over time, interaction with complete answer aggregates is similar to that in the RABBIT system.

3.9   BBQ and MIX

XML as a data format provides excellent opportunities for mixing operations for personal interaction, especially browsing and querying. Typically XML data elements are nested, making XML documents conducive to browsing via drill-down and roll-up metaphors. In addition, most XML query languages such as XML-QL are closed [32]. Thus, interactively blending browsing and querying of XML is quite natural.

Blending Browsing and Querying (BBQ) [65,68] is an information system which achieves precisely this objective. There are no system semantics dictating the order in which a user may apply the two information-seeking operations. Querying in BBQ [65], as opposed to more traditional XML query languages [32], may be performed by example via a drag and drop interface. Thus, querying in the BBQ system is interactive, as opposed to the one-shot style of interaction seen in other systems [37,41]. After a query is answered, the system infers a document type definition (DTD). This DTD assists the processing of subsequent queries.

We view BBQ as an information system which affords operators for personalization since querying is interactive and combined independently and at any interaction point with browsing in BBQ. The designers of BBQ do not recognize this aspect of their system. BBQ is currently absorbed by a larger project called MIX [69]. MIX is a mediator-based approach to integrating querying and navigation. While BBQ incorporates visualization, there also exist systems, focused solely on visualization, which afford operators for personalization as a convenient by product.

3.10   Operators for Interactive Visualization

Interactive information visualization is the main thrust of the systems we discuss in this section. These systems provide operators to bring aspects of interactivity to bear upon a visualization. Ultimately and as a by product, such operators tackle the mental mismatch issue endemic to personalization research. Therefore, we showcase these operations here in the context of the personalization they achieve. While there are a number of interactive information visualization systems, we focus on three which provide operators which affect user perception of an information base. Specifically, we analyze three data structures: user-defined hierarchies [109], polyarchies [83,84], and treemaps [98,103]. A unifying theme among these systems is their ability to provide visualizations and views which expose semantic relationships in an information base.

3.10.1 User-Defined Hierarchies

User-defined hierarchies (UDHs) are dynamic hierarchies. Systems incorporating UDHs champion multiple visual layouts of a single hierarchy and therefore support dynamic hierarchy specification and visualization. Multiple layouts facilitate the discovery of semantic relationships in data. A number of different layout algorithms, each with support for discovering different types of properties (e.g., level of clustering) efficiently, are discussed in [109]. Such algorithms modify a hierarchy dynamically based on user interaction. Dynamic hierarchies are generated directly from data and not as a result of operations or transformations on an 'unpersonalized' hierarchy or representation. Modeling interaction is thus not stressed in [109]. Figure 13 illustrates a possible reconstruction operator. A UDH, whose first, second, and third levels pertain to automobile year, model, and color respectively, is shown on the top side of Fig. 13. The bottom side of Fig. 13 might be the output of a goal-oriented reconstruction of the UDH description of Fig. 13 (top). This reconstruction reorga-

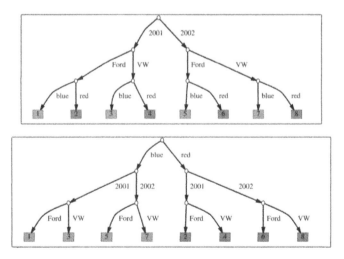

FIG. 13. Illustration of a possible reconstruction operator on a UDH. The UDH description of the hierarchy on the top is modified to restructure the levels of the hierarchy (bottom).

nizes the hierarchy by making automobile color, year, and model the first, second, and third levels respectively.

3.10.2 Polyarchies

Polyarchies [83,84] deal with predetermined (static) hierarchical structures. A polyarchy groups multiple intersecting hierarchies which share at least one node into a single hierarchical structure. Again, the main focus here is on visualization. A polyarchy helps to visualize both a single hierarchy and understand the relationships between multiple entities within that single hierarchy. In addition, a user may visualize more than one hierarchy simultaneously for a clear understanding of the relationships between multiple hierarchies. To facilitate these goals, manipulations such as sliding and pivot points are provided. Figure 14 illustrates adding a new object to a polyarchy. The left side of Fig. 14 shows one path in a management hierarchy—the path from 'Lowell, Lucy' to the root, 'Luther, Linus.' The right side of Fig. 14 shows the result of adding 'Smith, Greg' to the polyarchy—an additional path to the root. The use of this addition operator in this example illustrates the discovery of relationships between the selected entities. This approach distinguishes relationship discovery in polyarchies versus that from a general overview of an extremely large hierarchy.

3.10.3 Treemaps

Treemaps are yet another data structure approach to inferring relationships in an information base. Similar to polyarchies, treemaps deal with predetermined

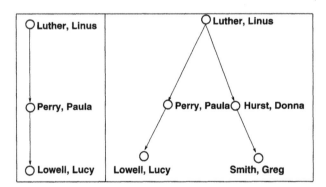

FIG. 14. Adding a person to a management polyarchy (adapted from [83]). (left) The path from 'Lowell, Lucy' to the root, 'Luther, Linus.' (right) The polyarchy resulting from adding 'Smith, Greg.' This figure illustrates how a user can incrementally add entities to a polyarchy which reveal resulting relationships. Such relationships are difficult to observe with a general overview of an extremely large hierarchy.

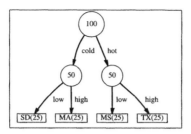

FIG. 15. A tree containing data about states (adapted from [108]).

structures—trees in this case. The traditional two dimensional treemap approach is discussed in [98]. The treemap3 system (see http://www.cs.umd.edu/hcil/treemap3/) extends this by allowing users to choose the aggregation order to form a tree of their choice. Layout difficulties in visualizing treemaps as opposed to supporting multiple aggregation orders are discussed in a newer article [103].

Figure 16 illustrates direct manipulation of treemap attribute weights to recompute the value of objects (e.g., the weight of states). The tree under consideration (Fig. 15) models attributes of states. The first level of the tree involves values for climate while the second level contains values for population. The number in a node represents the weight of the node which is equal to the sum of the weights of all the descendents of the node. The top of Fig. 16 displays a possible treemap and state weights for this data. Users may adjust the weight of attributes in this treemap by manipulating the dotted sliders. A user may move the sliders to explore the cumulative effect that different attribute weight values have on the objects (states, in this case). In Fig. 16, moving the sliders corresponds to adjusting the relative importance of preferences. Such an interface helps the user decide on, for example, relocation options. After manipulation the value of each object (e.g., state) is automatically recalculated as illustrated in the bottom side of Fig. 16. Such manipulations are critical to decision support systems as seen below. We now turn to interaction as a vehicle to analyze massive data sets.

3.11   Interactive Data Mining and Analysis

Close examination of data analysis in DBMSs, decision-support systems, and data mining packages from a user perspective reveals that analysis calls for iteration, intuition, and exploration. We have established that a query in a DBMS is a one-shot activity. Such an approach is effective when a user knows what he is seeking, but is not conducive to exploration. Thus, a user experiences frustration when using a query information-seeking strategy to search for information that the user does not

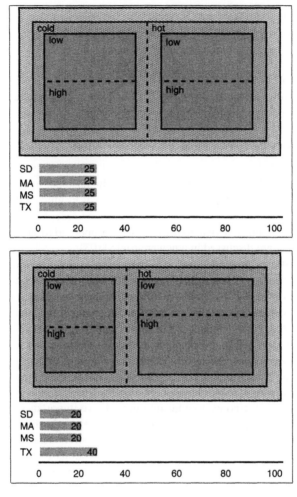

FIG. 16. Illustration of the slide operator to adjust weights of attributes in treemaps (adapted from [108]). (top) A possible treemap for the hierarchical data shown in Fig. 15. (bottom) Resulting treemap, which displays the recalculated state weights, from moving the sliders in (top).

know [13]. This problem is endemic when DBMSs and IR systems are used as inter-active systems. As discussed above, results refinement techniques such as relevance feedback are typically employed to combat this problem.

This issue is exasperated in decision-support systems and data mining applica-tions for the following reasons. Typically batch analysis of large data sets is costly and time consuming. Often the success of algorithms which discover patterns in data is predicated on and highly sensitive to algorithm-specific parameters (e.g., support and confidence) tuned by users. A poor choice of parameters may lead to useless results. The results of the first few runs on massive data sets may be correct, but undesirable or difficult to interpret. Furthermore, knowledge that a choice of parameters is poor is often unknown until results are returned. In summary, in traditional analysis systems, not only is querying, computation, and analysis one-shot, it also takes place in a 'black-box' [42]. Computation is conducted as efficiently as possible, but users have no control over it once begun.

A classic chicken and egg problem ensues. The difficulty is that users can neither precisely formulate their analysis goals nor tweak algorithmic-sensitive parameters until implicit properties of a dataset (e.g., dimensionality) are progressively revealed to them. While much research has been conducted on improving the efficiency of data analysis and mining algorithms in decision-support systems, little research has addressed improving usability and personalized interaction in such systems.

Applying techniques from human–computer interaction to data analysis is an approach. The goal of the Control project [42] is to afford users direct interaction with computation in order to refine results and control processing 'just-in-time.' Interaction tightens the data analysis process loop. Analogous to the nature of the operations of personalization of the information systems discussed in this section, Hellerstein et al. provide users of analysis tools with canned operations to facilitate interactive exploration. Rather than computations assuming a black-box model, operators for personal interaction in the Control project afford users direct insight into the ongoing analysis. Such operators trade quality and accuracy of results for direct control. A data mining user is typically willing to accept approximate and partial results in return for a handle into the computation.

The Control project supports many interactive algorithms for data analysis. The supported operations include online aggregation or drill-down online enumeration through user interface widgets to support 'eyeballing' and 'panning,' online data visualization through a technique called 'clouds,' and online data mining. Control employs random sampling and reordering to achieve online interactivity. In addition, Control implements ripple join algorithms to tackle online query-processing problems entailing multiple inputs.

Projects such as Control lie within the scope of data warehousing and OLAP. Data warehousing and OLAP technologies are critical to the success of decision-support systems which currently constitute a large segment of the database industry [22]. As OLAP technologies and resulting systems gain widespread acceptance, we expect the need for personalized interaction with them to increase. We view the design of systems such as Control as initial steps in this direction.

3.12   Social Network Navigation

While many sites on the web are organized along a hierarchical browsing motif, sites in certain domains are more effectively based on a social network navigation metaphor. A social network is a graph in which nodes represent entities (e.g., people, books, or movies) and edges represent relationships between entities (e.g., is-a-friend-of or have-co-authored-a-paper). Social networks are characterized by heterogeneous nodes and homogeneous edges. A simple example of a social network is one's network of family and friends. Examples of web sites based on a social network navigation metaphor are the Internet Movie Database at http://www.imdb.com, Barnes and Noble at http://www.bn.com, and the online computer science bibliography DBLP a http://www.informatik.uni-trier.de/~ley/db/ (see Fig. 17).

Social networks can be induced from an existing information base for later exploration and exploitation. An early project on social network analysis induced a communication network from email logs in order to discover shared interests [102]. For purposes here, we are interested in operators to explore and exploit already-induced social networks, in order to discover products of interest, serendipitous collaborations, or network resources [104]. Such operators enhance personal interaction and expedite the personalization process.

ReferralWeb [54] is a collaborative filtering recommender system which provides users with operators for exploration and exploitation in a person-person social network. Associations between people nodes are mined from close proximity of names in web documents subject to a set of heuristics. An induced network facilitates the search for experts, communities, or documents. ReferralWeb contains operators for several types of searches including a referral chain search (e.g., a user may be interested in finding the relationship chain between herself and a colleague and thus ask, "What is my relationship to John Doe?"), an expert search (e.g., by specifying a topic and a social radius a user may ask "What friends of mine or friends of friends of mine know about tourist attractions in Italy?"), and an expert controlled search (e.g., "List documents on the topic 'human factors and user interface components' close to Don Norman."). The examples of searches given here have been adapted from those in [54].

Consider how an editor of a journal may exploit a social network of authors in computer science to find an unbiased committee of reviewers for a communicated article. The editor surely does not desire individuals within close proximity of the author under review. The editor does however seek effective reviewers who must be close enough to the reviewees' research area to be qualified. The editor may therefore apply the available operators on a social network induced from a corpus to find all individuals within three degrees of separation from the author subject to review. Systems consisting of a social network and a suite of expressive operators foster relationship discovery and are thus classified here.

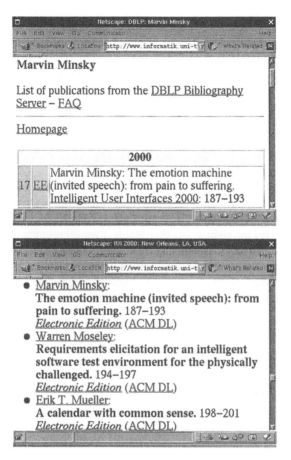

FIG. 17. An association in the social network at DBLP. Jumping from a author webpage (top) to a conference webpage (bottom).

4.   Representing and Reasoning about Interaction

Thus far this chapter has echoed the theme that personalization is advantageously approached by studying and understanding interaction [60]. In the previous two sections, the onus of personalization was on users. Templates are so over-specified that interaction is limited to filling out a form or writing a query to communicate an exact level of customization. While operators for personalization afford more freedom, interaction remains stifled by constraints on the applicability and composition of the available operators. If interaction is to guide the design of personalization systems, then beyond understanding and studying it, interaction must also be explicitly modeled and exploited. In other words, personalization should be approached from a user-centered design perspective [53]. In our opinion, representing and reasoning about interaction is the holy grail of personalization. The main premise of this section and chapter echoes that of Marchetti et al. [73], namely that '... information retrieval is an inherently interactive process, and that support of users should be support of their interaction, with all of the system resources.'

4.1   Why Model Interaction?

Ultimately, models of interaction serve as a representational basis to design an interactive system. They are more expressive than templates and operators and are thus at a finer level of granularity. Care must be taken however to ensure that interaction is not modeled too tightly. In other words, over-representation and excessive modeling can lead to bulky designs. Systems which fall victim to this trap run contrary to the goals of personalization. Representations which are too general should be avoided for obvious reasons as well. This problem suggests the need for structures of interaction at a personable level of granularity. Pednault motivates this issue as:

> "The representation should be as rich and fluid as the interaction itself, but at a level of abstraction that allows the relationships among stimuli and responses to be readily observed in the data collected". [79]

4.2   Information Seeking Strategies

Prior to designing an interactive system, we must first study, understand, and characterize the interactions which users desire of their information systems. Eventually designers shift from such understandings to system design representations which structure, support, and enhance interaction [11]. We begin by characterizing information-seeking behavior.

Belkin et al. [16] describe an information-seeking strategy (ISS) as a behavior a user engages in while interacting with a system. They have contributed a binary, four-dimensional ISS space (see Table I) containing 16 (i.e., 2^4) strategies. Each dimension can be considered as a factor of information-seeking and describes a dichotomy. The ISS space factors are method of interaction (scan or search), goal of interaction (learn or select), mode of retrieval (recognize or specify), and resource (information or meta-information).

For instance, ISS15 is indicative of a highly specified search [16]. A user is searching through an information base with the goal of selecting relevant items which match specification aspect input. ISS2, its complement, represents a prototypical example of a fuzzy and loose strategy. Here a user scans meta-information such as an

TABLE I

FOUR-DIMENSIONAL INFORMATION-SEEKING STRATEGY SPACE OF BELKIN ET AL. [16].

	Dimensions							
	Method		Goal		Mode		Resource	
ISSs	Scan	Search	Learn	Select	Recognize	Specify	Information	Meta-information
1	√		√		√		√	
2	√		√		√			√
3	√		√			√	√	
4	√		√			√		√
5	√			√	√		√	
6	√			√	√			√
7	√			√		√	√	
8	√			√		√		√
9		√	√		√		√	
10		√	√		√			√
11		√	√			√	√	
12		√	√			√		√
13		√		√	√		√	
14		√		√	√			√
15		√		√		√	√	
16		√		√		√		√

index in order to learn to recognize where topics are situated. Depending on specific strategy instances, the information-seeking strategies (ISSs) in this space may overlap. More importantly, users typically shift between ISSs in the course of an information-seeking session, called an episode in [16].

The following example illustrates such a shift. Consider a student who interacts with a university library information system to check out a reserved book for a course. If the student does not know the title of the book, he may interact with a directory indexed by course number to learn the title of the book (ISS12). After the student knows the title, he can use a search tool to find the book in the title-alphabetized reserve pages (ISS15).

Capturing and modeling such shifts is a way to support truly compelling experiences in information systems. The classification the space provides can be used to describe movement from one ISS to another. Design techniques to support combination through seamless movement from ISS to ISS are faithful to our vision of personalization through mixture of information-seeking activities as advocated throughout this chapter.

The single most striking aspect of this work is that Belkin et al. [16] view an ISS as an interaction with an information system. In other words, an interaction with an IR system is a dialogue between a user and a system. Other projects divorce the two and view each ISS as a query or functional requirement of a system. Therefore, such systems do not take advantage of the interaction inherent in use. Rather than supporting interaction, such systems constrain, tolerate [16], or react to it. This distinction goes to the heart of the difference between a one-way, reactive, interaction and a two-way, cooperative, dialogue.

Most designers make provisions for personalization in systems from the onset rather than supporting it through interaction. This trend is most salient in templates, but is also seen in operators designed to implement personalization. Due to these reasons, Belkin [12] feels that intelligent, agent-based approaches which circumvent the need for personal interaction with information resources are unlikely to be embraced by users.

These arguments have significant implications for the design of a system. Belkin et al. [16] prefer the design of a system to explicitly support such interaction, both at the individual ISS and inter-ISS level. The work of Belkin et al. is thus truly visionary in making these novel observations and contributions.

Details of the transition from high level ISSs and interaction models to concrete implementation details need to be pinned down. Through the construction of a prototypical interface to an IR system, Belkin et al. [16] explored this transition. The resulting system, called BRAQUE (BRowsing And QUEry formulation), is a two-level hypertext model of IR system DBs [73]. The system supports and validates the feasibility of the implementation of interaction as described here. In addition, and commensurate with systems presented above, BRAQUE blends query formulation and reformulation with browsing.

4.3   Structures of Interaction: Scripts, Cases, and Goal Trees

There are a number of formalisms applicable to modeling interaction. The goals, operators, methods and selection rules (GOMS) model of human–computer interaction, introduced by Card, Moran, and Newell [27–29] in the early 1980s, is accepted as the most mature formalism. Since then, three variations of the original GOMS formulation have been developed—the keystroke-level model (KLM), natural GOMS language (NGOMSL), and cognitive-perceptual-motor GOMS (CPM-GOMS)—and are surveyed in [48].

Belkin et. al. [16] however use a formal model called COR (conversational roles model), adept at representing dialogue structures for information-seeking. The model defines types of dialogue structures between two actors: the information provider and the information seeker. These structures capture turn taking, jumping out of dialogues, termination, and error recovery. COR models high-level dialogue structures while omitting details at the domain, task, and strategic levels. Therefore, a prescriptive interaction model in addition to the descriptive COR dialogue model is needed. Cases and scripts fill this void.

A dialogue is a specific instance of communication between a user and an information system. Dialogues may consist of many moves within a single ISS. For example, while employing an ISS, one user may decide to terminate interaction prematurely, while another may see the information-seeking goal to fruition. In either case, neither user has deviated from the particular ISS. The following is an example of a dialogue related to ISS12 of the course textbook example above.

Dialogue

1 System: May I have the course number please?
2 User: Yes. CS4604.
3 System: The title of the reserved book is "A First Course in Database Systems."
4 User: Thanks.

Intra-strategy shifts however make dialogues a poor model of interaction for system design.

An interaction script, which is better suited, is a pattern in a two-party interaction or dialogue. Belkin et al. [11] describe a script as a plan for dialogue between a user and an information system. Scripts are prototypes which model a class of concrete dialogues. Therefore, an actual dialogue is a specific instance of a script. A script is prototypical in that it implements an ISS. Scripts structure user interaction for the design of a system similar to how an interpreter structures the interaction of a program. The level of expressivity in scripts is correct for design. Scripts are written in plain English and intended to be easily understood by the layman as opposed to COR models.

An alternate representation of interaction is a goal tree. A goal tree is arranged as a hierarchy of goals which organize the set of necessary moves in an ISS. Goal trees are represented in a Prolog-style notation with goals corresponding to predicates. There are goal trees associated with each ISS. Furthermore, in order to model rich interaction, some goal trees may contain sub-goals (predicates) which represent jumps to other regions of the ISS space.

In a simple system design, scripts may be stored in a dialogue manager. Upon entrance, a user and the system execute a preamble script in order to determine and retrieve the desired or appropriate script. Such introduction, which is not specific to any ISS from [11] is given in Fig. 18. Combinations of scripts can also be used to achieve more expressive dialogues.

In practice, knowledge of how the dimensions of the ISS space affect each other is invaluable to reduce the number of script combinations which a system must support. Knowledge of these dimensional relationships also makes the prediction of moves

> **1 System:** Here's what we can do (offers choice).
> **2 User:** Let's do this (chooses one).
> **3 System:** OK, here's how we'll do it
>   (presents plan and means for accomplishing script).
> **4 User:** a. OK → 5
>   b. No, I don't like this. → 1

FIG. 18. Preamble sequence for interaction scripts from [16].

between the ISSs at decision points easier. Thus, these relationships help stir user interaction and form complex scripts. For instance, Xie [113] addresses how interaction intentions relate to ISSs. She identifies patterns of interaction revealing the circumstances under which certain ISSs are employed.

Another approach to interaction shifts is to mine patterns of usage in systems to anticipate which subset of the remaining 15 possible ISSs users will most desire to follow. For instance, if the leaf node in a goal tree cannot be simplified, it can be expanded and replaced with the goal tree of an alternate ISS. This leads to the broader question of where scripts come from.

Belkin et al. outline two approaches for deriving scripts in [11]. The first entails 'a general characterization of information-seeking goals and a related cognitive task analysis.' The second is driven by empirical observation of interaction patterns. This approach involves inducing patterns in system use akin to web log mining. Belkin et al. use case-based reasoning (CBR) for this purpose. The end-goal is to collect, analyze, and characterize cases in the ISS space.

In such an approach, the system and cases bootstrap each other. After collecting an initial set, the ISS space induces a partition on the gathered cases. Designers then attempt to select a prototypical case from each partition which leads to a script. Due to the iterative nature of CBR, it is acceptable to start the system with a prototype. MERIT [11] is an interactive IR system that embodies these ideas.

4.4   PIPE: Personalization by Partial Evaluation

PIPE [81] is a research project that employs representations similar to scripts for capturing information-seeking interactions. It is aimed as a modeling methodology for information personalization. However, PIPE makes no commitments to a particular algorithm, format for information resources, type of information-seeking activities or, more basically, the nature of personalization delivered. Instead, it emphasizes the modeling of an information space in a way where descriptions of information-

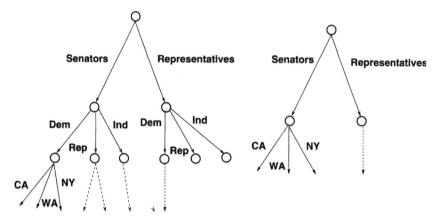

FIG. 19. Personalizing a browsing hierarchy. (left) Original information resource, depicting information about members of the US Congress. The labels on edges represent choices and selections made by a navigator. (right) Personalized hierarchy with respect to the criterion 'Democrats.' Notice that not only the pages, but also their structure is customized for (further browsing by) the user.

seeking activities can be represented as partial information. Such partial information is then exploited (in the model) by *partial evaluation*, a technique popular in the programming languages community [49].

It is easy to illustrate the basic concepts of PIPE by describing its application to personalizing a browsing hierarchy. Consider a congressional web site, organized in a hierarchical fashion, that provides information about US Senators, Representatives, their party and state affiliations (Fig. 19, left). Assume further that we wish to personalize the site so that a reduced or restructured hierarchy is made available for each user. The first step to modeling in PIPE involves thinking of information as being organized along a motif of interaction sequences. We can identify two such organizations—the site's layout and design that influences how a user interacts with it, and the user's mental model that indicates how best her information-seeking goals are specified and realized. In Fig. 19 (left), the designer has made a somewhat arbitrary partition, with type of politician as the root level dichotomy, the party as the second level, and state at the third. However the user might think of politicians by party first, a viewpoint that is not supported by the current site design. Site designs that are hardwired to disable some interaction sequences can be called 'unpersonalized' with respect to the user's mental model.

4.4.1 Example: Personalizing a Browsing Hierarchy

One typical personalization solution involves anticipating every type of interaction sequence beforehand, and implementing customized interfaces (algorithms) for all of them [43]. For independent levels of classification (such as in Fig. 19, left), this usually implies creating and storing separate trees of information hierarchies. Sometimes, the site designer chooses an intermediate solution that places a prior constraint on the types and forms of interaction sequences supported. This is frequently implemented by directing the user to one of several predefined categories (e.g., 'to search by State, click here.'). It is clear that such solutions can involve an exponential space of possibilities and lead to correspondingly cumbersome site designs.

The approach in PIPE is to create a programmatic representation of the space of possible interaction sequences, and then to use the technique of partial evaluation to realize individual interaction sequences. PIPE models the information space as a program, partially evaluates the program with respect to (any) user input, and recreates a personalized information space from the specialized program.

The input to a partial evaluator is a program and (some) static information about its arguments. Its output is a specialized version of this program (typically in the same language), that uses the static information to 'pre-compile' as many operations as possible. A simple example is how the C function pow can be specialized to create a new function, say pow2, that computes the square of an integer. Consider for example, the definition of a power function shown in the left part of Fig. 20 (grossly simplified for presentation purposes). If we knew that a particular user will utilize it only for computing squares of integers, we could specialize it (for that user) to produce the pow2 function. Thus, pow2 is obtained automatically (not by a human programmer) from pow by precomputing all expressions that involve exponent, unfolding the for-loop, and by various other compiler transformations such as *copy propagation* and *forward substitution*. Automatic program specializers are available for C, FORTRAN, PROLOG, LISP, and several other important languages. The interested reader is referred to [49] for a good introduction. While the traditional motivation for using partial evaluation is to achieve speedup and/or remove interpretation overhead [49], it can also be viewed as a technique for simplifying program presentation, by removing inapplicable, unnecessary, and 'uninteresting' information (based on user criteria) from a program.

```
int pow (int base, int exponent) {        int pow2 (int base) {
  int product = 1;                           return (base *base);
  for (int i = 0; i < exponent; i++)       }
    product = product *base;
  return product;
}
```

FIG. 20. Illustration of the partial evaluation technique. A general purpose power function written in C (left) and its specialized version (with exponent statically set to 2) to handle squares (right). Such specializations are performed automatically by partial evaluators such as C-Mix.

```
if (Sen)
  if (Dem)
    if (CA)
        .........            if (Sen)
    else if (NY)              if (CA)
        .........                .........
  else if (Rep)              else if (NY)
        .........                .........
  else if (Repr)            else if(Repr)
    if (Dem)                     .........
        .........
    else if (Rep)
        .........
```

FIG. 21. Using partial evaluation for personalization. (left) Programmatic input to partial evaluator, reflecting the organization of information in Fig. 19 (left). (right) Specialized program from the partial evaluator, used to create the personalized information space shown in Fig. 19 (right).

Thus we can abstract the situation in Fig. 19 (left) by the program of Fig. 21 (left) whose structure models the information resource (in this case, a hierarchy of web pages) and whose control-flow models the information-seeking activity within it (in this case, browsing through the hierarchy by making individual selections). The link labels are represented as program variables and semantic dependencies between links are captured by the mutually-exclusive if..else dichotomies. To personalize this site, for say, 'Democrats,' this program is partially evaluated with respect to the variable Dem (setting it to one and all conflicting variables such as Rep to zero). This produces the simplified program in the right part of Fig. 21 which can be used to recreate web pages with personalized web content (shown in Fig. 19, right). For hierarchies such as in Fig. 19, the representation afforded by PIPE (notice the nesting of conditionals in Fig. 21, left) is typically much smaller than expressing the same as a union of all possible interaction sequences.

Since the partial evaluation of a program results in another program, the PIPE personalization operator is closed. In terms of interaction, this means that any modes of information-seeking (such as browsing, in Fig. 21) originally modeled in the program are preserved. In the above example, personalizing a browsable hierarchy returns another browsable hierarchy. The closure property also means that the original information-seeking activity (browsing) and personalization can be interleaved in any order. Executing the program in the form and order in which it was modeled amounts to the system-initiated mode of browsing. 'Jumping ahead' to nested program segments by partially evaluating the program amounts to the user-directed

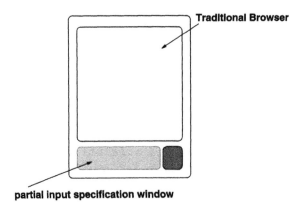

Traditional Browser

partial input specification window

FIG. 22. Sketch of a PIPE interface to a traditional browser. The interface retains the existing browsing functionality at all times. At any point in the interaction, in addition, the user has the option of supplying personalization parameters and conducting personalization (bottom two windows). Such an interface can be implemented as a toolbar option in existing systems.

mode of personalization. In Fig. 21 (right), the simplified program can be rendered and browsed in the traditional sense, or partially evaluated further with additional user inputs. PIPE's use of partial evaluation is thus central to realizing a mixed-initiative mode of information-seeking [85], without explicitly hardwiring all possible interaction sequences. With this approach, it is also possible to encode miscellaneous application logic (about the interaction) and use it to drive the personalization.

An interface design for such interaction is shown in Fig. 22. Figure 23 describes a sample scenario with the hypothetical web site of Fig. 19 (left). At the beginning of the session, the user is presented with the homepage that has options for choosing a branch of Congress. The user prefers, instead, to provide information about party ('Republican') and state ('South Dakota'). She uses the PIPE toolbar to specify this information out-of-turn (Fig. 23, left). Partial evaluation of the PIPE model with these details actually results in also setting the Representative variable to true (since the only Republican in South Dakota is the lone Representative from that state). This results in Fig. 23 (right) where information about the Representative is displayed. This simple example shows the importance of forming a representation of interaction as a basis for personalization.

4.4.2 Modeling in PIPE

Modeling an information space as a program that encapsulates the underlying information-seeking activity is key to the successful application of PIPE. For browsing hierarchies, a programmatic model can be trivially built by a depth-first crawl

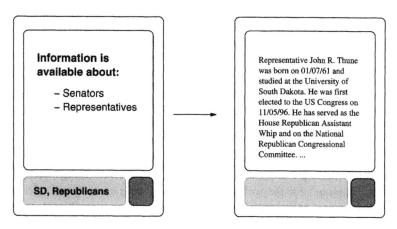

Information is available about:

- Senators
- Representatives

SD, Republicans

Representative John R. Thune was born on 01/07/61 and studied at the University of South Dakota. He was first elected to the US Congress on 11/05/96. He has served as the House Republican Assistant Whip and on the National Republican Congressional Committee. ...

FIG. 23. Example of using a PIPE interface to browse a web site about US Congressional Officials.

of the site. In addition, a variety of other information spaces and corresponding information-seeking activities can be modeled in PIPE. Modeling options for representing information integration, abstracting within a web page, interacting with recommender systems, modeling clickable maps, representing computed information, and capturing syntactic and semantic constraints pertaining to browsing hierarchies are described in [81,91]. Opportunities to curtail the cost of partial evaluation for large sites are also described in [91]. We will not address such modeling aspects here except to say that the effectiveness of a PIPE implementation depends on the particular modeling choices made *within* the programmatic representation (akin to [111]). We cannot overemphasize this aspect—an example such as Fig. 21 can be made 'more personalized' by conducting a more sophisticated modeling of the underlying domain. For example, individual politicians' web pages at the leaves of Fig. 19 could be modeled by a deeper nesting of conditionals involving address, education, precinct, and other attributes of the individual. In other words, a single page could be further modeled as a browsable hierarchy and 'attached' (functionally invoked) at various places in the program of Fig. 21 (left). Conversely, the example in Fig. 19 can be made 'less personalized' by requiring categorical information along with user input. For instance, replacing if (Dem) in Fig. 21 with if (Party==Dem) implies that the specification of the type of input (namely that 'Democrat' refers to the 'name of the party') is required in order for the statement to be partially evaluated. Personalization systems built with PIPE can thus be distinguished by what they model and the forms of customization enabled by applying partial evaluation to such a modeling.

5. Making It Work: Systems Support and Enabling Technologies

We now briefly mention some systems support technologies to bring personalization solutions into mainstream adoption and use.

5.1   Data Modeling

Researchers have identified data modeling as critical to the degree of personalization delivered [25,93]. For personalization purposes, data modeling often involves databases techniques for the web [1,36]. We focus here on content modeling and information integration techniques, such as web crawling and wrapping.

5.1.1   Web Wrappers and Information Integration

The main motivation for wrappers is bridging the gap between the abundance of data on the web and applications which have no direct access to the web [1,44]. WSQ [41] is an example of a system which can benefit from such modeling. The type of information extraction techniques employed are dependent on the type of personalization intended.

In template-based systems, a query typically drives the modeling process [4,52]. Manually designing a web wrapper and subsequently maintaining it is a painstaking process due to dependence on the source format. Therefore, research has been conducted on automatically generating wrappers. Such programs exploit structural cues in data. Ashish and Knoblock take a regular expression, grammar-based, approach to wrapper generation [4]. An alternate approach [95] is to exploit intermediate mappings between system-defined formats and standard formats, such as XML and DOM. The project culminated in the world wide web wrapper factory (W4F) toolkit [95].

All of these projects are focused on answering queries and thus approach wrapper generation from a within-page modeling standpoint. Others take a broader approach and model site structure or mediate inter-site differences [52]. Central to this approach is the flow of information within a site and across sites. In other words, information is integrated through data flow. The output of the first source is fed into the second source as input and so on. Such an approach can be contrasted to formalisms for information integration that use shared schemas and mediated queries [40,38,51].

These approaches suffer from a pitfall endemic to all wrappers, whether automatically generated or not. Crawling or wrapping a third party web site is error prone due to page irregularities, extensive use of stylish page formatting, and an abundance of semistructured data [1]. While many wrapper and crawling packages are freely available on the web, such tools are difficult to use out-of-the-box and typically require a level of manual customization for a particular site. It is often useful to conduct a preliminary inspection of page design and site layout before implementing such systems. In addition, a variety of semantic issues exist for effective information integration which are currently handled with heuristics.

Several distinct solutions to this problem have emerged. One idea is to focus modeling to specific document structures. Rus and Subramanian concentrate on capturing and modeling tabular structures and thus employ document segmentation and structural detection algorithms [93]. XTRACT [39], a system similar to [4], uses grammars and AI techniques to infer DTDs (document type definitions) for XML data. The endurance of such approaches are tested by richer standards for document types such as XSchema [33]. It is widely believed that XSchema may render DTDs obsolete. An alternate approach to webpage modeling, which also employs AI techniques, is wrapper induction [55]. Systems such as [39,55] scale well with regard to frequently changing sites due to the exploitation of machine learning techniques. Yet another solution uses program compaction techniques to infer schemas in semistructured data [74,75].

5.2   Requirements Gathering

Techniques discussed in this section address requirements gathering for personalization systems. This problem can be approached from two distinct angles. The first involves empirical and explicit requirements analysis techniques such as scenario-based design. An alternate approach involves web log mining to implicitly capture requirements. Ultimately these techniques are directed toward closing the gap between the goals of a system designer and the task model of a user [58].

5.2.1   Scenario-Based Methods

The techniques presented here are especially important with regard to representing and reasoning about interaction. Carroll and Rosson make an explicit science out of scenario-based design and claims analysis in [30] where they describe the 'task-artifact' methodology. The end-goal of this research, which lies at the intersection of human-computer interaction (HCI) and software engineering, is to develop an action science approach to HCI.

The first step in the methodology is to collect scenarios. Scenarios are narrative accounts of users performing tasks and can be generated empirically or analytically. Carroll and Rosson develop a classification of scenarios, or typology, which aids in analytical and empirical approaches to scenario collection.

The next step in the methodology is claims analysis. A claim is 'a specific psychological consequence of a system feature' [30]. While a scenario provides a narrative account, a claim provides a causal account. Claims analysis attempts to explain scenarios and must proceed in parallel with scenario generation. Scenarios and claims thus developed can be utilized by CBR as applied to script-directed information systems. For instance, they can be processed to yield cases and identify prototypical scripts.

This work also has important connections to requirements engineering in PIPE [91]. In particular, scenario-based design and claims analysis can be used to generate interaction sequences in a domain which lacks precise, explicit, and clear semantics. In existing systems, the task-artifact cycle can be used to characterize interaction sequences. This is particularly interesting in sites based on the metaphor of social network navigation. In such non-traditional information spaces, scenario-based design can be employed to either unroll unbounded interaction sequences to a manageable level or define personalization. The resulting scenarios (i.e., interaction sequences) would be invaluable to finding an appropriate programmatic design representation of interaction.

Rosson has researched the integration of task and object models [89] in software design. To facilitate this goal, she proposes using object-oriented analysis and design of scenarios. Scenarios are helpful in identifying an initial set of software objects. Claims analysis of the scenarios identifies constraints and opportunities. This work has ties to PIPE as well. In PIPE, a user's personalized experience, analogous to the task model, closely resembles the system's programmatic model of interaction, analogous to the object model.

These connections between scenario-based design and PIPE are explored in [92]. In addition, the authors discuss how explanation-based generalization (EBG) can be used to explain scenarios to provide a starting point for a personalization system. EBG is a machine learning technique which has strong ties to partial evaluation [49]. Proof trees in EBG used in explaining scenarios resemble the goal trees used by Belkin et al. [11].

An alternative approach to requirements gathering is metaphorical design [59]. It is well accepted by now that metaphors provide intuitive ways to think about interaction with information systems (e.g., the desktop). For instance, Wexelblat and Maes [112] explore the use of *footprints* as a navigation design metaphor.

5.2.2 Web Mining

The web is becoming fertile ground for what O'Leary calls 'AI Renaissance' [76]. The use of collaborative filtering in recommender systems was one of the first attempts at conducting personalization. Collaborative filtering is difficult, since the majority of web users are privacy conscious and dislike providing explicit feedback. When applying these techniques care must be taken to ensure that privacy is not compromised.

Web log mining is an alternate approach to capturing user interest and has been referred to as 'observational personalization' [58]. Web log mining is implicit, unobtrusive, and entails chartering the footprints left by visitors. One can analyze web logs to mine navigational patterns.

For instance, IndexFinder [78] mines patterns to guide a non-destructive and transformation approach to web site adaptation. Non-destructive adaptations are those that add structure, pages to sites, or links to pages, but do not destroy structure or otherwise remove information from a site. IndexFinder identifies co-occurring page visits and recommends candidate index pages to the web master. Thus, IndexFinder is a semi-automatic approach.

Web navigation patterns are sought to evaluate web site usability as well [100]. The focus here is on avoiding costly and error prone formative usability evaluations. The miner is looking for sequences of frequently visited pages and routes connecting pages frequently accessed together. Two popular web log mining software systems are MiDas and Web Utilization Miner (WUM) [100]. Another project which has user modeling goals is discussed in [64]. Here, weblog mining helps form associations which are used in a collaborative filtering style to aid a recommendation engine.

While web mining is data driven and therefore heuristic at best, it is inexpensive and can be applied more frequently than its manual counterparts discussed above. The projects described here show that mining access logs is a feasible approach to gathering requirements for personalization. This approach however suffers from problems of coordination and ethics. Therefore, social and operational issues need to be addressed to make such techniques practical and more appealing.

5.3   Transformation Algorithms

XML has matured from simple text markup for data interchange to a mature technology with a rich suite of associated tools. The eXtensible Stylesheet Language Transformation (XSLT) performs transformations from XML to XML and various other formats including plain text, HTML, and VoiceXML. The transformation capabilities of XSLT can be used to implement partial evaluation, among other operations, and to create a robust and easily maintainable personalization application.

Specifically, if an XML file models interaction with a web site, then an XSLT stylesheet representing partial input (i.e., a user request) can be matched against XML tag labels to simplify and personalize interaction. Since XSLT can transform XML into multiple output formats, transforming the model of interaction into a browsable web site (i.e., HTML) is also easy. XSLT thus unifies the processes required to conduct personalization into a single mature and well-accepted technology. Details regarding the use of these new and emerging W3C standards are presented in [23].

5.4   Delivery Mechanisms and Intermediaries

Intermediaries, which are 'programs or agents that meaningfully transform information as it flows for one computer to another,' [61] are critical to the success of personalization applications on the web. Examples of intermediaries are portals, proxies, and transcoders. IBM's WBI [61] provides a programming model for intermediaries akin to PIPE's contribution of a programming model for personalized interaction.

6.   Niche Domains

6.1   Adaptive Hypermedia

In the past 15 years, hypermedia has been extended to support personalization capabilities (e.g., the adaptive web [15]). Adaptive hypermedia lies at the intersection of hypermedia and user modeling [19]. Hypermedia services such as educational and online-help systems have been most impacted by personalization research.

Links in adaptive hypermedia systems are dynamic, leading to different destinations for different users. The techniques employed include direct guidance, adaptive link sorting, hiding, annotation, generation, and map adaptation. In addition to navigational adaptations, such applications modify the aesthetics of presentation to direct a user. We refer the interested reader to [18] and its sequel [19] for a comprehensive survey of methods and techniques of adaptive hypermedia systems and to [7] for a succinct introduction. Examples of browsing-oriented adaptive hypermedia systems are Syskill & Webert [80] and WebWatcher [47].

6.2   Mobile Environments

Mobile arenas, which host the fastest growing segment of web users, are plagued with low bandwidth networks, thin clients, and information appliances [14]. Furthermore, ubiquity is enriched and propelled by wireless portals, avatars [5,56], and information kiosks [63]. As these devices become commonplace, transcoding the information they present will not only become a necessity, but also vital to their widespread use and success [6,77]. Therefore, the use of personalization technology here extends past aesthetics. It is a requirement and no longer expendable. To introduce this application domain, we present the following two representative projects.

6.2.1   Proteus

Proteus [2] is a mobile personalization system developed at the University of Washington. The goal of the system is to both transcode and personalize web content based on mobile devices. To achieve the first goal, the designers segment webpages into screens using a probabilistic model. To achieve the goal of personalization, the designers collect training data from desktop computer usage to build user models.

Proteus supports both destructive and constructive within-page adaptations and implements three transformation operators—elide-content, swap-siblings, and add-shortcut. Creating a new webpage or adding new links between existing pages is not supported. The system can be contrasted to other adaptive systems such as IndexFinder [78]. While IndexFinder provides only non-destructive adaptation targeted by topic to all site visitors, Proteus is destructive as well and provides customization per individual. In addition, Proteus's user models are richer than those that result from web log mining, which are essentially limited to navigational usage patterns.

6.2.2 W^3IQ

W^3IQ [50] aims to provide asynchronous mobile access to the web. The designers explore collaborative information retrieval techniques to minimize resource use and information overload. W^3IQ employs intermediaries, such as proxy filters and cache servers, to facilitate disconnected browsing. In addition, it supports three types of transaction-like operations, which save state and are thus tolerant to disconnection.

6.3   Voice Interfaces and Multimodal Interaction

Speech and dialogue-based systems, which afford mixed-initiative interaction [45], provide ripe domains for personalization. Zadrozny et al. state that natural language is 'a compelling enabling technology for personalization' [114] and that mixed initiative dialogue is a form of personalization. Voice applications (e.g., voice portals[1]) and associated tools (e.g., VoiceXML) have collectively spawned the voice web [97]. Furthermore, this domain demonstrates how researchers in qualitatively different areas can work unconsciously on the same problem. We survey such connections below.

Sisl (several interfaces, single logic) [10], a primarily speech-based system, aims to minimize dialogue constraints to provide extensive flexibility to users. Thus, the motivations of Sisl are commensurate with those of PIPE. Furthermore, the authors of Sisl recognize the idea of engaging a system in a two-way dialogue as a means to provide personalization.

Sisl however takes a broader approach to personalization and supports multiple interfaces, error recovery, reversion, partial input, and partial orderings on specification aspects in dialogue. In contrast to PIPE, Sisl takes an event-based approach.

---

[1] Examples are Tellme (http://www.tellme.com) and BeVocal (http://www.bevocal.com).

The designers model application logic by event handling (reactive) mechanisms. The specification aspects of PIPE are called events in Sisl.

Sisl makes a distinction between partial orderings and partial information. Partial information is incomplete in that all specification aspects required to complete a dialogue or information-seeking activity are communicated incrementally. Partial orders, on the other hand, permit aspects to arrive in different orders. Furthermore, Sisl makes a distinction between *out-of-turn* aspects and *unsolicited* aspects. PIPE traditionally clubs these two together, because its support mechanism, partial evaluation, handles both uniformly.

Both Sisl and PIPE rely on the assumption that a representation of default order execution exists (e.g., a script). This representation involves anticipation in both approaches. PIPE eagerly (partially) evaluates that representation with respect to specification aspects, which may arrive in any order, to implement partial orderings in dialogues. Sisl, on the other hand, lazily evaluates aspects. In other words, when Sisl receives an aspect out-of-turn, which violates its representation, it logs that aspect in a queue. The system retrieves that aspect when the default order of execution solicits it later. At that time, the event is enabled and added to the activated set. The designers refer to this process, which handles unsolicited events and thus minimizes anticipation, as lookahead.

A closer connection between PIPE and speech-based systems is made in [85] where the form interpretation algorithm of VoiceXML [62] is shown to be a partial evaluator in disguise.

7. Conclusions

We have presented an overview of personalization systems according to the interaction they afford. The reader will have gathered that our personal preferences fall in the third tier of systems which explicitly represent and reason about interaction. As personalization systems become prevalent, the need to engage the user in compelling interactions will become more important.

Several factors lead us to be optimistic about the future of personalization as an academic discipline. For instance, the widespread use of physical computing devices, location-aware systems, and embedded Internet appliances means that personalization will transcend current delivery mechanisms. Such domains pose interesting problems that will continue to challenge our assumptions about personalization. Users create context in physical situations that can be stored and retrieved for use in electronic access paradigms. Thinking about how information access works in such multimodal settings will lead to a theory of human-information interaction, as espoused in [107].

We would like to end this chapter on a cautionary note. The contents of this chapter show that relevant work is becoming increasingly fragmented across many venues and sub-disciplines. Pertinent research is now published among the artificial intelligence, database systems, knowledge management, information retrieval, world wide web, user interfaces, and human–computer interaction conferences. We advocate periodic reconciliation and a back-to-basics approach to unify methodologies, when possible. For instance, in [82] we have highlighted the role of *partial* information in achieving various forms of personalization. Such models and modeling methodologies will help systematize the study of personalized interaction.

REFERENCES

[1] Abiteboul S., Buneman P., Suciu D., *Data on the Web: From Relations to Semistructured Data and XML*, Morgan Kaufmann, 2000.

[2] Anderson C.R., Domingos P., Weld D.S., "Personalizing web sites for mobile users", in: *Proceedings of the Tenth International World Wide Web Conference (WWW10), Hong Kong, May 2001*, ACM Press, 2001, pp. 565–575.

[3] Allen J.F., Guinn C.I., Horvitz E., "Mixed-initiative interaction", *IEEE Intelligent Systems* **14** (5) (1999) 14–23.

[4] Ashish N., Knoblock C., "Wrapper generation for semi-structured internet sources", *SIGMOD Record* **26** (4) (1997) 8–15.

[5] André E., Rist T., "From adaptive hypertext to personalized web companions", *Communications of the ACM* **45** (5) (2002) 43–46.

[6] Billsus D., Brunk C.A., Evans C., Gladish B., Pazzani M., "Adaptive interfaces for ubiquitous web access", *Communications of the ACM* **45** (5) (2002) 34–38.

[7] De Bra P., Brusilovsky P., Houben G.-J., "Adaptive hypermedia: From systems to framework", *ACM Computing Surveys* **31** (4es) (1999), Article No. 12.

[8] Belkin N.J., Croft W.B., "Information filtering and information retrieval: Two sides of the same coin?", *Communications of the ACM* **35** (12) (1992) 29–38.

[9] Bodner R., Chignell M., "Dynamic hypertext: Querying and linking", *ACM Computing Surveys* **31** (4es) (1999), Article No. 15.

[10] Ball T., Colby C., Danielsen P., Jagadeesan L.J., Jagadeesan R., Läufer K., Mataga P., Rehor K., "Sisl: Several interfaces, single logic", *International Journal of Speech Technology* **3** (2) (2000) 93–108.

[11] Belkin N.J., Cool C., Stein A., Thiel U., "Cases, scripts, and information seeking strategies: On the design of interactive information retrieval systems", *Expert Systems with Applications* **9** (3) (1995) 379–395.

[12] Belkin N.J., "An overview of results from Rutgers' investigations of interactive information retrieval", in: *Proceedings of the Thirty-Fourth Annual Clinic on Library Applications of Data Processing: Visualizing Subject Access for Twenty-First Century Information Resources*, 1997.

[13] Belkin N.J., "Helping people find what they don't know", *Communications of the ACM* **43** (8) (2000) 58–61.

[14] Bergman E. (Ed.), *Information Appliances and Beyond*, The Morgan Kaufmann Series on Interactive Technologies, Morgan Kaufmann, 2000.

[15] Brusilovsky P., Maybury M.T., "From adaptive hypermedia to the adaptive web", *Communications of the ACM* **45** (5) (2002) 31–33.

[16] Belkin N.J., Marchetti P.G., Cool C., "BRAQUE: Design of an interface to support user interaction in information retrieval", *Information Processing and Management* **29** (3) (1993) 325–344.

[17] Borgman C., "The user's mental model of an information retrieval system: An experiment on a prototype on-line catalogue", *International Journal of Man–Machine Studies* **24** (1) (1986) 47–64.

[18] Brusilovsky P., "Methods and techniques of adaptive hypermedia", *User Modeling and User-Adapted Interaction* **6** (2–3) (1996) 87–129.

[19] Brusilovsky P., "Adaptive hypermedia", *User Modeling and User-Adapted Interaction* **11** (1–2) (2001) 87–110.

[20] Bush V., "As we may think", *The Atlantic Monthly* **176** (1) (1945) 101–108.

[21] Croft W.B., Cronen-Townsend S., Larvrenko V., "Relevance feedback and personalization: A language modeling perspective", in: *Proceedings of the Joint DELOS-NSF Workshop on Personalisation and Recommender Systems in Digital Libraries, Dublin, Ireland, June 2001*, Dublin City University, 2001, pp. 49–54.

[22] Chaudhuri S., Dayal U., "An overview of data warehousing and OLAP technologies", in: *Proceedings of the 1997 ACM SIGMOD International Conference on Management of Data (SIGMOD'97), Tucson, AZ, May 1997*, ACM Press, 1997, pp. 65–74.

[23] Cingil I., Dogac A., Azgin A., "A broader approach to personalization", *Communications of the ACM* **43** (8) (2000) 136–141.

[24] Chawathe S.S., "Describing and manipulating XML data", *IEEE Data Engineering Bulletin* **22** (3) (1999) 3–9.

[25] Chiaramella Y., "Browsing and querying: Two complementary approaches for multimedia information retrieval", in: Fuhr N., Dittrich G., Tochtermann K. (Eds.), *Proceedings of Hypertext, Information Retrieval, Multimedia (HIM'97), Dortmund, Germany, 1997*, pp. 9–26.

[26] Cutting D., Karger D., Pedersen J., Tukey J.W., "Scatter/gather: A cluster-based approach to browsing large document collections", in: Belkin N.J., Ingwersen P., Pejtersen A.M. (Eds.), *Proceedings of the Fifteenth Annual International ACM SIGIR Conference on Research and Development in Information Retrieval, Copenhagen, Denmark, June 1992*, ACM Press, 1992, pp. 318–329.

[27] Card S.K., Moran T.P., Newell A., "Computer text-editing: An information-processing analysis of a routine cognitive skill", *Cognitive Psychology* **12** (1980) 32–74.

[28] Card S.K., Moran T.P., Newell A., "The Keystroke-level model for user performance time with interactive systems", *Communications of the ACM* **23** (7) (1980) 396–410.

[29] Card S.K., Moran T.P., Newell A., *The Psychology of Human–Computer Interaction*, Lawrence Erlbaum, Hillsdale, NJ, 1983.

[30] Carroll J.M., Rosson M.B., "Getting around the task-artifact cycle: How to make claims and design by scenario", *ACM Transactions on Information Systems* **10** (2) (1992) 181–212.

[31] Croft W.B., Thompson R.H., "I^{3}R: A new approach to the design of document retrieval systems", *Journal of the American Society for Information Science* **38** (6) (1987) 389–404.

[32] Deutsch A., Fernández M., Florescu D., Levy A., Maier D., Suciu D., "Querying XML data", *IEEE Data Engineering Bulletin* **22** (3) (1999) 10–18.

[33] Fallside D.C. (Ed.), *XML schema W3C recommendation document, Technical report*, World Wide Web Consortium, 2001.

[34] Fernández M., Florescu D., Kang J., Levy A., Suciu D., "Catching the boat with strudel: Experiences with a web-site management system", in: *Proceedings of the 1998 ACM SIGMOD International Conference on Management of Data (SIGMOD'98), Seattle, WA*, ACM Press, 1998, pp. 414–425.

[35] Fernández M., Florescu D., Levy A., Suciu D., "A query language for a web-site management system", *SIGMOD Record* **26** (3) (1997) 4–11.

[36] Florescu D., Levy A., Mendelzon A., "Database techniques for the world-wide web: A survey", *SIGMOD Record* **27** (3) (1998) 59–74.

[37] Fuhr N., Rölleke T., "A probabilistic relational algebra for the integration of information retrieval and database systems", *ACM Transactions on Information Systems* **15** (1) (1997) 32–66.

[38] Goh C.H., Bressan S., Madnick S., Siegel M., "Context interchange: New features and formalisms for the intelligent integration of information", *ACM Transactions on Information Systems* **17** (3) (1999) 270–293.

[39] Garofalakis M.N., Gionis A., Rastogi R., Seshadri S., Shim K., "XTRACT: A system for extracting document type descriptors from XML documents", in: *Proceedings of the 2000 ACM SIGMOD International Conference on Management of Data (SIGMOD'00), Dallas, TX, May 2000*, ACM Press, 2000, pp. 165–176.

[40] Garcia-Molina H., Papakonstantinou Y., Quass D., Rajaraman A., Sagiv Y., Ullman J.D., Widom J., "The TSIMMIS approach to mediation: Data models and languages", *Journal of Intelligent Information Systems* **8** (2) (1997) 117–132.

[41] Goldman R., Widom J., "WSQ/DSQ: A practical approach for combined querying of databases and the web", in: Chen W.C., Naughton J.F., Bernstein P.A. (Eds.), *Proceedings of the 2000 ACM SIGMOD International Conference on Management of Data (SIGMOD'00), Dallas, TX, May 2000*, ACM Press, 2000, pp. 285–296.

[42] Hellerstein J.M., Avnur R., Chou A., Hidber C., Olston C., Raman V., Roth T., Haas P.J., "Interactive data analysis: The control project", *IEEE Computer* **32** (8) (1999) 51–59.

[43] Hearst M.A., "Next generation web search: Setting our sites", *IEEE Data Engineering Bulletin* **23** (3) (2000) 38–48.

[44] Hammer J., Garcia-Molina H., Cho J., Crespo A., Aranha R., "Extracting semistructured information from the web", in: *Proceedings of the NSF–ESPRIT Workshop on Management of Semistructured Data, Tucson, AZ*, 1997, pp. 18–25.

[45] Haller S., McRoy S., "Computational models for mixed initiative interaction", in: *Papers from the 1997 AAAI Spring Symposium, Technical Report SS-97-04*, AAAI/MIT Press, 1997.

[46] Hiemstra D., Robertson S., "Relevance feedback for best match term weighting algorithms in information retrieval", in: Smeaton A.F., Callan J. (Eds.), *Proceedings of the Joint DELOS-NSF Workshop on Personalisation and Recommender Systems in Digital Libraries, Dublin, Ireland, June 2001*, Dublin City University, 2001, pp. 37–42.

[47] Joachims T., Freitag D., Mitchell T.M., "WebWatcher: A tour guide for the World Wide Web", in: *Proceedings of the Fifteenth International Joint Conference on Artificial Intelligence (IJCAI'97), Nagoya, Aichi, Japan, August 1997*, Morgan Kaufmann, 1997, pp. 770–777.

[48] John B.E., Kieras D.E., "The GOMS family of user interface analysis techniques: Comparison and contrast", *ACM Transactions on Computer–Human Interaction* **3** (4) (1996) 320–351.

[49] Jones N.D., "An introduction to partial evaluation", *ACM Computing Surveys* **28** (3) (1996) 480–503.

[50] Joshi A., Punyapu C., Karnam P., "Personalization and asynchronicity to support mobile web access", in: *Proceedings of the CIKM'98 Workshop on Web Information and Data Management, Bethesda, MD, November 1998*, ACM Press, 1998.

[51] Kirk T., Levy A.Y., Sagiv Y., Srivastava D., "The information manifold", in: Knoblock C., Levy A. (Eds.), *Information Gathering from Heterogeneous, Distributed Environments*, AAAI Press, Stanford, CA, 1995, pp. 85–91. AAAI Spring Symposium Series Technical Report.

[52] Knoblock C.A., Minton S., Ambite J.L., Ashish N., Modi P.J., Muslea I., Philpot A.G., Tejada S., "Modeling web sources for information integration", in: *Proceedings of the Fifteenth National Conference on Artificial Intelligence (AAAI-98), Madison, WI, July 1998*, AAAI Press, 1998, pp. 211–218.

[53] Kramer J., Noronha S., Vergo J., "A user-centered design approach to personalization", *Communications of the ACM* **43** (8) (2000) 45–48.

[54] Kautz H., Selman B., Shah M., "Referral web: Combining social networks and collaborative filtering", *Communications of the ACM* **40** (3) (1997) 63–65.

[55] Kushmerick N., Weld D.S., Doorenbos R., "Wrapper induction for information extraction", in: *Proceedings of the Fifteenth International Joint Conference on Artificial Intelligence (IJCAI'97), Nagoya, Aichi, Japan, August 1997*, Morgan Kaufmann, 1997, pp. 729–737.

[56] Lieberman H., Fry C., Weitzman L., "Exploring the web with reconnaissance agents", *Communications of the ACM* **44** (8) (2001) 69–75.

[57] Lacroix Z., Sahuguet A., Chandrasekar R., Srinivas B., "A novel approach to querying the web: Integrating retrieval and browsing", in: Embley D.W., Goldstein R.C. (Eds.), *Proceedings of the ER'97 Workshop on Conceptual Modeling of Multimedia Information Seeking, Los Angeles, CA, November 1997*, Springer, 1997.

[58] Mulvenna M.D., Anand S.S., Büchner A.G., "Personalization on the net using web mining", *Communications of the ACM* **43** (8) (2000) 122–125.

[59] Madsen K.H., "A guide to metaphorical design", *Communications of the ACM* **37** (12) (1994) 57–62.

[60] Marchionni G., *Information Seeking in Electronic Environments*, Cambridge Series on Human-Computer Interaction, Cambridge University Press, 1997.

[61] Maglio P., Barrett R., "Intermediaries personalize information streams", *Communications of the ACM* **43** (8) (2000) 96–101.

[62] McGlashan S., Burnett D., Danielsen P., Ferrans J., Hunt A., Karam G., Ladd D., Lucas B., Porter B., Rehor K., Tryphonas S., Voice eXtensible Markup Language: VoiceXML, Technical report, VoiceXML Forum, October 2001. Version 2.0.

[63] Mintzer F., Braudaway G.W., Giordano F.P., Lee J.C., Magerlein K.A., D'Auria S., Ribak A., Shapir G., Schiattarella F., Tolva J., Zelenkov A., "Populating the Hermitage Museum's new web site", *Communications of the ACM* **44** (8) (2001) 52–60.

[64] Mobashier B., Cooley R., Srivastava J., "Automatic personalization based on web usage mining", *Communications of the ACM* **43** (8) (2000) 142–151.

[65] Munroe K.D., Ludäscher B., Papakonstantinou Y., "Blending browsing and querying of XML in a lazy mediator system", in: Zaniolo C., Lockemann P.C., Scholl M.H., Grust T. (Eds.), *Proceedings of Seventh International Conference on Extending Database Technology (EDBT'00), Konstanz, Germany, March 2000*, Springer, 2000. In Exhibitions section.

[66] Miller R.C., Myers B.A., "Integrating a command shell into a web browser", in: *Proceedings of the 2000 USENIX Annual Technical Conference, San Diego, CA, June 2000*, The USENIX Association, 2000, pp. 158–166.

[67] Mostafa J., Mukhopadhyay S., Lam W., Palakal M., "A multilevel approach to intelligent information filtering: Model, system, and evaluation", *ACM Transactions on Information Systems* **15** (4) (1997) 368–399.

[68] Munroe K., Papakonstantinou Y., "BBQ: A visual interface for browsing and querying XML", in: Arisawa H., Catarci T. (Eds.), *Proceedings of Fifth Working Conference on Visual Database Systems (VDB5), Fukuoka, Japan, May 2000*, Kluwer Academic Publishers, 2000.

[69] Mukhopadhay P., Papakonstantinou Y., "Mixing querying and navigation in MIX", in: *Proceedings of the Eighteenth International Conference on Data Engineering (ICDE'02), San Jose, CA*, 2002.

[70] Manber U., Patel A., Robinson J., "Experience with personalization on Yahoo!", *Communications of the ACM* **43** (8) (2000) 35–39.

[71] Meuss H., Schulz K.U., "Complete answer aggregates for treelike databases: A novel approach to combine querying and navigation", *ACM Transactions on Information Systems* **19** (2) (2001) 161–215.

[72] Miller R.J., Tsatalos O.G., Williams J.H., "Integrating hierarchical navigation and querying: A user customizable solution", in: Cruz I.F., Marks J., Wittenburg K. (Eds.), *Proceedings of ACM Workshop on Effective Abstractions in Multimedia Layout, Presentation, and Interaction, San Francisco, CA, November 1995*, ACM Press, 1995.

[73] Marchetti P.G., Vazzana S., Panero R., Belkin N.J., "BRAQUE (abstract): An interface to support browsing and interactive query formulation in information retrieval

systems", in: *Proceedings of the Sixteenth Annual International ACM SIGIR Conference on Research and Development in Information Retrieval, Pittsburgh, PA, June–July 1993*, ACM Press, 1993, p. 358.

[74] Nestorov S., Abiteboul S., Motwani R., "Inferring structure in semistructured data", *SIGMOD Record* **26** (4) (1997) 39–43.

[75] Nestorov S., Abiteboul S., Motwani R., "Extracting schema from semistructured data", in: Haas L.M., Tiwary A. (Eds.), *Proceedings of the 1998 ACM SIGMOD International Conference on Management of Data (SIGMOD'98), Seattle, WA, June 1998*, ACM Press, 1998, pp. 295–306.

[76] O'Leary D., "The internet, intranets, and the AI renaissance", *IEEE Computer* **30** (1) (1997) 71–78.

[77] Pancake C., "The ubiquitous beauty of user-aware software", *Communications of the ACM* **44** (3) (2001) 130.

[78] Perkowitz M., Etzioni O., "Adaptive web sites", *Communications of the ACM* **43** (8) (2000) 152–158.

[79] Pednault E.P.D., "Representation is everything", *Communications of the ACM* **43** (8) (2000) 80–83.

[80] Pazzani M., Muramatsu J., Billsus D., "Syskill and Webert: Identifying interesting web sites", in: *Proceedings of the Thirteenth National Conference on Artificial Intelligence (AAAI-96), Portland, OR, August 1996*, AAAI Press, 1996, pp. 54–61.

[81] Ramakrishnan N., "PIPE: Web personalization by partial evaluation", *IEEE Internet Computing* **42** (9) (2000) 21–31.

[82] Ramakrishnan N., The traits of the personable, Technical Report cs.AI/0205022, Computing Research Repository (CoRR), May 2002.

[83] Robertson G.G., Cameron K., Czerwinski M., Robbins D., "Animated visualization of multiple intersecting hierarchies", *Information Visualization* **1** (2002) 50–65.

[84] Robertson G.G., Cameron K., Czerwinski M., Robbins D., "Polyarchy visualization: Visualizing multiple intersecting hierarchies", in: *Proceedings of the Conference on Human Factors in Computing Systems (CHI'02), Minneapolis, MN, April 2002*, ACM Press, 2002, pp. 423–430.

[85] Ramakrishnan N., Capra R., Pérez-Quiñones M.A., "Mixed-initiative interaction = mixed computation", in: Thiemann P. (Ed.), *Proceedings of the ACM SIGPLAN Workshop on Partial Evaluation and Semantics-Based Program Manipulation (PEPM'02), Portland, OR, January 2002*, ACM Press, 2002, pp. 119–130. Also appears in ACM SIGPLAN Notices 37, No. 3, March 2002.

[86] Riecken D., "Personal end-user tools", *Communications of the ACM* **43** (8) (2000) 89–91.

[87] Riecken D., "Personalized views of personalization", *Communications of the ACM* **43** (8) (2000) 27–28.

[88] Rocchio J.J., "Relevance feedback in information retrieval", in: Salton G. (Ed.), *The SMART Retrieval System: Experiments in Automatic Document Processing*, Prentice-Hall, Englewood Cliffs, NJ, 1971, pp. 313–323.

[89] Rosson M.B., "Integrating development of task and object models", *Communications of the ACM* **42** (1) (1999) 49–56.

[90] Rucker J., Polano M.J., "Siteseer: Personalized navigation for the web", *Communications of the ACM* **40** (3) (1997) 73–75.

[91] Ramakrishnan N., Perugini S., The partial evaluation approach to information personalization, Technical Report cs.IR/0108003, Computing Research Repository (CoRR), August 2001.

[92] Ramakrishnan N., Rosson M.B., Carroll J.M., Explaining scenarios for information personalization, Technical Report cs.HC/0111007, Computing Research Repository (CoRR), November 2001.

[93] Rus D., Subramanian D., "Customizing information capture and access", *ACM Transactions on Information Systems* **15** (1) (1997) 67–101.

[94] Resnick P., Varian H.R., "Recommender systems", *Communications of the ACM* **40** (3) (1997) 56–58.

[95] Sahuguet A., Azavant F., "Looking at the Web through XML glasses", in: *Proceedings of the Fourth IFCIS International Conference on Cooperative Information Systems (CoopIs'99), Edinburgh, Scotland, September 1999*, IEEE Computer Society, 1999, pp. 148–159.

[96] Sacco G.M., "Dynamic taxonomies: A model for large information bases", *IEEE Transactions on Knowledge and Data Engineering* **12** (3) (2000) 468–479.

[97] Srinivasan S., Brown E., "Is speech recognition becoming mainstream?", *IEEE Computer* **35** (4) (2002) 38–41.

[98] Shneiderman B., "Tree visualization with tree-maps: 2D space-filling approach", *ACM Transactions on Graphics* **11** (1) (1992) 92–99.

[99] Smith D.C., "Building personal tools by programming", *Communications of the ACM* **43** (8) (2000) 92–95.

[100] Spiliopoulou M., "Web usage mining for web site evaluation", *Communications of the ACM* **43** (8) (2000) 127–134.

[101] Suchman L.A., *Plans and Situated Actions: The Problem of Human–Machine Communication*, Cambridge University Press, 1987.

[102] Schwartz M.F., Wood D.C.M., "Discovering shared interests using graph analysis", *Communications of the ACM* **36** (8) (1993) 78–89.

[103] Shneiderman B., Wattenberg M., "Ordered treemap layouts", in: *Proceedings of the IEEE Symposium on Information Visualization (INFOVIS'01), San Diego, CA, October 2001*, IEEE Computer Society, 2001, pp. 73–78.

[104] Singh M.P., Yu B., Venkatraman M., "Community-based service location", *Communications of the ACM* **44** (4) (2001) 49–54.

[105] Terveen L., Hill W., Amento B., McDonald D., Creter J., "PHOAKS: A system for sharing recommendations", *Communications of the ACM* **40** (3) (1997) 59–62.

[106] Thomas B., "URL diving", *IEEE Internet Computing* **2** (3) (1998) 92–93.

[107] Thomas J.J., McGee D.R., Kuchar O.A., Graybeal J.W., McQuerry D.L., Novak P.L., "What is your relationship with your information space?", in: *Proceedings of Computer Graphics International, Bradford, UK*, 2002.

[108] Interactive Transactions of OR/MS (ITORMS): Visualization and Optimization. Available at http://catt.bus.okstate.edu/jones98/treemaps.htm.

[109] Wilson R.M., Bergeron R.D., "Dynamic hierarchy specification and visualization", in: *Proceedings of the IEEE Symposium on Information Visualization (INFOVIS'99), San Francisco, CA, October 1999*, IEEE Computer Society, 1999, pp. 65–72.

[110] Widom J., "Data management for XML: Research directions", *IEEE Data Engineering Bulletin* **22** (3) (1999) 44–52.

[111] Williams M.D., "What makes RABBIT run?", *International Journal of Man–Machine Studies* **21** (1984) 333–352.

[112] Wexelblat A., Maes P., "Footprints: History-rich tools for information foraging", in: *Proceedings of the Conference on Human Factors in Computing Systems (CHI'99), Pittsburgh, PA, May 1999*, ACM Press, 1999, pp. 270–277.

[113] Xie H., "Patterns between interactive intentions and information-seeking strategies", *Information Processing and Management* **38** (1) (2002) 55–77.

[114] Zadrozny W., Budzikowski M., Chai J., Kambhatla N., Levesque S., Nicolov N., "Natural language dialogue for personalized interaction", *Communications of the ACM* **43** (8) (2000) 116–120.

Author Index

Numbers in *italics* indicate the pages on which complete references are given.

383

Subject Index

Contents of Volumes in This Series

403

Printed and bound by CPI Group (UK) Ltd, Croydon, CR0 4YY

03/10/2024

01040410-0012